PHILIPPINE PRIVATE INTERNATIONAL LAW

This book is the first authoritative reference on Philippine private international law in English. It covers all facets of Philippine private international law and its inevitable intersection with family and succession issues, commercial matters, intellectual property, competition, cross-border insolvency, and environmental disputes.

This book goes beyond a systematic presentation of the traditional private international law issues on jurisdiction, applicable law, and enforcement mechanisms. Employing a problem-centred approach, the chapters also look into conflict of law questions arising in arbitration, and assess the Philippines' involvement in the harmonisation of private international law globally and regionally within ASEAN.

With the Philippine legal system uniquely blending common and civil law traditions, the book presents Philippine private international law through the perspectives and analytical techniques characteristic of both traditions. In doing so, the book provides readers worldwide with a more profound and comprehensive understanding of private international law in the Philippines.

Volume 16 in the series Studies in Private International Law – Asia

Studies in Private International Law – Asia

Editor: Anselmo Reyes
Advisory Editor: Paul Beaumont
Assistant Editors: Kazuaki Nishioka and Wilson Lui

Much has been written about private international law in the EU and the US. Less is known about the conflict of laws in Asia. Thus, little attention has been paid so far to the modernisation of private international law codes and rules that has been taking place over the last decade all over Asia. That trend continues. Now is the time to take stock of those reforms that have already taken place and suggest further improvements for the future.

Published under the celebrated series *Studies in Private International Law*, this monograph sub-series provides a forum for discussion and analysis of private international law in Asia. The series is not solely a survey of jurisdictions for practitioners. Comprising both in-depth thematic and country-specific studies, each volume considers the private international law of Asian countries from a variety of perspectives. An underlying assumption is that private international law in different jurisdictions follows broadly discernible patterns. Each volume in this sub-series highlights those patterns and discusses how rules in different Asian jurisdictions are either converging with, or diverging from, the patterns identified. Such an analytical framework will assist academics, judges, lawyers and legislators to envisage ways in which laws affecting cross-border relationships can be harmonised across jurisdictions and be made more responsive to the needs of citizens in Asia and elsewhere.

Volume 1: Recognition and Enforcement of Judgments in Civil and Commercial Matters
Edited by Anselmo Reyes

Volume 2: Indonesian Private International Law
Afifah Kusumadara

Volume 3: Chinese Private International Law
Edited by Xiaohong Liu and Zhengyi Zhang

Volume 4: Direct Jurisdiction: Asian Perspectives
Edited by Anselmo Reyes and Wilson Lui

Volume 5: Japanese Private International Law
Kazuaki Nishioka and Yuko Nishitani

Volume 6: Indian Private International Law
Stellina Jolly and Saloni Khanderia

Volume 7: Treatment of Foreign Law in Asia
Edited by Kazuaki Nishioka

Volume 8: Choice of Law and Recognition in Asian Family Law
Edited by Anselmo Reyes, Wilson Lui and Kazuaki Nishioka

Volume 9: Private International Law in East Asia: From Imitation to Innovation and Exportation
Edited by Olivier Gaillard and Krista Nadakavukaren Schefer

Volume 10: Overriding Mandatory Rules in International Commercial Disputes: Korean and Comparative Law
Min Kyung KIM

Volume 11: Privacy and Personal Data Protection Law in Asia
Edited by Adrian Mak, Ching Him Ho and Anselmo Reyes

Volume 12: Hong Kong Private International Law
Wilson Lui and Anselmo Reyes

Volume 13: Choice of Forum Clauses in Asia
Lemuel D Lopez

Volume 14: Cambodian Private International Law
Nobumichi Teramura

Volume 15: Multinationals and Human Rights in Asia
Edited by Jason Ho Ching Cheung and Kazuaki Nishioka

Volume 16: Philippine Private International Law
Edited by Jocelyn Cruz, Thomas Elliot Mondez and Justin Sucgang

Philippine Private International Law

Edited by
Jocelyn Cruz
Thomas Elliot Mondez
and
Justin Sucgang

•HART•
OXFORD • LONDON • NEW YORK • NEW DELHI • SYDNEY

HART PUBLISHING

Bloomsbury Publishing Plc

Kemp House, Chawley Park, Cumnor Hill, Oxford, OX2 9PH, UK

1385 Broadway, New York, NY 10018, USA

Bloomsbury Publishing Ireland Limited, 29 Earlsfort Terrace, Dublin 2, D02 AY28, Ireland

First published in Great Britain 2026

1

A catalogue record for this book is available from the British Library.

A catalogue record for this book is available from the Library of Congress.

ISBN: HB: 978-1-50994-858-1
ePDF: 978-1-50994-860-4
ePub: 978-1-50994-859-8

Typeset by Compuscript Ltd, Shannon
Printed and bound in Great Britain by TJ Books, Padstow, Cornwall

For product safety related questions contact productsafety@bloomsbury.com

To find out more about our authors and books visit www.hartpublishing.co.uk. Here you will find extracts, author information, details of forthcoming events and the option to sign up for our newsletters.

SERIES EDITORS' PREFACE

Philippine Private International Law is the seventh volume in the country sub-series of Hart's *Studies in Private International Law – Asia*.

An initial characteristic that emerges from a perusal of this book is that the Philippine system of private international law is largely judge-made. It is true that there are vestiges of provisions from the Spanish civil laws that applied to the Philippines in the 19th century and that there are sprinklings of what might be regarded as conflict-of-law principles in various contemporary Philippine codes and statutes. But there is no single code or statute that systematically sets out the private international law rules to be applied in given situations. Thus, although the Philippines is often categorised as a hybrid civil and common law country due to its history as a former Spanish and later American colony, its private international law is more common law than civil law in nature and development.

A second characteristic that strikes the reader is that, until lately, Philippine private international law has been conservative in nature. One thinks here, in particular, of the observation highlighted (critically) at various points of this book that, the Vatican apart, the Philippines is the only sovereign country in the world that still prohibits absolute divorce. However, the conservatism of the law is evident in many other aspects, possibly reflecting the Catholicism of a large part of the Philippine population. This traditionalism has, however, proved to be at odds with the realities of today's Filipino diaspora and the openness of the Philippines generally to foreign nationals.[1] It has meant that the courts have had, as acknowledged by the book's Preface, to become "quite dynamic … to adjust to the realities of a world where civil and commercial relations transcend borders". Reflecting on the dissonance between the law's conservatism (and concomitant bureaucracy) and the pressures of dealing pragmatically with the everyday transnational problems of the 21st century, the final chapter of this book is under no illusions. The chapter refers ruefully to the constant "thickening" of "the untamed jungle of Philippine laws" despite an urgent need "to coordinate the codification of local laws with the country's compliance with its treaty obligations". The chapter recognises that the task ahead is "herculean", such that rationalisation and modernisation of the law will require not just the judiciary's attention but more pertinently "the cooperation of the three co-equal branches of government".

A third characteristic, one that may not be immediately apparent to a reader, is that this work has been a labour of love which has been in the works for some time. It is no mean endeavour to produce a comprehensive treatise on modern Philippine private international law. Research has thrown up at least five such earlier works. The first is Justice Edgardo Lardizábal Paras' *Philippine Private International Law*, published by Villanueva Book Store in 1962. The second is the same author's *Philippine Conflict of Laws*, the sixth edition of which was published

[1] The book's Preface notes that there are 11 million Filipinos residing abroad, with about 4.1 million in the US, 2.3 million in the Middle East, 2.6 million in Asian and Pacific nations, and more than 650,000 in Europe, while some 153,651 foreign nationals have been resident in the Philippines since the COVID-19 pandemic.

by Rex Book Store in 1984. The third is Dean Jovito Salonga's *Private International Law*, published by Rex Book Store in 1995. The fourth is the much-loved *Conflict of Laws: Cases, Materials and Comments* by Professors Jorge Rioflorido Coquia and Elizabeth Aguiling-Pangalangan, published by Central Book Supply in 2000. The fifth and most recent is Professor Galahad Pe Benito's *Conflict of Laws*, published by Rex Book Store in 2020. But much has transpired since 2020, so that the book's editors and contributors have effectively had to map their own way through the ever-thickening "jungle of Philippine laws" to arrive at an authoritative statement of what the Philippine conflict of laws is today and might aspire to be tomorrow. All five previous treatises have been produced domestically for essentially a Filipino audience. This is the first account of Philippine private international law which is intended to be forward-looking, for a worldwide readership of lawyers, academic, students and interested lay persons.

The Editors
Kyoto
7 October 2025

PREFACE

The significance of private international law to Filipinos cannot be overstated. Private international law, or even international law in general, had been overlooked by Filipinos due to their focus on local legal and parochial concerns. Interest in the subject gained traction in the twenty-first century following key developments in Philippine law and jurisprudence. The repercussions of greater free trade in a globalised economy have also highlighted the importance of conflict of laws.

Philippine society, as well as its legal system, are products of an amalgamation of various influences. The Philippine Islands were colonised by Spain for over three centuries. In 1898, following the Treaty of Paris between the United States (US) and Spain, colonial control over the Philippine Islands was transferred to America. The Philippines was briefly occupied by the Japanese Empire during World War II. It gained independence from the US following the war in 1946.

Philippine society, cultural norms, language, traditions, and even its legal system are greatly influenced by a fusion of three cultures: the Spanish heritage of the Philippines, evidenced by its predominantly Catholic population and civil law system; America's profound influence, with English being the official business language of the Philippines and with its Constitution and system of government generally inspired by the US Constitution and Washington's government structure; and, the Asian vibe of the Philippines as a country geographically situated in the middle of East Asia's Pacific region.

The Philippines is also a member of the Association of Southeast Asian Nations (ASEAN), a regional bloc comprising of 11 Southeast Asian nations. While ASEAN has yet to develop a sophisticated integrated economy like the European Union (EU), it already has an ASEAN free trade area and it aspires to eventually create a single market.[1]

After gaining independence from the US, and despite its ASEAN membership, Philippine economic policies centred on domestic trade and import substitution, creating a powerful stranglehold of local oligarchs which is still present today. In the late 1980s, the Philippine government started to reform its economic policies by opening its doors to greater free trade. The policy shift gained momentum in the twenty-first century, with new laws and international business agreements designed to encourage foreign investments and greater commercial activity in a highly globalised economy.[2] Meanwhile, demand for foreign labour and greater accessibility of air travel allowed millions of Filipinos to seek employment abroad.

The above developments produced the following results: millions of Filipinos are residing overseas; Filipinos are frequently transacting business with foreign citizens and

[1] Article 1(5), ASEAN Charter. Association of Southeast Asian Nations (ASEAN), Charter of the Association of Southeast Asian Nations, Association of Southeast Asian Nations (ASEAN), 20 November 2007.

[2] TEA Mondez and JP Cruz in N Teramura, L Nottage, and B Jetin (eds), *Corruption and Illegality in Asian Investment Arbitration: The Philippines. Corruption and Illegality in Asian Investment Arbitration* (Springer, 2024) 345.

corporations; mass migration and technological advances such as communications via internet applications and mobile devices allow greater interactions that may lead to engagements with conflicting civil law consequences, such as marriage, producing offsprings of dual nationalities, and testate or intestate succession; and numerous foreign citizens are now residing in the Philippines.

The Philippine Statistics Authority (PSA) recorded that 78,396 foreign citizens reside in the Philippines based on its 2020 census. An additional 50,089 Filipinos with dual citizenship also reside in the country as of 2020. Nearly two out five foreign citizens live in the National Capital Region (NCR), which includes Manila and its adjoining metropolitan areas. The majority of the foreign citizens residing in the Philippines come from China and India. There are also numerous foreign citizens from the US, Japan, and South Korea residing in the Philippines.[3]

The number of foreign citizens in the Philippines significantly increased after the COVID-19 pandemic. The Philippine Bureau of Immigration (BI) recorded 153,651 foreigners who participated in its 2024 Annual Report, up by 13 per cent from the 136,065 foreign citizens who reported their stay in the Philippines in 2023. Foreign tourists and temporary visitors are not included in the BI data.[4] Undocumented foreigners are also excluded.

It is also significant to note that there are an estimated 2.16 million Filipinos working abroad. The majority of overseas Filipinos work in other Asian countries (77.4 per cent). Saudi Arabia, United Arab Emirates, and Qatar are the most popular destinations for Filipinos seeking employment abroad. Filipino workers are also deployed in North and South America (9.8 per cent), Europe (8.4 per cent), Australia (3 per cent), and Africa (1.3 per cent).[5]

However, the total number of Filipinos residing abroad is way higher than the 2.16 million documented Filipino migrant workers. Philippine migration data from the Commission on Filipinos Overseas reveals that there are nearly 11 million Filipinos residing abroad.[6] The US Census Bureau estimates that around 4.1 million Filipino Americans live in the US as of 2022.[7] Over 2.3 million Filipinos live in countries in the Middle East, while over 2.6 million reside in other Asian and Pacific nations. Over 650,000 Filipinos live in Europe.[8]

In 2024, the BI recorded 14,540,533 arrivals in the Philippines, comprising 7,922,052 Filipinos and 6,618,481 foreign nationals.[9]

The statistical data show that Filipinos are interacting with foreign citizens at a greater rate due to migration, tourism, business travel, and other commercial interactions. The private international law implications are significant, given that Philippine law recognises dual citizenships for qualified Filipinos, and that the Philippine Civil Code extends local laws which are relevant to family rights and duties, status, condition, and legal capacity of persons

[3] Data from the Philippine Statistics Authority. See psa.gov.ph/statistics/population-and-housing/node/1684059982.

[4] Data from the Philippine Bureau of Immigration. See immigration.gov.ph/bi-says-153k-aliens-took-part-in-2024-annual-report/.

[5] Data from the Philippine Statistics Authority. See psa.gov.ph/statistics/survey/labor-and-employment/survey-overseas-filipinos.

[6] Data from the Commission of Overseas Filipinos. See cfo.gov.ph/statistics-2/?appgw_azwaf_jsc=x9sXAV2D4Zr0Gy7_-m0K_QOLfR91NujnnRvN7MMYzBM.

[7] From Pew Research website, citing data from the US Census Bureau. See www.pewresearch.org/race-and-ethnicity/2024/08/06/filipino-americans-a-survey-data-snapshot/.

[8] Commission on Overseas Filipinos (n 7).

[9] Data from the Philippine Bureau of Immigration. See immigration.gov.ph/bi-highlights-2024-achievements-eyes-modernization-in-2025-as-it-moves-towards-bagong-immigration/#:~:text=MANILA, Philippines. The Bureau of, 8,348,283 Filipinos and 6,701,853 foreigners.

to all Philippine citizens even when living abroad.[10] It follows the nationality principle in international law.[11] Conflict of laws issues may arise, considering that many Filipino citizens are married to foreign nationals. This is especially true since the Philippines is one of two sovereign entities (The Holy See or Vatican City being the other) in the world which prohibit absolute divorce. Philippine jurisprudence on this matter, particularly when a divorce is obtained abroad, is quite dynamic and is evolving to adjust to the realities of a world where civil and commercial relations transcend borders.

The number of commercial transactions with possible private international law concerns is increasing. The Philippine government is committed to increase foreign investments by having robust economic relationships with other countries. However, conflicts arising from transactions covered by bilateral investment treaties (BIT) may occur, such as the controversial case between the Philippine government and Fraport AG Frankfurt Services Worldwide, a German company involved in the construction of one of the terminals of Manila's international airport. The controversy involved proceedings in both the International Centre for Settlement of Investment Disputes (ICSID) and local Philippine courts, proving how conflicts in jurisdiction as well as both substantive and procedural law may cause complications in commercial matters, even if covered by a BIT.[12]

Philippine legislation in the twentieth century focused on domestic concerns. The new realities of a highly globalised economy compelled lawmakers to enact laws that recognise, and adequately address, issues that may arise involving actors from different legal jurisdictions. These new laws include the Philippine Competition Act (2015),[13] Data Privacy Act of 2012,[14] Cybercrime Prevention Act of 2012[15] and the Expanded Anti-Human Trafficking in Persons Act of 2022,[16] among others. Foreign entities doing business in the Philippines and/or with Filipino entities may be covered by these new laws. For instance, the Data Privacy Act has a provision on extraterritorial application for acts involving the processing of personal information of Filipino citizens or if the act involves an entity that has an established business link in the country, whether committed or processed in the Philippines or abroad.[17] The Philippine Competition Act provides that it is applicable to matters involving international trade, including those that result from or are committed outside the Philippines, if the acts have direct, substantial, and reasonably foreseeable effects in trade, industry, or commerce in the country.[18] The extraterritorial application of the Philippine Competition Act is consistent with the effects doctrine in international law, which recognises that a state may exert jurisdiction over a matter where its effects are felt within the country's territory.[19] Entities and individuals doing business in the Philippines and/or with Filipino citizens and businesses, whether in the Philippines or abroad, must therefore take into account the possible extraterritorial application of concerned laws and regulatory actions by agencies such as the Philippine Competition Commission and the National Privacy Commission.

[10] Article 15, New Civil Code of the Philippines. Republic Act No. 386 (12 June 1949).
[11] AEB Nachura and J Gatdula, *Outline Introduction to Public International Law* (Manila, Rex Book Store, 2017) 72.
[12] Mondez and Cruz (n 2) 355–60.
[13] Republic Act No. 10667. 21 July 2015.
[14] Republic Act No. 10173. 15 August 2012.
[15] Republic Act No. 10175. 12 September 2012.
[16] Republic Act No. 11862. 23 June 2022.
[17] Section 6 (n 15).
[18] Section 3 (n 14).
[19] Nachura and Gatdula, *supra*, note 11, 74.

This book covers Philippine private international law as it relates to choice of law in matters such as family law, property law, corporate law, competition law, and intellectual property rights. It also includes local court recognition and enforcement of foreign judgments, international treaty and commercial arbitration, and the efforts taken by the Philippine government to harmonise Philippine private international law with the conflict of laws rules of other countries.

Jocelyn P Cruz
Thomas Elliot A Mondez
Justin DJ Sucgang
Manila, Philippines
3 November 2025

ACKNOWLEDGEMENTS

The editors are grateful to Anselmo Reyes, international judge of the Singapore International Commercial Court, for his patronage and support. Professor Reyes is an instrumental part of this collaborative project.

The contributing authors must be commended for sharing their expertise and valuable insights. They are acknowledged experts in their respective fields of law in the Philippines.

The institutional support of De La Salle University in Manila, Philippines for research publications is deeply appreciated. In particular, its Department of Commercial Law under the Ramon V. Del Rosario College of Business has consistently produced a strong pool of contributors in legal research and publication. The editors highly appreciate the contributions of their co-faculty and support staff in the Department of Commercial Law. The efforts of Attorney Andrei V. Elinzano deserve the highest praise. We also acknowledge the contribution of Attorney Luigi Bonoan.

The collaborative authorship of this publication significantly contributed to the enhancement of De La Salle University's legal management programme. The editors acknowledge the industrious efforts of Wileen Calisin and her fellow student assistants, Louis Miguel Ecat and Alecxis Bianca Libang. Finally, this project would not have been possible without the invaluable support of Lourdes Perez, whose assistance to the editors, authors, and student assistants has been indispensable.

Jocelyn P Cruz
Thomas Elliot A Mondez
Justin DJ Sucgang
Manila, Philippines.
3 November 2025

CONTENTS

LIST OF CONTRIBUTORS

Angela Ray T Abala is the Research and Development Lead at the Singapore International Dispute Resolution Academy. She holds a Master of Laws in International Legal Studies from Georgetown University and is licensed to practice law in the Philippines and the State of New York. Her work focuses on international dispute resolution, with particular expertise in mediation, arbitration, and investor-state disputes, and she regularly conducts training for legal professionals and government officials across the Asia-Pacific region. She is a part-time professor at the Department of Commercial Law of De La Salle University.

Emiliano S Bantog is the Vice Chair of Department of Commercial Law of the Ramon V Del Rosario College of Business at De La Salle University in the Philippines. He is an accomplished legal professional and advocate, serving as the Executive Director of Legal Engagement Advocating Development and Reform (LEADeR), with experience in public service, legal practice, and education, particularly in the fields of road safety, public health, and transportation reform.

Hilario S Caraan is an Associate Professor at the Department of Commercial Law, RVR College of Business, DLSU, Manila, and the Managing Lawyer of Caraan and Associates Law Offices. He handles civil, criminal, labour, and administrative cases and specialises in corporate governance, human resources management, educational management, and government compliance, areas which are also his research interests.

Christopher E Cruz is the University Legal Counsel, the Director of the DLSU Intellectual Property Office, and the Manager of the DLSU Innovation and Technology Office at De La Salle University (DLSU), Manila. He is a Full Professor at DLSU with 33 years of teaching experience and extensive work in intellectual property and technology transfer, both locally and internationally. He holds degrees in Philosophy and Law, as well as a Ph.D. in Philosophy. He is a registered patent agent, Co-Editor-in-Chief of the Asia Pacific Journal of Intellectual Property Management and Innovation, and serves on advisory bodies for intellectual property policy and technology grant evaluations. In 2023, he taught in the WIPO-Harvard PatentX programme and remains active in promoting technology transfer as a career in the Philippines, serving as President of the Alliance of Tech Transfer Professionals of the Philippines (ATOP).

Jocelyn P Cruz is an Associate Professor and the current Chair of the Department of Commercial Law at the Ramon V Del Rosario College of Business at De La Salle University in the Philippines. She was the former Vice Dean of the College of Law of De La Salle University.

Andrei V Elinzano is a full-time faculty member of the Commercial Law Department of the Ramon V. Del Rosario College of Business at De La Salle University. He is a practising lawyer with over three years of experience in the legal industry, specialising in litigation and dispute resolution. He currently serves as the Managing Partner at Gloria & Elinzano Law Offices.

Lambert Yancy B Garganta is a full-time faculty member of the Department of Commercial Law and currently the Undergraduate Practicum Coordinator of the Department of Commercial Law, RVR College of Business, De La Salle University. He teaches and researches on subjects such as commercial law, law on business organisations, law and society, and legal history.

Maria Jesse Anne B Gloria is a part-time faculty member of the Commercial Law Department of Ramon V. Del Rosario College of Business, De La Salle University. She is also a Partner at Gloria & Elinzano Law Offices. Her practice focuses on corporate and labour laws.

James Keith C Heffron is the Managing Partner at Heffron Cruz. He has published extensively on contemporary legal issues, including cybercrime, ASEAN economic integration, and artificial intelligence in corporate governance. He is a full-time faculty member of the Department of Commercial Law and a former Vice Dean of the Ramon V. Del Rosario College of Business.

Antonio A Ligon is a full-time professor of the Department of Commercial Law of De La Salle University specialising in business and commercial law. He was the former director of the university's Office of Personnel Management. He was honoured with the 2019 Dangal ng Lipi Award for his outstanding contributions to public service in the Province of Bulacan.

Severo C Madrona Jr is a Professional Lecturer at the Department of Commercial Law at RVR College of Business, De La Salle University, and a Professor and Dean at the City University of Pasay School of Law. He specialises in strategic leadership, labour economics, constitutional law, local governance, and fiscal policy, with recent publications including *The Handbook of Election Laws and Cases in the Philippines* (2025) and *A Treatise on the Local Government Law in the Philippines* (2024).

Thomas Elliot A Mondez is a professional lecturer at the Department of Commercial Law of De La Salle University in Manila. He is the author of *Geopolitics and International Law* (Central Books, 2021) and a contributing author in *Corruption and Illegality in Asian Investment Arbitration* (Springer, 2024). He has extensive experience in administrative and legal matters as a civil servant in various Philippine government agencies.

Richard J Nethercott holds a Mechanical Engineering degree from De La Salle University–Manila, a Juris Doctor from Ateneo de Manila University, and an MBA from De La Salle University, where he is pursuing a Doctorate, while serving as the founding partner of Nethercott Law, an Associate Professor at multiple law schools, and the President and CEO of the Independent Electricity Market Operator of the Philippines (IEMOP). He is a part-time faculty member of the Department of Commercial Law.

Arvin Kristopher A Razon is a lawyer with an MBA and LLM specialising in technology law, with extensive leadership experience in digital banking and fintech. Previously the Regional Director of Legal, Compliance, and Regulatory Affairs at a leading Open Finance fintech provider in SEA, and has also contributed to technology law research and lectured on Digital Law and Banking & Fintech Law and Regulation. He is a part-time faculty member of the Department of Commercial Law.

Ryan Jay I Roset is a Juris Doctor and LLM graduate, is a senior legal counsel with expertise in litigation, corporate law, human rights, and policy development, currently serving as Coordinator for Direct Legal Service at the Legal Rights and Natural Resources Center-Friends of the Earth Philippines (LRC-FOE), and with a strong background in working with marginalised communities, public sector reforms, and legislative development. He is a part-time faculty member of the Department of Commercial Law.

Justin DJ Sucgang is Associate Professor of Law at the De La Salle University Tañada-Diokno School of Law, where he also obtained his Juris Doctor degree as part of the inaugural batch. He obtained his Master of Laws from the University of Michigan Law School on a Fulbright Scholarship and DeWitt Fellowship. Currently, he is finishing his Doctor of Juridical Sciences program in the Fordham University School of Law. He was appointed by the former President as Commissioner of the Legal Education Board, the national government agency regulating law schools. He teaches Civil Law subjects, Philosophy of Law, and Legal Writing and Research in the law school. He previously taught at the Diliman and Iloilo campuses of the University of the Philippines College of Law.

Pamela Raye M Tadeo is the University Intellectual Property Officer of De La Salle University. She serves as the Programme Manager of the DLSU Strategic Management of IP Certificate Course and the upcoming WIPO-IPOPHL-DLSU Master's Programme in IP Management and Innovation. She is a fellow of the Royal Academy of Engineering Leaders in Innovation Fellowship (Batch 5, 2019) and the current Secretary of the Alliance of Tech Transfer Professionals of the Philippines, Inc. (ATOP Inc.).

Peter Immanuel dL Tenido is a Project Director of the DLSU Innovation and Technology Office. In that capacity, he renders patent services and technology transfer support services, including patent searching, drafting, and prosecution, technology licence negotiations, and IP management support. His research interests include: use of patent information to draw technical and business insights, IP management in academic institutions, and IP human resource development and capacity building.

Rio Mei L Uy is a lawyer and certified public accountant (CPA) who placed 8th in the 2022 Bar Examinations and 19th in the 2014 CPA Licensure Examination. She graduated as valedictorian with a Juris Doctor degree from Ateneo Law School and earned her Accountancy degree with honors from De La Salle University. She currently serves as a Legal Officer at the Bangko Sentral ng Pilipinas, following previous roles in top-tier law and audit firms. She is a part-time faculty member of the Department of Commercial Law.

TABLE OF CASES

Canada

International Court of Justice

Philippines

United Kingdom

United States

TABLE OF LEGISLATION

Philippine Laws

Philippine Government and Regulatory Documents

TABLE OF INTERNATIONAL INSTRUMENTS

1

Introduction to Private International Law

RYAN JAY I ROSET AND MARIA JESSE ANNE B GLORIA

I. The Subject Matter of Private International Law

Private international law is that body of conventions, model laws, national laws, legal guides, and other documents and instruments that regulate private relationships across national borders.[1] It refers to that part of law where a foreign element, by way of a fact, event or transaction, is closely connected to more than one state or legal system.[2] In other words, it pertains to that branch of law that deals with conflicts in the domestic law of different nations related to private transactions between those countries.[3] This, consequently, gives rise to three separate but interrelated issues: jurisdiction, choice of law, and recognition and enforcement of a foreign judgment.[4]

Private international law possesses a dualistic character, which balances international consensus with domestic recognition and implementation, as well as balancing sovereign actions with those of the private sector.[5] It can arise in a variety of topics such as contracts, marriage and divorce, jurisdiction, recognition of judgments, child adoption and abduction, and the like.[6] The most complex equitable claim might need private international law to solve a problem.

Inasmuch as private international law has a sovereign aspect, it cannot be divorced from the phenomenon of state-building itself. There are nearly 200 member states in the United Nations. Each of these comprise independent entities with their own laws, histories, identities, and cultures; in the exercise of their sovereignty and self-determination, these states have the power to enact laws, rules, and regulations to govern subjects within their respective municipal domains, consistent with their social and political values.

There are times when these municipal laws are consistent with the laws of other states; there are instances as well when they are not. In times past, it was not such a common problem in view of the vast spatial distances between states. With the advent of globalisation and advances in transportation, industry, and telecommunications technology, the world, in many ways, has gotten smaller. A simple click of a mouse in Thailand triggers a financial transaction involving

[1] D Ford and American Society of International Law, 'Private International Law' (Electronic Source Guide, 2013), www.asil.org/sites/default/files/ERG_PRIVATE_INT.pdf.

[2] E Aguiling-Pangalangan, 'International Judicial Cooperation Through The Hague Conference On Private International Law (Hcch) Conventions' (2017) *Philippine Yearbook Of International Law* 158–60, law.upd.edu.ph/wp-content/uploads/2021/09/IJC-The-Hague.pdf.

[3] International Legal Research, 'Private International Law', (n.d.), law.duke.edu/ilrt/def_terms_3.htm.

[4] Aguiling-Pangalanan (n 2).

[5] Ford (n 1).

[6] International Legal Research (n 3).

a payment of a Philippine bank to a United States incorporated company, which then orders its supplier in Japan to ship goods manufactured and located in China, to some location in Guam. It is also noteworthy that advances in environmental science link large-scale corporate business conduct to transboundary harms. This will become more prominent in climate litigation, and the area of attribution science, which seeks to ascertain liability for human-induced greenhouse gases that increased the likelihood of climate impacts for communities. Even amorous matters have increasingly become more complicated. Not only are prospective love found online, even marriages can now be celebrated virtually.[7]

As life becomes more complex, conflicts of law problems involving family relations, property matters, contracts, torts, and business multiply at a rate deemed unfathomable years before.[8] Transactions today have ceased to be limited to municipal spheres but are instead characterised by an intricate web of tangled connections. On this score, it may be well worth to quote the prophetic and sagacious Jovito Salonga (1920–2016), a known Filipino legal luminary and former Senate President, whose words decades ago on the present subject matter still ring true today:

> As life becomes more complex, conflicts problems involving family relations, property matters, contracts, torts, business associations multiply at a rate that would have been incredible many years ago. Transactions today are seldom confined within national, territorial limits. The expansion of international trade, the influx of foreign investments almost everywhere x x x, the encouragement given to the tourist industry, the massive migration of persons from one country to another due to economic or political difficulties at home, and the lifting of many barriers to international commerce and intercourse as a result of the 'information revolution' x x x are among the factors that make Private International Law an important department of law.

A. As Distinguished from Public International Law

Public international law concerns state-to-state relations and intergovernmental bodies, whereas private international law involves relationships between private parties across international jurisdictions including commercial affairs and family law.[9] As to subjects, public international law concerns itself with states, and international organisations. On the other hand, private international law deals with, as a general rule, individuals and entities.[10]

However, recent developments in environmental rights and human rights law have started to consider corporate entities as the subject of human rights. The Supreme Court of Canada's ruling in *Nevsun Resources Ltd. v Araya*[11] illustrates the modern understanding of how public international law concepts affect private law claims, especially when it involves alleged violations of international humanitarian law. In *Nevsun Resources Ltd. v Araya*, the Court summarised the facts of the case as follows:

> Three Eritrean workers claim that they were indefinitely conscripted through Eritrea's military service into a forced labour regime where they were required to work at a mine in Eritrea. They claim they

[7] R Amjad, 'How To Get Married Online in Utah (Step-by-Step Guide)' (30 August 2024), www.courtly.com/resources/how-to-get-married-online-in-utah-step-by-step-guide.

[8] J Salonga, *Private International Law* (Rex Bookstore, 1995) 32.

[9] G Pe Benito, *Conflicts of Law* (Rex Bookstore, 2020) 2.

[10] ibid.

[11] *Nevsun Resources Ltd. v Araya*, 2020 SCC 5, [2020] 1 S.C.R. 166, (2020), decisions.scc-csc.ca/scc-csc/scc-csc/en/item/18169/index.do.

> were subjected to violent, cruel, inhuman and degrading treatment. The mine is owned by a Canadian company, Nevsun Resources Ltd. The Eritrean workers started proceedings in British Columbia against Nevsun and sought damages for breaches of customary international law prohibitions against forced labour, slavery, cruel, inhuman or degrading treatment, and crimes against humanity. They also sought damages for breaches of domestic torts including conversion, battery, unlawful confinement, conspiracy and negligence. Nevsun brought a motion to strike the pleadings on the basis of the act of state doctrine, which precludes domestic courts from assessing the sovereign acts of a foreign government. Nevsun also took the position that the claims based on customary international law should be struck because they have no reasonable prospect of success. The chambers judge dismissed Nevsun's motion to strike, and the Court of Appeal agreed.

As earlier mentioned, the subject of public international law are states and intergovernmental bodies. It is clear from the facts of *Nevsun Resources Ltd. v Araya* that Nevsun, being a mining corporation, is neither a state nor an intergovernmental body that could generally be held responsible for human rights violations. It is noteworthy that, based on the facts of the case, it was the Eritrean government who conscripted the claimants and subjected them to violent, cruel, inhuman, and degrading treatment. It was, thus, only natural for Nevsun to raise the act of state doctrine as a defence. Interestingly, the courts of British Columbia consistently held that the act of state doctrine is not a bar to the claim of the Eritrean workers, to wit:

> The act of state doctrine and its underlying principles as developed in Canadian jurisprudence are not a bar to the Eritrean workers' claims. The act of state doctrine has played no role in Canadian law and is not part of Canadian common law. Whereas English jurisprudence has reaffirmed and reconstructed the act of state doctrine, Canadian law has developed its own approach to addressing the twin principles underlying the doctrine: conflict of laws and judicial restraint. Both principles have developed separately in Canadian jurisprudence rather than as elements of an all-encompassing act of state doctrine. As such, in Canada, the principles underlying the act of state doctrine have been completely subsumed within this jurisprudence. Canadian courts determine questions dealing with the enforcement of foreign laws according to ordinary private international law principles which generally call for deference, but allow for judicial discretion to decline to enforce foreign laws where such laws are contrary to public policy, including respect for public international law.

However, the Court in *Nevsun Resources Ltd. v Araya* did not stop at explaining the inapplicability of the act of state doctrine. The Court also explained the impact of the development of international human rights law on the international law framework; particularly, the recognition that the prohibition against slavery, forced labour, and cruel, inhuman and degrading treatment have attained the status of *jus cogens*.

> Modern international human rights law is the phoenix that rose from the ashes of World War II and declared global war on human rights abuses. Its mandate was to prevent breaches of internationally of accepted norms. Those norms were not meant to be theoretical aspirations or legal luxuries, but moral imperatives and legal necessities. Conduct that undermined the norms was to be identified and addressed.
>
> While states were historically the main subjects of international law, it has long-since evolved from this state-centric template. The past 70 years have seen a proliferation of human rights law that transformed international law and made the individual an integral part of this legal domain, reflected in the creation of a complex network of conventions and normative instruments intended to protect human rights and ensure compliance with those rights. The rapid emergence of human rights signified a revolutionary shift in international law to a human-centric conception of global order. The result of these developments is that international law now works not only to maintain peace between states, but to protect the lives of individuals, their liberty, their health, and their education. The context in which international human rights norms must be interpreted and applied today is one in which such norms are routinely

> applied to private actors. It is therefore not plain and obvious that corporations today enjoy a blanket exclusion under customary international law from direct liability for violations of obligatory, definable, and universal norms of international law.

The Court then explained that 'Canada has long followed the conventional path of automatically incorporating customary international law into domestic law via the doctrine of adoption, making it part of the law of Canada. Therefore, customary international law is automatically adopted into domestic law without any need for legislative action.' Consequently, international human rights law has the same force and effect in Canada and must be treated with the same respect as domestic law. In light of the application of the doctrine of adoption, the Court ruled to dismiss the appeal of Nevsun.

> A compelling argument can therefore be made that since customary international law is part of Canadian common law, a breach by a Canadian company can theoretically be directly remedied. Since the workers' claims are based on norms that already form part of our common law, it is not 'plain and obvious' that our domestic common law cannot recognize a direct remedy for their breach. Appropriately remedying the violations of *jus cogens* and norms of customary international law requires different and stronger responses than typical tort claims, given the public nature and importance of the violated rights involved, the gravity of their breach, the impact on the domestic and global rights objectives, and the need to deter subsequent breaches.
>
> Nevsun has not demonstrated that the Eritrean workers' claim based on breaches of customary international law should be struck at this preliminary stage. The Court is not required to determine definitively whether the Eritrean workers should be awarded damages for the alleged breaches of customary international law. It is enough to conclude that the breaches of customary international law, or *jus cogens*, relied on by the Eritrean workers may well apply to Nevsun. Since the customary international law norms raised by the Eritrean workers form part of the Canadian common law, and since Nevsun is a company bound by Canadian law, the claims of the Eritrean workers for breaches of customary international law should be allowed to proceed.

The case of *Nevsun Resources Ltd. v Araya* illustrates not only the development of public international law but also its convergence with private international law. As international law on environment and human rights continue to develop, the traditional delineation between public and private international law slowly fades away. In fact, the ruling in *Nevsun Resources Ltd. v Araya* is consistent with the principles adopted by the Philippines concerning environmental law, as it relates to commercial activities. Recent legislation, Philippine Supreme Court guidelines, and jurisprudence have set a trend towards greater government and private sector accountability on matters involving environmental issues. Philippine domestic law, as it involves foreign and local companies with mining operations and other analogous activities that may harm the environment or cause human rights violations, is affected by the modern understanding of how private actors are held accountable within the framework of both public international law and Philippine municipal laws.

II. History of Private International Law

Integration and diversity are two dominant features of modern society that inevitably give rise to conflicts of laws.[12] In the midst of all these is the plurality of legal systems, which exercise

[12] HE Yntema, 'The Historic Bases of Private International Law' (1953) 2(3) *The American Journal of Comparative Law* 297, doi.org/10.2307/837480.

sovereignty within their own territories, and which exercise power over their legal subjects, and the reality of interstate transactions, arising out of commerce, or personal connections with a foreign element.[13]

The conundrum of overlapping legal systems is by no means a modern phenomenon. In fact, in the Greek cities of the Hellenic period, there were special courts for cases involving foreigners.[14] In Rome too, customary laws were recognised in the courts of the provincial governor.[15] As Yntema noted:

> That specialized courts with special laws for racial groups within a political community existed in the ancient world, is indicated by one of the Fayoum papyri, x x x Among the royal decrees of the Ptolomies, the document includes a text prescribing that contracts between Greeks – who had established colonies in Egypt – and Egyptians, if in Greek form, should be tried before *chrematists*, the Greek courts; if in Egyptian form, before the *laocrits*, the native courts, in accordance with the laws of the country.[16]

Although these edicts did not deal specifically with the application of foreign law to foreign cases, they nonetheless dealt with the challenge of plurality of native laws, which served as the precursor to modern private international law.

The emergence of Italian city-states in the late middle ages, such as Florence, Bologna, Milan, Pisa, Venice, Padua, and Medina, paved the way for the development of private international law. These flourishing city-states, brimming with wealth and progress arising from trade, and commerce, developed their own unique customs and municipal laws. The resulting legal skirmishes concerning which laws to apply incited the minds of eminent thinkers of that time, including the jurist Bartolus (1314–57), to grapple with the issue.[17] Their approach was through the lens of statutory interpretation, which allowed them to apply the law of Rome, and the special local laws, or *statuta*, of the autonomous municipalities within the feudal structure; in many ways this approach limited the jurists' imagination, nonetheless, they were able to conveniently take advantage of the wealth of literature on Roman law and apply it to the existing native laws.[18]

Eventually, a theory of statutes was formulated and laws were further subdivided into real (*statuta realia*), personal (*statuta personalia*), and mixed (*statuta mixta*). Real statutes were those that applied to immovables within the territory. Personal statutes were those that applied to movables and persons outside of their domicile, such as laws on personal status. Mixed statutes applied to objects that cannot be siloed into either, but they were mostly applied to contracts.[19] By the fourteenth century, however, a number of principles have been developed to resolve statutory conflicts according to the nature and subject matter of the provision. Among these were as follows:

> *Lex loci actus* is a legal term that means the laws to a particular action or agreement are determined by the laws of the place where it took place;
>
> *Litis ordinatio* which states that questions of procedure are governed by the place where the suit is filed;
>
> *Litis decisio* which pertains to matters affecting the performance of a contract, if arising conformably to the contract at the time of its conclusion, shall be governed by the law of the place of contract. However, liability for delicts is governed by the *lex loci delicti* except when a foreigner may justifiably plead ignorance for a particular law;

[13] ibid.
[14] ibid 300.
[15] ibid.
[16] ibid 300–301.
[17] Salonga (n 8) 15.
[18] Yntema (n 12) 303.
[19] Salonga (n 8) 15–16.

> *Lex rei sitae* is Latin for 'the law where the property is situated, and real estate or immovable property is exclusively subject to the laws of the government within whose territory it is situated'.[20]

In the sixteenth century, French legal thinkers, informed by the French tradition of *coutime* or customs, where provinces had separate legal systems, introduced their own innovations to the development of private international law. Charles Dumoulin (1500–66), an ardent monarchist who resisted the idea of federalism, introduced the notion that parties to a contract could choose the law that was to govern their agreement.[21] In other words, the intentions of the parties, rather than territoriality, governs the validity and consequences of the contract. In effect, Dumoulin's idea, anchored on contractual autonomy, proved pivotal in expanding the consequences of statutes beyond their parochial limits, while enfeebling territorial moorings.

On the other side of the spectrum was Dumoulin's chief critic, Bertrand D'Argentre (1519–90). D'Argentre was a Breton, who ardently believed in the historical independence of Brittany, and the autonomy of its ancestral customs.[22] This fervour, wittingly or unwittingly, defined his thought, which espoused the superiority of territorial sovereignty; drawing on the Italian trinity of *statute*. D'Argentre asserted that, except for a limited group of purely personal statutes, that is, those that pertain to personal status, capacity, or movables,[23] all laws are real, that is, territorial in their application.[24] This predilection for *real statuta* led D'Argentre to advocate that even in matters of succession, the law of the country where the movable is situated should apply.[25] Although both Dumoulin and D'Argentre believed in *coutime* and its transboundary application, they diverged in their points of departure; Dumoulin anchored his theory on contractual autonomy, while D'Argentre's theoretical bearings laid in territorialism.

By the seventeenth century, the wave of independence movements, which followed the conclusion of continental Europe's Thirty Years War, ushered in a new era for private international law. Emboldened by their recent independence, erudite jurists, such as Ulrich Huber, formulated three maxims upon which private international law rests, to wit: (1) the laws of each state *(imperii)* have force within the limits of that government and bind all subjects to it, but not beyond; (2) all persons within the limits of a government, whether they live there permanently or temporarily, are deemed to be subjects thereof; and (3) sovereigns will so act by way of *comity* so that rights acquired within the limits of a government retain their force everywhere so far as they do not cause prejudice to the powers or rights of such government or of their subjects.[26] Huber regarded *comity* as a political concession, which might be granted depending upon the sovereign;[27] the recognition in each state of so-called foreign-created rights was a mere concession, which was granted based on the basis of convenience and utility, and not as the result of a binding obligation or duty.[28] In simple terms, the courts of sovereign states do not apply foreign law; they merely recognise the consequences of the operation of foreign law.

Huber's *comitas gentium* was widely accepted and his emphasis on sovereignty prompted continental Europe to conveniently codify private international law rules in their own civil code.

[20] Yntema (n 12) 305.
[21] Salonga (n 8) 16.
[22] Yntema (n 12) 305.
[23] Salonga (n 8) 17.
[24] Yntema (n 12) 306.
[25] Salonga (n 8) 17.
[26] EG Lorenzen and Huber, 'Huber's De Conflictu Legum' (1918) 13 *Illinois Law Review* 376, openyls.law.yale.edu/bitstream/handle/20.500.13051/4068/Huber_s_De_Conflictu_Legum.pdf?sequence=2&isAllowed=y.
[27] ibid.
[28] ibid 376.

Among these rules, which can be found in the Philippine Civil Code, is *lex situs*, that is, real property as well as personal property are subject to the law of the country where it is located.[29]

In the nineteenth century, three prominent jurists defined the development of private international law scholarship: Joseph Story, Friedrich Karl von Savigny, and Pasquale Stanislao Mancini.

Story was greatly influenced by Huber's work. He proposed three maxims: (i) every nation possesses an exclusive sovereignty and jurisdiction within its own territory; (ii) no state or nation can, by its laws, directly affect, or bind property out of its own territory, or persons not resident therein, whether they are natural born subjects or others; and, (iii) whatever force and obligations the laws of one country have in another depends solely upon the laws, and municipal regulations of the latter, that is to say, upon its own proper jurisprudence and polity, and upon its own express or tacit consent.[30]

Savigny, on the other hand, had a different view and maintained that in resolving conflicts of law issues, it is essential to always bear in mind the existence of an international community of nations having intercourse with one another.[31] Rather than enquiring whether rules pertained to property, persons, or acts, an approach which confined prior jurists, Savigny proposed to ascertain fundamentally where legal problem or relationship, according to its nature, has its seat.[32] Here the seat is the place where the thing is situated or in case of a person, where he or she is domiciled.

The Italian jurist Mancini argued that the rational basis of international law is the nation and the *nazionalista*.[33] According to Mancini, by nature, and history, people are grouped in different nations.[34] Components of nationality, he asserted, are the traditions, religion, customs of life, the language, the race of people, its history and traditions, even its landscape of the country and its climate, all of which create a spiritual unity through the common consciousness of nationality.[35] This identity is inextricably linked to the concept of nation. In matters of personal character, the citizen of the state is protected by state law. These include matters on status, capacity, and family relationships.[36] This of course was later codified and became the basis of the Philippines's nationality principle found under Article 15 of the Civil Code, that is, a person's status and capacity are governed by a person's nationality, even though living abroad.

In matters of contract, on the other hand, Mancini asserted 'autonomy of the parties' as an adjunct of 'personal freedom,' which in many ways, echoes Dumoulin's perspective. With respect to property, however, particularly real property, a certain authority was still conceded to the local law, ie *lex situs*. And finally other matters, related to the hazy category of 'public policy,' remained under the sway of territorial rules, mainly those enacted by the *lex fori*; under this category are laws pertaining to public order, such as criminal laws.[37]

By the twentieth century, private international law came to be defined by three distinct schools. The first of these were the neo-statuists, which were mostly adherents of the Italian school. The

[29] Republic Act No. 386, Civil Code of the Philippines, (1949) Article 15, www.officialgazette.gov.ph/1949/06/18/republic-act-no-386/.

[30] R Michaels, 'Forthcoming in Elgar Encyclopedia of Private International Law' (n.d.) 8, scholarship.law.duke.edu/cgi/viewcontent.cgi?article=6387&context=faculty_scholarship.

[31] Salonga (n 8) 23.

[32] ibid 24.

[33] ibid 25.

[34] R De Nova, 'New Trends in Italian Private International Law' (1963) 28(4) *Law and Contemporary Problems* 808, doi.org/10.2307/1190566.

[35] Salonga (n 8) 25.

[36] De Nova (n 34) 808.

[37] Salonga (n 8) 25.

Philippines falls under this category.[38] The second were the internationalists, who asserted that the problem is not to classify laws according to their object, but to discover for every legal relation the appropriate local law to which in its proper nature it belongs.[39] The internationalists, who fervently believed in the existence of an international community of nations having intercourse with one another, advocated for a single body of international rules that could resolve problems with a foreign element.[40] The most outstanding merit of this particular theory is that it tries to decide on each conflict the basis of its circumstances and most relevant set of laws. It supports the application of laws of that legal system to which the parties/things concerned naturally belong. To the third group belongs the territorialists, who believed that 'courts of sovereign states do not apply foreign law but merely recognize the consequences of the operation of foreign law.' This means that courts of a country apply foreign law only to the extent to which they are permitted to do so by the sovereign. In effect, it means that judges cannot by their will apply any foreign law or judgment to any case they are deciding; a judge essentially applies the law of the land to govern all the cases that have a foreign element.[41]

III. Sources of Private International Law

Private international law is governed mostly by the domestic law of the countries in question.[42] For instance, whether, a foreign judgment shall be enforced by a Philippine court is determined by Philippine domestic laws. There has been initiative to create a more unified system, through bilateral or multilateral treatises, codifications, conventions, and practices. These efforts remain laudable for purposes of uniformity and practicality but as things stand, much of private international law remains subject-specific, ie contracts or family law, which have their own governing rules.[43]

A. Codes and Other Domestic Laws

Private international law exerted great influence in the codifications of continental Europe. For instance, Article 3 of the Napoleonic Code, which followed the nationality rule, was later adopted in the development of the Spanish Civil Code, and later on the New Civil Code of the Philippines, among other former colonies of European countries.

There are special statutes too that have been passed in the Philippines that have conflicts of law provisions. Among these are the Corporation Code, the Anti-Dummy Law, the Revised Penal Code, Carriage of Goods in Sea Act, General Banking Act, Investments Act, Insurance Code, Intellectual Property Code, among others. Of course, the 1987 Philippine Constitution too, contains provisions on nationality, and *comity*, and thus a source of private international law.

[38] ibid 27.

[39] S Gandhi, 'Theories Of Private International Law And Their Application' (2021) II(I) *Indian Journal of Integrated Research in Law* 4.

[40] Salonga (n 8) 27.

[41] Gandhi (n 39) 6.

[42] LibGuides, UCLA School of Law Hugh and Hazel Darling Law Library, 'Private International Law' (n.d.) Introduction, libguides.law.ucla.edu/privateinternational.

[43] ibid.

B. Treatises

The Philippines entered into treatises and conventions that pertain to private international law. Out of the 39 Hague Conference on Private International Law Conventions, the Philippines is a state party to five: (1) Intercountry Adoption (in 1996), (2) Civil Aspects of International Child Abduction (in 2016), (3) Apostille (in 2019), (4) Service (in 2020), and (5) Recovery of Child Support (in 2022).

The Philippines also acceded to the Convention on International Civil Aviation, the Warsaw Convention, Convention on Offenses Committed Onboard Aircraft, the Convention on the Carriage of Goods by Sea Act, the Convention on the Recognition of Foreign Judgment on Civil and Commercial Matters, Convention Establishing the World Intellectual Property Organisation, among others.

Also included under treatises and conventions as the source of private law are the standards issued by international rule-making bodies, such as the United Nations Commission for International Trade Law.

C. Case Law

The rules on private international law are to a large extent, judge-made.[44] Courts have to operate almost without any written rules. As a consequence, the rules become flexible and incomplete, rather than petrified. As Ronald H Graveson said, private international law is more completely judge-made than most any other branch of law.

D. Preliminary Matters

In understanding the concept of private international law, there are several matters that must be preliminarily considered. The challenge in private international law is resolving a dispute while respecting the respective jurisdiction of states and safeguarding equally important but conflicting interests. As will be further discussed below, it is crucial to properly characterise issues and identify connecting factors when resolving conflict of laws disputes.

E. Characterisation and Incidental Question

Characterisation refers to the process by which a court assigns a fact-based situation in the proper legal category to determine the applicable laws to apply.[45] This characterisation is necessary inasmuch as different legal systems may classify a particular set of facts as a tort issue, while another one considers it as a property issue, or even a purely contractual one, which may then lead to different legal outcomes. The process of characterisation, therefore, is meant to ensure that the court identifies the correct category before deciding which law to apply.

Two approaches have developed out of much legal writing: the first holds that all incidental questions should be governed by the relevant choice-of-law rule of the forum; the second

[44] Salonga (n 8) 39.
[45] JR Coquia and EA Pangalanan, *Conflict of Laws, Materials and Cases* (Central Books, 2000) 83.

considers that the law governing the principal issue in the case should determine what law governs the subsidiary questions.[46] Characterisation is often complicated by the 'incidental question' which may arise as a preliminary or subsequent enquiry.[47] The issue of the incidental question is best illustrated by way of an example:

> Suppose a Greek national (H) dies intestate with a domicile in Greece leaving goods in England. The forum (F) is England. Under F's conflicts rule the law of the domicile governs the succession. Suppose further that W, H's wife, claims to be entitled to a share in the estate which is under the control of F. By what law is the existence of the marital relation to be determined? Suppose by the English law, *locus regit actum*. The parties having married in England by a civil ceremony, the marriage is valid by F's conflicts rule. But by Greek law (the domicile) the law of nationality (also Greek law) determines the validity of the marriage. Since a priest was not present, as required by Greek law, the marriage was a nullity. The principal question in Wolff's illustration is one of succession. It involves the selection of the country whose system of law will provide rules governing the devolution of the estate on intestacy. The incidental question is, Is W the wife of H? The question is so styled because it arises incidentally in a question of intestate succession. Whether or not W is really the wife of H is said to raise a 'preliminary question', because she first must prove the marital status. But it is obvious that the issue of her status cannot arise until after the selection of a domestic system whose succession laws provide that a wife may claim a share in the estate of a husband dying intestate. In other words, the selection of the *lex causae* on the principal issue must precede the 'preliminary question.'[48]

There are two general approaches to characterisation. The first is called the single-aspect approach where one element of the situation is considered in order to connect a case.[49] The more modern approach, however, is to consider all important factors, both territorial and non-territorial, and rationally elaborate the policies and purposes underlying the particular rules that come into question, as well as the needs of international intercourse.[50] The Philippines, however, follows the single-aspect method, as may be culled from the following provisions of its New Civil Code:

> Article 15. Laws relating to family rights and duties, or to the status, condition and legal capacity of persons are binding upon citizens of the Philippines, even though living abroad. (9a)
>
> Article 16. Real property as well as personal property is subject to the law of the country where it is stipulated.
>
> However, intestate and testamentary successions, both with respect to the order of succession and to the amount of successional rights and to the intrinsic validity of testamentary provisions, shall be regulated by the national law of the person whose succession is under consideration, whatever may be the nature of the property and regardless of the country wherein said property may be found. (10a)
>
> Article 17. The forms and solemnities of contracts, wills, and other public instruments shall be governed by the laws of the country in which they are executed.
>
> When the acts referred to are executed before the diplomatic or consular officials of the Republic of the Philippines in a foreign country, the solemnities established by Philippine laws shall be observed in their execution.

[46] ibid 529.

[47] AE Gotlieb, 'The Incidental Question in Anglo-American Conflict of Law' (1955) XXXIII *The Canadian Bar Review* 525.

[48] ibid 529–30.

[49] Coquia and Pangalanan (n 45) 82.

[50] ibid.

> Prohibitive laws concerning persons, their acts or property, and those which have for their object public order, public policy and good customs shall not be rendered ineffective by laws or judgments promulgated, or by determinations or conventions agreed upon in a foreign country. (11a)

F. *Dépecage*

Inextricably related to the incidental question is *Dépeçage*, which literally means dismemberment in French, and pertains to that concept in private international law where different aspects of a case with a foreign element are governed by different legal systems. This may be relevant in the context of autonomy of contracts where different aspects thereof are governed by different laws. This may also find application in the context for instance of testate succession, the formalities of which, in the Philippine context, is governed by the law where they are executed, while the successional rights are ruled by the nationality of the testator.[51]

G. *Renvoi* and Transmission

Renvoi is a procedure whereby a jural matter presented is referred by the conflict of laws rules of the forum to a foreign state, the conflict of rules of which, in turn refers the matter to the law of the forum of a third state.[52] The referral back to the law of the forum is called 'remission' while a referral to a third state is called 'transmission'.[53] The principle of *renvoi*, as applied in the Philippines, is best illustrated in *Aznar v Garcia*,[54] which involves the will of an American citizen from the State of California in the United States who died while domiciled in the Philippines.

In *Aznar v Garcia*, the decedent, Edward E Christensen, was a citizen of the United States and of the State of California. At the time of his death, he was domiciled in the Philippines. In his will, he indicated that he had but one (1) child, named, Maria Lucy Christensen (Lucy), who shall inherit most of his estate. The decedent further stated that he is devising and bequeathing a certain amount to Maria Helen Christensen (Helen), who, while baptised as Christensen, was not, at any time, adopted by the decedent. Particularly, the will stated:

> 3. I declare … that I have but ONE (1) child, named MARIA LUCY CHRISTENSEN (now Mrs. Bernard Daney), who was born in the Philippines about twenty-eight years ago, and who is now residing at No. 665 Rodger Young Village, Los Angeles, California, U.S.A.
>
> 4. I further declare that I now have no living ascendants, and no descendants except my above named daughter, MARIA LUCY CHRISTENSEN DANEY.
>
> xxx xxx xxx
>
> 7. I give, devise and bequeath unto MARIA HELEN CHRISTENSEN, now married to Eduardo Garcia, about eighteen years of age and who, notwithstanding the fact that she was baptized Christensen, is not in any way related to me, nor has she been at any time adopted by me, and who, from all information

[51] Republic Act No. 386, Civil Code of the Philippines, (1949), Articles 16 and 17, www.officialgazette.gov.ph/1949/06/18/republic-act-no-386/.

[52] Coquia and Pangalanan (n 45) 102.

[53] ibid.

[54] *In The Matter of The Testate Estate of Edward E. Christensen, Deceased, Adolfo C. Aznar and Lucy Christensen v Helen Christensen Garcia*, G.R. No. L-16749, 117 Phil 96–110, (31 January 1963).

> I have now resides in Egpit, Digos, Davao, Philippines, the sum of THREE THOUSAND SIX HUNDRED PESOS (P3,600.00), Philippine Currency the same to be deposited in trust for the said Maria Helen Christensen with the Davao Branch of the Philippine National Bank, and paid to her at the rate of One Hundred Pesos (P100.00), Philippine Currency per month until the principal thereof as well as any interest which may have accrued thereon, is exhausted …
>
> xxx xxx xxx
>
> 12. I hereby give, devise and bequeath, unto my well-beloved daughter, the said MARIA LUCY CHRISTENSEN DANEY (Mrs. Bernard Daney), now residing as aforesaid at No. 665 Rodger Young Village, Los Angeles, California, U.S.A., all the income from the rest, remainder, and residue of my property and estate, real, personal and/or mixed, of whatsoever kind or character, and wheresoever situated, of which I may be possessed at my death and which may have come to me from any source whatsoever, during her lifetime: …

In accordance with the will of the decedent, the executor, in his proposed project of partition, ratified the devise to Helen and proposed that the residue of the estate be transferred to Lucy. Helen opposed the approval of the project of partition. The Philippine Supreme Court, in the case of *Aznar v Garcia*, explained that:

> Opposition to the approval of the project of partition was filed by Helen Christensen Garcia, insofar as it deprives her (Helen) of her legitime as an acknowledged natural child. The legal grounds of opposition are (a) that the distribution should be governed by the laws of the Philippines, and (b) that said order of distribution is contrary thereto insofar as it denies to Helen Christensen, one of two acknowledged natural children, one-half of the estate in full ownership. It was alleged that the law that should govern the estate of the deceased Christensen should not be the internal law of California alone, but the entire law thereof because several foreign elements are involved, that the forum is the Philippines and even if the case were decided in California, Section 946 of the California Civil Code, which requires that the domicile of the decedent should apply, should be applicable.
>
> The court below ruled that as Edward E. Christensen was a citizen of the United States and of the State of California at the time of his death, the successional rights and intrinsic validity of the provisions in his will are to be governed by the law of California, in accordance with which a testator has the right to dispose of his property in the way he desires, because the right of absolute dominion over his property is sacred and inviolable (In re McDaniel's Estate, 77 Cal. Appl. 2d 877, 176 P. 2d 952, and In re Kaufman, 117 Cal. 286, 49 Pac. 192, cited in page 179, Record on Appeal). Oppositor Maria Helen Christensen, through counsel, filed various motions for reconsideration, but these were denied. Hence this appeal.

At this point, it is clear that the foreign element, the fact that the decedent is a foreign national, had made a simple issue of succession into a complex one. If the decedent was a Filipino, the rules of succession provided by the Civil Code of the Philippines would have applied without question. However, the Court was reluctant in applying the domestic law on succession outright because of the fact that the decedent was a foreign national. Instead, the Court was guided by the conflict of laws provision of the Civil Code of the Philippines and the concept of renvoi in resolving the issue in *Aznar v Garcia*.

In order to determine which law should apply, it was imperative to resolve the factual issue of the citizenship and domicile of the decedent because the citizenship of the decedent shall determine which between the laws of the Philippines and the laws of the State of California shall apply. Meanwhile, the determination that the decedent was indeed domiciled in the Philippines and that he left properties located in the Philippines shall support the conclusion that the property forum is indeed the Philippines. After going through the record of the case, the Court observed that:

> In arriving at the conclusion that the domicile of the deceased is the Philippines, we are persuaded by the fact that he was born in New York, migrated to California and resided there for nine years, and since he

came to the Philippines in 1913 he returned to California very rarely and only for short visits (perhaps to relatives), and considering that he appears never to have owned or acquired a home or properties in that state, which would indicate that he would ultimately abandon the Philippines and make home in the State of California.

Sec. 16. Residence is a term used with many shades of meaning from mere temporary presence to the most permanent abode. Generally, however, it is used to denote something more than mere physical presence. (Goodrich on Conflict of Laws, p. 29)

As to his citizenship, however, We find that the citizenship that he acquired in California when he resided in Sacramento, California from 1904 to 1913, was never lost by his stay in the Philippines, for the latter was a territory of the United States (not a state) until 1946 and the deceased appears to have considered himself as a citizen of California by the fact that when he executed his will in 1951 he declared that he was a citizen of that State; so that he appears never to have intended to abandon his California citizenship by acquiring another. This conclusion is in accordance with the following principle expounded by Goodrich in his Conflict of Laws.

The terms 'residence' and 'domicile' might well be taken to mean the same thing, a place of permanent abode. But domicile, as has been shown, has acquired a technical meaning. Thus one may be domiciled in a place where he has never been. And he may reside in a place where he has no domicile. The man with two homes, between which he divides his time, certainly resides in each one, while living in it. But if he went on business which would require his presence for several weeks or months, he might properly be said to have sufficient connection with the place to be called a resident. It is clear, however, that, if he treated his settlement as continuing only for the particular business in hand, not giving up his former 'home,' he could not be a domiciled New Yorker. Acquisition of a domicile of choice requires the exercise of intention as well as physical presence. 'Residence simply requires bodily presence of an inhabitant in a given place, while domicile requires bodily presence in that place and also an intention to make it one's domicile.' Residence, however, is a term used with many shades of meaning, from the merest temporary presence to the most permanent abode, and it is not safe to insist that any one use is the only proper one. (Goodrich, p. 29)

The law that governs the validity of his testamentary dispositions is defined in Article 16 of the Civil Code of the Philippines, which is as follows:

ART. 16. Real property as well as personal property is subject to the law of the country where it is situated.

However, intestate and testamentary successions, both with respect to the order of succession and to the amount of successional rights and to the intrinsic validity of testamentary provisions, shall be regulated by the national law of the person whose succession is under consideration, whatever may be the nature of the property and regardless of the country where said property may be found.

The application of this article in the case at bar requires the determination of the meaning of the term '*national law*' is used therein.

There is no single American law governing the validity of testamentary provisions in the United States, each state of the Union having its own private law applicable to its citizens only and in force only within the state. The 'national law' indicated in Article 16 of the Civil Code above quoted can not, therefore, possibly mean or apply to any general American law. So it can refer to no other than the private law of the State of California.

In the Philippines, courts do not take judicial notice of the existence and content of foreign laws. Thus, litigants who would need to refer to foreign laws must present proof of the existence of the said foreign law. In this case, the executor has already proven that the decedent was a citizen of the State of California even though he was domiciled in the Philippines for a considerable length of time. During the proceedings before the lower court in *Aznar v Garcia*, the executor presented an authenticated copy of the California Probate Code, the pertinent law of the State of California on succession.

The position of the appellee (the executor of the estate of the decedent) is that, according to the California Probate Code, a testator may dispose of his property by will in the form and manner he desires. In support of this position, the executor-appellee cited the case of Estate of McDaniel, 77 Cal. Appl. 2d 877, 176 P. 2d 952. Meanwhile, the appellant (Helen) invoked Article 946 of the Civil Code of California, which provided that, if there is no law to the contrary, in the place where personal property is situated, it is deemed to follow the person of its owner, and is thus governed by the law of his domicile. In accordance with this provision and following the doctrine of renvoi, the question of the validity of the testamentary provision in question should be referred back to the law of the decedent's domicile, which is the Philippines. It is at this point that the Court exhaustively explained the doctrine of renvoi, to wit:

> The theory of doctrine of *renvoi* has been defined by various authors, thus:
>
> The problem has been stated in this way: 'When the Conflict of Laws rule of the forum refers a jural matter to a foreign law for decision, is the reference to the purely internal rules of law of the foreign system; i.e., to the totality of the foreign law minus its Conflict of Laws rules?'
>
> x x x   x x x   x x x
>
> 'This is one type of *renvoi*. A jural matter is presented which the conflict-of-laws rule of the forum refers to a foreign law, the conflict-of-laws rule of which, in turn, refers the matter back again to the law of the forum. This is renvoi in the narrower sense. The German term for this judicial process is "Ruckverweisung."' (Harvard Law Review, Vol. 31, pp. 523–571.)
>
> After a decision has been arrived at that a foreign law is to be resorted to as governing a particular case, the further question may arise: Are the rules as to the conflict of laws contained in such foreign law also to be resorted to? This is a question which, while it has been considered by the courts in but a few instances, has been the subject of frequent discussion by textwriters and essayists; and the doctrine involved has been descriptively designated by them as the 'Renvoyer' to send back, or the 'Ruchversweisung', or the 'Weiterverweisung', since an affirmative answer to the question postulated and the operation of the adoption of the foreign law in toto would in many cases result in returning the main controversy to be decided according to the law of the forum. … (16 C.J.S. 872.)
>
> Another theory, known as the 'doctrine of *renvoi*', has been advanced. The theory of the doctrine of *renvoi* is that the court of the forum, in determining the question before it, must take into account the whole law of the other jurisdiction, but also its rules as to conflict of laws, and then apply the law to the actual question which the rules of the other jurisdiction prescribe. This may be the law of the forum. The doctrine of the *renvoi* has generally been repudiated by the American authorities. (2 Am. Jur. 296)
>
> The scope of the theory of *renvoi* has also been defined and the reasons for its application in a country explained by Prof. Lorenzen in an article in the Yale Law Journal, Vol. 27, 1917–1918, pp. 529–531. The pertinent parts of the article are quoted herein below:
>
> The recognition of the *renvoi* theory implies that the rules of the conflict of laws are to be understood as incorporating not only the ordinary or internal law of the foreign state or country, but its rules of the conflict of laws as well. According to this theory 'the law of a country' means the whole of its law.
>
> x x x   x x x   x x x
>
> Von Bar presented his views at the meeting of the Institute of International Law, at Neuchatel, in 1900, in the form of the following theses:
>
> (1) Every court shall observe the law of its country as regards the application of foreign laws.
> (2) Provided that no express provision to the contrary exists, the court shall respect:
>
> (a) The provisions of a foreign law which disclaims the right to bind its nationals abroad as regards their personal statute, and desires that said personal statute shall be determined by the law of the domicile, or even by the law of the place where the act in question occurred.

(b) The decision of two or more foreign systems of law, provided it be certain that one of them is necessarily competent, which agree in attributing the determination of a question to the same system of law.

x x x x x x x x x

The Court in *Aznar v Garcia* aptly observed that Article 946 of the California Civil Code is the conflict of laws rule, while the rule applied in *In re Kaufman*, the case cited by the executor-appellee, is the internal law of the State of California. From this observation, the Court explained that:

> If the law on succession and the conflict of laws rules of California are to be enforced jointly, each in its own intended and appropriate sphere, the principle cited In re Kaufman should apply to citizens living in the State, but Article 946 should apply to such of its citizens as are not domiciled in California but in other jurisdictions. The rule laid down of resorting to the law of the domicile in the determination of matters with foreign element involved is in accord with the general principle of American law that the domiciliary law should govern in most matters or rights which follow the person of the owner.
>
> When a man dies leaving personal property in one or more states, and leaves a will directing the manner of distribution of the property, the law of the state where he was domiciled at the time of his death will be looked to in deciding legal questions about the will, almost as completely as the law of situs is consulted in questions about the devise of land. It is logical that, since the domiciliary rules control devolution of the personal estate in case of intestate succession, the same rules should determine the validity of an attempted testamentary disposition of the property. Here, also, it is not that the domiciliary has effect beyond the borders of the domiciliary state. The rules of the domicile are recognized as controlling by the Conflict of Laws rules at the situs property, and the reason for the recognition as in the case of intestate succession, is the general convenience of the doctrine. The New York court has said on the point: 'The general principle that a disposition of a personal property, valid at the domicile of the owner, is valid anywhere, is one of the universal application. It had its origin in that international *comity* which was one of the first fruits of civilization, and it this age, when business intercourse and the process of accumulating property take but little notice of boundary lines, the practical wisdom and justice of the rule is more apparent than ever. (Goodrich, Conflict of Laws, Sec. 164, pp. 442–443.)

Guided by the conflict of laws principles of the State of California and of the Philippines, as well as by the doctrine of renvoi, the Court in *Aznar v Garcia* denied the appeal of the appellant (Helen). The Court explained that, since the law of the State of California provides for a set of laws for its citizens domiciled abroad, it was duty-bound to enforce said laws. The Court ratiocinated as follows:

> It is argued on appellees' behalf that the clause 'if there is no law to the contrary in the place where the property is situated' in Sec. 946 of the California Civil Code refers to Article 16 of the Civil Code of the Philippines and that the law to the contrary in the Philippines is the provision in said Article 16 that the *national law* of the deceased should govern. This contention can not be sustained. As explained in the various authorities cited above the national law mentioned in Article 16 of our Civil Code is the law on conflict of laws in the California Civil Code, i.e., Article 946, which authorizes the reference or return of the question to the law of the testator's domicile. The conflict of laws rule in California, Article 946, Civil Code, precisely refers back the case, when a decedent is not domiciled in California, to the law of his domicile, the Philippines in the case at bar. The court of the domicile can not and should not refer the case back to California; such action would leave the issue incapable of determination because the case will then be like a football, tossed back and forth between the two states, between the country of which the decedent was a citizen and the country of his domicile. The Philippine court must apply its own law as directed in the conflict of laws rule of the state of the decedent, if the question has to be decided, especially as the application of the internal law of California provides no legitime for children while the Philippine law, Arts. 887(4) and 894, Civil Code of the Philippines, makes natural children legally acknowledged forced heirs of the parent recognizing them.

> The Philippine cases (In re Estate of Johnson, 39 Phil. 156; Riera vs. Palmaroli, 40 Phil. 105; Miciano vs. Brimo, 50 Phil. 867; Babcock Templeton vs. Rider Babcock, 52 Phil. 130; and Gibbs vs. Government, 59 Phil. 293.) cited by appellees to support the decision can not possibly apply in the case at bar, for two important reasons, i.e., the subject in each case does not appear to be a citizen of a state in the United States but with domicile in the Philippines, and it does not appear in each case that there exists in the state of which the subject is a citizen, a law similar to or identical with Art. 946 of the California Civil Code.
>
> We therefore find that as the domicile of the deceased Christensen, a citizen of California, is the Philippines, the validity of the provisions of his will depriving his acknowledged natural child, the appellant, should be governed by the Philippine Law, the domicile, pursuant to Art. 946 of the Civil Code of California, not by the internal law of California.

Based on the foregoing, the Court clearly referred the jural matter on the validity of the testamentary provisions of the will of Edward E Christensen to his national law, the California Probate Code. However, there was a remission back to the law of the forum (the law of the Philippines) because the California Probate Code clearly provides that the laws of the domicile of its citizens residing abroad shall apply. Since the domicile and the forum in *Aznar v Garcia* are one and the same (the Philippines), remission and not transmission took place. Through the referral of the jural matter back to the Court, the application of the doctrine of renvoi was completed.

After its issuance, the ruling of the Court in *Aznar v Garcia* became a guidepost for the Philippine bench and bar on the appropriate application of the doctrine of renvoi. It is also considered as an important landmark case on conflict of laws in the Philippines because, more than just an explanation on the concept of the doctrine of renvoi and its proper application, the case of *Aznar v Garcia* is a masterclass on characterisation for Philippine law practitioners.

IV. Connecting Factors

The concept of connecting factors is intimately related to the concept of characterisation. In the case of *Saudi Arabian Airlines v Court of Appeals*,[55] the Philippine Supreme Court elucidated the concept of connecting factors as follows:

> Before a choice can be made, it is necessary for us to determine under what category a certain set of facts or rules fall. This process is known as 'characterization', or the 'doctrine of qualification'. It is the 'process of deciding whether or not the facts relate to the kind of question specified in a conflicts rule.' The purpose of 'characterization' is to enable the forum to select the proper law.
>
> Our starting point of analysis here is not a legal relation, but a factual situation, event, or operative fact. An essential element of conflict rules is the indication of a 'test' or 'connecting factor' or 'point of contact'. Choice-of-law rules invariably consist of a factual relationship (such as property right, contract claim) and a connecting factor or point of contact, such as the *situs* of the *res*, the place of celebration, the place of performance, or the place of wrongdoing.
>
> Note that one or more circumstances may be present to serve as the possible test for the determination of the applicable law. These 'test factors' or 'points of contact' or 'connecting factors' could be any of the following:
>
> (1) The nationality of a person, his domicile, his residence, his place of sojourn, or his origin;
> (2) the seat of a legal or juridical person, such as a corporation;

[55] *Saudi Arabian Airlines v Court of Appeals*, G.R. No. 122191, 358 Phil 105–129 (8 October 1998).

(3) the situs of a thing, that is, the place where a thing is, or is deemed to be situated. In particular, the *lex situs* is decisive when real rights are involved;

(4) *the place where an act has been done, the locus actus, such as the place where a contract has been made, a marriage celebrated, a will signed or a tort committed. The lex loci actus is particularly important in contracts and torts*:

(5) the place where an act is intended to come into effect, e.g., the place of performance of contractual duties, or the place where a power of attorney is to be exercised;

(6) the intention of the contracting parties as to the law that should govern their agreement, the *lex loci intentionis*;

(7) the place where judicial or administrative proceedings are instituted or done. The *lex fori* – the law of the forum – is particularly important because, as we have seen earlier, matters of 'procedure' not going to the substance of the claim involved are governed by it; and because the *lex fori* applies whenever the content of the otherwise applicable foreign law is excluded from application in a given case for the reason that it falls under one of the exceptions to the applications of foreign law, and

(8) the flag of a ship, which in many cases is decisive of practically all legal relationships of the ship and of its master or owner as such. It also covers contractual relationships particularly contracts of affreightment.

For the purpose of this chapter, the connecting factors or nationality and domicile shall be further discussed below.

A. Nationality

The concept of nationality does not exclusively apply to natural persons and juridical entities, as it also applies to ships and aircrafts. The rules for nationality of natural persons are different from juridical entities. Furthermore, international law provides for a unique set of rules to determine the nationality of ships and aircrafts.

i. Nationality of Natural Persons

The terms 'citizenship' and 'nationality' have both been used – and mostly as interchangeable notions, as is often done in international legal studies on nationality and citizenship.[56] In the landmark case of *Nottebohm*,[57] the International Court of Justice famously defined nationality as a legal bond between a person and a state 'having as its basis a social fact of attachment, a genuine connection of existence, interests and sentiments, together with the existence of reciprocal rights and duties.' It has also considered as a legal device denoting political affiliation. It is the 'right to have rights.'[58] The Philippine Supreme Court described citizenship as one's personal and permanent membership in a political community. The core of citizenship is the capacity to enjoy political rights, that is, the right to participate in government principally through the right to vote, the right to hold public office, and the right to petition the government for redress of grievance.[59] Citizenship also entails obligations to the political community of which one is

[56] M Adjami and J Harrington, 'The Scope and Content of Article 15 of the Universal Declaration of Human Rights' (2008) 27(3) *Refugee Survey Quarterly* 94, ssrn.com/abstract=1443012.

[57] Nottebohm (*Liechtenstein v Guatemala*) ICJ Reports (1955) 4–23.

[58] CJ Warren, Dissenting Opinion in *Perez v Brownwell*, 356 U.S. 44 (1958).

[59] *Go v Republic of the Philippines*, G.R. 202809, 729 SCRA 138, 149 (2 July 2014), citing J Bernas, 'The 1987 Constitution Of The Republic Of The Philippines, A Commentary' (2009 edition).

part.[60] Citizenship, therefore, is intimately tied with the notion that loyalty is owed to the state, considering the benefits and protection provided by it. This is particularly so if these benefits and protections have been enjoyed from the moment of the citizen's birth.

According to the eminent jurist Mancini, the traditions, religion, customs of life, the language, the race of people, even the landscape of the country and its climate, create a spiritual unity through the common consciousness of nationality.[61] An individual's nationality, from a political standpoint, suggests an identity, a belongingness to a political community, which is a fundamental element of a state. Naturally, this belongingness carries with it an obligation on the part of the individual to his or her nation, most especially insofar as private affairs are concerned. The Italian jurists, who fervently believed in *customa* or native law, believed that laws of each state were made for particular ethnicities, thus nationality was used to establish a link between an individual and a state. This principle has been adopted in the Philippine context under Article 15 of the New Civil Code, which provides that laws relating to family rights and duties, or to the status, condition and legal capacity of persons are binding upon citizens of the Philippines, even though living abroad.

Generally, each state is free to determine by its own laws, the persons whom it considers as its citizens, as embodied in Article I of the 1930 Convention of Certain Questions Relating to the Conflict of Nationality Law, which provides that it is for each state to determine under its own law who are its nationals. This law shall be recognised by other states in so far as it is consistent with international conventions, international custom, and the principles of law generally recognised with regard to nationality.[62] Any question as to whether a person possesses the nationality of a particular state shall be determined in accordance with the law of the state.[63] The power of a state to define who its nationals are is limited by international treaties, international customs, and generally accepted principles of international law.

This independent authority of each state to define who its nationals are gives rise to dual or multiple nationalities. In this regard, Article 3 of the Convention on Certain Questions Relating to the Conflict of Nationality Law provides that a person having two or more nationalities may be regarded as its national by each of the states whose nationality he or she possesses. In the event, however, that litigation arises in a third state, persons having more than one nationality shall be treated as if they had only one. Without prejudice to the application of its law in matters of personal status and of any conventions in force, a third state shall, of the nationalities which any such person possesses, recognise exclusively in its territory either the nationality of the country in which he or she is habitually and principally resident, or the nationality of the country with which in the circumstances the person appears to be in fact most closely connected.[64]

In the Philippine context, dual citizenship is not necessarily inimical, what the 1987 Philippine Constitution proscribes is dual allegiance. Nationality may be determined at the time of birth, ie natural-born, or acquired subsequently through a legal act or process after birth, ie naturalisation. Among the laws that govern naturalisation are Republic Act No. 9139, otherwise known as the Administrative Naturalization Law of 2000, and Commonwealth Act 473, otherwise known as the Revised Naturalization Law. One who desires to acquire Filipino citizenship by naturalisation is generally required to file a verified petition. The applicant must establish, among others,

[60] ibid.
[61] Salonga (n 8) 25.
[62] League of Nations, 'Convention on Certain Questions Relating to the Conflict of Nationality Law' (1930) 179(4137) *Treaty Series* 89.
[63] ibid Article 2.
[64] ibid Article 5.

that he or she is of legal age, is of good moral character, and has the capacity to adapt to Filipino culture, tradition, and principles, or otherwise has resided in the Philippines for a significant period of time. Further, the applicant must show that he or she will not be a threat to the state, to the public, and to the Filipinos' core beliefs.

There are two principles by which nationality is determined at birth. The first is *jus soli*, meaning 'right of soil', which determines nationality or citizenship on the basis of place of birth. The second is the principle of *jus sanguinis*, which literally translated means right of blood. It determines the nationality or citizenship based on the nationality of a person's parents regardless of the place of his or her birth, as opposed to the doctrine of *jus soli*. The Philippines adheres to the *jus sanguinis* principle under Article IV, Sections 1 and 2 of the 1987 Constitution.[65]

Implied in *jus sanguinis*, however, is the fact that the supposed bloodline could actually be determined. Insofar as foundlings are concerned, however, the same may not be established conclusively but a presumption may arise depending upon the circumstances. The Philippine Supreme Court discussed in detail the history of the citizenship rules of the Philippines in *David v Senate Electoral Tribunal* and *Poe-Llamanzares v Commission on Elections*.[66] The said cases involved the candidacy for presidency and qualification as an incumbent senator of Grace Poe, a Filipino whose status as a natural-born Filipino citizen, a qualification to be elected as president and senator, was questioned. Grace was a foundling who was found as an abandoned newborn in a church in Iloilo City, Philippines. She was later on adopted by Filipino citizens. Interestingly, Grace's adoptive father, who also previously ran for the presidency but narrowly lost in the 2004 Philippine elections, also had his status as a natural-born Filipino citizen affirmed by the Supreme Court after a challenge to his citizenship was filed.[67] In Grace's case, her Filipino citizenship was affirmed after the Court in *David v Senate Electoral Tribunal* ruled that foundlings are natural-born citizens. The Court pointed out that, while there was no express provision found in the 1987 Philippine Constitution on the citizenship of foundlings, the same was implied from its very text. Furthermore, the Court highlighted that Grace did not do anything in order to acquire her citizenship unlike naturalised individuals. Finally, the Court in *David v Senate Electoral Tribunal* explained that, based on the factual milieu of the case, it was highly probable that the biological parents of Grace were likewise Filipino citizens because she was found within the territory of the Philippines and there were no indications that her biological parents were foreigners. Despite the lengthy explanation of the Court on the determination of the citizenship of Grace, who was a foundling, the Court interestingly declared that this case certainly does not decide with finality the citizenship of every single

[65] The Constitution of the Republic of the Philippines, Article IV, Sections 1 and 2, (1987), www.officialgazette.gov.ph/constitutions/1987-constitution/, states that:

> Section 1. The following are citizens of the Philippines:
>
> 1. Those who are citizens of the Philippines at the time of the adoption of this Constitution;
> 2. Those whose fathers or mothers are citizens of the Philippines;
> 3. Those born before January 17, 1973, of Filipino mothers, who elect Philippine Citizenship upon reaching the age of majority; and
> 4. Those who are naturalized in the accordance with law.
>
> Section 2. Natural-born citizens are those who are citizens of the Philippines from birth without having to perform any act to acquire or perfect their Philippine citizenship. Those who elect Philippine citizenship in accordance with paragraph (3), Section 1 hereof shall be deemed natural-born citizens.

[66] *David v Senate Electoral Tribunal*, G.R. No. 221538, 803 SCRA 435 (20 September 2016); *Poe-Llamanzares v Commission on Elections*, G.R. No. 221697, 786 SCRA 1 (8 March 2016).

[67] *Tecson et. al. v Commission on Elections*, G.R. No. 161434, 424 SCRA 277 (3 March 2004).

foundling as natural-born. The circumstances of each case are unique, and substantial proof may exist to show that a foundling is not natural-born.

ii. Nationality of Corporations

There are two approaches to determine the nationality of a corporation. The common law rule is that a corporation's nationality is determined by its place of incorporation. On the other hand, the civil law countries in general determine the nationality of a corporation based on its seat, also called its central administration. The Philippines follows primarily the place of incorporation to determine nationality. This rule is found under Sections 2–4 of the Revised Corporation Code.[68]

The rational for the place of incorporation test is that a corporation exists only in contemplation of law and by force of the law, and where that law ceases to operate and is no longer obligatory, the corporation can have no existence.[69] It must dwell in the place of its creation, and cannot migrate to another sovereignty.[70]

Although the Philippines primarily follows the place of incorporation test to determine a corporation's nationality, there are instances when the Control Test, and its complement, the Grandfather Rule, are resorted to determine the nationality of a corporation. Under the Control Test, the nationality of a corporation with alien equity is determined based on the percentage of capital owned by Filipino citizens.[71] On the other hand, the Grandfather Rule looks into the citizenship of the individuals who ultimately own and control the shares of stock of a corporation for purposes of determining compliance with the constitutional requirement of Filipino ownership.[72] The reason for the Control Test and its adjunct, the Grandfather Rule, may be gleaned from the ruling of the Philippine Supreme Court in *Daimler Co Ltd v Continental Tyre and Rubber Co (Great Britain) Ltd.*,[73] which stated as follows:

> The acts of a company's organs, its directors, managers, secretary, and so forth, functioning within the scope of their authority, are the company's acts and may invest it definitively with enemy character. It seems to me that similarly the character of those who can make and unmake those officers, dictate their conduct mediately or immediately, prescribe their duties and call them to account, may also be material in a question of the enemy character of the company. If not definite and conclusive, it must at least be prima facie relevant, as raising a presumption that those who are purporting to act in the name of the company are, in fact, under the control of those whom it is their interest to satisfy. Certainly I have found no authority to the contrary. Such a view reconciles the positions of natural and artificial persons in this regard, and the opposite view leads to the paradoxical result that the King's enemies, who chance during war to constitute the entire body of corporators in a company registered in England, thereby pass out of the range of legal vision, and, instead, the corporation, which in itself is incapable of loyalty, or enmity, or residence, or of anything but bare existence in contemplation of law and registration under some system of law, takes their place for almost the most important of all purposes, that of being classed among the King's friends or among his foes in time of war.

[68] Republic Act No. 11232, Revised Corporation Code of the Philippines, Section 2, elibrary.judiciary.gov.ph/thebookshelf/showdocs/2/86463, states that:

> Section 2. Corporation Defined. – A corporation is an artificial being created by operation of law, having the right of succession and the powers, attributes, and properties expressly authorised by law or incidental to its existence.

[69] *Bank of Augusta v Earle*, 38 U.S. 519 (1839).

[70] ibid.

[71] *Gamboa v Teves*, G.R. No. 176579, 625 SCRA 690 (28 June 2011).

[72] *Narra Nickel Mining and Development Corp., et al v Redmont Consolidated Mines Corp.*, G.R. No. 195580, 722 SCRA 382 (28 January 2015).

[73] *Daimler Co Ltd v Continental Tyre Rubber Co (Great Britain) Ltd*, 2 AC 307 (1916).

The Control Test and the Grandfather Rule are critical in determining compliance with the nationality requirements under Philippine law, *viz*:

1. Article XII, Section 11 of the Philippine Constitution limits foreign equity participation in public utilities to a maximum of 40%, meaning that at least 60% of the capital must be owned by Filipino citizens or Filipino corporations.
2. Under Article XII, Section 2 of the Constitution, the State may enter into co-production, joint venture, or production-sharing agreements involving the exploration, development, and utilization of natural resources provided foreign ownership is limited to 40%.
3. Article XVI, Section 11 of the Constitution mandates that ownership and management of mass media be wholly owned by Filipino citizens or Filipino-controlled corporations.
4. Only Filipino citizens or corporations at least 60% owned by Filipinos may own private land in the Philippines.

As such, while the place of incorporation may generally determine whether a corporation is a Filipino corporation, the failure of a corporation to comply with the Control Test and the Grandfather Rule in instances required by the 1987 Philippine Constitution may result in the corporation being considered as a foreign corporation, the nationality of which is determined by the nationality of the majority of its stockholders. The concept of the Control Test and the Grandfather Rule is significantly important in determining whether an act of a corporation is valid. Otherwise, its responsible officers may be held liable for *ultra vires* acts.

iii. Ships and Aircraft

Ships have the nationality of the state whose flag they are entitled to fly,[74] which grants the flag-state the right to exercise jurisdiction over the vessel. Every state shall fix the conditions for the grant of its nationality to ships, for the registration of ships in its territory, and for the right to fly its flag. More importantly, there must exist a *genuine link* between a ship and the state purporting to confer its nationality upon that ship.[75] The purpose of the 'genuine link' requirement is to secure more effective implementation of the duties of the flag state to effectively exercise its jurisdiction and control in administrative, technical and social matters over ships flying its flag.[76]

Under the Convention on International Civil Aviation concluded at Chicago on 7 December 1944,[77] aircraft should have a nationality in the state in which it was registered,[78] and that no aircraft could be validly registered in more than one state.[79] The principle that every aircraft, at least every one that flies outside its country of origin, must have a nationality enables a number of rights and duties to be attached onto the aircraft or channeled through the aircraft to a variety of persons. At the international level, moreover, it ensures that there will be no aircraft for which there is no accountable state.

Notably, under Article 3 of the Convention on the Reduction of Statelessness, birth on a ship or in an aircraft shall be deemed to have taken place in the territory of the state whose flag the ship flies or in the territory of the state in which the aircraft is registered, as the case may be.

[74] UN General Assembly, 'United Nations Convention on the Law of the Sea', Article 91 (10 December 1982).

[75] ibid.

[76] ibid Article 94.

[77] NB The Philippines is a signatory to the Convention on International Civil Aviation concluded at Chicago on December 7, 1944, and deposited its instrument of ratification of said Convention on 1 March 1947.

[78] International Civil Aviation Organization (ICAO), 'Convention on International Civil Aviation ("Chicago Convention)', 15 U.N.T.S. 295, Article 17 (7 December 1944).

[79] ibid Article 18.

iv. Domicile and Residence

In *In the Matter of the Testate Estate of Christensen Garcia*,[80] the Philippine Supreme Court, generously citing Herbert F Goodrich, had the opportunity to distinguish between residence and domicile, to wit:

> The terms 'residence' and 'domicile' might well be taken to mean the same thing, a place of permanent abode. But domicile, as has been shown, has acquired a technical meaning. Thus, one may be domiciled in a place where he has never been. And he may reside in a place where he has no domicile. The man with two homes, between which he divides his time, certainly resides in each one, while living in it. But if he went on business which would require his presence for several weeks or months, he might properly be said to have sufficient connection with the place to be called a resident. It is clear, however, that, if he treated his settlement as continuing: only for the particular business in hand, not giving up his former 'home,' he could not be a domiciled New Yorker. Acquisition of a domicile of choice requires the exercise of intention as well as physical presence. 'Residence simply requires bodily presence as an inhabitant in a given places while domicile requires bodily presence in that place and also an intention to make it one's domicile.' Residence, however, is a term used with many shades of meaning, from the merest temporary presence to the most permanent abode, and it is not safe to insist that any one use is the only proper one.

Under Philippine law, there are further nuances between the domicile of natural persons as compared to corporations as will be elucidated below.

v. Natural Persons

Article 50 of the Civil Code decrees that '[f]or the exercise of civil rights and the fulfillment of civil obligations, the domicile of natural persons is their place of habitual residence.' This concept of domicile has taken to mean an individual's 'permanent home,' 'a place to which, whenever absent for business or for pleasure, one intends to return, and depends on facts and circumstances in the sense that they disclose intent.' Domicile includes the twin elements of 'the fact of residing or physical presence in a fixed place' and *animus manendi*, or the intention to remain. Residence, in its ordinary conception, implies the factual relationship of an individual to a certain place.[81] It is the physical presence of a person in a given area, community or country.[82] The essential distinction between residence and domicile in law is that residence involves the intent to leave when the purpose for which the resident has taken up his or her abode ends.[83] One may seek a place for purposes such as pleasure, business, or health.[84] If a person's intent is to remain, it becomes his or her domicile; if the person's intent is to leave as soon as his or her purpose is established, it is merely the person's residence. It is thus quite perfectly normal for an individual to have different residences in various places. However, a person can only have a single domicile, unless, for various reasons, he or she successfully abandons the original domicile in favour of another domicile of choice.

A person may have a residence in one place and a domicile in another.[85] Residence is not domicile, but domicile is residence coupled with the intention to remain for an unlimited time. A person can have but one domicile for the same purpose at any time, but they may have numerous places of residence. A person's place of residence is generally their place of domicile, but it is not by any means necessarily so since no length of residence without intention of remaining will constitute domicile.

[80] *Aznar v Garcia* (n 54).
[81] *Macalintal v COMELEC*, G.R. No. 157013, 405 SCRA 514 (10 July 2003).
[82] ibid.
[83] ibid.
[84] ibid.
[85] *Uytengsu v Republic*, G.R. No. L-6379, 95 Phil 890 (29 September 1954).

A person must have a residence or domicile somewhere. Also, domicile, once established, remains until a new one is acquired. Lastly, a person can have but one residence or domicile at a time.

Domicile is classified into three, namely: (1) domicile of origin, which is acquired by every person at birth; (2) domicile of choice, which is acquired upon abandonment of the domicile of origin to establish a new domicile of choice, personal presence in the place must be coupled with conduct indicative of this intention – it requires not only such bodily presence in that place but also a declared and probable intent to make it one's fixed and permanent place of abode; and, (3) domicile by operation of law, which the law attributes to a person independently of his or her residence or intention.

Domicile, however, is different from residence. In *Arnado v COMELEC*,[86] the Philippine Supreme Court expounded on the difference between citizenship and domicile, to wit:

> Domicile requires both physical presence and *animus revertendi* or intent to return. Citizenship may be presumed from one's domicile, but this presumption is disputable. Further proof other than domicile may be required to prove citizenship.

A person residing in the Philippines is presumed to be a Filipino citizen. Domicile, however, does not *ipso facto* prove his or her citizenship. A Filipino may reside in the United States but still remain a Filipino citizen. An American may also reside in the Philippines and still remain an American citizen. The presumption created by residency is not conclusive of one's citizenship.

While domicile is not a significant connecting factor in the conflict of laws provisions found under Articles 15, 16, and 17 of the Civil Code of the Philippines, it may be so in foreign laws. In *Aznar v Garcia*,[87] there was remission because the California Probate Code provided that the intrinsic validity of the testamentary provisions of a will shall be determined by the laws of the domicile of the decedent. In resolving *Aznar v Garcia*, domicile was an important connecting factor between California Law and Philippine Law on succession.

vi. Corporations

Determining the domicile of corporations is essential in the context of venue and jurisdiction. This becomes more significant in light of the increasingly globalised nature of business. Under Article 51 of the New Civil Code, when the law creating or recognising them, or any other provision does not fix the domicile of juridical persons, the same shall be understood to be the place where their legal representation is established or where they exercise their principal functions.

Under the Corporation Code, a foreign corporation is one formed, organised or existing under laws other than those of the Philippines and whose laws allow Filipino citizens and corporations to do business in its own country or state. It shall have the right to transact business in the Philippines after obtaining a licence. Securing of a licence, however, does not equate to acquisition of residence status. As the Philippine Supreme Court opined in *State Investment House, Inc v Citibank*:[88]

> [A] foreign corporation licitly doing business in the Philippines, which is a defendant in a civil suit, may not be considered a non-resident within the scope of the legal provision authorizing attachment against a defendant not residing in the Philippine Islands; in other words, a preliminary attachment may not be applied for and granted solely on the asserted fact that the defendant is a foreign corporation authorized to do business in the Philippines – and is consequently and necessarily, 'a party who resides out of the Philippines.' Parenthetically, if it may not be considered as a party not residing in the Philippines, or as a

[86] *Arnado v COMELEC*, G.R. No. 210164, 767 SCRA 168 (18 August 2015).

[87] See above n 14.

[88] *State Investment House, Inc v Citibank*, G.R. Nos. 79926-27, 203 SCRA 9 (17 October 1991).

party who resides out of the country, then, logically, it must be considered a party who does reside in the Philippines, who is a resident of the country. Be this as it may, this Court pointed out that:

> … Our laws and jurisprudence indicate a purpose to assimilate foreign corporations, duly licensed to do business here, to the status of domestic corporations. (Cf. Section 73, Act No. 1459, and Marshall Wells Co. vs. Henry W. Elser & Co., 46 Phil. 70, 76; Yu; Cong Eng vs. Trinidad, 47 Phil. 385, 411) We think it would be entirely out of line with this policy should we make a discrimination against a foreign corporation, like the petitioner, and subject its property to the harsh writ of seizure by attachment when it has complied not only with every requirement of law made specially of foreign corporations, but in addition with every requirement of law made of domestic corporations. …

Obviously, the assimilation of foreign corporations authorized to do business in the Philippines 'to the status of domestic corporations,' subsumes their being found and operating as corporations, hence, residing, in the country.

The same principle is recognized in American law: that the 'residence of a corporation, if it can be said to have a residence, is necessarily where it exercises corporate functions …;' that it is (sic) considered as dwelling 'in the place where its business is done …,' as being 'located where its franchises are exercised …,' and as being 'present where it is engaged in the prosecution of the corporate enterprise;' that a 'foreign corporation licensed to do business in a state is a resident of any country where it maintains an office or agent for transaction of its usual and customary business for venue purposes;' and that the 'necessary element in its signification is locality of existence.' Courts have held that 'a domestic corporation is regarded as having a residence within the state at any place where it is engaged in the particulars of the corporate enterprise, and not only at its chief place or home office;' that 'a corporation may be domiciled in one state and resident in another; its legal domicile in the state of its creation presents no impediment to its residence in a real and practical sense in the state of its business activities.'

The foregoing propositions are in accord with the dictionary concept of residence as applied to juridical persons, a term which appears to comprehend permanent as well as temporary residence.

The Court cannot thus accept the petitioners' theory that corporations may not have a residence (i.e., the place where they operate and transact business) separate from their domicile (i.e., the state of their formation or organization), and that they may be considered by other states as residents only for limited and exclusive purposes. Of course, as petitioners correctly aver, it is not really the grant of a license to a foreign corporation to do business in this country that makes it a resident; the license merely gives legitimacy to its doing business here. What effectively makes such a foreign corporation a resident corporation in the Philippines is its actually being in the Philippines and licitly doing business here, 'locality of existence' being, to repeat, the 'necessary element in … (the) signification' of the term, resident corporation.

Thus, the functions served by domicile, whether domicile of a natural person or of a corporate entity, insofar as Private International Law is concerned are as follows: (1) judicial jurisdiction, that is, whether a court has jurisdiction based on the residence or domicile of one of the parties; (2) choice of law; and, (3) governmental benefits.[89]

V. Substance and Procedure

Matters of procedure are governed by the *lex fori*, the law of the forum, whereas matters of substance are governed by the *lex causae*, the law of the cause, or foreign law. The reason for such rule is articulated in the 1934 Restatement of the Law of Conflict of Laws:

> One of the chief ends secured by a rational system of Conflicts of Laws rules is that the rights and duties of parties arising from a legal situation shall not be substantially varied because of the forum in which

[89] Salonga (n 8) 191.

> an action is brought to settle disputed questions arising out of the situation. International commerce, to give but one example, could hardly continue if parties were frequently exposed to the hazards and unknown requirements of foreign laws. For this reason, when a case involving foreign elements is presented, the courts of all civilized states now decline the easy and obvious solution of ignoring foreign law and treating the case as a purely domestic one; instead they seek, by reference to the foreign law deemed appropriate, to protect the parties against a substantial change of position because of the fortuitous circumstances that suit is brought in that particular case.
>
> If theoretically complete uniformity of right and duty were to be attained, a court having before it a case in which reference to the foreign rule of law had been appropriately made would apply the foreign law to furnish the rule or decision for both the existence of the right or duty, and those things ordinarily thought of by lawyers as the means by which the prevailing party could, by that law, compel the other to perform the legal duty found to exist. Conversely, the means of compulsion against the defeated party to the action would be no more than that provided by the law designated as the appropriate one to govern the transaction. The means provided for compulsion, or limitation upon the compulsion, which may be brought against the alleged wrongdoer are, in many cases, of almost equal practical importance to the declaration of the validity of a plaintiff's claim.

Such all-inclusive reference to the foreign law is never made. The difficulties involved would be very great; so great as to be impossible in many instances. A heavy burden would be thrown upon the courts of the forum and the orderly administration of justice there would be hampered and delayed. A limitation upon the scope of foreign law is thus necessary. Such limitation excludes those phases of the case which make administration of the foreign law by the local tribunal impracticable, inconvenient, or violative of local policy. In these instances, the local rules at the forum are applied and are classified as matters of procedure.[90]

A. Proof of Foreign Laws and Other Evidentiary Matters

As earlier mentioned, in the Philippines, courts do not take judicial notice of foreign law. The party who wants to have a foreign law applied to a dispute or case has the burden of proving the foreign law. The foreign law is treated as a question of fact to be properly pleaded and proved as the judge cannot take judicial notice of a foreign law.[91] The judge is presumed to know only domestic or forum law.[92] If the foreign law is not pleaded, or if pleaded, is not proved, then the foreign law is presumed to be the same as Philippine law, in accordance with the doctrine of processual presumption.[93]

To prove a foreign law, the party invoking it must present a copy thereof and comply with Sections 24 and 25 of Rule 132 of the Revised Rules of Court which read:

> SEC. 24. Proof of official record. – The record of public documents referred to in paragraph (a) of Section 19, when admissible for any purpose, may be evidenced by an official publication thereof or by a copy attested by the officer having the legal custody of the record, or by his deputy, and accompanied, if the record is not kept in the Philippines, with a certificate that such officer has the custody. If the office in which the record is kept is in a foreign country, the certificate may be made by a secretary of the embassy or legation, consul general, consul, vice consul, or consular agent or by any officer in the foreign service of the Philippines stationed in the foreign country in which the record is kept, and authenticated by the seal of his office.

[90] American Law Institute, 'Restatement of the Law of Conflicts of Law', Introductory Note to Chapter XII, Section 585 (1934).

[91] *In the Matter of Testate Estate of Bambao v Sekito*, G.R. No. 237449, 965 SCRA 169 (2 December 2020).

[92] ibid.

[93] *Cargill Philippines Inc v Commissioner of Internal Revenue*, G.R. No. 203346, 951 SCRA 494 (9 September 2020); *Saura Import & Export Co, Inc v Philippine International Surety Co, Inc*, G.R. No. L-15184,8 SCRA 143 (28 April 1970).

> SEC. 25. What attestation of copy must state. – Whenever a copy of a document or record is attested for the purpose of the evidence, the attestation must state, in substance, that the copy is a correct copy of the original, or a specific part thereof, as the case may be. The attestation must be under the official seal of the attesting officer, if there be any, or if he be the clerk of a court having a seal, under the seal of such court.

The above-quoted provisions, however, do not exclude proof by any other competent evidence, such as testimonial evidence.[94]

B. Taking Evidence Abroad for Use in Philippine Proceedings

The procedure for taking evidence abroad is governed by Philippine laws, including the Rules of Court and applicable treaties or international conventions. The Hague Convention on the Taking of Evidence Abroad in Civil or Commercial Matters is one such international instrument, though the Philippines is not a signatory. However, similar processes may be implemented through bilateral treaties or the use of discovery procedures in the Philippine context. The Philippine Supreme Court in *Dulay v Dulay*[95] explained these mechanisms:

> Deposition is chiefly a mode of discovery, the primary function of which is to supplement the pleadings for the purpose of disclosing the real points of dispute between the parties and affording an adequate factual basis during the preparation for trial. It may be taken with leave of court after jurisdiction has been obtained over any defendant or over property that is the subject of the action; or, without such leave, after an answer has been served. A party's right to avail itself of this procedure is "well-nigh unrestricted" if the matters inquired into are otherwise relevant and not privileged, and the inquiry is made in good faith and within the bounds of the law. Nevertheless, the use of discovery procedures is directed to the sound discretion of the trial courts, which, in general, are given wide latitude in granting motions for discovery in order to enable the parties to prepare for trial or otherwise to settle the controversy prior thereto.
>
> While the letters rogatory issued by the trial court specifically directed the Clerk of Court of Boston to take the depositions needed in the case, it became impossible to follow the directive since the Clerk of Court of Boston merely brushed it aside and refused to cooperate. Respondent cannot be faulted for the resultant delay brought about by this circumstance. Neither can the trial court be faulted for allowing the admission of the depositions taken not in strict adherence to its original directive, nor for directing the petitioner to have the depositions authenticated. Obviously, it was not within the trial court's power, much less the respondent's to force the Clerk of Court of Boston to have the deposition taken before it. It would be illogical and unreasonable to expect respondent to comply with the letters rogatory without the cooperation of the very institution or personality named in the letters rogatory and requested to examine the witnesses. After all, while a court had the authority to entertain a discovery request, it is not required to provide judicial assistance thereto. This reality was recognized by the trial court when it ordered respondent to have the questioned depositions authenticated by the Philippine consulate. Indeed, refusing the allowance of the depositions in issue would be going directly against the purpose of taking the depositions in the first place, that is, the disclosure of facts which are relevant to the proceedings in court.
>
> x x x x x x x x x
>
> In our jurisdiction, depositions in foreign countries may be taken: (a) on notice before a secretary of embassy or legation, consul general, consul, vice consul, or consular agent of the Republic of the Philippines; (b) before such person or officer as may be appointed by commission or under letters rogatory; or (c) before any person authorized to administer oaths as stipulated in writing by the parties.

[94] *Willlamete Iron & Steel Works v Muzzal*, G.R. No. 42538, 61 Phil 471 (21 May 1935).
[95] *Dulay v Dulay*, G.R. No. 158857, 474 SCRA 674 (11 November 2005).

While letters rogatory are requests to foreign tribunals, commissions are directives to officials of the issuing jurisdiction.

Generally, a commission is an instrument issued by a court of justice, or other competent tribunal, directed to a magistrate by his official designation or to an individual by name, authorizing him to take the depositions of the witnesses named therein, while a letter rogatory is a request to a foreign court to give its aid, backed by its power, to secure desired information. Commissions are taken in accordance with the rules laid down by the court issuing the commission, while in letters rogatory, the methods of procedure are under the control of the foreign tribunal.

Leave of court is not required when the deposition is to be taken before a secretary of embassy or legation, consul general, consul, vice-consul or consular agent of the Republic of the Philippines and the defendant's answer has already been served. However, if the deposition is to be taken in a foreign country where the Philippines has no secretary of embassy or legation, consul general, consul, vice-consul or consular agent, it may be taken only before such person or officer as may be appointed by commission or under letters rogatory.

C. Taking Evidence in the Philippines for Proceedings Abroad

Under private international law, foreign courts have the right to ask Philippine courts to help them get evidence that is housed in the Philippines. Philippine procedural laws and international legal cooperation instruments, such as letters rogatory or certain treaties including those pertaining to mutual legal assistance, regulate this process.

Evidence collected in the Philippines for foreign use, however, must still comply with local legal standards. For instance, any evidence obtained must respect Philippine laws on admissibility, such as the rules on hearsay and authentication. Evidence that does not meet these standards may not be considered valid or admissible in foreign courts.

D. Mandatory Rules, *Ordre Public*, Public Law, and the Evasion of Law

i. *Mandatory Rules*

The concept of mandatory rules in essence provides that foreign laws should not undermine domestic laws inasmuch as this is an adjunct of a state's sovereignty. In this regard, Article 17 of the Civil Code of the Philippines, states, in part that:

> Prohibitive laws concerning persons, their acts or property, and those which have for their object public order, public policy and good customs shall not be rendered ineffective by laws or judgments promulgated, or by determinations or conventions agreed upon in a foreign country.

ii. Ordre Public *(Public Order)*

The Civil Code of the Philippines also provides that foreign laws or judgments that are contrary to public policy may be refused application. This is reflected in Article 15, which relates to the status, condition, and legal capacity of persons, and Article 17, which includes *ordre public* considerations when it comes to laws that contradict Philippine values or principles. As the Philippine Supreme Court opined in *Querubin v Querubin*,[96] prohibitive laws concerning persons, their acts

[96] *Querubin v Querubin*, G.R. No. L-3693, 87 Phil 124 (1950).

or their property, and those aimed at public order and morals, shall not be rendered null and void by laws or judgments handed down, or by agreed provisions or conventions, in foreign countries.

iii. Public Law

Public law principles are emphasised in both doctrine and judicial decisions, confirming that public law (such as criminal, tax, and administrative laws) is territorial and should not be applied extraterritorially. The rule that public laws do not travel outside of their jurisdiction is a well-established principle in international law. This of course, is without exceptions. Under Article 2 of the Revised Penal Code, Philippine penal laws may be given extraterritorial effect when: (1) the offenses is committed while on a Philippine ship or airship; (2) the offense involves forging or counterfeiting any coin or currency note of the Philippine Islands or obligations and securities issued by the Government of the Philippine Islands; (3) the offense involves acts connected with the introduction into these islands of the obligations and securities mentioned in the presiding number; (4) the offense involves public officers or employees, who commit the acts in the exercise of their functions; or, (5) the offense involves any of the crimes against national security and the law of nations.

iv. Evasion of Law

The evasion of law principle is supported by the idea of preventing fraud or abuse of legal provisions. The concept of evasion of law has been invoked in cases where parties seek to avoid domestic law by creating artificial foreign elements. Philippine jurisprudence has dealt with these issues in cases related to family law, such as marriages and divorces obtained abroad. In *Tenchavez v Escaño*,[97] the Philippine Supreme Court refused to recognise the absolute divorce obtained in the United States by two Filipinos. It opined that:

> The Civil Code of the Philippines, now in force, does not admit absolute divorce, *quo ad vinculo matrimonii;* and in fact does not even use that term, to further emphasize its restrictive policy on the matter, in contrast to the preceding legislation that admitted absolute divorce on grounds of adultery of the wife or concubinage of the husband (Act 2710). Instead of divorce, the present Civil Code only provides for legal separation (Title IV, Book 1, Arts. 97 to 108), and, even in that case, it expressly prescribes that "the marriage bonds shall not be severed" (Art. 106, subpar. 1).
>
> For the Philippine courts to recognize and give recognition or effect to a foreign decree of absolute divorce between Filipino citizens could be a patent violation of the declared public policy of the state, specially in view of the third paragraph of Article 17 of the Civil Code that prescribes the following:
>
> Prohibitive laws concerning persons, their acts or property, and those which have for their object public order, policy and good customs, shall not be rendered ineffective by laws or judgments promulgated, or by determinations or conventions agreed upon in a foreign country.
>
> Even more, the grant of effectivity in this jurisdiction to such foreign divorce decrees would, in effect, give rise to an irritating and scandalous discrimination in favor of wealthy citizens, to the detriment of those members of our polity whose means do not permit them to sojourn abroad and obtain absolute divorces outside the Philippines.

In sum, private international law finds increasing relevance because of globalisation. As more transborder transactions take place, concepts and principles of private international law also evolve to aid in the resolution of disputes. In particular to the Philippines, substantive and

[97] *Tenchavez v Escaño*, G.R. No. L-19671, 15 SCRA 355 (29 November 1965).

procedural laws are laid in statutes, such as the Civil Code of the Philippines, to aid its bench and bar.

Despite its evolution, the concept of characterisation still hold a significant role in resolving conflict of laws issues. In fact, characterisation is seemingly a mandatory step in dispute resolution of conflict of laws issues. Without characterisation, it would be difficult to determine the appropriate and applicable law and procedure. In characterising conflict of laws issues, it is important to identify connecting factors such as the concepts of nationality and domicile. Ultimately, proper characterisation can guide courts and litigants in navigating the complexities of conflict of laws issues.

2

Jurisdiction

ARVIN KRISTOPHER A RAZON

I. Introduction

The Philippines has one of the few legal systems in the world with a mixture of both common law and civil law systems. Philippine conflict of laws rules on jurisdiction are primarily based on the country's civil law heritage. Republic Act (RA) No. 386 or the Civil Code of the Philippines codifies the various laws spanning general obligations and contracts, property relations and succession: a reiteration, if not legal transplant, of the Civil Code of Spain of 1888, which was introduced in the Philippines towards the latter decades of the more than 300-year Spanish period of colonisation.[1] That does not mean that Anglo-American common law played no part in shaping Philippine private international law. As a consequence of American colonial rule that effectively lasted for over five decades,[2] Philippine Supreme Court decisions, which form part of the Philippine common law regime,[3] make several references to American decisions in analysis of conflict of laws cases. It is important to keep in mind the country's unique civil law-common law system when understanding Philippine conflict of laws on jurisdiction, as their continuing developments and interpretation still largely draw from these traditions. To put it simply, one cannot understand Philippine private international law without a proper appreciation of its Spanish civil law roots, interpreted in the light of the doctrine of precedent introduced by American common law.

II. Jurisdiction *In Personam*

A. General Principles

This section discusses the manner by which Philippine courts deal with the question of jurisdiction in actions *in personam* or those cases intended to impose a personal liability on the defendant or their successors-in-interest. In a dispute with a cross-border element, a Philippine court may dismiss it on the ground of lack of jurisdiction or, even when it has determined to have jurisdiction over the matter, for *forum non-conveniens*. If the court decides to exercise jurisdiction and

[1] JR Salonga, *Private International Law* (Pasig, Regina Publishing, 1995).
[2] ibid.
[3] Civil Code, Art 8.

try the case, it will then consider whether to apply Philippine or foreign law. This is applicable in cases involving contractual disputes or recovery of debt.

i. Establishing Jurisdiction

In the Philippines, resolution of a conflict-of-laws problem starts with an inquiry into the jurisdiction of local courts. To proceed with a case, a Philippine court must assert jurisdiction over one or more of the following: (1) a property or *res*, (2) the persons involved as plaintiff and the defendant, or (3) the subject matter of the dispute.[4] The discussion on jurisdiction against property (referred to as jurisdiction *in rem*) is discussed below. For the plaintiff, jurisdiction over their person, *in personam*, is established by filing a lawsuit in a Philippine court, thereby consenting to the court's jurisdiction over the case and any related proceedings, including counterclaims from the defendant.[5] Conversely, jurisdiction over a defendant is secured either through the defendant's voluntary appearance in court, usually by submitting a responsive pleading, or through proper service of legal documents within the Philippines (known as the service of summons).[6] For actions *in personam*, Rule 14 of the Rules of Civil Procedure (as amended) governs.[7]

As a general rule, service of summons must be done personally, to the defendant, as laid out in Section 5 of the Rules of Civil Procedure. If this fails for whatever reason, such as the defendant cannot be located or refuses to personally receive the summons, the modes of substituted service come into effect, as set out in Section 6 of the said Rules. With this recent amendment, Rule 14 expanded the modes of substituted service. Previously, it allowed service of summons at the defendant's residence, office, or regular place of business (and therefore imposing a *de facto* territorial limit of the service to the local jurisdiction). Now, under Section 9 of Rule 14, it allows service to the electronic mail address of the defendant or counsel, or through other electronic means of transmission, raising the question of whether summons may be made to a defendant outside of the Philippines.[8]

The Philippine Supreme Court has not had the occasion to decide as to whether this amendment enables local courts to exercise jurisdiction over a defendant located outside of the Philippines, considering that there is a specific provision that deals with extraterritorial service: Section 17. In any case, Sections 12 and 14 potentially offer some indication. Section 12, which refers to service upon a domestic private juridical entity, states that refusal on the persons required to receive summons despite at least three (3) attempts on two (2) different dates may result in the court allowing service to be made electronically. Section 14 refers to service upon foreign private juridical entities, defined as an entity that has transacted (presumably, even on an isolated basis) or is doing business in the Philippines, as defined by law: if the foreign private juridical entity is not registered in the Philippines, or has no resident agent, a Philippine court may allow service to be effected outside of the Philippines through any of the following means:

(a) By personal service coursed through the appropriate court in the foreign country with the assistance of the Department of Foreign Affairs;
(b) By publication once in a newspaper of general circulation in the country where the defendant may be found and by serving a copy of the summons and the court order by registered mail at the last known address of the defendant;

[4] JR Coquia and E Aguiling-Pangalangan, *Conflict of Laws: Cases, Materials and Comments* (Quezon, Central Book Supply, 2000) 20.
[5] ibid.
[6] *Banco Espanol Filipino v Palanca* GR No 11390 (1918).
[7] Rules of Civil Procedure (AM No 19-10-20-SC). The amendments to the Rules of Civil Procedure came into effect on 1 May 2020.
[8] Rules of Civil Procedure, Rule 14, s 9.

(c) By facsimile;
(d) By electronic means with the prescribed proof of service; or,
(e) By such other means as the court, in its discretion, may direct.

Substituted service upon foreign juridical entities is a new introduction into the procedural rules taking effect in 2020, in what appears to be a broadening of the Philippine court's powers to obtain jurisdiction upon a defendant who may not be within its territorial limits. This provision is significant. Before the amendment was introduced and took effect in 2020, there was no clear way to serve summons on foreign entities that did not have a presence in the Philippines. It is not difficult to imagine a situation where the local court sanctions the substituted service of summons to a foreign company based on a breach of contract claim by a plaintiff, where the contract was entirely negotiated and transacted online. Whether this would be effective in impleading a foreign entity has not been decided in a binding court decision. Moreover, there is no common law rule that can provide further guidance on this point just yet.

Jurisdiction over subject matter or subject matter competence is the general power for courts to try cases of a general class under which the complaint falls.[9] That it is a matter of law and cannot be agreed upon by the parties, finds basis in the Philippine Constitution and the Judiciary Reorganization Act,[10] which outlines the cases that are within the jurisdiction of local courts, from the municipal trial courts (the lowest court in the judicial hierarchy) to the Court of Appeals (the highest appellate body). Matters within the Supreme Court's original and exclusive jurisdiction are defined in the Philippine Constitution.

Conflict of laws rules typically apply when local courts are either requested to exercise or refrain from exercising jurisdiction, which either party to an action claim to fall under a foreign court or a Philippine court's jurisdiction. An example is *Zapanta v Local Civil Registrar of Davao*, where the claimant filed an action for the enforcement of a joint custody arrangement, one which was characterised as an action for specific performance: a civil case incapable of pecuniary estimation that rightfully belongs to the regional trial court.[11] The regional trial court initially refused to entertain the action, thinking that a divorce decree issued by a foreign court, the Illinois court, stripped it of its jurisdiction. The Supreme Court held that the jurisdiction that the Illinois court pertain to the enforcement of the various provisions of its judgment for dissolution, but did not strip the Philippine court of post-divorce matters, including the matter of joint child custody; this remained beyond the Illinois court's jurisdiction.

ii. *Applying* Forum Non Conveniens

Procedural rules yield to common law when it comes to the matter of Philippine courts exercising jurisdiction, and case law is replete with Supreme Court cases deciding that jurisdiction may be established despite what the rules may otherwise provide under the doctrine of *forum non conveniens*. Faced with the question of whether a Philippine court could properly exercise jurisdiction over an employment contract that was executed in the US considering that the employee returned and sent the executed contract there, the Supreme Court decided, in quite interesting language, that 'a Philippine court in a conflict-of-laws case may assume jurisdiction *if it chooses to do so*,' setting the following requisites: (1) that the parties may conveniently resort to Philippine courts (as opposed to a foreign one); (2) that the Philippine court is in a position to make an

[9] *Caluag v Pecson* GR No 1403 (1948).
[10] B.P. 129, as amended by RA No 7691 (1954).
[11] *In Re: Petition for Correction of Entry in the Register of Deaths of the Civil Registry of Davao City, from The Name 'Flaviano Castro Zapanta' To 'Florencio B. Zapanta,' Gliceria S. Zapanta* GR No 55380 (1994).

intelligent decision on the law and the facts; and, (3) the Philippine court has or is likely to have the power to enforce its decision.[12]

In the same vein, just because a Philippine court may exercise jurisdiction over a case does not mean that it will do so, if it is not the most convenient available forum and parties may be able to seek a remedy elsewhere, in a more appropriate and convenient forum. Essentially, it may use the same doctrine to conclude that another forum would be able to serve the interests of justice. Evidently, the doctrine of *forum non conveniens* is rooted in the factual determination of the court. Certain factors in American common law may be considered, such as whether witnesses or evidence may readily be presented in the Philippines, justice may be administered swiftly considering the court's caseload, or a Philippine judgment will be enforceable in a foreign jurisdiction where the subject matter lies.[13] The Supreme Court recognised the 'well-established practice in the application of the principle of *forum non conveniens* that unless the balance is strongly in favour of the defendant, the plaintiff's choice of forum should rarely be disturbed, and that, furthermore, the consideration of inadequacy to enforce the judgment, which is one of the important factors to be considered in the application of said principle, would precisely constitute a problem to the plaintiffs if the local courts decline to assume jurisdiction on the basis of said principle, considering that the defendant is a resident of the Philippines.'[14]

Some other factors that the Philippine courts may consider when assessing whether it can assume jurisdiction over a case with a foreign element, under the guise of properly considering private interests of the parties involved, are: (1) the court's competency to access evidence, considering that evidence may not be easily accessible or presentable to the court, (2) the compellability of witnesses who may be unwilling to attend, (3) the property in question that may be easily accessed by the court if necessary, and (4) any issue that would make litigation inexpensive and the administration of justice expeditious. They may also consider the public interest in deciding whether jurisdiction is properly exercisable, including the congestion of the court's dockets and whether they would have the confidence and competence to apply foreign law.[15]

The determination of whether a Philippine court may exercise jurisdiction over a matter is a sovereign prerogative of the country where the case is filed.[16] Perhaps this is the reason why in *Raytheon International Inc v Rouzie*, the Supreme Court held that a local court that has jurisdiction over the subject matter, the parties and the *res*, may proceed to try a case although the conflict of laws rules point to a foreign court as a more convenient forum. This highlights the nature of the doctrine of *forum non conveniens* as an exception rather than a general rule. It also demonstrates a seeming reluctance on the part of Philippine courts to part with its authority to exercise jurisdiction where all three jurisdictional factors are present, even where they may not be the most convenient forum and where a governing law is other than Philippine law. *Raytheon* involved a dispute between a company incorporated in Connecticut and an American citizen, concerning the negotiation of government projects in the Philippines for an agreed 10 per cent commission over the sales receipts. Even where the underlying contract provides that Connecticut law would govern, the Supreme Court clarified that Philippine courts are not precluded from hearing the action.

[12] *Continental Micronesia Inc v Basso* GR Nos 178382-83 (2015).

[13] AV Sempio-Diy, *Handbook on Conflict of Laws* (Quezon, Joer Printing, 2004) 14–5, citing *Canada Malting Co Ltd v Patterson Steamships Ltd* 285 US 413 and *Heine v New York Life Insurance Co* 45 F 2d 426.

[14] *Wing On Co v SYYAP* 64 OG 8311 (1967).

[15] *Gulf Oil Corp v Gilbert* 330 US 501 (1947).

[16] *Raytheon International Inc v Rouzie* GR No 162894 (2008).

iii. Service of Process Outside of the Philippines

Summonses as a general rule must be effected by personal service or, in the event of failure to do this, by substituted service. As discussed, substituted service now allows the service of summonses by means of sending an electronic mail to a defendant, which may include a foreign private juridical entity which has transacted or is doing business in the Philippines. To carry out this summons outside of the Philippines, Rule 14, Section 17 of the Rules of Court requires concurrence of various elements. As to the *defendant*, he should not reside in and is not found in the Philippines. As to the *action*, (a) it affects the personal status of the plaintiff, (b) it relates to property within the Philippines, or (c) the subject of which is property within the Philippines. As to the *prejudice to the defendant*, it must be due to (a) possession or claim of possession of a lien or interest, actual or contingent, (b) the property of the defendant has been attached within the Philippines, or (c) the relief demanded by the plaintiff consists, wholly or in part, in excluding the defendant from any interest therein. As to the *implementation of the service*, it must be effected out of the Philippines by (a) personal service, following the requirements under Section 5, (b) following the requirements provided for in international conventions to which the Philippines is a party, or (c) by publication in a newspaper of general circulation in such places and for such time as the court may order, in which case a copy of the summons and order of the court shall be sent by registered mail to the last known address of the defendant, or in any other manner the court may deem sufficient. Lastly, service of process outside the Philippines is not discretionary. It requires *securing of leave of court*, where a judge, upon granting such leave, shall specify a reasonable time, which shall not be less than sixty (60) calendar days after notice, within which the defendant must answer.[17]

The above rule on extraterritorial service must be read in conjunction with Rule 14, Section 14 on service upon foreign private juridical entities, which, as discussed above, allows for service of summonses outside of the Philippines on a foreign private juridical entity, by leave of court through the means previously outlined.

Judicial precedent decided before the amendment to the procedural rules in 2020 does not allow for service of process outside of the Philippines in an action *in personam*.[18] Sections 14 and 17 have diluted the effect of this ruling, considering that service outside of the Philippines in *in personam* actions may be made against a foreign private juridical entity or a defendant that does not reside in and is not found in the Philippines in the same way that service may be made on a defendant outside of the Philippines in actions *in rem* and *quasi in rem*. The nature of these actions is discussed below.

iv. Service of Foreign Proceedings within the Philippines

The difficulty of coordinating local cases with a foreign element has been discussed in *Dulay et al. v Dulay*.[19] In this case, a petition for the issuance of letters rogatory was filed before a Philippine court in order to get depositions of several witnesses residing abroad. Sections 11 and 12 of Rule 23 allow depositions to be taken in foreign countries (a) on notice before a secretary of embassy or legation, consul general, consul, vice consul, or consular agent of the Republic of the Philippines; (b) before such person or officer as may be appointed by commission or under letters rogatory; or, (c) before any person authorised to administer oaths as stipulated in writing by the

[17] Rules of Civil Procedure, Rule 14, s 17.
[18] *Pantaleon v Asuncion* GR No 13141 (1959).
[19] GR No 158857 (2005).

parties.[20] The request was made to the Clerk of Court in Boston, Massachusetts, USA. However, the Clerk of Court, upon receipt of the letters Rogatory, merely brushed it aside and refused to cooperate. The Philippine court then allowed that the depositions be taken by a notary public then authenticated by a Philippine consul in the United States. The opposing party contested this, with the Supreme Court recognising that 'it was not within the [Philippine] trial court's power, much less the respondent's to force the Clerk of Court of Boston to have the deposition taken before it.' In the end, the Supreme Court found that there was substantial compliance with the requirements for depositions even if its original directive was not complied with.

Citing US authorities, the Supreme Court defined two types of foreign instructions to take depositions: a commission issued by a court of justice or other competent tribunal, directed to a magistrate by his or her official designation or to an individual by name, authorising the taking of deposition; and, a letter rogatory requesting a foreign court to give its aid to secure the desired information. Commissions are issued in accordance with the rules of the issuing court, while letters rogatory are under the control of the foreign tribunal.[21] By parity, in practice, and not as a matter of formal rule, service of ongoing foreign proceedings within the Philippines may be done by letters rogatory issued by the foreign court and addressed to a defendant in the Philippines. The letters rogatory will request a Philippine court, often with the assistance of diplomatic channels, to enforce the request, which may be the taking of a deposition or service of documents.

Section 48 of Rule 39 sets out the effect of foreign judgments or final orders, in what is the only clear rule on how foreign proceedings can be effected in the Philippines. A foreign judgment with a Philippine nexus is issued by a foreign court upon a thing or against a person located in the Philippines.[22] In case of a foreign judgment or final order upon a specific thing, the judgment or final order is conclusive upon the title of a thing, while a foreign judgment or final order against a person is presumptive evidence of a right as between the parties and their successors in interest by a subsequent title.[23] A specific petition is first required to enforce the foreign judgment or final order. The merits of the case need not be re-tried by the Philippine court, except if there is evidence of a want of jurisdiction, failure to notify the party, collusion, fraud or clear mistake of law or fact. If these exceptions apply, the foreign judgment or final order may be repelled altogether.[24]

Service of such documents is now bound to be more expedient, given the recent entry into force in the Philippines of the Convention on the Service Abroad of Judicial and Extrajudicial Documents in Civil or Commercial Matters.[25]

B. Special Rules for Establishing Jurisdiction

The next step to a Philippine court's determination that it can properly assume jurisdiction over a case with a conflict of laws problem is to decide whether it would apply *lexi fori* (ie, local Philippine law) or *lex causae* (ie, foreign law). There are three instances when *lex fori* will be

[20] Rules of Civil Procedure, Rule 23, s 11.

[21] *Pantaleon v Asuncion* GR No 13141 (1959).

[22] Foreign arbitral awards are also recognised in the Philippines, as it is a party to the 1958 New York Convention on the Recognition and Enforcement of Foreign Arbitral Awards. This is also reflected in the Alternative Dispute Resolution Act of 2004 (RA No 9285).

[23] Rules of Civil Procedure, Rule 39, s 48.

[24] ibid.

[25] Registration No. 9432 (1965) (the 'Service Convention'). See 'Service Convention enters into force for the Philippines' (1 October 2020) at www.hcch.net/en/news-archive/details/?varevent=752.

applied: (1) when Philippine law expressly provides in its conflict rules that its local law should apply, (2) proper foreign law is not properly pleaded and proved, and (3) the case involves an exception to the application of foreign law as the proper law.

There are certain provisions in the conflict rules in statutory law, mostly found in the Philippine Civil Code, that expressly requires the application of Philippine law. The second instance, on the other hand, contemplates a scenario where foreign law would have been the proper law, except that it was not properly proven by evidence; foreign law is not a matter of judicial notice in the Philippines and therefore has to be proven as a fact by the rules of evidence.[26] When applying Philippine law in this manner, the court applies the doctrine of processual presumption, in which foreign law is presumed to be the same as Philippine law.[27] The third instance involves the Philippine court making an assessment of the substantive foreign law, and determining that there is some reason why it must be set aside to give way to the application of Philippine law. These exceptions can range from the foreign law being contrary to good morals or public policy or might endanger the vital interest of the state to the matter being purely fiscal and administrative in nature.

A determination that foreign law is the proper *lex causae* does not automatically cause a Philippine court to decline jurisdiction. A decision that the *lex causae* is foreign does not by itself oblige the court to dismiss the case or send the parties elsewhere. Even where foreign law has been properly proven by evidence (as mentioned in the second instance above), the Philippine court will still need to consider whether it should decline jurisdiction under the doctrine of *forum non conveniens*. This will allow a Philippine court, even if it has jurisdiction, to refuse to exercise it if it is not the most convenient or available forum for resolving a dispute with foreign elements. Applying foreign law presents significant challenges, as the process of providing foreign law as an evidentiary fact may be a cumbersome process for both the court and the parties. Further, local courts may misinterpret or misapply foreign law, as the foreign court is still the more competent authority to adjudge based on its legal regime. The case of *Manila Hotel Corp v National Labor Relations Commission* used one factor in determining when a Philippine court may assume jurisdiction over a case: whether the Philippine court is in a position to make an intelligent decision as to the law and the facts.[28] Although the Supreme Court also discussed other factors like the importance of the local court having the power to enforce the decision, this precedent highlights the 'serious inconvenience,' as the Supreme Court highlights, of using the local fora in resolving disputes. While applying this doctrine in an employment dispute involving two foreign jurisdictions with the employee being a Philippine citizen, the Supreme Court made certain to qualify that '[t]his is not to say that Philippine courts and agencies have no power to solve controversies involving foreign employers' and that it is not 'saying that [it does] not have power over an employment contract executed in a foreign country'.

The Supreme Court has established that the Philippines follows the nationality theory in conflict of laws, in which a person's nationality determines subject matter jurisdiction, especially as they relate to personal status such as capacity to act and contract, and family relations such as marriage and divorce.[29] Article 15 of the Civil Code provides: 'Laws relating to family rights and duties, or to status, condition and capacity of persons are binding upon citizens of the Philippines, even though living abroad.' Although limited in its application to Philippine citizens, it has been

[26] *In re Testate Estate of Suntay* GR No 3087 (1954).
[27] *Arreza v Toyo* GR No 213198 (2019).
[28] GR No 120077 (2000).
[29] *Ellis v Republic* GR No 16922 (1963).

used as the legal basis for determining the personal status, and therefore the applicable national law, of foreign citizens in conflict of laws disputes with a question on personal status.[30]

C. After Determining the Applicable Law: Effect on Jurisdiction and *Forum Non Conveniens*

Once a Philippine court identifies the law governing the dispute (whether *lex fori* or a foreign *lex causae*), the case proceeds under that applicable law. The choice of law itself does not dictate whether the court retains or relinquishes jurisdiction. By the time the court decides the applicable law, it has already assumed jurisdiction over the case (having found that it can properly hear the dispute). The next step is simply to apply the chosen law to the merits. In other words, determining the applicable law does not automatically trigger a re-examination of jurisdiction or a need to decline the case in favour of another forum. The court will move forward and adjudicate the controversy under the selected law, whether that be Philippine law or a foreign law, so long as jurisdiction is proper.

If the applicable law is foreign, the Philippine court does not on that basis divest itself of jurisdiction or hand off the case to foreign courts. Philippine conflict of laws rules allow (and expect) local courts to apply foreign law when appropriate. In such instances, the foreign law is treated as a matter of fact that must be pleaded and proved by the party invoking it.[31] The court will require evidence (usually official publications or a copy of the law attested by the officer having legal custody of the record) to establish the content of the foreign law.[32] If the foreign law cannot be adequately proven, the court will apply Philippine law by default, under the doctrine of processual presumption.[33] This doctrine holds that when a foreign law is not properly proven, it is presumed to be the same as Philippine domestic law – thereby ensuring the court can still resolve the case. The key point is that the need to apply foreign law does not strip the court of competence or jurisdiction. Philippine courts are capable of interpreting and applying foreign law as long as it is duly proved, and they do so in many conflict of laws cases. Only if the foreign law is contrary to an important public policy or moral imperative would the court refuse to apply it – in which case Philippine law (*lex fori*) would be applied instead, to the extent necessary, rather than dismissing the case outright.[34]

Importantly, the choice of applicable law has no automatic bearing on whether the court should accept or decline jurisdiction. The determination that a foreign law governs an issue does not mean the Philippine court must reconsider the propriety of hearing the case or defer to a foreign tribunal. In Philippine practice, the questions of jurisdiction (including the possible dismissal of a case for being a seriously inconvenient forum) and choice of law are distinct steps in the analysis. The Supreme Court has outlined *three phases* in resolving conflict of laws problems: (1) jurisdiction (does the court have authority, and will it exercise it?), (2) choice of law (which law governs the dispute?), and (3) recognition or enforcement of the resulting judgment.[35] By the

[30] *Gibbs v Government of the Philippines* GR No 35694 (1933).

[31] 2019 Proposed Amendments to the Revised Rules on Evidence, ss 24 and 25.

[32] *Wildvalley Shipping v Court of Appeals* G.R. No. 119602, 6 October 2000; *Manufacturers Hanover Trust Co. v Guerrero* G.R. No. 136804, 19 February 2003.

[33] *Industrial Personnel & Management Services Inc v De Vera*, 785 SCRA 563, 582 (2016); *Edi-staff Builders International v NLRC* G.R. No. 145587, 26 October2007.

[34] *SAUDIA v Rebensio et al* G.R. No. 198587, 14 January 2015; *Philippine Export and Foreign Loan Guarantee v V.P. Eusebio Construction, Inc.*, 478 Phil. 269 (2004); *Pakistan International Airlines Corporation v Ople* 268 Phil. 92 (1990).

[35] *Raytheon International, Inc. v Rouzie, Jr.* G.R. No. 162894, 26 February 2008.

time the court reaches the choice of law stage, it has *already decided to entertain the case* (ie, not to dismiss on jurisdictional grounds). Thus, after identifying the proper law, the court generally proceeds to adjudicate the case on the merits using that law. There is no subsequent step requiring the court to decline jurisdiction simply because a foreign law applies.

A decision that the *lex causae* is foreign (eg, the law of another country) does not by itself oblige the court to dismiss the case or send the parties elsewhere. The doctrine of *forum non conveniens* – which allows a court to dismiss a case when another forum is clearly more suitable and convenient – is separate from the choice of law determination. *Forum non conveniens* is a *discretionary* tool used to ensure that litigation is pursued in the most appropriate location; it relates to the forum, not to the choice of governing law.[36] In other words, the fact that foreign law would govern the dispute is *merely one factor* and not determinative of the proper forum. The Philippine Supreme Court has explicitly held that invoking foreign law does not automatically make the Philippines an inconvenient forum.[37] A foreign applicable law is considered an *incident* of the case, not a decisive criterion for jurisdiction. Thus, a Philippine court will not decline jurisdiction *solely* because it must apply foreign law; it will still hear the case if the forum is otherwise appropriate.

Forum non conveniens comes into play only if a party timely raises it and persuades the court that there is a more convenient and competent forum elsewhere to hear the case.[38] Even when a conflict of laws scenario exists, a Philippine court may assume jurisdiction if it chooses to do so, provided that certain conditions are met. These conditions, as the Supreme Court has noted, are that: (1) the Philippine forum is convenient for the parties or witnesses, (2) the court is capable of intelligently applying the appropriate law (including foreign law) to resolve the facts, and (3) the court has or is likely to have the ability to enforce its decision.[39] If these requisites are satisfied – for example, if the Philippines has a significant connection to the case or the plaintiff resides here, and the court can obtain evidence and apply foreign law with no insurmountable difficulty – then the court will continue to hear the case despite the foreign law elements. The mere applicability of foreign law is not enough to render the Philippine forum inconvenient under these standards.

In practice, a determination that foreign law applies does not trigger an automatic *forum non conveniens* dismissal. Philippine courts will typically honour the plaintiff's choice of forum unless the defendant (or occasionally the court on its own) shows that the Philippine forum is so inconvenient that the ends of justice would be better served if the case were heard elsewhere. This is a high bar. Philippine jurisprudence, echoing international practice, holds that the plaintiff's choice of forum should rarely be disturbed unless the balance is strongly in favour of the defendant's claim of inconvenience.[40] Factors like the availability of witnesses, the location of evidence, the connection of the dispute to the Philippines, and the existence of an alternative forum are weighed. If, after deciding the applicable law, it remains clear that the Philippine court is a reasonable forum, the court will proceed with the case even if that means applying foreign substantive law. On the other hand, if a party had convincingly demonstrated early on that the Philippines is a seriously inappropriate venue (for instance, if virtually all relevant facts and parties are overseas and a foreign court would be much better suited to apply its own law), the Philippine court could

[36] *SAUDIA* (n 34).
[37] ibid.
[38] ibid.
[39] *Continental Micronesia, Inc. v Joseph Basso*, G.R. Nos. 178382–83, 23 September 2015; *Bank of America, NT&SA v Court of Appeals*, G.R. No. 120135, 31 March 2003, 400 SCRA 156, 169.
[40] *Saudi Arabian Airlines v Court of Appeals*, G.R. No. 122191, 8 October 1998.

dismiss on *forum non conveniens* grounds *before* delving into the merits. But that decision is made at the outset, not as a consequence of the choice of law outcome.

To sum up, once the Philippine court has decided which law to apply, that choice does not, in itself, determine whether the court keeps or declines the case. The court will apply the chosen law and resolve the dispute. A finding that *foreign law* governs a matter does not oblige the court to decline jurisdiction in favour of a foreign tribunal. The court will only refuse to hear the case if an appropriate motion to dismiss for *forum non conveniens* has been granted based on a full consideration of convenience and justice – a decision that is conceptually independent from the choice of law analysis.[41] In other words, the Philippine court will not automatically invoke *forum non conveniens* just because foreign law is involved. Absent extraordinary circumstances, it will adjudicate the case to its conclusion, applying either *lex fori* or the proven foreign *lex causae*, as justice requires.

i. Law of Obligations

a. Contracts

In construing the applicable law of a contract with foreign elements, depending on the issue in dispute, a Philippine court will assess either the extrinsic or intrinsic validity of the contract, as well as the contracting parties' capacity to enter into the contract.

The principle of party autonomy of the contracting parties is codified in Article 1306 of the Civil Code: 'Contracting parties may establish such stipulations, clauses, terms and conditions as they may deem convenient, provided that they are not contrary to Philippine laws, morals, good customs, public order, or public policy.'[42] This is relevant in private international law insofar as it allows the contracting parties to agree to a governing law other than Philippine law when entering into a contractual arrangement under the principle of *lex loci intentionis*. Parties can agree on the governing law, which will then determine the intrinsic validity of their contract, in a choice-of-law clause. The intrinsic validity of the contract refers to the interpretation of its essential elements such as the consideration for the contract, the cause impelling the parties and the nature of remedies for its non-performance or breach.

As for the extrinsic validity, *lex loci contractus* governs the contract's formal or extrinsic validity. In order to be extrinsically valid, the contract must conform to the form required by the law of the place where the contract was made. Article 17 of the Civil Code provides the guiding rule: "The forms and solemnities of contracts, wills and other public instruments shall be governed by the laws of the country in which they are executed."[43] The rule expressly recognises the extrinsic validity of contracts executed in conformity with another country's laws, and are then presented for adjudication before Philippine courts. In the Philippines, the basal rule is that contracts are binding in whatever form the parties agree on, with certain exceptions where the contract must be in a certain form to be valid[44] or enforceable.[45]

Regardless of the governing law stated and agreed upon in the contract, the Supreme Court has demonstrated a willingness to delve further into the legal system that controls a given situation

[41] *SAUDIA* (n 34).

[42] Civil Code, Art 1306.

[43] ibid, Art 17.

[44] ibid, Art 1356. Certain documents which are intended to serve as records in a public registry, such as contracts that create, transmit, modify or extinguish real rights over immovable property, need to be executed or acknowledged before a notary. Otherwise, they are void: ibid, Arts 1771, 1773.

[45] Civil Code, Art 1403(2) of the Statute of Frauds.

depending on the choice of the parties and the place where significant facts occurred. With the private interest of the litigant as a paramount interest, Philippine courts may weigh the relative claim of the parties and look into where the litigant maintains substantial connections so as not to cause fundamental unfairness to them.[46] In that regard, the choice of law clause of the parties must have 'connecting factors' to the dispute, which may be the law of the place of contracting, the law of the place of negotiation or performance, or the 'state of the most significant relationship.'[47] Although the court may have found that *lex loci voluntatis* or *lex loci intentionis* ought to apply in a dispute, it may nonetheless set it aside and apply Philippine law if the foreign law is contrary to public order, public policy and good customs. In *Bank of America NT & SA v American Realty Corp*, the Supreme Court set aside the foreign law for being contrary to the sound and established policy in Philippine law that the remedies available to a creditor foreclosing on a mortgage are deemed alternative and not cumulative, explaining that prohibitive laws in the Philippines concerning property (as well as those concerning persons or have for their object public order and public policy) shall not be rendered ineffective by foreign laws or judgments.[48]

In other words, the foreign law, even if properly pleaded and proved, may still be set aside to give way to the application of domestic law, if the Philippine policy so requires. This doctrine is hardly surprising, and merely continues the line of reasoning that Philippine law may prevail in conflict of laws disputes before Philippine courts if they deem it appropriate under certain circumstances.[49] One way that this has been done is by applying the doctrine of *forum non conveniens*. Could there be a scenario where Philippine courts would most likely respect the parties' choice without exercising their discretion in applying these exceptions? An agreement with an arbitration clause will most likely be considered contractually binding and considered by a court as a condition precedent before it exercises its jurisdiction, even if the clause requires arbitration to be conducted outside of the Philippines. In one case, the Supreme Court has held that the parties must comply with the arbitration clause providing for London as the venue of arbitration in accordance with the Arbitration Act 1950.[50]

The matter of deciding whether it has jurisdiction over a case is the first important step that a Philippine court must navigate in a contractual dispute with an international element, the next one being the more contentious rules on whether foreign or domestic law should apply. This is often a multilayered challenge, considering the need to look into the intrinsic and extrinsic validity of the contract. There are even more specific rules for different types of contracts. For example, in a loan agreement by a bank, the law of its permanent place of business is the proper governing law. A loan with an individual would be governed by the law of the place where the loan was executed. Contracts of sale, barter, donation or security, as well as antichresis, would have the *lex situs* or the governing law of the place where the property is located.[51]

Employment contracts are considered as contracts for service, with *lex loci contractus* governing extrinsic validity and *lex loci voluntatis* or *lex loci intentionis* determining the intrinsic validity. The protection of employees is paramount, and Philippine courts will interpret such contracts to ensure that an aggrieved employee obtains social justice, even if the services were performed outside of the Philippines. These were the circumstances considered by the Supreme Court in *Pakistan International Airlines v Ople*, where it held that the employment contract, although not executed in

[46] *Saudi Arabian Airlines* (n 40).
[47] *Hasegawa v Kitamura* GR No 149177 (2007).
[48] *Bank of America NT & SA v American Realty Corp* GR No 133876 (1999).
[49] *Pakistan International Airlines Corp v Ople* GR No 61594 (1990).
[50] *Puromines Inc v Court of Appeals* GR No 91228 (1993).
[51] The Personal Property Security Act (RA No 1057) repealed the Civil Code provisions on chattel mortgage and pledge.

the Philippines, between an employer that is a foreign corporation (although licensed to do business in the Philippines) and employees performing their services in between the Middle East and Europe, does not divest Philippine courts and the labour administrative agencies of its jurisdiction over the case. The venue clause in the contract, providing that the settlement of the dispute must be resolved only in courts before Karachi, Pakistan, was invalidated. As contracts relating to labour and employment are impressed with public interest, the principle of party autonomy must be counter-balanced with public policy considerations.[52] To be clear, courts will not indiscriminately exercise jurisdiction over a contract just because it relates to employment. In *Manila Hotel v National Labor Relations Commission*,[53] labour courts were not the proper forum for adjudication in a case where the dispute involved foreign jurisdictions, and the rule of *forum non conveniens* was held to be inapplicable.

The contract for transportation of goods across international borders are governed by the law of the country of their destination, in the event of their loss, destruction or deterioration.[54] Philippine law would be the governing law of the contract, and the extraordinary due diligence of the common carrier begins, from the moment that the goods are unconditionally placed in the carrier's possession.[55]

b. Torts

The concept of tort under Philippine law is derived from the Spanish civil law on quasi-delict or *culpa aquilana*. It is defined in Article 2176 of the Civil Code as an act or omission causing damage to another, there being fault or negligence, if there is no pre-existing contractual relation between the parties. Philippine law has also codified tort in the Civil Code in its law on damages: 'Every person who, contrary to law, wilfully or negligently causes damage to another, shall indemnify the latter for the same.'[56]

In an action for tort, the applicable law would be the *lex loci delicti commissi* or the law of the place where the alleged tort was committed. Identifying the situs can be complicated when the tort happens over a period of time, and the place of conduct, injury and the tortfeasor may be governed by different legal rules. Philippine courts, in such conflicting cases, have time and again shown their lack of hesitation to step in when necessary. In the 1910 case of *United States v H.N. Bull*, which was decided during the American colonisation of the Philippines, the Philippine Supreme Court had occasion to interpret the laws Act No. 55 and Act No. 400, which provided for the organisation of the courts of the Philippine islands.[57] The tortious act – the unlawful carrying and transportation of 677 cattle and carabao without providing means for securing them while in transit – was done in a Norwegian vessel not registered or licensed in the Philippines. The Supreme Court started its analysis by stating that local courts did not have jurisdiction over offenses committed on the high seas – until the vessel comes within Philippine territorial waters, in this case 3 miles from Manila Bay. At that point, the continuing offence – and every element necessary to constitute it – is done within Philippine jurisdiction, and the local court therefore had jurisdiction over the subject matter of the offence and the person of the offender.

Almost a century later, the doctrine has been broadened to the 'State of the most significant relationship' rule, with local courts able to exercise jurisdiction in a case where the 'point of

[52] *Pakistan International Airlines Corp v Ople* GR No 61594 (1990).
[53] GR No 120077 (2000).
[54] Civil Code, Art 1753.
[55] ibid, Arts 1367–68. See also *American President Lines Ltd v Klepper* GR No 15671 (1960).
[56] Civil Code, Art 20.
[57] GR No. 5270 (1910).

contact' or 'connecting factor' of the tortious conduct took place is the Philippines. In a complaint for damages filed by a flight attendant who was employed by a foreign airline company, a resident foreign corporation engaged in the business of international carriage, the Supreme Court held that there is basis for the injury occurred in the Philippines. The complainant was a resident Philippine national, and although part of her work entailed flying to different overseas locations and certain acts or parts of the injury allegedly occurred in another country, the overall harm or the fatality of the alleged injury to her person, reputation, social standing and human rights occurred in the Philippines. The Supreme Court fleshed out the application of the 'State of the most significant relationship' rule, which it deemed to be appropriate given the factual context of the case. In applying this rule, the following 'points of contact' were taken into account and considered as relevant to the issue: (1) the place where the injury occurred, (2) the place where the conduct causing the injury occurred, (3) the domicile, residence, nationality, place of incorporation, or place of business of the parties, and (4) the place where the relationship, if any, between the parties was centered.[58]

ii. Property

a. Real and Personal Property

The general rule under Philippine law for real and personal property follows the international custom of *lex situs*. This is mirrored in Article 16 of the Civil Code which states that the law of the country where a real or personal property is situated shall govern. However, regardless of the nature of the property and the country where it may be found, the national law of the person whose succession is under consideration shall govern intestate and testamentary succession, both with respect to the order of succession and to the amount of successional rights and to the intrinsic validity of testamentary provisions.

There are several nuances and exceptions to this general rule, which is hardly surprising, considering the universal complexity of property law regimes around the world, the different transactions that contemplate the alienation of property, and even the diversity of types of what is classifiable as 'property.' Article 16 qualifies that in the case of testate and intestate succession, it is the national law of the decedent that governs. This would encompass the intrinsic validity of a testamentary disposition, the order of succession and the amount of succession rights, as well as the capacity of beneficiaries to succeed.[59]

Another exception is where the transaction does not affect the title or ownership over the real property; in this case, either *lex voluntatis* or *lex loci intentionis* governs. Where real property is offered as a security or collateral for the performance of a principal obligation, the security transaction is governed by the *lex situs*, whilst the principal obligation remains to be governed by the same rules as ordinary contracts.

The rules for personal property also have considerable variation. Where the situs of the movable property is not significant, the court may set aside the *lex situs* as the governing law. Otherwise, the variation often depends on the type of movable property, particularly intangible properties that do not have a clear situs. Philippine law infers the appropriate situs for them. Loans remain to be governed by *lex situs*. Negotiable instruments are governed by the law stated in the contract or the place of delivery. Choses in possession are governed by the law of the place where the property is located at the time that the contract was entered into. It has been suggested

[58] *Saudi Arabian Airlines* (n 40).
[59] Civil Code, Art 1039.

that for debts, the rule to be applied should be based on the contract from which the debt arises.[60] A quite different rule applies when it comes to garnishment, which should be where the debtor can be served with summons.

The governing law relating to the sale of corporate shares is the law of the place of the corporation's principal office. The Philippine Corporation Code provides for additional requirements applicable to local corporations – that the sale be recorded in the books of that corporation.[61] However, one must be aware that as between private parties to the share sale contract, the governing law is either *lex loci voluntatis* or *lex loci intentionis*. For goods in transit, the law of destination is the governing law, augmented by the Carriage of Goods by Sea Act.[62]

b. Intellectual Property

The conflict rules for intellectual property are based on a combination of local and international sources: the locally enacted Intellectual Property Code and the treaties 1883 Paris Convention for the Protection of Industrial Property and 1886 Berne Convention for the Protection of Literary and Artistic Works. Unlike other areas of law where the Philippines has seemingly lagged behind in signing private international law treaties, intellectual property is an area where the Philippines is attuned to the international order. The requirement under the Paris Convention to protect trade names that are not necessarily locally registered is found in the Intellectual Property Code, which affords protection to trade or business names, even those without registration.[63]

Recognising the importance of a harmonious international order in the protection of intellectual property, the Intellectual Property Code has enacted the principle of mutual protection and reciprocity. As such, any person who is a national or who is domiciled or has a real and effective industrial establishment in a country which is a party to any convention, treaty or agreement relating to intellectual property rights or the repression of unfair competition, to which the Philippines is also a party, or extends reciprocal rights to nationals of the Philippines by law, shall be entitled to benefits to the extent necessary to give effect to any provision of such convention, treaty or reciprocal law, in addition to the rights under the Intellectual Property Code.

Even before the Paris Convention and Berne Convention, foreign corporations not doing business in the Philippines has been entitled to intellectual property protection as early as 1927. In *Western Equipment and Supply Co v Reyes*, Western Electric Co, a foreign corporation incorporated in New York and not doing business in the Philippines filed a case to restrain a local applicant that attempted to incorporate a domestic corporation with the name Western Electric Company Inc.[64] The Supreme Court considered a corporation's right to use its trade name as a right *in rem*, such that a foreign corporation can seek protection from an attempted trademark infringement.[65]

The interpretation of the Paris Convention alongside local intellectual property law was tested in *Philip Morris v Fortune Tobacco Corporation*, a case that involved the alleged trademark infringement of Fortune Tobacco Corporation of a trademark owned by Philip Morris, a foreign-registered corporation. The Supreme Court held that even if countries where the disputing parties registered are members of the Paris Convention, it does not automatically entitle the foreign corporation to the protection of their trademarks in the Philippines absent actual use of the marks in local commerce and trade in the Philippines. While the Philippines' adherence to the Paris Convention effectively obligates the Philippines to honour and enforce its provisions as

[60] Coquia and Aguiling-Pangalangan (n 4) 314.
[61] Revised Corporation Code (RA No 11232), s 62.
[62] Carriage of Goods by Sea Act (Commonwealth Act No. 65).
[63] Paris Convention, Art 8. Intellectual Property Code (RA No 8293), s 165.2.
[64] GR No 27897 (1927).
[65] *Philips Export BV v Court of Appeals* GR No 96161 (1992).

regards the protection of industrial property of foreign nationals in the Philippines, the protection accorded has to be made subject to the limitations of Philippine laws.[66] In any case, a foreign corporation not registered in the Philippines may file a local action to recover damages for the local infringement of its trademark, as well as unfair competition.[67] As for copyright protection, the Philippines being party to the Berne Convention guarantees the rights of foreign copyright holders. Article 5 provides that foreign authors shall enjoy the same rights which the laws of the Contracting States grant to nationals, without any formality requirements.

iii. Family

a. Marriage

The validity of a marriage solemnised in other countries depends on whether it conforms with the applicable governing law for its extrinsic or intrinsic validity. While the basal rules are set out in the Civil Code and the later Family Code,[68] common law has since carved out many nuances that makes the conflict rules on marriages less statute-based than it is substantially jurisprudence-based. The intrinsic validity of a marriage celebrated abroad depends on compliance with essential requisites, while the extrinsic validity depends on compliance with formal requisites.[69] Intrinsic validity is controlled by the parties' personal laws (either domiciliary or nationality), while the extrinsic validity is governed by the *lex loci celebrationis*.

In order for a marriage to be legally recognised in the Philippines, it must comply with the requirements imposed by the law of the place of celebration. A foreigner intending to marry in the Philippines must prove capacity to marry by obtaining a certificate of legal capacity to contract marriage from the relevant consular official of their home country. A stateless person or refugee would be able to comply with this requirement by submitting an affidavit evidencing their capacity.[70] The validity of marriages between Filipinos celebrated abroad has been a matter of discussion by the Supreme Court in several cases. The statutory basis for this is the Family Code which recognises the validity of all marriages performed outside the Philippines as long as they were in accordance with the laws in force in the country where they were solemnised and valid there as such.[71] The following exceptions mean that a marriage that would otherwise be compliant in the foreign jurisdiction would nonetheless be considered invalid in the Philippines:[72]

(1) Either or both parties did not have legal capacity to marry under Philippine law;[73]
(2) The marriage is bigamous or polygamous;[74]
(3) The consent of one party was vitiated by a mistake as to the identity of the other party;[75]
(4) At the time of the marriage, a party was psychologically incapable of complying with essential marital obligations;[76]
(5) The marriage is incestuous;[77]
(6) The marriage is void by reason of public policy.[78]

[66] GR No 158589 (2006).
[67] Intellectual Property Code, ss 156, 160.
[68] Family Code (Executive Order No 209).
[69] ibid Arts 2–3.
[70] ibid Art 21.
[71] ibid Art 26.
[72] ibid.
[73] ibid Art 35(1).
[74] ibid Art 34(4).
[75] ibid Art 35(5).
[76] ibid Art 36.
[77] ibid Art 37.
[78] ibid Art 38.

Notice that these exceptions pertain to the essential requisites of marriage. Because the intrinsic validity of a Filipino's marriage is determined by their personal law, even if their marriage abroad complied with all the formal requisites of that jurisdiction, it would nonetheless be invalidated if they fall under any of these exceptions.

While marital relations are considered by law as personal in nature beyond court intervention, the Family Code provides guiding principles for them couched in broad language that are not strictly enforceable, including maintaining mutual fidelity, respect, cohabitation and support, the wife's right to use the husband's surname, and the establishment of a family.[79] In cases where the spouses are of different nationalities, legislators have commented that Philippine law would govern their relations, regardless of which one of them has Philippine nationality.[80] Philippine law is also the default rule in governing the property relations of spouses of different nationalities, where there are no contrary stipulations in their marriage settlement.[81] The legislators' intent in applying Philippine law as the default governing law in certain legal aspects of a marriage reveals a desire to protect Filipinos from a foreign law that may be unfamiliar to the Filipino spouse.[82] The legislators may have been well-intentioned in assuming that Filipino citizens would prefer Philippine law to govern their rights and obligations. However, this may in the end shortchange a Filipino spouse who cannot seek protection in a foreign law that might in the end provide better and more robust protection to them. At the very least, there is room for a mixed-nationality marriage to opt for a different governing law – one that might be better than Philippine law – when it comes to their marriage settlement.

b. Divorce, Nullity and Separation

The Philippines, apart from the Vatican, is the only country in the world where divorce is not legal.[83] Previous attempts to enact a divorce law have thus far failed. The modes of severing marital ties are limited to a nullification or annulment of marriage, with legal separation as a de facto separation that merely dissolves the spouses' marital duties and property relations, but not the bond of marriage.[84] This has been complicated by Filipinos who are able to successfully obtain divorce abroad with the view of applying its effect in the Philippines, only to find out that a foreign decree of divorce would have no effect in the Philippines.[85] One can imagine the legal confusion that might arise where a divorce granted and recognised in one jurisdiction is sternly rejected in the Philippines. Philippine courts, applying the nationality theory (and therefore Philippine law) to Filipino citizens, exercise jurisdiction over nullity and annulment cases involving Filipinos. A Filipino citizen that does not hold residence in the Philippines would therefore still be bound by Philippine law insofar as their marriage status is concerned, and judgments of Philippine courts may still affect them even if they did not participate in the proceedings. The grounds to nullify a marriage were previously limited to those permitted by the *lex loci celebrationis*. The strict rules in recognising

[79] ibid Arts 68, 70–1.

[80] Sempio-Diy (n 13) 105, citing the 15, 22 and 24 November minutes of the Civil Code Revision and Family Law Committee Meetings.

[81] Family Code, Art 80.

[82] Sempio-Diy (n 13) 102.

[83] 'Why the Philippines is the only country where divorce is illegal' *The Economist* (London, 15 February 2020), available online at www.economist.com/asia/2020/02/13/why-the-philippines-is-the-only-country-where-divorce-is-illegal. However, divorce is allowed in the Philippines insofar as Muslim marriages are concerned: Code of Muslim Personal Laws (Presidential Decree No 1083) Title II.

[84] Family Code, Art 63.

[85] *Techaves v Escano* GR No 19671 (1965).

foreign divorces or annulments of marriage have seen a gradual change over time, starting with the statutory requirement that a foreign decree of divorce between a Filipino and a foreign spouse must have been obtained, thus enabling the Filipino spouse to remarry. This starting point provides for quite a niche scenario as to when a foreign divorce might be recognised in the Philippines: first, the marriage must be between a Filipino and non-Filipino and, second, the non-Filipino spouse must have been the one to obtain the divorce.[86] Several decisions that have come before the Supreme Court have interpreted this statutory requirement quite strictly. For example, a Filipino spouse who was able to obtain foreign nationality and then subsequently obtain a divorce could not enforce their foreign divorce decree in the Philippines, because Philippine law still applied at the point of their marriage.[87] After decades of refusing to recognise foreign divorce decrees that did not fall into the specific exception laid out in the statute, the Supreme Court has finally determined the effects of obtaining a foreign divorce decree involving a Filipino spouse that has obtained foreign citizenship, thus allowing the other Filipino spouse to remarry in the Philippines.[88] Perhaps the biggest change, however, happened in 2018 with the case *Republic of the Philippines v Manalo*, completely nullifying the requirement that the non-Filipino spouse must have been the one that obtained the divorce.[89] This has made the process for getting a foreign divorce decree recognised in the Philippines slightly less cumbersome for the Filipino spouse, although the Philippine court will still need to look into whether it was validly issued abroad in accordance with the applicable foreign law.[90] The latest case in this saga was in February 2024, when the Supreme Court clarified that the type of divorce – whether administratively issued or judicially decreed – does not matter, as long as the divorce is valid under the foreign spouse's national law.[91]

iv. Corporations and Insolvency

The old pre-2020 procedural rules only allowed summons to be served on foreign corporations doing business in the Philippines through their resident agent or officer in the Philippines, or through a local regulator.[92] The 2020 procedural rules now allow summons to be served on foreign corporations that do business in the Philippines but have no local presence or resident agent. Permission of court is still a requirement, but non-registered foreign corporations may now be served summons in any of the following ways:

(1) personal service through the appropriate foreign country with the assistance of the Philippine Department of Foreign Affairs;
(2) publication in a newspaper of general circulation in the country where the defendant may be found and serving a copy of the summons by registered mail to the defendant's last known address;
(3) facsimile transmission or any recognised electronic means that can generate proof of service; or,
(4) such other means as the court may direct.[93]

[86] Family Code, Art 26.
[87] *Republic of the Philippines v Iyoy* GR No 152577 (2005).
[88] *Republic of the Philippines v Orbecido* GR No 154380 (2005).
[89] *Republic of the Philippines v Manalo* GR No 221029 (2018).
[90] *Garcia v Recio* GR No 138322 (2001).
[91] *Republic of the Philippines v Ng* GR No 249238 (2024).
[92] Rules of Civil Procedure, Rule 14, s 12.
[93] Amendment of Section 12, Rule 14 of the Rules of Court on Service upon Foreign Private Juridical Entity (AM No 11-3-6-SC).

III. Jurisdiction *In Rem*

A. General Principles

The previous section discussed actions *in personam*, which addresses questions relating to the status of the persons involved in the action. Rules regarding the proper service of documents on the parties are thus important to ensure that the decision of the court would not be futile. In an action *in rem*, Philippine courts have jurisdiction over the property or *res*, so their decisions will affect the subject matter of the suit and become binding on the whole world, regardless of the persons who bring the case before them. Courts are able to exercise jurisdiction not because of the proper service of summons on the defendant, but because of the presence of the property within their territorial jurisdiction. Examples of *in rem* proceedings are land registration and admiralty cases, where courts may impose judgment concerning the subject land or vessel, rendering judgment binding against the world, and not just the interested persons. A *quasi in rem* action is a hybrid of an *in rem* and *in personam action;* it is *in rem* as it affects property within the court's jurisdiction, but *in personam* insofar as it is directed only against a particular person with the purpose of subjecting their property to the lien burdening it. An example of a *quasi in rem* action would be subjecting property to the payment of a claim, foreclosure of a mortgage, or partitioning of land.

The strictest rules for summons apply in actions *in personam*, although the rules have been somewhat relaxed to allow for extraterritorial service in the latest amendments to the procedural rules. Actions *in rem* or *quasi in rem* do not require personal service, and may be served outside of the Philippines, as long as they fall under the following general classes: (1) affects the claimant's personal status, (2) relates to property located in the Philippines that the defendant claims to have an interest in, (3) seeks to exclude the defendant from an interest in property located in the Philippines, or (4) pertains to defendant's property subject to attachment in the Philippines.[94] Although personal service is not required, due process considerations require that the parties at least be given adequate notice and opportunity to be heard. These requirements may be satisfied by publication, without requiring personal service.

B. Ship Arrest

Shipping cases often involve a conflict element, considering the cross-border nature of maritime activities. The statutory basis for dealing with admiralty and maritime matters is the Judiciary Reorganization Act,[95] granting Regional Trial Courts (RTCs) the exclusive original jurisdiction over such cases. Despite their mobile nature, ships are considered subject of an *in rem* action under Philippine law, with the Ship Mortgage Decree stipulating that maritime liens over a ship may be enforced in any foreign country in which the ship may be located, in accordance with the foreign country's laws for enforcing ship mortgages.[96] The presidential issuance, having the status of statutory law, is a unique case of the Executive branch of government exercising its quasi-legislative power over a matter of private international law. In order to enforce a lien on a ship and facilitate a ship arrest, the claimant-creditor must file a petition for judicial foreclosure on a

[94] *Gomez v Court of Appeals* GR No 127692 (2004).
[95] Judiciary Reorganization Act of 1980 (Batas Pambansa Blg 129).
[96] Ship Mortgage Decree (Presidential Decree No 1521), s 10.

ship mortgage. The creditor may then apply, without knowledge of the ship owner, for an order to arrest the vessel, providing evidence of the mortgage default and executing a bond to be determined by the judge. Because ship arrest proceedings are *in rem*, the court is empowered to order its sale by public auction upon a finding that the interests of the parties will be properly served by its sale or that the property is considered perishable.[97] Conflicting claims over the same vessel during rehabilitation proceedings have been the subject of two cases consolidated by the Supreme Court, *Negros Navigation Co v Court of Appeals*[98] and *Tsuneishi Heavy Industries (Cebu) Inc v Negros Navigation Co*,[99] illustrating the difficulty of enforcing liens over vessels as a unique specie of property, especially in the context of rehabilitation proceedings. The case involves Tsuneishi filing a maritime lien claim over the vessel with the Cebu RTC, alleging that it had not been paid for repairs it had done to the vessels. Meanwhile, the maritime company owning the vessels, Negros, commenced rehabilitation proceedings in the Manila RTC, another RTC branch, to suspend payments and to stay all claims filed against it. The Cebu RTC nonetheless proceeded to seize the vessels, prompting Negros to seek to suspend the proceedings. Ultimately, the Supreme Cour decided that the Manila RTC proceedings had not divested the Cebu RTC of jurisdiction over the maritime lien, although the maritime lien could only be enforced after the rehabilitation proceedings had been suspended or Negros dissolved as a corporate entity.

IV. Immunities from Jurisdiction

A. Establishing Immunity

Because generally accepted principles of international law are adopted by the Philippine Constitution, the principles of diplomatic and sovereign immunity are considered as part of Philippine law. Foreign governments or diplomats may avail of these immunities in cases they face before Philippine courts. In order to do so, they must inform the local courts of their intent to benefit from an immunity by an endorsement from the Executive Department through the Department of Foreign Affairs. The process is more practical than rule-based, and usually involves the Secretary of Foreign Affairs endorsing by way of a letter or telegram the immunity to the local court.[100] Whatever form the endorsement takes, the local court is expected to accept the immunity claim endorsed by its co-equal branch.[101]

B. Diplomatic Immunity

The Philippine Constitution effectively converts the generally accepted principles of international law into local law by express recognition under the doctrine of incorporation.[102] The personal inviolability or immunity of diplomatic representatives, recognised in customary international law, is incorporated into Philippine law. The Philippines is also a signatory to the 1961 Vienna Convention on Diplomatic Relations, so foreign diplomats may seek immunities from arrest, prosecution and

[97] ibid s 11.
[98] *Negros Navigation Co v Court of Appeals* GR No 163156 (2008).
[99] *Tsuneishi Heavy Industries (Cebu) Inc v Negros Navigation Co* GR No 166845 (2008).
[100] *The Holy See v Rosario* GR No 101949 (1994).
[101] *World Health Organization v Aquino* GR No 35131 (1972).
[102] Constitution, Art II, s 2.

punishment for violation of criminal law. Diplomatic representatives are therefore exempt from the criminal jurisdiction of Philippine courts and cannot be subject to arrest, prosecution and punishment for violation of the criminal law.[103] They are also exempt from the court's civil jurisdiction, and cannot be defendants in a case or their property attached or subject to lien.[104] These immunities will not apply in the following actions, as provided in the 1961 Vienna Convention:

(1) relating to privately owned immovable property located in the Philippines, unless the property is held for the purpose of a mission;
(2) relating to the diplomatic representative acting in their private capacity, and not on behalf of the state, as an executor, administrator, heir or legatee; or,
(3) relating to the diplomatic representative's professional or commercial activities in the Philippines outside the scope of official duties.[105]

The interplay of the rules and their exceptions was made evident in *Liang v People*,[106] where the diplomatic representative was an economist employed at the Asian Development Bank (ADB), accused of slander against a colleague. The Department of Foreign Affairs, in accordance with protocol, issued a certification as to the immunity of the foreign diplomat, on the basis of an agreement between the ADB and the Philippines as to the headquarters of the ADB in the country. The Supreme Court rejected the immunity claim, arguing that the government communication is not binding on the court as it can only be applied to acts done in official course of duties. While diplomatic representatives have broad protections from criminal prosecution, representatives of international organisations are differently situated and can only be protected from criminal prosecution for acts done in their official capacity.

C. Sovereign Immunity

Sovereign immunity is similarly protected in the Philippine Constitution, specifically stating that the state may not be sued without its consent.[107] This doctrine has been extended to cover actions against foreign states being sued without their consent.[108] In a suit for ejection and the recovery of payment of property rentals, contracts for lease of apartments were executed by US army officers purportedly in the name of the US government for the billeting and quartering of US soldiers stationed in the Philippines. Entered into at the height of the Japanese-Philippines conflict during World War II in 1945, the agreement was for the lease to be terminated six (6) months after the war has ended or unless terminated sooner by the US. When the war ended on 2 September 1945, the US army refused to leave and advised that they will only be able to do so on 1 February 1947, prompting the lessors to file the case. The Philippine Supreme Court ultimately affirmed the dismissal of the case by the lower courts, concluding that the real defendant was the US government. The Supreme Court then dismissed the case for lack of jurisdiction, anchored on the sovereign immunity of the US government:

> The question of lack of jurisdiction was raised and interposed at the very beginning of the action. The US Government has not given its consent to the filing of this suit which is essentially against her, though

[103] 1961 Vienna Convention on Diplomatic Relations, Arts 29, 31.
[104] ibid Art 31.
[105] ibid Art 31(1).
[106] *Liang v People of the Philippines* GR No 125865 (2000).
[107] Constitution, Art XVI, s 3.
[108] *Syquia v Lopez* GR No 1648 (1949).

> not in name. Moreover, this is not only a case of a citizen filing a suit against his own Government without the latter's consent but it is of a citizen filing an action against a foreign government without said government's consent, which renders more obvious the lack of jurisdiction of the courts of his country. The principles of the law behind this rule are so elementary and of such general acceptance that we deem it unnecessary to cite authorities in support thereof.[109]

Almost four decades after this ruling was made, the Philippines has made a distinction as to the cases in which sovereign immunity may be properly invoked: governmental acts of a state are entitled to sovereign immunity, while commercial and proprietary, or private acts, are not:

> [A] State may be said to have descended to the level of an individual and can thus be deemed to have tacitly given its consent to be sued only when it enters into business contracts. It does not apply where the contract relates to the exercise of its sovereign functions. In this case the projects are an integral part of the naval base which is devoted to the defense of both the United States and the Philippines, indisputably a function of the government of the highest order; they are not utilized for nor dedicated to commercial or business purposes.[110]

To be clear, certain commercial acts entered into by a foreign state may still attract sovereign immunity if, for example, it is for the purpose of or incidental to a sovereign activity.[111] A stipulation that Philippine law governs a contract entered into by a foreign government does not necessarily result in a waiver of sovereign immunity.[112]

State immunity is not limited to foreign governments and applies to those acting on behalf of foreign states. Quite separate from diplomatic representatives, a foreign officer or agent acting under the instructions of the foreign state and with the consent of the hosting state, in this case the Philippines, can equally claim sovereign immunity. Insofar as their actions can be imputed to the foreign state, they can properly be characterised as agents acting in the discharge of their official duties. The foreign state they represent will be officially held accountable for their actions.[113] Whether a foreign government agency or entity of a foreign state may claim sovereign immunity depends on a test laid down by the Philippine Supreme Court, primarily based on whether it was incorporated under the foreign state's law:

> An incorporated agency has a charter of its own that invests it with a separate juridical personality, like the Social Security System, the University of the Philippines, and the City of Manila. By contrast, the unincorporated agency is so called because it has no separate juridical personality but is merged in the general machinery of the government, like the Department of Justice, the Bureau of Mines and the Government Printing Office.
>
> If the agency is incorporated, the test of its suability is found in its charter. The simple rule is that it is suable if its charter says so, and this is true regardless of the functions it is performing. Municipal corporations, for example, like provinces and cities, are agencies of the State when they are engaged in governmental functions and therefore should enjoy the sovereign immunity from suit. Nevertheless, they are subject to suit even in the performance of such functions because their charter provides that they can sue and be sued.[114]

[109] *Syquia v Lopez* GR No 1648 (1949).
[110] *United States of America v Ruiz* GR No 35645 (1985).
[111] *Republic of Indonesia v Vinzon* GR No 154705 (2003).
[112] ibid.
[113] *United States of America v Guinto* GR No 76607 (1990).
[114] *Deutsche Gesellschaft für Technische Zusammenarbeit v Court of Appeals* GR No 152318 (2009).

3

The Law of Obligations

HILARIO S CARAAN

I. Law of Obligations

Globalisation challenges had significantly posted a uniformising conflict of laws in the Association of Southeast Asian Nations (ASEAN) where to be able to compete effectively in the global economy the region needs supranational legal infrastructure that facilitates international business transactions. However, sovereignty and independence of states serve as hindering factors regarding the nexus between legal infrastructure and economic development. Among the major areas of conflict of laws that need to be dealt with is the uniformisation of 'choice of law' in the region.

In the Philippines, legal issues involving conflict of laws are addressed by courts ascertaining which law shall be applied. Philippine laws are generally enforced when the area of law or the contract involved specifically requires the application thereof, *or* when a party fails to show that foreign laws properly apply therein. Even if a Philippine court had already assumed jurisdiction, it may still decline to decide on the case following the doctrine of *forum non conveniens.*[1]

The cross-cultural exchange of ideas had been bolstered by technological globalisation which resulted in an incessantly increasing number of stipulations from natural and juridical persons of different nationalities and in multifarious consequential legal responsibilities. It is significant that states have diversified laws on how obligations of persons are created.

In the Philippines, obligations emanate from either: (a) obligations mandated by specific provisions of law which may be in the nature of a crime or delict, quasi-contract or quasi-delict, or (b) a plain contractual stipulation entered into by parties.[2] This globalisation challenge complicated the conflict of laws problems encountered by various countries especially in terms of varying rules on contract formation, formalities, interpretation, and enforcement. The Philippine legal system has a hybrid combination of the Spanish and American civil and common law traditions, which differs from other states, even among its neighbour ASEAN countries.

These varied rules create a need for the forum court, dealing with interpretation and enforcement of cases with foreign law components, to assess what the parties actually intended at the time of constitution of obligation particularly in resolving issues presented before it. More so, the forum court must be prepared to substitute its forum law with that of other countries.

[1] JR Coquia and E Aquiling-Pangalangan, *Conflict of Laws: Cases, Materials and Comments (Quezon City, Central Book Supply, 2000) 40, citing Wing On Company v Syyap* (64 O.G. 8311, 1967).

[2] Civil Code, Republic Act No. 386, Art 1157.

A. Contracts

As humankind entered the twenty-first century, methods of communication became highly advanced due to the technological boom. From handwritten snail mail and the uncertainty of whether one's missives would reach their designated recipients, people are now able to send their messages across the world with the press of a button.

As methods of communication became highly advanced, so did other ways in which humans handle their business dealings and contracts. It has become regular practice now to send contracts via electronic mail and parties are able to sign documents using electronic signatures, regardless of their location, without having to physically meet. This is how foreign elements become involved in contractual relations and choice of law issues may arise. The forum court would be in charge of determining which law is applicable if the parties' intentions (*lex loci intentionis*) cannot be ascertained based on the contract.

If the intention of parties cannot be ascertained, one authority presents the situation to the forum court:

> Where a choice of law is not made expressly, giving effect to that choice is significantly more difficult. In such circumstances, the common law provides that the proper law of the contract is the system of law that the parties impliedly choose as the law governing their contract. The common law model is beset by divergent [conceptualizations] of the implied proper law and [skepticism] as to the reality or artificiality of the connecting factor of inferred intention by which it is ascertained. Of equal concern is the scope of the proper law, brought about by: ambiguity surrounding the concept of 'choice'; the leniency of the standards by which a choice of law is inferred; and the probity and propriety of various indicia of inferred intention.[3]

Under Philippine law, a contract is 'a meeting of minds between two persons whereby one binds himself, with respect to the other, to give something or to render some service.'[4] A contract is perfected by mere consent, or the meeting of minds, between the parties in which 'there is a concurrence between the offer and the acceptance upon the subject matter, consideration, and terms of payment.'[5] Since a contract can be perfected by mere consent, it generally takes effect only between the parties involved, their assigns, and heirs.[6] This is called the relativity of contracts wherein the terms stipulated in a contract are binding only to the parties who entered into it.[7]

The Philippine Supreme Court[8] recognises that in general, contracts undergo three distinct stages of negotiation, perfection or birth, and consummation. Negotiation begins from the time the prospective contracting parties manifest their interest in the contract and ends at the moment of their agreement. Thereafter, perfection or birth of the contract takes place when the parties agree upon the essential elements of the contract. Finally, consummation occurs when the parties fulfill or perform the terms agreed upon in the contract, culminating in the extinguishment thereof.

Once parties have entered into a contract, they are obligated to comply with it in good faith since it has the force of law between the parties.[9] The contract they entered into equally binds

[3] B Marshall, 'Reconsidering the Proper Law of the Contract' (2012) 13 *Melbourne Journal of International Law* 505–39, ssrn.com/abstract=2718853.

[4] Civil Code, Art. 1305.

[5] *Heirs of Ignacio v Home Bankers Savings and Trust Company, Spouses Rodriguez and Zuniga*, G.R. No. 177783 (2013).

[6] Civil Code, Art 1311.

[7] *CCC Insurance Corporation v Kawasaki Steel Corporation, F.F. Mañacop Construction Co. Inc. and Mañacop*, G.R. No. 156162 (2015).

[8] *CF. Sharp & Co., Inc. v Pioneer Insurance & Surety Corporation*, 682 Phil. 198, 207 (2012).

[9] Civil Code, Art 1159.

both parties, compliance with which cannot be left to the will of only one party.[10] This is known as the mutuality of contracts. The contract is void if the fulfillment of the contract is dependent exclusively upon the sole discretion and will of only one of the contracting parties.[11]

It is a source of obligation for those entering into a contract (the contracting parties), a juridical necessity[12] whereby the parties agree on the fulfillment of a prestation to give, to do, or not to do[13] through the intervention of courts, if necessary. In an obligation to give, fulfillment may be through giving either a determinate (specific) or indeterminate (generic) property.[14] In an obligation to do, the fulfillment is done through the performance of an act or the rendering of a service;[15] whereas in an obligation not to do, the fulfillment is by abstaining from the prohibited act.[16]

i. Governing Law of a Contract

The parties are given autonomy to have any and all stipulations they may deem necessary for their agreement to come into fruition, to the point they can choose which law or state would govern their contract. If a choice of law issue is submitted to the forum court, the first consideration would be what the parties intended.

The forum court is faced with three phases involved in resolving a choice of law issue: jurisdiction, choice of law, then recognition and enforcement of judgment.[17] The Philippine Supreme Court listed the following as questions to be asked by the forum court:

1. Under the law, do I have jurisdiction over the subject matter and the parties to this case?
2. If the answer is yes, is this a convenient forum to the parties, in light of the facts?
3. If the answer is yes, what is the conflicts rule for this particular problem?
4. If the conflicts rule points to a foreign law, has said law been properly pleaded and proved by the one invoking it?
5. If so, is the application or enforcement of the foreign law in the forum one of the basic exceptions to the application of foreign law? In short, is there any strong policy or vital interest of the forum that is at stake in this case and which should preclude the application of foreign law?[18]

The governing law in the Philippines for contracts is the Civil Code. Under the Civil Code, the contracting parties are free to establish any stipulations, clauses, terms and conditions that they may deem convenient as long as these are not contrary to existing law, morals, good customs, public order, or public policy.[19] This is called freedom to contract or autonomy of contracts in the Philippine setting.[20]

[10] Civil Code, Art 1308.

[11] *Villa Crista Monte Realty & Development Corporation v Equitable PCI Bank (now known as Banco De Oro Unibank, Inc.) et al* G.R. No. 208336 (2018).

[12] Civil Code, Art 1156.

[13] *Asuncion et al v CA and Buen Realty Development Corporation*, G.R. No. 109125 (1994).

[14] Civil Code, Art 1165.

[15] Civil Code, Art 1167.

[16] Civil Code, Art 1168.

[17] *Continental Micronesia, Inc. v Basso*, G.R. Nos. 178382-83 (2015) citing *Hasegawa v Kitamura*, G.R. No. 149177 (2007) 538 SCRA 261, 272–73.

[18] ibid and J Salonga, *Private International Law* (Rex Bookstore, 1995) 111.

[19] Civil Code, Art 1306.

[20] *Bricktown Development Corp. and Veralde v Amor Tierra Development Corporation*, G.R. No. 112182 (1994).

The 1987 Philippine Constitution expressly prohibits any law to be passed that would impair the obligation of contracts.[21] This implies that the freedom to contract, as well as the corresponding obligations of parties, is a constitutionally guaranteed freedom[22] to enter legally valid contracts.[23]

ii. Determination of the Applicable Law

The applicable law in a contract, first and foremost, is what is stipulated between the parties and their intent.[24] With the autonomy given to parties, they equally bind themselves to the terms and conditions they set upon themselves including the determination of which state law will control their terms. Courts have leaned toward the disposition of choice of law issues based on parties' presumed intent.[25]

Since a contract is the law between parties,[26] they are free to agree on which jurisdiction will govern their contract. This is called *lex contractus* or the 'law voluntarily agreed upon by the parties.'[27] Settlement of choice of law issues arising from contracts will always give priority consideration to the intention of the parties.[28] If the parties fail to stipulate on certain provisions, the law is deemed incorporated and written into that contract.

All the terms and conditions of a contract shall be interpreted together and the parties are free to stipulate which law would govern their contract.[29] Courts are not empowered to dictate on what the terms and stipulations in a contract should be and alter the law to be followed in interpreting the contract terms if the parties themselves did not voluntarily consent to it.[30]

However, regardless of stipulation and intent of the parties, there are certain kinds of contracts wherein Philippine law will automatically apply. An example of this is the sale of immovable property where the property is located in the Philippines (*lex situs*).[31] *Lex situs* is the generally accepted rule in choice of law issues that when the immovable property is found in a certain state or country, that country or state's laws will apply given the property's fixed location.[32]

iii. Formal Validity

A contract, regardless of form, is always obligatory.[33] However, there are certain contracts that are required by law to be in a certain form in order to be valid.[34]

[21] 1987 Philippine Constitution, Art III, s 10.
[22] *The Philippine American Life Insurance Company v The Auditor General*, G.R. No. L-19255 (1968), Concurring Opinion by J. Fernando.
[23] *San Diego v Mun. of Naujan, Oriental Mindoro*, G.R. No. L-9920 (1960).
[24] Civil Code, Art 1370.
[25] Columbia Law Review Association, 'Conflict of Laws: "Party Autonomy" in Contracts' (1957) 57(4) *Columbia Law Review* 553–76, doi.org/10.2307/1119750.
[26] *IP E-game Ventures, Inc. v Tan*, G.R. No. 239576 (2021).
[27] HS De Leon and HM De Leon Jr. *Comments and Cases on Obligations and Contracts* (Rex Book Store, 2014) 559.
[28] R Johnston, 'Party Autonomy in Contracts Specifying Foreign Law' (1966) 7(1) *William & Mary Law Review* 37–60, scholarship.law.wm.edu/wmlr/vol7/iss1/3/.
[29] *Dupasquier, et. al. v Ascend As (Philippines) Corporation*, G.R. No. 211044 (2019).
[30] *Norton Resources and Development Corporation v All Asia Bank Corporation*, G.R. No. 162523 (2009).
[31] Civil Code, Art 16.
[32] B Phukon, 'The Concept of Lex Situs and Tangible Movable Properties under Private International Law' (2021) 4(3) *International Journal of Law Management and Humanities* 385–93, doij.org/10.10000/IJLMH.11486.
[33] Civil Code, Art 1356.
[34] ibid.

Philippine law will apply to the required form and solemnity of the contract when it is made and executed in the country (*lex loci celebrationis*).[35] *Lex loci celebrationis* comes into choice of law issues when the contracting parties' place of citizenship differs from the place where the contract was entered into.[36]

Examples of contracts required to be in a certain form are: donation of real or immovable property which has to be in a public instrument,[37] donation of personal property when the value exceeds Php 5,000.00 which has to be in writing,[38] negotiable instruments which have to be in writing,[39] and sale of land through an agent wherein the authority of the agent must be made in writing.[40]

If such contracts are not made in the form specified by law, they will not be considered valid.

In the event that parties consented to enter into a contract but their true intention was not expressed in the written form or instrument they executed as the embodiment of their agreement, one of the parties may ask for the reformation of the instrument.[41] Reformation is a remedy available where there is already a valid existing contract between the parties, only that the instrument embodying the contract would need to be revised in order to express the true intention of the parties.[42]

iv. Material Validity

The following are the necessary requisites in order for there to be a valid contract:

(1) Consent of the contracting parties;
(2) Object certain which is the subject matter of the contract; [and]
(3) Cause of the obligation which is established.[43]

If one of these requisites is not present, there is no contract and it will not have any legal effect.

Consent of the contracting parties is demonstrated when there is a certain offer and absolute acceptance upon the subject matter and cause of the contract.[44] Should the acceptance be qualified, it is deemed a counter-offer and there is no contract.[45] Consent must be freely given by both parties such that if 'consent is given through mistake, violence, intimidation, undue influence, or fraud,' the contract is voidable.[46]

A voidable contract, though defective, is binding to the parties, unless the contract is either ratified[47] wherein it becomes absolutely valid or annulled by the court which causes it to be set aside.[48] The action for annulment must be brought within four years.[49]

The subject matter of the contract is the object certain in an obligation sourced from a contract.[50] If it consists in an obligation to give, the thing must not be outside the commerce

[35] Civil Code, Art 17.
[36] *Ambrose v Suque-Ambrose*, G.R. No. 206761 (2021).
[37] Civil Code, Art 749.
[38] Civil Code, Art 748.
[39] The Negotiable Instruments Law, Act No. 2031, s 1.
[40] Civil Code, Art 1874.
[41] Civil Code, Art 1359.
[42] *Makati Tuscany Condominium Corporation v Multi-Realty Development Corporation*, G.R. No. 185530 (2018).
[43] Civil Code, Art 1318.
[44] *Sps. Beltran v Sps. Cangayda*, G.R. No. 225033 (2018).
[45] Civil Code, Art 1319.
[46] Civil Code, Art 1330.
[47] Civil Code, Art 1390.
[48] *Leonardo v CA*, G.R. No. 125485 (2004).
[49] Civil Code, Art 1391.
[50] De Leon and De Leon, Jr (n 27) 659.

of man,[51] such as property of public dominion which is inalienable.[52] On the other hand, if it consists in an obligation to do, the service must not be contrary to law, morals, good customs, public order, or public policy.[53] The Civil Code provides that the object certain must not be an impossible thing or service.[54]

The cause of the contract is the purpose, consideration, or essential reason as to why the parties entered into a contract.[55] At the time of entering into the contract, the cause must be in existence already or at least must have a potential existence as specified by law; otherwise, the contract will be considered void *ab initio*.[56] Similarly, the cause must also be true and lawful.[57]

v. Capacity

In the Philippines, capacity to contract is restricted based on 'minority, insanity, imbecility, the state of being a deaf-mute, prodigality, and civil interdiction.'[58] The age of majority in the Philippines is 18.[59] Everyone is presumed to have the capacity to enter into a contract, until such time that 'satisfactory proof to the contrary is presented.'[60]

If a contract was entered into wherein both parties are incapable of giving consent or where both are lacking the capacity to contract, the contract is unenforceable unless the contract is ratified.[61] However, if a contract was entered into with one of the parties having a restriction on their capacity to act, the contract is voidable akin to an instance where there is vitiated consent upon entering into the contract.[62] A voidable contract is binding to the parties, though defective, and deemed valid even as regarding the one with the restriction on their capacity to act, unless the contract is either ratified[63] where the legal consequence of such defect is waived, or annulled by the court[64] where the voidable contract is declared void in view of such defect on that essential element.

vi. Mandatory Rules

Even though valid contracts are always obligatory regardless of form, there are contracts which are required by law to be in writing. Otherwise, if they fail to conform to the written form, they shall be valid but unenforceable until such time that the contract is executed in writing or there is secondary evidence of its contents.[65] This is called the 'Statute of Frauds' wherein the contracting parties are not deprived of their right to stipulate on the matters involved, only that the

[51] Civil Code, Art 1347.

[52] *Villarico v Sarmiento, Spouses Del Mundo, Andok's Litson Corporation and Marites' Carinderia*, G.R. No. 136438 (2004).

[53] Civil Code, Art 1347.

[54] Civil Code, Art 1348.

[55] *Uy v CA*, G.R. No. 120465 (1999).

[56] Civil Code, Art 1409.

[57] Civil Code, Art 1353.

[58] Civil Code, Art 38.

[59] An Act Lowering the Age of Majority from Twenty-One to Eighteen Years, Amending for the Purpose Executive Order Numbered Two Hundred Nine, and for Other Purposes, Republic Act No. 6809, s 1.

[60] *First Philippine Holdings Corporation v Trans Middle East (Phils.) Equities Inc.*, G.R. No. 179505 (2009).

[61] Civil Code, Art 1403(3).

[62] Civil Code, Art 1390.

[63] ibid.

[64] *Leonardo v CA*, G.R. No. 125485 (2004).

[65] Civil Code, Art 1403.

Statute regulates the formalities of the contract necessary to render it enforceable[66] such as in the following:

(a) An agreement that by its terms is not to be performed within a year from the making thereof;
(b) A special promise to answer for the debt, default, or miscarriage of another;
(c) An agreement made in consideration of marriage, other than a mutual promise to marry;
(d) An agreement for the sale of goods, chattels or things in action, at a price not less than five hundred pesos, unless the buyer accept and receive part of such goods and chattels, or the evidences, or some of them, of such things in action or pay at the time some part of the purchase money; but when a sale is made by auction and entry is made by the auctioneer in his sales book, at the time of the sale, of the amount and kind of property sold, terms of sale, price, names of the purchasers and person on whose account the sale is made, it is a sufficient memorandum;
(e) An agreement of the leasing for a longer period than one year, or for the sale of real property or of an interest therein; [or]
(f) A representation as to the credit of a third person.[67]

An unenforceable contract that infringes on the Statute of Frauds could be ratified by 'accepting and retaining the benefits of a contract'[68] whether partial or complete. Only the parties to a contract may question its enforceability. Non-parties may not assail an unenforceable contract.[69]

B. Specific Contracts

The advancement of communication methods brought about by modern technology introduced even more complex dealings and transactions. Contracts in their general sense of being mutual agreements between parties became the be-all and end-all solution to ensure rights and interests involving any subject matter. Contracts became increasingly detailed as various needs arose. By virtue of *lex loci intentionis* and the principle of autonomy of contracts, parties could choose and stipulate on which country or state law would govern their contract. Such placement and indication of which law would govern the contract has become common practice.

However, if the parties enter into a contract with a foreign element or the parties fail to specify their terms and conditions on choice of law issues, the forum court may infer from the parties' intentions or it would need to assess which state law has to apply based on facts and be prepared to substitute its own forum law with that of another country. The forum court also has to take into consideration the kind of contract and the interests of parties involved. Considering the varied agreements that people may execute on a day-to-day basis, choice of law issues have become more complex today given the varying rules per law or country vis-a-vis the specific contracts entered into.

i. Consumer Contracts

Consumer contracts, like an order slip or delivery invoice, are issued by the seller in the ordinary course of business and are given leeway by the courts as to the construction or interpretation of said contracts. Such contracts are not required to follow strict formality and are often lacking in content as ordinary commercial transactions would only need the description, price, and

[66] *Orduña, et. al. v Fuentebella, et. al.*, G.R. No. 176841 (2010).
[67] Civil Code, Art 1403.
[68] *Francisco v Herrera*, G.R. No. 139982 (2002).
[69] Civil Code, Art 1408.

quantity of an item before the next customer is dealt with. These are still recognised as valid between parties as long as proof that such a consumer transaction occurred can be presented.[70]

Due to the rise in technology and the ease in which transactions are made regardless of where one is in the world, cross-border transactions have become an ordinary part of consumers' lives. In the event that there is a choice of law matter arising from a consumer contract absent a clear choice from the parties who entered into the transaction, the law of the consumer's habitual residence will generally govern the contract in the interest of consumer protection.[71]

In the Philippines, a 'consumer' is defined as 'a *natural person* who is a purchaser, lessee, recipient or prospective purchaser, lessor or recipient of consumer products, services or credit'; thus, juridical persons are not covered by the protections laid down in the Consumer Act of the Philippines.[72] Juridical persons would have to find their recourse under existing laws other than the Consumer Act.

ii. Employment Contracts

Employment contracts, like any other contract, may contain such stipulations, terms, and even conditions as agreed by the parties,[73] and usually, they state which set of laws would govern in case of conflict. As a means of protection for both the employer and employee, these contracts are written and signed by the parties as concrete proof of their agreement on the employment terms and conditions, which may include provisions on choice of law.

In the Philippines, there is a large and constantly growing number of workers who seek employment in other countries, since employment opportunities in their country appear to be limited, or not as lucrative as those on foreign soil.[74] It is a reality the country has acknowledged – the 'foreign dream' – and therefore multifarious Philippine laws have been enacted for the protection of Overseas Filipino Workers (OFWs).[75]

While employment contracts of these OFWs might state the home country of the employer to have jurisdiction over conflicts arising from employment, the Philippine Supreme Court also adheres to the *doctrine of processual presumption*. If the stated foreign law in the contract is not pleaded and properly proved in court, the court will presume that Philippine law is the same as foreign law and will thus use Philippine laws to rule on the matter.[76] As added protection for the OFWs, manning or placement agencies involved in their overseas deployment are held, by law and administrative regulations, jointly and severally liable with foreign principals insofar as monetary awards are concerned.

iii. Insurance Contracts

Insurance contracts are often specific as to the terms and conditions on the coverage for the insured but they do not usually contain provisions on choice of law issues even though such

[70] *Donato C. Cruz Trading Corp. v CA*, G.R. No. 129189 (2000).

[71] G Ruhl, 'Consumer Protection in Choice of Law' (2011) 44(3) *Cornell International Law Journal* 570–601, scholarship.law.cornell.edu/cilj/vol44/iss3/4/.

[72] Consumer Act of the Philippines, Republic Act No. 7394, Art 4(n).

[73] *Sagun v ANZ Global Services and Operations (Manila), Inc.*, G.R. No. 220399 (2016).

[74] *Industrial Personnel & Management Services, Inc. (IPAMS), SNC Lavalin Engineers & Contractors, Inc. and Hernandez v De Vera and Arriola*, G.R. No. 205703 (2016).

[75] *Industrial Personnel & Management Services, Inc. (IPAMS), SNC Lavalin Engineers & Contractors, Inc. and Hernandez v De Vera and Arriola*, G.R. No. 205703 (2016).

[76] *EDI-Staffbuilders International, Inc. v NLRC*, G.R. No. 145587 (2007).

provisions have been added as a staple to any commercial contract.[77] There are several approaches on how to deal with choice of law issues arising from an insurance contract and the forum court handles choice of law issues on a case-by-case basis.

There are generally two approaches to deciding which set of laws would govern a choice of law issue in an insurance contract: the Claim-Specific approach and the Policyholder's Headquarters approach.[78]

The Claim-Specific approach is based on where the loss, damage, or injury occurs. The state with the most significant relationship is where the injury occurred, since the injury is the basis on which the insurance contract will take effect.[79] On the other hand, the Policyholder's Headquarters approach is based on where the principal place of business of the policyholder is located.[80] This approach is consistent with *lex loci contractus* or the law of the place where the contract was made[81] since an insurance contract is entered into with the parties' principal addresses in mind.

iv. Contracts for the Sale of Immovable Property

In a contract of sale, one party is obligated to transfer ownership and to deliver a specific thing whereas the other party is obligated to pay for it in terms of money or its equivalent.[82] The property laws of the place where the immovable property, as the object of sale, is located shall govern it (*lex situs*),[83] including other contracts such as a lease involving said real property.

Lex situs is generally considered as decisive when it comes to ownership transfers of real property and/or rights on the same.[84] In consideration of the location where the property is situated, it is naturally expected that the law of that place would govern. There is, however, an exception to the generally applicable *lex situs* rule. When the ownership of the land is being passed to another by virtue of succession, the national law of the decedent would govern.[85]

If the immovable property is situated in the Philippines, formal validity of the contract of sale involving said immovable property is dependent on it being written and in a public instrument in order for the sale to be valid as between parties and as against the whole world.[86] Neither Philippine law nor its courts recognise the oral sale of immovable property as this is deemed unenforceable[87] and cannot be registered at the government property registry (Registry of Deeds).

As to capacity of the parties in order for the contract to be valid, they must have the capacity to act[88] and the seller must have the right to transfer the ownership of the immovable property upon delivery.[89] In addition to the seller having the right to transfer the ownership, if they are married, the selling spouse must acquire the consent of the other spouse in order to dispose of or

[77] J Coyle, 'The Mystery of the Missing Choice-of-Law Clause' (2021) 56(2) *University of California Davis Law Review* 707–58, dx.doi.org/10.2139/ssrn.3976508.

[78] S Klepper, 'Choice of Law for CGL Insurance Policies: Toward a Uniform Rule' (2009) 45(1) *Tort Trial & Insurance Practice Law Journal* 31–56, www.jstor.org/stable/25763950.

[79] The Insurance Code, Republic Act No. 10607, s 2.

[80] A Woodhouse, 'The Importance of Jurisdiction and Choice of Law Clauses: A European Perspective' (2007) 42(4) *Tort Trial & Insurance Practice Law Journal* 1027–41, www.jstor.org/stable/25763867.

[81] *Hasegawa, et. al. v Kitamura*, G.R. No. 149177 (2007).

[82] Civil Code, Art 1458.

[83] B Akkermans, 'The Influence of the Four (or five) Freedoms on Property Law' in *Research Handbook on European Union Property Law* (Edward Elgar, 2022) dx.doi.org/10.2139/ssrn.4232332.

[84] *Alcala v Alcañeses*, G.R. No. 187847 (2021).

[85] Civil Code, Art 16.

[86] Civil Code, Art 1358.

[87] *Heirs of Alido v Campano*, G.R. No. 226065 (2019).

[88] Civil Code, Art 39.

[89] Civil Code, Art 1459.

sell any immovable property that is conjugally owned[90] or owned under the absolute community property relationship of spouses.

If such consent of the other spouse is not acquired, the sale of the immovable conjugal property is void[91] but shall be considered as a 'continuing offer on the part of the consenting spouse and the third person, and may be perfected as a binding contract upon the acceptance by the other spouse or authorisation by the court before the offer is withdrawn by either or both offerors.'[92]

v. Contracts for Sale of Goods

In a contract of sale of goods or personal property, *lex rei sitae* generally applies such that the law of the place where the goods are located shall govern it.[93]

Lex rei sitae, similar to *lex situs*, is considered as an expression of territorial sovereignty since it is dependent on the location of the property and would therefore make use of the laws of the country where it is located.[94]

In the Philippines, the object or the goods must be licit.[95] As to form, a contract of sale must be in writing if the sale of the goods would amount to at least Php 500.00; otherwise, the contract shall be unenforceable.[96] This kind of contract falls under the mandate of the 'Statute of Frauds' wherein the contract must be in writing or such stipulation is found in other secondary evidence to render it enforceable.[97] As earlier cited, this is however subject to the exceptions of ratification and/or partial or complete delivery of the object or partial or complete payment of the purchase price.[98]

The parties must have the capacity to act[99] in the contract of sale and the seller must have the right to transfer the ownership of the property upon delivery.[100] However, there is an exception with regard to one's capacity to act when the contract of sale of goods is for necessaries such as sustenance or medicine.[101] Hence, if the buyer has no capacity to act, such as when they are a minor, but necessaries are sold, the contract is valid and the buyer must pay a reasonable price for it.[102]

vi. Contracts for the Hire of Goods

A contract for the hire of goods involves the transfer of possession of goods for a specific period of time. For the protection of parties' interests, such contracts may be made in writing in order to

[90] *Spouses Cueno v Spouses Bautista, et. al.*, G.R. No. 246445 (2021).
[91] Family Code of the Philippines, Executive Order No. 209, Arts 96 and 124.
[92] *Alejo v Spouses Cortez, et. al.*, G.R. No. 206114 (2017).
[93] Civil Code, Art 16.
[94] B Akkermans, 'Lex Rei Sitae and the EU Internal Market – Towards Mutual Recognition of Property Relations' (2018) 7(3) *European Property Law Journal* 246–66, doi.org/10.1515/eplj-2018-0012.
[95] Civil Code, Art 1459.
[96] Civil Code, Art 1403.
[97] ibid.
[98] *University of Mindanao, Inc. v Bangko Sentral Pilipinas, et. al.*, G.R. No. 194964-65 (2016) citing *Yasuma v Heirs of Cecilio S. de Villa*, 531 Phil. 62, 68 (2006).
[99] Civil Code, Art 39.
[100] Civil Code, Art 1459.
[101] Family Code, Art 194; *Necessaries*. Legal Information Institute. www.law.cornell.edu/wex/necessaries.
[102] Civil Code, Art 1489.

define the terms and period for which the hiring of goods would last and the quality of goods to be hired,[103] inclusive of choice of law provisions.

Under Philippine law, the temporary transfer of possession of things (personal property) is called a *lease* and it is defined as follows: 'In the lease of things, one of the parties binds himself to give to another the enjoyment of use of a thing for a price certain, and for a period which may be definite or indefinite. However, no lease for more than ninety-nine years shall be valid.'[104] Ownership remains in the lessor's hands even as possession is transferred to the lessee.[105]

Given the temporary nature of such contract of lease, consumable goods cannot be the subject matter, unless such goods are only to be displayed or are an accessory to an industrial establishment.[106]

A contract of lease of personal property need not follow a certain form in order to be valid. It may be impliedly renewed if upon the end of the contract the lessee would continue to enjoy the use of the things with the consent of the lessor, unless a previous notice to the contrary was given by either party.[107] Such implied renewal of the period, no matter how many times it would occur, does not amount to consenting to all other stipulations nor does it grant the lessee an option to purchase the thing.[108]

vii. Contracts for the Carriage of Goods by Sea, Air, or Land

Cross-border carriage of goods by sea, air, or land has become an ordinary part of consumers' lives due to the dawn of the modern age. Regardless of where one is in the world, goods may be delivered to one's doorstep with the click of a button. Choice of law issues certainly arise when the goods would be transported to a different country from its point of origin.

The United Nations Convention on the Carriage of Goods by Sea (Hamburg Rules) and the United Nations Convention on Contracts for the International Carriage of Goods Wholly or Partly by Sea (Rotterdam Rules) were established to standardise the rules with regard to the rights and obligations of shippers and carriers under contracts of carriage of goods.[109] Under the Hamburg Rules, goods 'includes live animals; where the goods are consolidated in a container, pallet or similar article of transport or where they are packed, "goods" includes such article of transport or packaging if supplied by the shipper.'[110] The Rotterdam Rules cover the carriage of goods by sea between two different states. Under the Rotterdam Rules, there is recognition that goods may be transported through other means, not only through sea, and that such transactions may be covered by electronic documents due to modern technology.[111]

In the Philippines, common carriers are those engaged in the business of transporting or carrying goods by land, water, or air for compensation.[112] While the contracts to hire such common carriers

[103] Supply of Goods and Services Act 1982, Ch 29, s 9 (UK).
[104] Civil Code, Art 1643.
[105] *Tamio v Ticson*, G.R. No. 154895 (2004).
[106] Civil Code, Art 1645.
[107] Civil Code, Art 1670.
[108] *Mañas v Nicolasora, et. al.*, G.R. No. 208845 (2020).
[109] United Nations Commission on International Trade Law. (n.d.). *International Transport of Goods*. uncitral.un.org/en/texts/transportgoods.
[110] United Nations Convention on the Carriage of Goods by Sea (Hamburg, 1978). uncitral.un.org/sites/uncitral.un.org/files/media-documents/uncitral/en/hamburg_rules_e.pdf.
[111] United Nations Convention on Contracts for the International Carriage of Goods Wholly or Partly by Sea (New York, 2008). uncitral.un.org/sites/uncitral.un.org/files/media-documents/uncitral/en/rotterdam-rules-e.pdf.
[112] Civil Code, Art 1732.

are not required to be in a specific form, the law requires extraordinary diligence in terms of vigilance over the goods to be transported.[113] This kind of diligence is different from what is normally expected from other kinds of contracts or obligations, which is only ordinary diligence.

The law imposes the extraordinary responsibility upon the common carrier from the time the goods are placed in the carrier's possession until such time that the goods are delivered to the consignee.[114]

viii. Negotiable Instruments (Including Bills of Exchange)

Negotiable instruments are written promises or orders involving the payment of money.[115] Choice of law issues involving negotiable instruments arise when the instrument is made or drawn, negotiated, and paid in more than one jurisdiction.[116] Generally, these are governed by the law of the place of the contract.[117]

In the Philippines, the most common forms of negotiable instruments are promissory notes, bills of exchange, or bank checks.[118] Negotiable instruments are one of the kinds of contracts wherein the form is necessary for it to be valid. The following are the requisites for a negotiable instrument:

(a) It must be in writing and signed by the maker or drawer;
(b) Must contain an unconditional promise or order to pay a sum certain in money;
(c) Must be payable on demand, or at a fixed or determinable future time;
(d) Must be payable to order or to bearer; and
(e) Where the instrument is addressed to a drawee, he must be named or otherwise indicated therein with reasonable certainty.[119]

While a bill of exchange is a kind of negotiable instrument, it is more specifically defined as 'an unconditional order in writing addressed by one person to another, signed by the person giving it, requiring the person to whom it is addressed to pay on demand or at a fixed or determinable future time a sum certain in money to order or to bearer.'[120]

When a negotiable instrument is issued in writing, the following are some of the legal presumptions that are attached to it:

1. The date of the instrument, if any, is presumed to be the 'true date of the making, drawing, acceptance, or indorsement, as the case may be';[121]
2. Intentional and valid delivery of the instrument is presumed when it is 'no longer in the possession of a party whose signature appears thereon';[122] and,
3. The instrument is presumed to have been issued for a 'valuable consideration'.[123]

Such legal presumptions are considered binding and conclusive unless satisfactorily rebutted or overturned through contrary evidence.[124]

113 Civil Code, Arts 1733 and 1737.
114 Civil Code, Art 1736.
115 *Negotiable instruments*. Legal Information Institute. www.law.cornell.edu/wex/negotiable_instruments.
116 W Morris, 'Some Conflict of Laws Problems Relating to Negotiable Instruments' (1964) 66(2) *West Virginia Law Review* 91–108. researchrepository.wvu.edu/wvlr/vol66/iss2/3.
117 'Conflict of Laws in Negotiable Instruments' (1902) 2(4) *Columbia Law Review* 253–55. doi.org/10.2307/1109884.
118 The Negotiable Instruments Law, Act No. 2031, ss 184, 126 and 185.
119 ibid s 1.
120 Note 118, s 126.
121 Note 118, s 11.
122 Note 118, s 16.
123 Note 118, s 24.
124 *Travel-On, Inc. v CA and Miranda*, G.R. No. 56169 (1992).

ix. Letters of Credit

Letters of credit are financial devices wherein the buyer asks the bank to shoulder the payment to the seller, and the buyer is then obligated to pay the bank in return.[125]

The International Chamber of Commerce released the Uniform Customs & Practice for Documentary Credits (UCP 600) and it has become the worldwide standard in transactions involving letters of credit,[126] but it does not mention a governing law for letters of credit or how to resolve choice of law issues arising from such.[127] General rules on choice of law will apply and first depend on the agreement contained in the letter of credit, as such is the law between the parties, before the forum court would take into consideration other choice of law principles.

A letter of credit involves three different contracts: first, the buyer and seller for the delivery of the goods; second, the buyer and the bank for the payment terms to be made to the seller and terms for reimbursement of the buyer; and third, the seller and the bank for the receipt of the payment. The Philippine Supreme Court has summarised it as thus:

> A letter of credit is a financial device developed by merchants as a convenient and relatively safe mode of dealing with sales of goods to satisfy the seemingly irreconcilable interests of a seller, who refuses to part with his goods before he is paid, and a buyer, who wants to have control of the goods before paying. To break the impasse, the buyer may be required to contract a bank to issue a letter of credit in favor of the seller so that, by virtue of the letter of credit, the issuing bank can authorize the seller to draw drafts and engage to pay them upon their presentment simultaneously with the tender of documents required by the letter of credit. The buyer and the seller agree on what documents are to be presented for payment, but ordinarily they are documents of title evidencing or attesting to the shipment of the goods to the buyer.
>
> Once the credit is established, the seller ships the goods to the buyer and in the process secures the required shipping documents or documents of title. To get paid, the seller executes a draft and presents it together with the required documents to the issuing bank. The issuing bank redeems the draft and pays cash to the seller if it finds that the documents submitted by the seller conform with what the letter of credit requires. The bank then obtains possession of the documents upon paying the seller. The transaction is completed when the buyer reimburses the issuing bank and acquires the documents entitling him to the goods. Under this arrangement, **the seller gets paid only if he delivers the documents of title over the goods, while the buyer acquires the said documents and control over the goods only after reimbursing the bank.**[128] (Emphasis supplied.)

x. Contracts Involving the Transfer of Foreign Currency

Like similar transactions discussed above, a contract that involves the transfer of foreign currency automatically places a foreign element in the contract and is open to choice of law issues. In order to protect the interests of the parties involved, these contracts are executed in writing with specific provisions on choice of law matters as well as currency fluctuation clauses. General rules in resolving choice of law matters would necessitate the forum court to first determine what the parties' intent was as to which state or country's law would govern the terms of the contract.

[125] R Gewolb, 'The Law Applicable to International Letters of Credit' (1966) 11(4) *Villanova Law Review* 742–70, digitalcommons.law.villanova.edu/vlr/vol11/iss4/9.

[126] *The Hongkong & Shanghai Banking Corporation, Limited v National Steel Corporation, et. al.*, G.R. No. 183486 (2016).

[127] A Markstein, 'The Law Governing Letters of Credit' (2010) 16 *Auckland University Law Review* 138–63, www.nzlii.org/nz/journals/AukULawRw/2010/7.html.

[128] *Bank of America, NT & SA v CA, Inter-Resin Industrial Corporation, Trajano, John Doe and Jane Doe*, G.R. No. 105395 (1993).

Given the autonomy of parties to enter into a contract with such stipulations as they may decide as necessary, currency fluctuation clauses are often added since the transfer of foreign currency is open to the risk in variation of exchange rate.

In the Philippines, parties may agree upon which currency the contract be paid in. If the delivery or payment of the stipulated currency is not possible, then the legal tender in the Philippines (Philippine peso) would be substituted.[129] This is further reinforced by both law and Supreme Court decisions stating that transactions, contracts, or obligations may be paid in the currency agreed upon even if it is not in Philippine peso, subject to the possibility of substitution of Philippine peso in the applicable exchange rate.[130]

xi. Agency

In a contract of agency, the agent binds themselves to do or to render service in representation or on behalf of the principal, with the latter's consent.[131] As a means to ensure the protection of the principal, a contract of agency is usually written, but not generally required to be in writing, to provide the specific terms and duties necessary on how the agent is going to act on behalf of the principal inclusive of provisions on choice of law matters.

In the Philippines, a contract of agency is not generally required to be in a specific form, except for those enumerated in the law[132] as involving not mere matters of administration but an exercise of strict dominion such as when there is a sale of property made through an agent. If a sale of the property is made through an agent, the authority of said agent to represent a party must be written.[133] In all other circumstances, agency may be oral, or even expressly or impliedly made.[134]

No matter how the contract of agency is formed, the agent's acts are limited by the scope of authority conferred upon them by the principal.[135] This is because agency is based on representation and the fact that '[s]uch acts [of the agent] have the same legal effect as if they were personally done by the principal. By this legal fiction of representation, the actual or legal absence of the principal is converted into his legal or juridical presence.'[136]

C. Torts

A tort is an act or omission which would give rise to damage or injury to another such that the person who caused the damage or injury would be made liable.[137] The source of liability is the fact that one person has caused damage to another and the damage needs to be rectified.

In choice of law cases, *lex loci delicti commissi* or the law of the place where the tort was committed is often the basis to determine tort liability.[138] However, this principle is not ironclad without an

[129] Civil Code, Art 1249.

[130] An Act Repealing Republic Act Numbered Five Hundred Twenty-Nine As Amended, Entitled 'An Act To Assure The Uniform Value of Philippine Coin and Currency', Republic Act No. 8183, s 1 and *C.F. Sharp & Co., Inc. v Northwest Airlines, Inc.*, G.R. No. 133498 (2002).

[131] Civil Code, Art 1868.

[132] Please see Civil Code, Art 1878, for a complete list.

[133] Civil Code, Art 1874.

[134] Civil Code, Art 1869.

[135] *Country Bankers Insurance Corporation v Keppel Cebu Shipyard, et. al.*, G.R. No. 166044 (2012).

[136] *Country Bankers Insurance Corporation v Keppel Cebu Shipyard, et. al.*, G.R. No. 166044 (2012) citing *Siredy Enterprises, Inc. v Court of Appeals*, 437 Phil. 580, 591 (2002).

[137] *Tort*. Legal Information Institute, www.law.cornell.edu/wex/tort#:~:text=A%20tort%20is%20an%20act,1.

[138] S Özel, 'The Determination of Applicable Law to Torts based on "the Law which is more closely connected"' (2021) 41(2) *Public and Private International Law Bulletin* 483–515, doi.org/10.26650/ppil.2021.41.2.939398.

adequate set of rules on how to determine which law to follow[139] since the commission of a tort may occur in more than one place and the damage caused may also be in more than one place.

To determine where the tort was committed, courts may resort to the use of the 'state with the most significant relationship' test in determining the choice of law when it comes to tort liability.[140] Following this test, the court chooses which state 'has the most substantial connection to the occurrence and the parties' in order to determine which state law to apply to a particular dispute or issue.[141]

The Philippine Supreme Court has ruled that there must be a determination of 'points of contact' or 'connecting factors' in order to locate the state with the most significant relationship, which could be *any* of the following:

1. The nationality of a person, his domicile, his residence, his place of sojourn, or his origin;
2. The seat of a legal or juridical person, such as a corporation;
3. The situs of a thing, that is, the place where a thing is, or is deemed to be situated. In particular, the *lex situs* is decisive when real rights are involved;
4. The place where an act has been done, the locus actus, such as the place where a contract has been made, a marriage celebrated, a will signed or a tort committed. The *lex loci actus* is particularly important in contracts and torts;
5. The place where an act is intended to come into effect, e.g., the place of performance of contractual duties, or the place where a power of attorney is to be exercised;
6. The intention of the contracting parties as to the law that should govern their agreement, the *lex loci intentionis*;
7. The place where judicial or administrative proceedings are instituted or done. The *lex fori* – the law of the forum – is particularly important because, as we have seen earlier, matters of 'procedure' not going to the substance of the claim involved are governed by it; and because the *lex fori* applies whenever the content of the otherwise applicable foreign law is excluded from application in a given case for the reason that it falls under one of the exceptions to the applications of foreign law; and
8. The flag of a ship, which in many cases is decisive of practically all legal relationships of the ship and of its master or owner as such. It also covers contractual relationships particularly contracts of affreightment.[142]

Under Philippine law, should the Philippines be deemed as the state with the most significant relationship, torts are more commonly called as 'Quasi-Delicts' and these are one of the sources of obligations.[143] Quasi-delicts or torts are defined as an act or omission which causes damage to another, through fault or negligence, and that there is no pre-existing contractual relationship between the parties.[144]

The elements in order for quasi-delict to exist are:

1. Damages to the plaintiff;
2. Negligence through act or omission by the defendant; and,
3. Connection of cause and effect between the negligence and damages.[145]

139 B Rodger, 'Ascertaining the Statutory Lex Loci Delicti: Certain Difficulties under the Private International Law (Miscellaneous Provisions) Act 1995' (1998) 47(1) *The International and Comparative Law Quarterly* 205–11, doi:10.1017/S0020589300061625.

140 *Alcala v Alcañeses, et. al.*, G.R. No. 187847 (2021).

141 *Hasegawa v Kitamura*, G.R. No. 149177 (2007).

142 *Saudi Arabian Airlines v CA, Morada, and Ortiz*, G.R. No. 122191 (1998).

143 Civil Code, Art 1157.

144 Civil Code, Art 2176.

145 *Torreon and Abellana v Aparra, Jr. et. al.*, G.R. No. 188493 (2017) citing *Vergara v Court of Appeals*, 238 Phil. 565 (1987).

The Supreme Court also emphasised the difference between negligence committed with a pre-existing contract (contractual breach) and without a pre-existing contract between the parties (tort or quasi-delict), as follows:

> Actions based on contractual negligence and actions based on quasi-delicts differ in terms of conditions, defenses, and proof. They generally cannot co-exist. Once a breach of contract is proved, the defendant is presumed negligent and must prove not being at fault. In a quasi-delict, however, the complaining party has the burden of proving the other party's negligence. In *Huang v. Phil. Hoteliers, Inc.*:
>
> [T]his Court finds it significant to take note of the following differences between quasi-delict (*culpa aquiliana*) and breach of contract (*culpa contractual*). In quasi-delict, negligence is direct, substantive and independent, while in breach of contract, negligence is merely incidental to the performance of the contractual obligation; there is a pre-existing contract or obligation, In *quasi-delict*, the defense of 'good father of a family' is a complete and proper defense insofar as parents, guardians and employers are concerned, while in breach of contract, such is not a complete and proper defense in the selection and supervision of employees. In *quasi-delict*, there is no presumption of negligence and it is incumbent upon the injured party to prove the negligence of the defendant, otherwise, the former's complaint will be dismissed, while in breach of contract, negligence is presumed so long as it can be proved that there was breach of the contract and the burden is on the defendant to prove that there was no negligence in the carrying out of the terms of the contract; the rule of *respondeat superior* is followed.[146] (Underscoring in the original text.)

i. Governing Law in Tort Generally

The governing law in the Philippines for torts or quasi-delicts is the Civil Code. Under the Civil Code, the person who caused damage to another through fault or negligence is obligated to indemnify the damage done.[147] This person is called the tortfeasor.

The defendant's liability or responsibility to indemnify for the damage they caused may be regulated by the courts in accordance with the circumstances.[148] Such liability is all-encompassing such that the defendant can be made liable for all damages which were the natural and probable consequences of one's negligent act or omission.[149] The Supreme Court has ruled that it is not necessary that the damages were foreseen or could have been reasonably foreseen, so long as it is duly proved that the damages were a direct or natural consequence of the negligent act or omission.[150]

In order to determine whether the plaintiff, or the person who has the right to receive damages, is entitled to full or mitigated damages, whoever is the 'immediate and proximate cause'[151] of the injury should be determined.

Immediate cause refers to the 'final act in a series of provocations leading to a particular result or event, directly producing such result without the intervention of any further provocation'[152]

[146] *Orient Freight International, Inc. v Keihin-Everett Forwarding Company, Inc.*, G.R. No. 191937 (2017) citing *Fores v Miranda*, 105 Phil. 266, 275 (1959); *Consolidated Bank and Trust Corp. v Court of Appeals*, 457 Phi]. 688, 708 (2003) & *Huang v Phil. Hoteliers, Inc.*, 700 Phil. 327 (2012).

[147] Civil Code, Art 2176.

[148] Civil Code, Art 1172.

[149] Civil Code, Art 2202.

[150] *Mendoza and Lim v Spouses Gomez*, G.R. No. 160110 (2014).

[151] Civil Code, Art 2179.

[152] *Immediate Cause.* Legal Dictionary. legal-dictionary.thefreedictionary.com/Immediate+Cause.

whereas *proximate* cause pertains to 'that which, in natural and continuous sequence, unbroken by any new cause, produces an event, and without which the event would not have occurred.'[153] The proximate cause need not have happened immediately in relation to when the injury was incurred, as long as the happening of such set other foreseeable events into motion that ultimately resulted in the damage to the plaintiff.[154]

Should the immediate and proximate cause of the injury be the plaintiff's own negligence, they cannot recover damages.[155] If the immediate and proximate cause of the injury is the defendant's lack of due care or negligence, but that the plaintiff had contributory negligence to their own injury, then the plaintiff would be entitled only to mitigated damages.[156]

It is also possible for a defendant to be made liable even if said defendant was not directly responsible for the damage caused, so long as the defendant is responsible for the actions or conduct of the person who caused the damage. The following are those made responsible for another person's actions:[157]

1. The father and mother, for damages caused by their minor children who live with them;
2. Guardians, for damages caused by minors or incapacitated people who live with them under their authority;
3. The owner of a motor vehicle, for damages caused by the person driving the vehicle during a vehicular mishap;
4. Owners and managers of an establishment, for damages caused by employees while in service by reason of their functions;
5. Employers, for damages caused by their employees and household helpers acting within the scope of their assigned tasks;
6. Teachers or heads of establishments of arts and trades, for damages caused by their students or apprentices under their custody; and,
7. The state, when it acts through a special agent, unless the damage is caused by the official or person to whom the task properly pertains.

The above-enumerated persons shall be free from liability if they sufficiently prove that they 'observed all the diligence of a good father of a family to prevent damage.'[158]

ii. Specific Torts

In choice of law issues, torts are generally resolved on the basis of *lex loci delicti commissi* or the law of the place where the tort was committed to determine tort liability.[159] This follows that not all torts may be legally classified as torts, or that a specific tort may not be called or classified as a tort based on the elements encompassing said specific tort, depending on the place or jurisdiction which would rule on it.

[153] *Abrogar v Cosmos Bottling Company and Intergames, Inc.*, G.R. No. 164749 (2017).
[154] *Abrogar v Cosmos Bottling Company and Intergames, Inc.*, G.R. No. 164749 (2017) citing *Pullman Palace Car Co. v Laack*, 143 111. 242, 32 N.E. 285, 18 L.R.A. 215.
[155] Note 151.
[156] Note 151.
[157] Civil Code, Art 2180.
[158] ibid.
[159] Özel (n 138).

In the Philippines, the specific kinds of torts with corresponding civil liability are limited to what is defined under the Civil Code. Some examples that can be cited are as follows:

1. The owner or possessor of an animal or whoever may make use of the same is liable for the damage caused by said animal, even if it escapes or is lost, unless it is proven that the damage came from *force majeure* or the fault of the plaintiff;[160]
2. The owner of a motor vehicle is made solely liable for the damage caused by the driver in motor vehicle mishaps, unless if the owner is in the vehicle and could have prevented the damage through due diligence;[161]
3. The manufacturer and processor of goods and articles are liable for the death or injuries caused by harmful substances used by them;[162]
4. The province, city, and municipality are liable for the death or injuries caused by the defective condition of roads, streets, and other public works and structures under their control or supervision;[163] and,
5. The proprietor or owner of a building or structure is liable for damages caused by total or partial collapse if said collapse is due to the lack of necessary repairs.[164]

a. Negligence

In the Philippines, negligence is naturally presumed in a quasi-delict or tort, and is governed by the Civil Code. On the other hand, the Revised Penal Code governs *criminal* negligence which is a punishable act through imprudence or negligence that resulted in a felony as defined by law.[165] The Civil Code distinguishes the two, quasi-delict as opposed to criminal negligence, in such a way that even with the civil liability arising from such criminal negligence, the plaintiff cannot recover damages twice for the same negligent act or omission.[166]

Negligence is defined as 'the failure to observe for the protection of the interests of another person that degree of care, precaution, and vigilance which the circumstances justly demand, whereby such other person suffers injury.'[167] As a general rule, the test of whether negligence existed is the determination of whether the defendant, as a prudent person, lacked diligence or had want of care which is required of them given the particular time, place, and circumstance.[168]

The Supreme Court has long-established the following statement as the *standard* of such test of negligence: 'Did the defendant in doing the alleged negligent act use that reasonable care and caution which an ordinarily prudent person would have used in the same situation? If not, then he is guilty of negligence.'[169]

However, such test only applies when the standard of diligence required is not specified by law. There are certain instances when the law dictates a standard of diligence to be observed, such as extraordinary diligence for common carriers in the transport of goods or passengers[170]

[160] Civil Code, Art 2183.
[161] Civil Code, Art 2184.
[162] Civil Code, Art 2187.
[163] Civil Code, Art.2189.
[164] Civil Code, Art 2190.
[165] Revised Penal Code, Act No. 3815 as amended by Republic Act No. 10951, Art 365.
[166] Civil Code, Art 2177.
[167] *Dela Cruz v Octaviano*, G.R. No. 219649 (2017).
[168] Civil Code, Art 1173.
[169] *Dela Cruz v Octaviano*, G.R. No. 219649 (2017) & *Philippine National Construction Corporation v CA*, G.R. No. 159270 (2005) citing *Picart v Smith*, G.R. No. L-12219 (1918).
[170] Civil Code, Art 1733.

or ordinary skill, care and diligence for medical practitioners that is generally employed by the profession under similar conditions and in like surrounding circumstances.[171]

b. Nuisance

A nuisance is a kind of tort under Philippine law which is

> any act, omission, establishment, condition of property, or anything else which:
> (1) Injures or endangers the health or safety of others;
> (2) Annoys or offends the senses;
> (3) Shocks, defies or disregards decency or morality;
> (4) Obstructs or interferes with the free passage of any public highway or street, or any body of water; or,
> (5) Hinders or impairs the use of property.[172]

Since nuisance is a kind of tort, damages may be recovered by the plaintiff in addition to having the nuisance abated.[173]

Determining the kind of nuisance is important as this would determine the procedure on how to abate it.[174] The Civil Code classified a nuisance as either a public or a private nuisance,[175] and jurisprudence has further classified these into either a nuisance *per se* or a nuisance *per accidens*.[176]

A public nuisance violates the exercise of a public right, affects public property, or causes injury to the public at large; whereas a private nuisance causes damage to only one or few individuals.[177] On the other hand, a nuisance *per se* is a nuisance at all times and under any circumstances, regardless of location or surroundings,[178] and this may be summarily abated,[179] such that there is no need for judicial intervention. On the other hand, a nuisance *per accidens* is a nuisance which is dependent upon certain conditions and circumstances, location or surroundings, and this cannot be abated without due hearing by an authorised tribunal.[180]

c. Wrongful Interference with Goods

The concept of 'wrongful interference with goods' is found under the law of the United Kingdom, governed by their Act 1977, Chapter 32.[181] Under said Act, 'wrongful interference with goods' is defined as:

> (a) conversion of goods (also called trover),
> (b) trespass to goods,
> (c) negligence so far at it results in damage to goods or to an interest in goods,
> (d) xxx any other tort so far as it results in damage to goods or to an interest in goods.[182]

171 *Casumpang, et. al. v Cortejo*, G.R. Nos. 171127, 171217, 171228 (2015).
172 Civil Code, Art 694.
173 *Rana v Wong*, G.R. Nos. 192861-862 (2014).
174 ibid.
175 Civil Code, Art 695.
176 Note 173.
177 *Frabelle Properties Corp. v AC Enterprises, Inc.*, G.R. No. 245438 (2020).
178 *Types of Nuisances*. US Legal Information, nuisances.uslegal.com/types-of-nuisances/#:~:text=A%20nuisance%20per%20se%20is,not%20constitute%20nuisance%20per%20se.
179 *Lucena Grand Central Terminal, Inc. v JAC Liner, Inc.*, G.R. No. 148339 (2005).
180 *North Greenhills Association, Inc. v Atty. Morales*, G.R. No. 222821 (2017).
181 *Torts (Interference with Goods) Act 1977 Chapter 32* (UK).
182 *Torts (Interference with Goods) Act 1977 Chapter 32* s.1 (UK).

Under this Act, the defendant may raise the defence of *jus tertii* wherein the defendant would claim that a third person has a better right than that of the plaintiff to the goods in question.[183]

Such does not exist under torts in the Philippine context in its entirety. When a person converts or trespasses on goods that do not belong to him or are not in his rightful possession, such act is theft and it is a crime punishable by imprisonment.[184] Furthermore, *jus tertii* is not an automatic defence and can only be raised in the Philippines if it can be shown that the third person cannot assert one's own right.[185]

In the Philippines, tortuous interference does involve a particular participation of a third person and it does not necessarily involve goods, but a *contract*. Under the Civil Code, a person shall be liable for tortuous interference if they 'induces another to violate his contract.'[186] It necessitates that: (a) there is an existing valid contract between parties, (b) that the third person interfering has knowledge of the existence of said contract, and (c) that such interference by the third person has no legal justification.[187]

Unlike in *jus tertii*, the third person liable for tortuous interference does not have a better right. They instead interfered with the fulfillment of a contract between two other parties.

d. Defamation

While defamation in some jurisdictions is deemed a tort, under Philippine law, defamation is not a tort, but a crime requiring malicious intent punishable by imprisonment or a fine, depending on the nature of the defamation.[188] The crime is further delineated between defamation through spoken means (slander) or defamation through written means (libel). If a defamatory imputation is made through slander or libel, it is automatically presumed to be malicious even if true, unless proven otherwise.[189]

Slander has the following elements:

1. There must be an imputation of a crime, or of a vice or defect, real or imaginary, or any act, omission, status or circumstances;
2. The imputation was made orally;
3. The imputation was made publicly;
4. The imputation was made maliciously;
5. The imputation is directed to a natural or juridical person, or one who is dead; and,
6. It tends to cause dishonour, discredit or contempt of the person defamed.[190]

On the other hand, libel is defined as a 'public and malicious imputation of a crime, or of a vice or defect, real or imaginary, or any act, omission, condition, status, or circumstance tending to cause the dishonor, discredit, or contempt of a natural or juridical person, or to blacken the memory of one who is dead.'[191] It has the following elements, for which if one is missing, a case for libel will not prosper:

1. It must be defamatory;
2. It must be malicious;

[183] *Torts (Interference with Goods) Act 1977 Chapter 32* s.8.1 (UK).
[184] Revised Penal Code, Art 308.
[185] *Telecommunications and Broadcast Attorneys of the Philippines, Inc. v COMELEC*, G.R. No. 132922 (1998).
[186] Civil Code, Art 1314.
[187] *Go v Cordero*, G.R. No. 164703 & 164747 (2010).
[188] Revised Penal Code, Art 358.
[189] Revised Penal Code, Art 354.
[190] *Ramos v People*, G.R. No. 226454 (2017) citing *De Leon v People*, G.R. No. 212623, 11 January 2016, 779 SCRA 84.
[191] Revised Penal Code, Art 353.

3. It must be given publicity; and,
4. The victim must be identifiable.[192]

Despite defamation being classified as a crime, the rule on claiming damages or the civil liability differs from that of other crimes. The general rule is that civil liability is automatically attached to the criminal liability; however, damages for defamation may be claimed in an independent civil action which can proceed separately and independently of the criminal prosecution.[193] As such, the independent civil action for damages shall only require a preponderance of evidence whereas the determination of criminal liability shall require proof of guilt beyond reasonable doubt.[194]

It is noteworthy that the plaintiff may recover damages for defamation even if the defendant will not be found guilty of the crime, as long as the plaintiff does not recover twice for the same act of defamation.[195]

e. Environmental Damage and Pollution

In the Philippines, the Constitution is unequivocal in mandating that: 'The State shall protect and advance the right of the people to a balanced and healthful ecology in accord with the rhythm and harmony of nature.'[196]

Environmental tort is a hybrid of both tort law and environmental law.[197] For the action to prosper, there must be 'actual injury' in order for environmental damage incurred to be corrected based upon the defendant's fault. Similar to any claim for tort, the plaintiff may recover damages sustained if the defendant neglected their duties specifically enjoined by law such that it resulted in the plaintiff's injury.[198] In this regard, the Supreme Court ruled that this right is all-encompassing to all generations, such that injury to the environment at the present time would also injure the rights of generations to come.[199] As such, future generations are given capacity to sue when there is an injury to their right to a balanced and healthful ecology.

The Supreme Court likewise emphasised the need to protect the environment by establishing the Rules of Procedure for Environmental Cases, wherein there are special remedies afforded in order '[t]o protect and advance the constitutional right of the people to a balanced and healthful ecology'.[200] Included in these Rules is the Writ of Kalikasan (Nature) which affords stronger protection of one's right to a balanced and healthful ecology[201] and the Writ of Continuing Mandamus which orders or directs any government agency or instrumentality to perform an act or series of acts in relation to the protection of one's right to a balanced and healthful ecology.[202]

These Rules have highlighted further the importance of natural resources as they are vital to the survival of our society,[203] and that management of natural resources is a public trust since all natural resources are deemed owned by the state for the benefit of citizens.[204]

[192] *Diaz v People of the Philippines*, G.R. No. 159787 (2007) citing *Novicio v Aggabao*, G.R. No. 141332, 11 December 2003, 418 SCRA 138, 143, further citing *Alonzo v Court of Appeals*, 241 SCRA 51 (1995).
[193] Civil Code, Art 33.
[194] *Jose-Consing, Jr. v People of the Philippines*, G.R. No. 161075 (2013).
[195] *Supreme Transportation Liner, Inc. & Ruz v San Andres*, G.R. No. 200444 (2018).
[196] 1987 Constitution, Art. III, s 16.
[197] *Sanggacala, et. al. v National Power Corporation*, G.R. No. 209538 (2021).
[198] Rules of Procedure for Environmental Cases, A.M. No. 09-6-8-SC, Rule 8, s 1.
[199] *Oposa v Factoran*, G.R. No. 101083 (1993).
[200] The Rules of Procedure for Environmental Cases, A.M. No. 09-6-8-SC, s 3(a).
[201] Note 200, Rule 7.
[202] Note 200, Rule 8.
[203] *Republic of the Philippines v N. Dela Merced & Sons, Inc.*, G.R. No. 201501 (2018).
[204] *Maynilad Water Services, Inc. v DENR Secretary, et. al.*, G.R. No. 202897 (2019).

D. Unjust Enrichment

Choice of law presents the issue of whether varying jurisdictions have rules for 'unjust enrichment' or simple 'restitution' though the term used is unjust enrichment.[205] This in itself shows the peculiarity of unjust enrichment, and with the inclusion of states with their respective sovereignty and independence, it is a matter often handled based on territory even though the peculiarity of unjust enrichment is not solved by simplifying it in terms of territory.[206] Authorities are at odds as to which law to choose in terms of unjust enrichment. It is possible that unjust enrichment occurs across different countries or jurisdictions. On one hand, there are some who argue that the law of the place of enrichment is to be followed, whereas others argue that the law of the place of the act of enrichment should be followed.[207]

In the Philippines, unjust enrichment exists 'when a person unjustly retains a benefit to the loss of another, or when a person retains money or property of another against the fundamental principles of justice, equity and good conscience.'[208] Should the person unjustly enrich themselves at the expense of another without just or legal ground, that person is liable to return that which they unjustly benefitted from.[209]

In the Philippine legal system, it is important to note that simply benefitting from another is not enough for the claim of unjust enrichment to suffice. The defendant must have benefitted from the plaintiff in such a way that the benefit was acquired *without just or legal ground*.[210] Furthermore, for a plaintiff to pursue the claim of unjust enrichment, the plaintiff must have no other cause of action based on contract, crime, or otherwise.[211]

With the concept embedded in the Civil Code under the 'Human Relations' section, Philippine law is guaranteeing that even if such is a matter of equity, a plaintiff is not without recourse or remedy to obtain relief for the damage they sustained.[212]

E. Trusts and Charitable Foundations

A trust in its general sense is a right of property, regardless if real or personal, held by one party for the benefit of another person.[213] It may be express, wherein the trust is specifically created with intent, or implied, wherein the trust came into existence by operation of law.[214] Choice of law issues stem from when the elements that comprise the trust are spread out in more than one jurisdiction, such as when the trust encompasses multiple properties located in several countries.[215] When a choice of law issue does arise in trusts, the intent of the trustor must be determined as

[205] A Chong, 'Choice of Law for Unjust Enrichment/Restitution and the Rome II Regulation' (2008) 57(4) *The International and Comparative Law Quarterly* 863–98, www.jstor.org/stable/20488256.

[206] TW Bennett, 'Choice of Law Rules in Claims of Unjust Enrichment' (1990) 39(1) *The International and Comparative Law Quarterly* 136–68, www.jstor.org/stable/760323.

[207] Note 205.

[208] *Filinvest Land, Inc., et. al. v Backy, et. al.*, G.R. No. 174715 (2012).

[209] Civil Code, Art 22.

[210] *Philippine Stock Exchange, Inc. v Litonjua*, G.R. No. 204014 (2016).

[211] *Shinryo v RRN Incorporated*, G.R. No. 172525 (2010).

[212] *California Clothing Inc. & Ybañez v Quiñones*, G.R. No. 175822 (2013).

[213] *Estate of Cabacungan v Laigo, et. al.*, G.R. No. 175073 (2011).

[214] Civil Code, Art 1441.

[215] A Wallace, 'Choice of Law for Trusts in Australia and the United Kingdom' (1987) 36(3) *The International and Comparative Law Quarterly* 454–82, www.jstor.org/stable/760478.

to what law shall be used.[216] However, if such intent cannot be determined or it is a case of an implied trust, the 'most significant relationship' test shall be used.[217]

In the Philippines, when a person dies without any heirs or beneficiaries, the estate is inherited by the state.[218] In this event, the properties composing the estate shall be assigned to the municipality or city where the deceased last resided or where the properties are located, if the deceased never resided in the Philippines and the estate left behind shall be used for the benefit of public schools or charitable institutions.[219]

In this regard, charitable institutions or foundations in the Philippines are exempted from taxation[220] and the land, buildings, and improvements that these foundations actually, directly, and exclusively use for charitable purposes are also exempt from real property taxes.[221] Choice of law issues arise when the activities of a certain charitable institution extend over another country or jurisdiction. It is also possible that the charitable act of the institution, if done over a different jurisdiction, be prohibited in that jurisdiction.[222]

216 ibid.
217 *Hasegawa v Kitamura*, G.R. No. 149177 (2007).
218 Civil Code, Art 1011.
219 Civil Code, Art 1013.
220 1987 Constitution, Art. VI, s 28(3).
221 1987 Constitution, Art XIV, s 4(3).
222 K Roosevelt, *Choice of Law Issues in the Nonprofit Arena* (New York University School of Law, 2006) ncpl.law.nyu.edu/wp-content/uploads/pdfs/2006/Conf2006_Roosevelt_FINAL.pdf.

4

Law of Property

RICHARD J NETHERCOTT AND RIO MEI L UY

I. Kinds of Property

The *lex situs* governs immovable and movable property. For the purposes of characterisation, it may be useful to set out precisely what constitute 'immovable,' 'movable,' and other types of property and their incidents as a matter of Philippine law.

A property, defined as a thing which is or may be the object of appropriation, may be classified either as: (a) immovable or real property; or (b) movable or personal property.[1] A property may also be classified based on the ownership. Further, a property, in relation to the person to whom it belongs, is either of public dominion or of private ownership.[2]

Classification of properties as movable or immovable and if it is of public dominion or private ownership carries significant legal implications, as the rules governing acquisition, ownership, possession, loss, transfer, registration, and even taxation differ depending on the classification of the property involved. For example, immovable property generally requires formal documentation and registration with the proper government agency to affect third parties, whereas movable property is typically governed by principles of possession and delivery. On the other hand, properties of public dominion are generally not subject to real property tax.

A. Immovable Property

The Civil Code enumerates those properties which may be considered as immovable. They are:

(1) Land, buildings, roads and constructions of all kinds adhered to the soil;
(2) Trees, plants, and growing fruits, while they are attached to the land or form an integral part of an immovable;
(3) Everything attached to an immovable in a fixed manner, in such a way that it cannot be separated therefrom without breaking the material or deterioration of the object;
(4) Statues, reliefs, paintings or other objects for use or ornamentation, placed in buildings or on lands by the owner of the immovable in such a manner that it reveals the intention to attach them permanently to the tenements;

[1] Civil Code, Art 414.
[2] Civil Code, Art 419.

(5) Machinery, receptacles, instruments or implements intended by the owner of the tenement for an industry or works which may be carried on in a building or on a piece of land, and which tend directly to meet the needs of the said industry or works;
(6) Animal houses, pigeon-houses, beehives, fish ponds or breeding places of similar nature, in case their owner has placed them or preserves them with the intention to have them permanently attached to the land, and forming a permanent part of it; the animals in these places are included;
(7) Fertiliser actually used on a piece of land;
(8) Mines, quarries, and slag dumps, while the matter thereof forms part of the bed, and waters either running or stagnant;
(9) Docks and structures which, though floating, are intended by their nature and object to remain at a fixed place on a river, lake, or coast; and,
(10) Contracts for public works, and servitudes and other real rights over immovable property.

The foregoing notwithstanding, parties to a contract may validly stipulate that a real property be considered as personal. After agreeing to such stipulation, they are estopped from claiming otherwise.[3]

From this enumeration, immovable properties may be further classified as real property by: (a) **nature**, which pertains to properties which cannot be carried from place to place (items 1, 2, and 8); (b) **incorporation**, which pertains to properties attached to an immovable in a fixed manner to be an integral part thereof (items 1 to 4 and 6); (c) **destination**, which pertains to properties placed in an immovable for the utility it gives to the activity carried thereon (items 4 to 7 and 9); and (d) **analogy**, or those properties classified as such by express provision of law (item 10).

i. Those Adhered to the Soil

Land is the best example of an immovable property. It is real property by nature since it cannot be carried from one place to another. A shovelful of land, however, is considered personal property since it is no longer adhered to the soil. Independent of and regardless of the ownership of the land, buildings are classified as immovable properties by incorporation. A building is considered immovable property by reason of its adherence to the soil on which it is built. However, once it is demolished, it ceases to exist as such and hence its character as immovable likewise ceases.[4] To be considered immovable under this provision, the building must be more or less a permanent structure, and not mere impositions on the land like a shanty.

ii. Those Attached to the Land or which Form an Integral Part of an Immovable

They are immovable property (by nature or incorporation) on the theory that they derive their existence or sustenance from the soil. Trees and plants are immovable by nature if they are the spontaneous products of the soil, and by incorporation if they are produced by lands of any kind through cultivation or labour. However, once the tree or plant is cut or uprooted (or its incorporation otherwise ceases), it becomes a movable property.

[3] *Serg's Products, Inc. v PCI Leasing & Finance, Inc* GR No 137705 (2000).
[4] *Bicerra v Teneza* GR No L-16218 (1962).

iii. Those Attached to an Immovable in a Fixed Manner, in Such a Way that it cannot be Separated Therefrom without Breaking the Material or Deterioration of the Object

These are classified as immovable by incorporation. To be considered as immovable property, the injury or breakage or deterioration in case of separation, must be substantial. An example of this would be a fixed fire escape stairway firmly embedded in the walls of a house, an aqueduct, a sewer, or a well. It must be stressed that unlike in item five (5), the attachment under item three (3) need not be made by the owner of the immovable, provided that (a) it cannot be separated from the immovable without breaking the material; and (b) the attachment was intended or is material.

iv. Those Placed in Buildings or on Lands by the Owner of the Immovable in Such a Manner that it Reveals the Intention to Attach them Permanently to the Tenements

These are classified as immovable by incorporation and destination. The following must concur in order to be considered as immovable under this: (a) the object, which must be an object of ornamentation or use, must be placed in the immovable by the owner of the latter or their agent, such as a lessee or usufructuary, otherwise, the object will not attain the character of an immovable;[5] (b) the object must be placed on a building or land; and, (c) there is an intention of permanent annexation or attachment, even if adherence will not involve breakage or injury. The latter is the defining characteristic.

Compared to those attached to an immovable in a fixed manner where real property cannot be separated from the immovable without breaking its material, and the attachment need not be by the owner, real property placed in such a manner that it reveals the intention to attach permanently can be separated from the immovable without breaking or deterioration, and must be placed/attached by the owner of the immovable (or by their agent).

v. Those Intended by the Owner of the Tenement for an Industry or Works which may be Carried on in a Building or on a Piece of Land, and which Tend Directly to Meet the Needs of the Said Industry or Works

These are classified as immovable by destination. The properties listed need not be attached to an immovable. Their immovable character depends upon their use in the industry or works carried on in a building or on a piece of land. For instance, machinery of breweries used in the manufacture of liquor and soft drinks, though movable in nature, are immobilised because they are essential to said industries.[6] To be considered as immovable under this, (a) the object must be placed by the owner of the tenement or their agent, (b) some industry or work is carried on in the tenement, and (c) the object tends directly to meet the needs of such industry or work. The last element satisfies the Test of Essentiality, *that is*, that the machineries must be an essential and principal element of the industry or works, without which such industry or works would be

[5] *Davao Sawmill v Castillo* GR No L-4041 (1935).

[6] *Mindanao Bus Co. v City Assessor and Treasurer* GR No L-17870 (1962).

unable to function or carry on the industrial purpose for which it was established, and not merely incidental.[7]

vi. Those Used for Animal Housing or Breeding Places of Similar Nature

These structures, classified as immovable by destination and incorporation, are considered real property if (a) their owner has placed them or preserves them, (b) with the intention to have them permanently attached to the land, and (c) forming a permanent part of it. Likewise, the animals in these places are considered as real property.

Suppose the animals are outside, their houses may still be considered as real properties if the animals intend to return, as in the case of a homing pigeon. On the other hand, a temporary bird cage which may be easily removable, or which may be carried from place to place, is considered a movable property.

vii. Fertiliser Actually Used on a Piece of Land

It is classified as immovable by destination. The term 'actually used' means that it has been spread over the land. Otherwise, if kept in a container, they are considered movable.

viii. Mines, Quarries, and Slag Dumps, while the Matter Thereof Forms Part of the Bed, and Waters Either Running or Stagnant

These are classified as immovable by nature. Once severed, they become movable. However, 'waters' which are immovables, such as a sea, river, or lake, must not be confused with 'water' itself which is plainly movable property. Waters, either running or stagnant, are classified as immovables.

ix. Those Structures which, Though Floating, are Intended by their Nature and Object to Remain at a Fixed Place on a River, Lake, or Coast

These are classified as immovable by destination. Vessels are considered as movables, although they partake the nature of real property, in view of their importance in the world of commerce.

x. Contracts for Public Works, and Servitudes and Other Real Rights Over Immovable Property

They are classified as immovable by analogy (eg, usufruct of real property for a period of one year and registered). Properties referred herein are not material things but rights, which are necessarily intangible but are nevertheless considered immovable by provision of law.

B. Movable Property

Movables properties are those: (a) not included in the above enumeration; (b) those considered personal property by special provision of law; (c) forces of nature; (d) obligations and actions,

[7] ibid.

including the infinite variety of contracts, promises, or obligations which confer on one party the right to recover movable property or a sum of money from another by action.; (e) shares of stocks; and, (f) other incorporeal personal property.

Three tests may generally be applied for a property to be identified as movable: (a) whether the property can be transported or carried from place to place; (b) whether such change of location can be made without injuring the immovable to which the object may be attached; and (c) whether the object does not fall within any of the ten cases enumerated in Article 415 of the Civil Code.

For taxation of properties, the Local Government Code – being a special law that delegates to local government units the authority to impose real property taxes – takes precedence over the Civil Code, which is a general law on property and property relations. Thus, the Local Government Code governs the determination of which properties are subject to real property tax. In *Manila Electric Company v City Assessor*,[8] the Supreme Court held that transformers, electric posts, transmission lines, insulators, and electric meters of Manila Electric Company may be classified as 'machinery' under the Local Government Code and are therefore subject to real property tax. Similarly, in *Capitol Wireless, Inc. v Provincial Treasurer of Batangas*,[9] the Supreme Court ruled that submarine or undersea communication cables entering Philippine territory are comparable to electric transmission lines and may also be considered 'machinery' liable for real property taxation under the Local Government Code. The Local Government Code was recently amended by the Real Property Valuation and Assessment Reform Act[10] which defines 'machinery' as follows '[m]achinery refers to machines, equipment, mechanical contrivances, instruments, appliances, or apparatus which may or may not be attached, permanently or temporarily, to the real property. It includes the physical facilities for production, the installations and appurtenant service facilities, those which are mobile, self-powered or self-propelled, and those not permanently attached to the real property which are actually, directly, and exclusively used to meet the needs of the particular industry, business or activity, and which, by their very nature and purpose, are designed for or necessary to its manufacturing, mining, logging, commercial, industrial or agricultural purposes[.]'[11]

II. Public Dominion or Private Ownership

Pursuant to Article 419 of the Civil Code, property, in relation to the person to whom it belongs, is either of public dominion or of private ownership. As such, properties are owned either in a public capacity (*dominio publico*) or in a private capacity (*propiedad privado*).[12]

Property of public dominion is outside the commerce of man. Consequently, it can neither be appropriated nor be the subject of contracts; hence, they cannot be alienated or encumbered.[13] There are three kinds of property of public dominion: (a) property intended for public use; (b) property intended for some specific public service; and, (c) property intended for the development of the national welfare.[14]

[8] *Manila Electric Company v City Assessor* G.R. No. 166102 (2015).
[9] *Capitol Wireless, Inc. v Provincial Treasurer of Batangas* G.R. No. 180110 (2016).
[10] RA No. 12001.
[11] RA No. 12001, s 4(k).
[12] *Republic v Spouses Alejandre* G.R. No. 217336 (2018).
[13] *Republic v Pasig Rizal Co., Inc* GR No 213207 (2022).
[14] Civil Code, Art 420.

On the other hand, private property is either: (a) patrimonial property, which is the property owned by the state and its political subdivisions in their private capacity, and all property of the state not included in Article 420 of the Civil Code;[15] or (b) possession of which belongs to private persons either personally or through predecessors-in-interest, openly, continuously and exclusively for 20 years immediately preceding the filing of the application for confirmation title except when prevented by war or *force majeure*.[16]

Properties of public domain include properties owned by government instrumentalities. These properties are not subject to local taxes and real property taxes if actually used by the government instrumentality.[17]

In *Philippine Heart Center v Local Government of Quezon City*,[18] the Supreme Court ruled that the Philippine Heart Centre (PHC) is a government instrumentality with corporate powers exempt from local taxes, including real property tax. The properties of the PHC are properties of public dominion devoted to public use and welfare and, therefore, exempt from real property taxes and levy, without prejudice to the liability of taxable persons to whom the beneficial use of any of these properties has been granted. The Court further explained that properties of public dominion are outside the commerce of man. These properties are exempt from levy, encumbrance or disposition through public or private sale.

However, even if the property is owned by a government instrumentality, it is deemed patrimonial in character when it is utilised for commercial or profit-generating purposes. In *PNOC Alternative Fuels Corp. v National Grid Corporation of the Philippines*,[19] the subject property owned by PAFC is classified as patrimonial because the same is declared by law to be an industrial and commercial estate that may be transferred or conveyed to private persons so that business activities may be conducted therein. It is thus apparent from the law and its corresponding implementing rules and regulations that the industrial estate is being owned, managed, and operated by the state, not in its sovereign capacity, but rather in its private capacity. Simply stated, the management and operation of the industrial estate is proprietary in character, serving the economic ends of the state.

In *Government Service Insurance System v City Treasurer and City Assessor of the City of Manila*,[20] the Court also nullified the real property tax assessments issued by the City of Manila to the Government Service Insurance System (GSIS), with the exception of the assessment on the Katigbak property that was leased to the Manila Hotel Corporation, a subsidiary corporation under the GSIS formed to manage the Manila Hotel which had actual and beneficial use of the premises. The Court held that the properties registered under the name of GSIS are, in fact, owned by the Republic, and that GSIS merely holds them in trust, either having been transferred to it by the Government or acquired for the enhancement of the system.

III. Expropriation

Private properties may be taken by the government for public use through expropriation in the exercise of its power of eminent domain, proscribed by the restraint of public use and just

[15] Civil Code, Arts 421–424.
[16] RA No 11573.
[17] Local Government Code, ss 133 and 234(a).
[18] G.R. No. 225409 (2020).
[19] G.R. No. 224936, 4 September 2019.
[20] G.R. No. 215955, 13 January 2021.

compensation. Rule 67 of the Rules of Court provides guidelines to ensure that due process is observed and just compensation is rightly paid to private owners.

The taking of private property for public use, to be compensable, need not be an actual physical taking or appropriation. It also includes any form of destruction, restriction, diminution, or interruption of the rights of ownership or of the common and necessary use and enjoyment of the property in the lawful manner, lessening or destroying its value. It is neither necessary that the owner be wholly deprived of the use of their property nor material whether the property is removed from the possession of the owner, or in any respect changes hands.

There are two types of expropriation. The first one is ordinary expropriation, where the purpose of the taking must be strictly for public use. An example of this would be the building of market sites and market stalls, roads, public buildings, or railroads. However, there is no more cogent point for the government's retention of the expropriated land when the public necessity ceases or disappears, or when the government devotes the property to another public use very much different from the original or deviates from the declared purpose to benefit another person.

The second is extraordinary expropriation, where the purpose of taking is for private use, but there is still a connotation of public use: for the benefit of certain individuals. For instance, the implementation of the Agrarian Reform Programme which recognised the right of farmers and regular farmworkers, who are landless, to own directly and collectively the lands they till, or in case of other farmworkers, to receive a just share of the fruits thereof. The main purpose of this type of expropriation is to uphold social justice to the end that public welfare will be enhanced.

IV. Modes of Acquiring Ownership of Property

The modes of acquisition of ownership over immovable and movable properties may be through (1) occupation, (2) law, (3) donation, (4) tradition, (5) intellectual creation, (6) prescription, and (7) succession.[21]

A. Occupation

This is a mode of acquiring ownership by seizure of corporeal things that have no owner, with the intention of acquiring them, and according to the rules laid down by law. The requisites for this mode of acquisition are as follows: (i) the thing must be *res nullius* – a thing which has no owner, either because a former owner has finally abandoned it, or because it has never been appropriated by any person, or because (in the Roman Law) it is not susceptible to private ownership;[22] (ii) it must be appropriable by nature or one that can be seized or apprehended (or it must be corporeal); (iii) it must be brought into the actual possession or control of the person professing to acquire it; and, (iv) the person must acquire it with the intention of acquiring ownership. They must therefore have the necessary capacity to consent.[23]

Properties which may be acquired by occupation include animals that are objects of hunting and fishing, hidden treasure, and the abandoned movables.[24]

[21] Civil Code, Art 712.
[22] *Republic v Guzman* G.R. No. 132964 (2000), citing *Black's Dictionary of Law*, 4th edn (2023) 1470.
[23] 3 Sanchez 210: 2 Castan 140.
[24] Civil Code, Art 713.

However, the ownership of a piece of land cannot be acquired by occupation.[25] The Regalian Doctrine provides that when a piece of land is without an owner, it becomes patrimonial land of the state, susceptible to acquisition through prescription.

B. Law

These are special legal provisions which directly vest ownership or real rights in favour of certain persons, independently of the other modes of acquiring and transmitting ownership or other real rights. For instance, fruits that naturally fall onto adjoining land become the property of the said landowner.[26] Similarly, if a person, not originally the owner of a property, sells or alienates and delivers it and subsequently acquires ownership, the title automatically vests in the buyer or transferee by operation of law.[27]

C. Donation

Donation is an act of liberality whereby a person disposes gratuitously of a thing or right in favour of another, who accepts it.[28] Donation has three indispensable elements: (1) the reduction of the patrimony of the donor; (2) the increase in the patrimony of the donee; and (3) the intent to commit an act of liberality or *animus donandi*.[29] Donative intent is a creature of the mind and cannot be perceived except by the material and tangible acts which manifest its presence. Accordingly, donative intent is presumed present when one gives a part of one's patrimony to another without consideration and it is not negated when the person donating has other intentions, motives or purposes which do not contradict the donative intent.[30]

Donation is a mode of acquisition as the Civil Code treats donation as a contract that transfers ownership. As explained in *Liguez v Court of Appeals*, donation is one of the modes of acquiring ownership. It need not be completed by tradition since Article 712 of the Civil Code prescribes that ownership and rights therein are acquired and transmitted – by donation, succession and in consequence of certain contracts by tradition, thereby implying that donation is not one of the contracts requiring tradition.[31]

When it comes to real property, such as land, donation must be executed through a public instrument. Failure to comply with this formality renders the alienation invalid, even as between the parties to the transaction.[32]

For movable property, the formal requirements differ based on the value of the property.[33] If the value exceeds Php 5,000, the donation must be made in writing, which may be done through a private instrument. In this case, both the donation and the acceptance must be in writing. For example, the donation of an automobile worth Php 1.7 million must comply with these requirements. If the donation is made in writing (eg, through an affidavit), but the donee merely accepts it orally, the donation is void. If the value of the movable property is Php 5,000 or less, the donation may be made

[25] Civil Code, Art 714.
[26] Civil Code, Art 681.
[27] Civil Code, Art 1434.
[28] Civil Code, Art 725.
[29] *Bacala v Heirs of Poliño* G.R. No. 200608 (2021).
[30] *Abello v Commissioner of Internal Revenue and Court of Appeals* G.R. No. 120721 (2005).
[31] *Liguez v Court of Appeals* GR No. L-11240 (1958).
[32] Civil Code, Art 749.
[33] Civil Code, Art 748.

orally, but it must be accompanied by simultaneous delivery of the item or of the document representing the right donated. While the law permits the donation to be in writing even in such cases, it does not require the acceptance to also be in writing. In all cases, compliance with the formal requirements of donation is essential. Failure to do so results in the nullity of the donation.

D. Tradition or Delivery

Tradition or delivery, as a method of acquiring and transferring ownership and other real rights, involves the delivery of possession coupled with the intent to transfer such ownership or rights. The requisites of tradition are as follows: (1) pre-existence of the right to be transmitted in the estate of the grantor, the same being a derivative mode of acquiring ownership; (2) just cause or title for the transmission, such as sale; (3) intention on the part of the grantor to grant and on the part of the grantee to acquire; (4) capacity to transmit (on the part of the grantor) and capacity to acquire (on the part of the grantee); and, (5) an act which gives it outward form, physically, symbolically, or legally.

In all forms of delivery, it is necessary that the act of delivery, whether constructive or actual, should be coupled with the intention of delivering the thing. The act, without the intention, is insufficient. The critical factor in the different modes of effecting delivery which gives legal effect to the act, is the actual intention of the vendor to deliver, and its acceptance by the vendee. Without that intention, there is no tradition.[34]

i. Types of Tradition (or Delivery)

(a) Actual or Real Tradition – This refers to the physical transfer of the item to the grantee. If the item is movable, it is delivered by handing it directly from one person to another. If immovable, delivery is carried out through certain visible or possessory actions by the grantee, done with the grantor's consent, such as entering the property or collecting its fruits.

(b) Constructive (or Symbolic) Tradition – Delivery may occur even without an actual, physical transfer. Instead, it is represented by actions or indications that signify the intent to transfer possession, making it a constructive form of delivery.

(c) Quasi-Tradition – This applies to the transfer of incorporeal rights or intangible assets, accomplished when the grantee begins to exercise the rights with the acquiescence of the grantor.

ii. Forms of Constructive Delivery

(a) *Traditio symbolica* (Delivery through symbolic acts) – The transfer of ownership is effected by the delivery of symbols or things which represent those to be delivered. For movable property, delivery can be carried out by handing over the keys to the storage or location where the item is kept.[35] For immovable property, symbolic delivery is made through the execution of a public instrument, which the law recognises as equivalent to the actual delivery of the property that is the object of the contract.

[34] *Union Motor Corporation v Court of Appeals* G.R. No. 117187 (2001).
[35] Civil Code, Art. 1498.

(b) *Traditio longa manu:* The transfer of ownership is effected by the grantor by pointing out or identifying the thing to be delivered to the grantee. For example, a seller points to a piece of furniture sold within a warehouse.
(c) *Traditio brevi manu* – This form of delivery happens when the grantee is already in possession of the thing – such as when it has been leased to them – and the grantor subsequently declares that the grantee shall now hold the item, which is already under their control, as owner. This declaration constitutes delivery. For example, a lessee buys the leased property; there is no need for physical transfer.
(d) *Traditio constitutum possessorium* – The delivery is affected by a mere declaration by the grantor that he will now hold the thing on behalf of the grantee. This typically occurs when the owner transfers ownership but retains possession under a different legal relationship, such as through a lease. For instance, the owner may sell a property and then lease it back from the new owner.

A contract of sale is an agreement wherein one party undertakes to transfer ownership and deliver a specific thing, while the other agrees to pay therefore a certain price in money or its equivalent.[36] A contract of sale is a consensual contract which means that the sale is perfected by mere consent. The deliver of the thing sold or the payment of the price is not required for the contract to be perfected. Instead, upon perfection, the parties become bound to fulfill their respective obligations, which is to deliver the thing sold and to pay the price thereof. Thus, a contract of sale is not a mode of acquiring ownership, it only creates title. It is tradition or delivery, as a consequence of sale, that actually transfers ownership.

As to the validity of sale, no particular form is required in a contract of sale for its validity.[37] A contract of sale may be made in writing, or by word of mouth, or partly in writing and partly by word of mouth, or may be inferred from the conduct of the parties subject only to the provisions of the Statute of Frauds and of any other applicable statute.[38]

The following must be in writing to be enforceable: (a) personal property at a price not less than Five Hundred Pesos (Php500.00); (b) real property or an interest therein regardless of price; (c) property or of an interest not to be performed within a year from the date thereof regardless of the nature of the property and price; and, (d) when an applicable statute requires that the contract of sale be in a certain form.

It is worthy of mentioning that a sale of real property, though not contained in a public instrument or formal writing, is nevertheless valid and binding, for even a verbal contract of sale or real estate produces legal effects between the parties. Hence, a defective notarisation of deed does not affect the validity of the sale. The formalities required by law are not essential for the validity of the contract but are simply for its greater efficacy or convenience, or to bind third persons, and are merely a coercive means granted to the contracting parties to enable them to reciprocally compel the observance of the prescribed form.[39]

In cases involving a double sale, where a property is sold to two different buyers with conflicting interests, the ownership of an immovable property shall belong to the person acquiring it in good faith who first recorded it in the Registry of Property. Should there be no inscription, the ownership shall pertain to the person who in good faith was first in the possession of the property. In the absence thereof, the ownership pertains to the person possessing the property who

[36] Civil Code, Art 1544.
[37] *Dalion v Court of Appeals* G.R. No. 78903 (1990).
[38] Civil Code, Art 1483.
[39] *Diampoc v Buenaventura* GR No 200383 (2018).

presents the oldest title. Meanwhile for movable property, the ownership of the property shall be transferred to the person who may have first taken possession thereof in good faith.[40]

E. Intellectual Creation

Intellectual property refers to creations of the mind such as inventions; literary and artistic works; designs; and symbols, names and images used in commerce.[41]
The following persons acquire ownership through their intellectual creations:

1. Authors, for their literary, dramatic, historical, legal, philosophical, scientific, or similar works;
2. Composers, for their musical compositions;
3. Painters, sculptors, and other artists, for the products of their art; and,
4. Scientists, technologists, or any other persons, for their discoveries or inventions.[42]

A letter or other private written communication becomes the property of the person to whom it is addressed and delivered. However, it cannot be published or shared with others without the consent of the author or the author's heirs. The court may, nonetheless, permit its publication or dissemination if it determines that doing so serves the public good or the interests of justice.[43]

F. Prescription

Prescription is another mode of acquiring ownership and other real rights over immovable property. It is concerned with lapse of time in the manner and under conditions laid down by law, namely, that the possession should be (in relation to an owner) public, peaceful, uninterrupted and adverse. Possession is open when it is patent, visible, apparent, notorious and not clandestine. It is continuous when uninterrupted, unbroken and not intermittent or occasional; exclusive when the adverse possessor can show exclusive dominion over the land and an appropriation of it to their own use and benefit; and notorious when it is so conspicuous that it is generally known and talked about by the public.[44]

Acquisitive prescription has two types – ordinary and extraordinary. Ordinary prescription requires possession of things in good faith and with just title for the time fixed by law.[45] On the other hand, extraordinary prescription does not require good faith and just title.[46]

For example, the ownership of a real property may be acquired by prescription, when there is bad faith, after an interrupted adverse possession of 30 years.[47] Conversely, acquisition in bad faith of a personal property needs only uninterrupted possession of eight years.[48] However, if there is good faith possession, ownership and other real rights over immovable property are

[40] Civil Code, Art 1544.
[41] What is Intellectual Property, www.wipo.int/en/web/about-ip.
[42] Civil Code, Art 721.
[43] Civil Code, Art 723.
[44] *Republic of the Philippines v Northern Cement Corporation* G.R. No. 200256 (2018) citing *Heirs of Crisologo v Rañon* G.R. No. 171068 (2007).
[45] Civil Code, Art 1117.
[46] Civil Code, Art 1137.
[47] Civil Code, Art 1137.
[48] Civil Code, Art 1132.

acquired by ordinary prescription of ten years,[49] meanwhile those over movable property may be acquired through uninterrupted and continuous possession for four years.[50]

The Doctrine of Irrevendicability provides that possession of movable property is presumed ownership. It is equivalent to title and no further proof is necessary. This is essential to facilitate transactions involving movables, which do not require special formalities. However, the possessor's title is not absolute but merely presumptive. Hence, it can be defeated by the true owner. Nevertheless, the doctrine has two exceptions, when the owner has lost the thing, or has been unlawfully deprived thereof. In these cases, the possessor cannot retain the thing as against the owner, who may recover it without paying any indemnity. The only exception is acquisition in good faith of the possession at a public sale.[51]

G. Succession

As to succession, where the ownership is transferred from the decedent to an heir or heirs, the same will be further discussed below.

Ownership of property may be acquired through two general classifications: **original** mode and **derivative** mode. Under the original mode, the ownership of property is acquired independently of any pre-existing or preceding title or right of another, like occupation and intellectual creation or work. Meanwhile for derivative mode, the property is previously owned by somebody else, such as in cases of succession, donation, prescription, and tradition.

i. General Considerations

Succession is a mode of acquisition by virtue of which the property, rights, and obligations, to the extent of the value of the inheritance, of a person are transmitted through death to another or others either by will or by operation of law.[52]

The rights to the succession are transmitted from the moment of the death of the decedent.[53] Accordingly, the moment of death is the determining point when an heir acquires a definite right to the inheritance. The rights to a person's succession do not vest in their heirs until such time.[54]

The scope of inheritance is, generally, all the property, rights, and obligations of a person which are not extinguished by such person's death; and the property and the transmissible rights and obligations which have accrued thereto since the opening of the succession.[55]

Nonetheless, the transmissibility of rights and obligations by succession is subject to certain exceptions. These exceptions include rights and obligations which are not transmissible[56] such as those that are intransmissible by nature and those that are strictly personal (*intuitu personae*). Such intransmissible rights and obligations include: (1) those relating to family relations; (2) those arising from public law; (3) those which involve or require the personal skills, qualifications, characteristics or circumstances of a particular individual; and, (4) criminal responsibility

[49] Civil Code, Art 1134.
[50] See n 14.
[51] Civil Code, Art 559.
[52] Civil Code, Art 774.
[53] Civil Code, Art 777.
[54] *Locsin v Court of Appeals* G.R. No. 89783 (1992).
[55] Civil Code, Art 781.
[56] Civil Code, Art 1311.

(exception: In case of death of any of the parties to a complaint for illegal dismissal during the pendency of the proceedings, they may be substituted by their heirs).[57]

Other exceptions may also be those that are intransmissible by stipulation, and those that are intransmissible by provision of law, like usufruct, agency, and commodatum.

Another exception is the monetary debt left by the decedent which remains intransmissible since it is paid from the estate of the decedent and only the net estate or remainder goes to the heirs. If the decedent's estate is not sufficient to pay their debts, their heirs cannot be held liable for said debts in their personal capacity.[58]

ii. Kinds of Succession

Succession may be classified into the following types:

1. Testamentary Succession – This form of succession arises from the express designation of an heir in a will duly executed in accordance with the formalities prescribed by law.[59]
2. Legal or Intestate Succession – This occurs if a person dies without a will, or when the will is void or one which has subsequently lost its validity.[60] In such cases, the law determines the heirs and their respective shares.
3. Mixed Succession – This type of succession arises partly by will and partly by operation of law, such as when a decedent disposes of only a portion of their estate through testamentary provisions in their will.
4. Compulsory Succession – This takes place by operation of law with respect to the legitime, which is reserved by law for compulsory heirs and cannot be impaired by the will of the testator.

iii. Laws Governing Succession

In accordance with Article 16, paragraph 2, and Article 1039 of the Civil Code, the national law of the decedent shall govern both intestate and testamentary successions in relation to the following matters: (1) the order of succession; (2) the amount of successional rights; (3) the intrinsic validity of the provisions of the will; and, (4) the capacity to succeed. For instance, the intrinsic validity of will and the determination of the heirs are governed by the law of the decedent's nationality. In one case, the Supreme Court held that the Philippine law on legitime does not apply to foreign decedents, since the governing law in such case is the national law of the decedent.[61]

When any of the above matters is at issue, the applicable law is that in force at the time of the decedent's death. This is in keeping with the principle that succession rights vest upon death; hence, subsequent changes in the governing law cannot impair those rights, whether they pertain to the identification of heirs, their respective shares, the validity of testamentary provisions, or the capacity to inherit.

As a general rule, the formalities and modes of execution of wills are determined by the law of the country where the will is executed.[62] A Filipino abroad may execute a will in accordance

[57] *Nedira v NJ World Corporation* GR No 240005 (2022).
[58] Rules of Court, Rules 88–90.
[59] Civil Code, Art 799.
[60] *Heirs of Conti v Court of Appeals*, G.R. No. 118464 (1998).
[61] *Bellis v Bellis* G.R. No. L-23678 (1967).
[62] Civil Code, Art 17, para 1.

with the formal requirements of the host country, and such will may be admitted to probate in the Philippines.[63] However, an exception exists with respect to joint wills: joint wills executed by Filipino citizens in a foreign country shall not be valid or enforceable in the Philippines, even if valid under the law of the place of execution.[64]

Where the applicable law concerning forms and solemnities has changed, the governing law is the one in force at the time of the will's execution.[65] This preserves the validity of a will that complied with the law at the time it was made.

With regard to the legal capacity of the decedent, the same is governed by their national law.[66] More specifically, the capacity to make a will is determined by the law in force at the time of its execution. Thus, if the testator possessed testamentary capacity at that time, a later change in the law rendering them incapable will not invalidate the will.[67] Conversely, a will executed by a person lacking capacity at the time cannot be validated by a supervening change in the law conferring capacity after the fact.

iv. Wills

Testamentary succession is that which results from the designation of an heir, made in a will executed in the form prescribed by law.[68]

A will is an act whereby a person (called as a testator) is permitted, with the formalities prescribed by law, to control to a certain degree the disposition of their estate to take effect after their death.[69]

There are two kinds of wills, namely: (a) ordinary or attested/notarial, which must comply with formal requirements provided by law, including notarisation and attestation, among others;[70] and (b) holographic, which is entirely written, dated and signed by the hand of the testator.[71]

The execution of an ordinary or attested will is governed by Articles 804 to 809 of the Civil Code. This type of will, also referred to as a notarial will, must be acknowledged before a notary public by both the testator and the attesting witnesses. In contrast, Article 810 of the Civil Code provides for the execution of a holographic will, which must be entirely written, dated, and signed by the testator in their own handwriting. Unlike an ordinary will, a holographic will does not require attestation by witnesses. However, if the will is not fully handwritten by the testator, it must then adhere to the formalities prescribed for an ordinary will in order to be considered valid.

Both wills are required to be: (1) in writing, except that a holographic will is required to be written entirely in the testator's own handwriting; and (2) it must be executed in a language or dialect known to the testator.

The main consideration of a will is the intention of the testator on how they will dispose of their properties upon death. Even in the absence of dispositive provisions, a will disinheriting a

[63] Civil Code, Art 815.
[64] Civil Code, Art 819, in relation to Art 818.
[65] Civil Code, Art 795.
[66] Civil Code, Art 15.
[67] Civil Code, Art 801.
[68] Civil Code, Art 779.
[69] Civil Code, Art 783.
[70] Civil Code, Arts 804–808.
[71] Civil Code, Art 810.

compulsory heir is still a dispositive will because a disinheritance has the effect of disposing the legitime of the disinherited compulsory heir in favour of other compulsory heirs.[72]

A testator must have the testamentary capacity to execute a will. Meaning, the testator must not be expressly prohibited by law to make a will, must be at least 18 years old,[73] and must be of sound mind at the time of execution.[74] The execution of a will is a statutory grant, not a constitutional right. Hence, all the requirements laid down under the law should be complied with.

A will is a purely personal act, and it cannot be left in whole or in part to the discretion of a third person. Likewise, it cannot be accomplished through an agent or attorney. Nevertheless, there are certain matters that the testator may delegate to a third person, particularly (a) the designation of a person/institution falling under a class specified by the testator, and (b) the manner of distribution of property specified by the testator.[75] However, for this delegation to be valid, the testator must first specify the class and the amount of property for proper delegation.

It is likewise a unilateral act which does not involve an exchange of values or depend on simultaneous offer and acceptance. Further, the execution of a will is an individual act. Two or more persons cannot make a will jointly, or in the same instrument, either for their reciprocal benefit or for the benefit of a third person.[76]

A will is a free and intelligent act.[77] Its execution should not be tainted by any vices affecting the free will of the testator: if proven otherwise, it will be disallowed. Being a solemn or formal act, the law prescribes specific formalities for the execution of a will. Failure to observe these formalities may render the will void.[78]

A will can be revoked at any time before the testator's death.[79] However, once the testator dies, the will shall take effect since it is in the nature of *mortis causa*.[80]

v. Intestacy

Intestacy takes place by operation of law in default of compulsory and testamentary succession. Legal or intestate succession operates in the following situations:[81]

(a) If a person dies without a will, or with a void will, or will has subsequently lost its validity;
(b) When the will does not institute an heir;
(c) When the will does not dispose of all the property belonging to the testator. Legal succession shall take place only with respect to the property which the testator has not disposed (mixed succession);
(d) If the suspensive condition attached to the institution of the heir does not happen or is not fulfilled;
(e) If the heir dies before the testator;
(f) If the heir repudiates the inheritance, there being no substitution, and no right of accretion takes place;

[72] *Seangio v Reyes* G.R. Nos. 140371–72 (2006).
[73] Civil Code, Art 797.
[74] Civil Code, Art 798.
[75] Civil Code, Art 786.
[76] Civil Code, Art 818.
[77] Civil Code, Art 839.
[78] Civil Code, Art 839.
[79] Civil Code, Art 828.
[80] Civil Code, Art 783.
[81] Civil Code, Art 960.

(g) When the heir instituted is incapable of succeeding, except in cases provided in the Civil Code;
(h) Upon the expiration of term, or period of institution of heir;
(i) Upon fulfillment of a resolutory condition attached to the institution of heir, rendering the will ineffective;
(j) Preterition – Intestacy may be total or partial depending on whether or not there are legacies or devises;[82] and,
(k) When a testamentary disposition is impossible of compliance or is ineffective.[83]

As a general rule, only relatives by blood may inherit, up to the fifth degree of consanguinity in the collateral line (ie, the child of a first cousin). However, certain exceptions are recognised by law, allowing the surviving spouse, an adopted child, and, in cases of escheat proceedings, the state, to likewise succeed to the decedent's estate.

For transfers, Philippine law follows the *rule of preference between lines* which provides that those in the direct descending line shall exclude those in the direct ascending and collateral lines while those in the direct ascending line shall, in turn, exclude those in the collateral line. A direct line refers to the succession of degrees among ascendants and descendants. Examples of relatives within the direct line include parents, children, and grandparents. The direct line may be classified as either descending or ascending. The descending direct line connects the head of the family to those who descend from them while the ascending direct line links a person to those from whom they descend. In contrast, a collateral line is formed by a series of degrees among individuals who are neither ascendants nor descendants, but who share a common ancestor. For instance, siblings are collateral relatives, their common ancestors being their parents.

Pertinent to this is the *rule of proximity of degree* where the nearer excludes the more remote, without prejudice to the right of representation.[84] Thus, legitimate children exclude the legitimate grandchildren and great-grandchildren of the decedent. If all legitimate children are living, possess capacity to inherit, and none have been disinherited, they alone shall succeed to the estate, to the exclusion of other legitimate descendants. However, if any child is predeceased, disinherited, or incapacitated, the law allows for the right of representation, whereby the descendant of such child may step into their place and inherit in their stead.

Similarly, the *rule of equality* among relatives of the same degree provides that those of equal degree inherit in equal shares, subject to the rule that the full blood relative shall inherit double than that of the half-blood relative.

If the decedent has legitimate and illegitimate children, such children must inherit with their respective legitime first before giving the free portion pro rata (which includes the illegitimate children).

vi. Administration of Deceased's Estate

The appointment of the administrator of the estate and the manner of the administration and the rights and obligations of the administrator are governed by the Rules of Court. An administration proceeding is a proceeding for the liquidation of the estate and the distribution of the residue among the heirs. It is conducted by an administrator who is the person appointed by the court to administer the intestate estate of the decedent, through a Letter of Administration. The Letter

[82] Professor RF Balane, *Jottings and Jurisprudence in Civil Law (Succession)* (2016).
[83] DP Jurado, *Comments and Jurisprudence on Succession* (Rex Book Store, 2009).
[84] Civil Code, Art 962, para 1.

of Administration is the grant of authority to administer the intestate estate of a deceased person issued by the court to a person appointed by it, in the absence of a valid will.

If no executor is named in the will, or the executor/s are incompetent, refuse the trust, or fail to give bond, or a person dies intestate, administration shall be granted to the following: (a) to the surviving husband or wife, as the case may be, or next of kin, or both, in the discretion of the court, or to such person as such surviving husband or wife, or next of kin, requests to have appointed, if competent and willing to serve; (b) if such surviving husband or wife, as the case may be, or next of kin, or the person selected by them, be incompetent or unwilling, or if the husband or widow, or next of kin, neglects for 30 days after the death of the person to apply for administration or to request that administration be granted to some other person, it may be granted to one or more of the principal creditors, if competent and willing to serve; and, (c) if there is no such creditor competent and willing to serve, it may be granted to such other person as the court may select.

A Letter of Administration must be filed by an interested person, who would benefit by the estate, such as an heir, or one who has claim against the estate, such as a creditor. The interest must be material and direct. There is an order of preference in the appointment of an administrator which is as follows: (a) to the surviving husband or wife, as the case may be, or next of kin, or both, in the discretion of the court, or to such person as such surviving husband or wife, or next of kin, requests to have appointed, if competent and willing to serve; (b) if such surviving husband or wife, as the case may be, or next of kin, or the person selected by them, be incompetent or unwilling, or if the husband or widow, or next of kin, neglects for 30 days after the death of the person to apply for administration or to request that administration be granted to some other person, it may be granted to one or more of the principal creditors, if competent and willing to serve; and, (c) if there is no such creditor competent and willing to serve, it may be granted to such other person as the court may select.[85]

On the other hand, if the will of the deceased is proved and allowed by the court, a Letter Testamentary is issued which grants authority to administer the estate of a deceased person, issued by the court to the executor appointed in the will, provided that the executor is: (a) competent, (b) accepts the trust, and (c) gives a bond as required by the relevant rules.

An executor designated and charged by the testator in their will shall carry out the provisions thereof and, upon the allowance of the will, said person, unless they are unfit to discharge the trust as executor, takes over the administration of the estate. Not everyone can be an executor. Those who are not competent to serve as an executor or administer are disqualified such as: (a) minors, (b) non-residents of the Philippines, and, (c) in the opinion of the court, those who are unfit to execute the duties of the trust by reason of drunkenness, improvidence, or want of understanding or integrity, or by reason of conviction of an offence involving moral turpitude.

[85] Rules of Court, Rule 78, s 6.

5

Family Law

JUSTIN DJ SUCGANG AND ANTONIO A LIGON

I. Introduction

Socially and culturally, the family plays a central role in the Philippines.[1] The 1987 Constitution of the Republic of the Philippines acknowledges this centrality. The state recognises the family as the foundation of the Filipino nation,[2] and the sanctity of the family life.[3] It is a declared state policy to protect the family as a basic autonomous social institution.[4] Accordingly, the state shall strengthen the family's solidarity and actively promote its total development.[5] The state is likewise obligated to defend the following rights:[6]

(1) of spouses to found a family in accordance with their religious convictions and the demands of responsible parenthood;
(2) of children to assistance, including proper care and nutrition, and special protection from all forms of neglect, abuse, cruelty, exploitation, and other conditions prejudicial to their development;
(3) of the family to a family living wage and income; and,
(4) of families or family associations to participate in the planning and implementation of policies and programmes that affect them.

The earliest rules on family law can be traced to civil law, as a consequence of the Spanish occupation of the Philippine islands which lasted for 333 years. The 1680 *Recopilación de las Leyes de los Reynos de las Indias* (Compilation of the Laws of the Kingdom of the Indies) incorporated a 1530 royal ordinance, establishing a hierarchy of preference of the laws governing the colonies: (a) the most recent law for the colonies; (b) the Compilation; (c) the *Novisima Recopilación*; (d) the *Nueva Recopilación*; (e) the *Leyes de Toro*; (f) the royal ordinances of Castile; (g) the *Ordenamiento de Alcalá*; (h) the *Fuero Juzgo*; and (i) the *Siete Partidas*.[7] Since no provisions of a civil law in nature were found in the Compilation, application of supplementary laws was not unusual in the

[1] VA Miralao, 'The Family, Traditional Values and the Socicultural Transformation of Philippine Society' (1994) 45(1) *Philippine Sociological Review* 189–215.
[2] The 1987 Philippine Constitution ('Constitution'), Art XV, s 1.
[3] Constitution, Art II, s 12.
[4] ibid.
[5] Constitution, Art XV, s 1.
[6] Constitution, Art XV, s 3.
[7] RF Balane, *Civil Law Florilegium: Essays on the Philippine Variant of the Civil Law Tradition* (Quezon City, University of the Philippines College of Law, 2012).

Philippines.[8] For instance, the *Leyes de Toro* was applied for matters concerning children's successional rights, while the *Siete Partidas* were cited for bigamous marriage.[9] In July 1889, the *Codigo Civil* (Civil Code of Spain) was promulgated, regulating all major aspects of civil law in Spain. A week after, a royal decree was issued extending the application of the Civil Code of Spain to Cuba, Puerto Rico, and the Philippines.[10] Book I of the Civil Code of Spain refers to the law on persons, which include family relations. Being non-political in nature, the Civil Code of Spain remained effective throughout the almost five-decade American rule in the Philippines.

A year after gaining independence from the United States, President Manuel Roxas issued Executive Order (EO) No. 48 which called for the framing of a new Civil Code. In 1949, Congress enacted Republic Act (RA) No. 386 or the Civil Code of the Philippines. Scholars observed that this resembles the Civil Code of Spain so closely that they consider it as an English version.[11]

In 1987, President Corazon Aquino issued EO No. 209 which promulgated the Family Code of the Philippines. It expressly repealed almost the entire Book I of the Civil Code of the Philippines. The Family Code includes provisions on marriage; legal separation; the spouses' rights, obligations, and property relations; family members and home, paternity, filiation and adoption, support, parental authority, emancipation; and family matters, incidents, and disputes allowing summary judicial proceedings.

II. Marriage

Both the Philippine Constitution[12] and the Family Code[13] declare that marriage is the foundation of the family and an inviolable social institution. Any discussion on Philippine family law must, therefore, begin with the discussion of the institution of marriage.[14]

Article 1 of the Family Code defines marriage as a special contract of permanent union between a man and a woman entered into in accordance with law for the establishment of conjugal and family life.

While marriage is a contract, it is not just any other civil contract. As a special contract, marriage is imbued with public interest. Since the break-up of families weakens the social and moral fabric, their preservation is a concern not only of the family members alone.[15] The public is deeply interested in its maintenance.[16] This is the reason why, although a contract, the nature, consequences and incidents of marriage are governed by law and may not be subject to any stipulation by the contracting parties, with the sole exception of agreements concerning property relations.[17]

As a social institution, it is in the interest 'of each and every member of the community to prevent the bringing about of a condition that would shake its foundation and ultimately lead to its destruction.'[18] The task of protecting the institution of marriage requires vigilant and zealous

[8] ibid.
[9] ibid citing *Jayme v Gamboa* 75 Phil 479 (1945) and *Ker v Cauden* 6 Phil 732 (1906).
[10] ibid.
[11] RF Balane, 'The Spanish Roots of Philippine Law' (2018) 66(1) *Estudios de Deusto* 23–31.
[12] Constitution, Art XV, s 2.
[13] Family Code (Executive Order No 209), Art 1.
[14] Balane (n 7).
[15] *Ancheta v Ancheta* GR No 143570 (2004).
[16] *Tilar v Tilar* GR No 214529 (2017).
[17] Family Code, Art 1.
[18] *Jimenez v Cañizares* GR No L-12790 (1960).

participation of the state, via the public prosecutor or the Solicitor General.[19] According to the Philippine Supreme Court, a mere *pro forma* compliance or semblance of participation by the state in proceedings concerning marriage is insufficient. Moreover, even if the law states that the purpose of the participation of the prosecutor is to determine and prevent collusion between the parties to obtain a decree,[20] it is legitimate for the prosecutor to bring to light any circumstances that could give rise to the interference that either party will be able to obtain a decree without regard to the legal merits of the case.[21]

Marriage is not only a mere institution; it is an inviolable one. According to the Supreme Court, this inviolability is central to the traditional and religious concepts of morality in the Philippines, which provide the very bedrock on which the Filipino society finds stability. That is why the Family Code emphasises the permanent nature of marriage – it is 'immutable and when both spouses give their consent to enter it, their consent becomes irrevocable, unchanged even by their independent wills.'[22] Nonetheless, this inviolability depends upon whether the marriage exists and is valid.[23]

A. Formal Requisites

The Family Code provides for the three formal requisites of a valid marriage.[24] While the absence of any of them generally renders the marriage void *ab initio*, a mere irregularity shall not affect the validity of marriage. Nonetheless, the party or parties responsible shall be civilly, criminally or administratively liable.[25] For instance, the Revised Penal Code declares the performance of an illegal marriage ceremony by a priest, minister, or a civil authority to be criminal.[26] A local civil registrar who fails to file registrable documents presented to them for entry shall be punished.[27]

i. Valid Marriage Licence

Parties who wish to contract a valid marriage shall apply for a marriage licence with the local civil registrar of the place where either of them habitually resides,[28] by filing separately a sworn application with the information or documents required under Articles 13 to 16 of the Family Code. A notice shall be prepared by the registrar and posted for ten days outside the office. After this period, the licence shall be issued which shall be valid in any part of the Philippines for 120 days and shall be deemed automatically cancelled upon the expiration of the period.[29] If the Filipino citizens shall marry abroad, the above duties of the civil registrar shall be performed by the consul-general, consul, or vice-consul of the Republic of the Philippines.

If one or both parties are citizens of a foreign country, they shall be required to produce a certificate of legal capacity to contract marriage, issued by their diplomatic or consular officials. An affidavit showing such capacity shall suffice if either is a stateless person or a refugee.[30]

[19] *Malcampo-Sin v Sin* GR No 137590 (2001).
[20] Family Code, Arts 48 and 60. Notably, these provisions were adopted from Civil Code (RA No 386), Art 101.
[21] *Brown v Yambao* GR No L-10699 (1957).
[22] *Malcampo-Sin v Sin* GR No 137590 (2001).
[23] ibid.
[24] Family Code, Art 3.
[25] Family Code, Art 4, paras 1 and 3.
[26] Revised Penal Code (Act No 3815), Art 352.
[27] Act No 3753, ss 12 and 18.
[28] Family Code, Art 9.
[29] Family Code, Art 20.
[30] Family Code, Art 21.

The lack or absence of a marriage licence renders the marriage void *ab initio*,[31] which may be proven by a certificate issued by the civil registrar that the document does not exist notwithstanding diligent search.[32] But the issuance of a marriage licence in a place that is not the residence of either of the contracting parties, or despite the absence of publication or prior to the completion of the ten-day period for publication, are considered mere irregularities that do not affect the validity of the marriage.[33]

Nonetheless, the Family Code considers a marriage valid despite the absence of a marriage licence in the following circumstances:

(a) Marriages in *articulo mortis* (when either or both contracting parties are at the point of death), even if the ailing party subsequently survives;[34]
(b) Marriages solemnised in a remote location, when there is no means of transportation to enable a party to appear personally before the local civil registrar;[35]
(c) Marriages celebrated among members of the same ethnic cultural community, provided they are solemnised according to their customs;[36] and
(d) Marriages solemnised after a five-year exclusive cohabitation between parties who carry no legal impediment to marry each other.[37] This period should be characterised by a perfect union, valid under the law but rendered imperfect only by the lack of a marriage contract.[38]

ii. Authority of Solemnising Officer

The Family Code[39] and the Local Government Code authorises the following individuals to solemnise marriages:

(a) Incumbent members of the judiciary. However, the marriage must be performed within the court's territorial jurisdiction. Otherwise, while the marriage may be valid, the judge may be held liable;[40]
(b) Municipal or city mayors, within their territorial jurisdiction;[41]
(c) Consuls-general, consuls, or vice-consuls of the Republic of the Philippines, if the parties are Filipino citizens and the marriage is celebrated abroad;[42] and,
(d) Priests, rabbis, imams, or ministers of any religious sect. They, however, must be duly authorised by their respective congregation and must act within the limits of such authority, and be registered with the civil registrar general. While Article 7 of the Family Code states that at least one of the contracting parties must belong to the congregation of the officiant, the formal requisite pertains to the authority. Hence, the fact that one or both of the contracting parties are not members of the congregation is a mere irregularity.

[31] Family Code, Art 4, para 1.
[32] *Kho v Republic of the Philippines* GR No 187462 (2016).
[33] *Alcantara v Alcantara* GR No 167746 (2007).
[34] Family Code, Art 27.
[35] Family Code, Art 28.
[36] Family Code, Art 33.
[37] Family Code, Art 33.
[38] *Niñal v Bayadog* GR No 133778 (2000).
[39] Family Code, Art 7.
[40] *Arañes v Judge Occiano* AM No MTJ-02-1390 (2002).
[41] Local Government Code (RA No 7160), ss 444(b)(1)(xviii) and 455 (b)(1)(xviii).
[42] Family Code, Art 10.

In case of marriages in *articulo mortis*, a ship captain, airplane pilot, and a commissioned military commander of a unit to which a chaplain is assigned, are likewise authorised to solemnise a marriage. If performed by a ship captain or airplane pilot, the marriage must be between passengers or crew members during the voyage or event during stopovers at ports of call.[43] If performed by a military commander, the marriage must be between persons within the zone of military operation, whether civilians or members of the armed forces.[44]

Although the lack or absence of legal authority renders the marriage void *ab initio*,[45] the good faith of one or both contracting parties that the officiant had the authority to solemnise the marriage between them makes the marriage perfectly legal under statutory law[46] and case law.[47]

iii. Marriage Ceremony

The Family Code does not prescribe a specific form or ceremony for a marriage to be valid. It is enough that the contracting parties appear personally before the solemnising officer, and freely declare that they take each other as husband and wife.[48] While the mere signing of the marriage contract without the presence of the solemnising officer does not satisfy this requisite factor,[49] the absence of witnesses is only an irregularity.

Any marriage celebrated abroad by Filipino citizens shall be considered valid in the Philippines as long as such foreign marriage is in accordance with the law in force in the country, and is considered valid in that country.[50] In this regard, the doctrine of processual presumption may come into play.[51] However, since the Philippines subscribe to the nationality principle, any marriage, although formally valid abroad, may still be considered void under Philippine law if it is considered void in the Philippines.[52] Hence, see the exceptions found in the first paragraph of Article 26 of the Family Code.

B. Essential Requisites

The Family Code provides for the two essential requisites of a valid marriage.[53] While the absence of any of them generally renders the marriage void *ab initio*, a defect in either of them shall only render the marriage voidable.[54]

i. Capacity

Legal capacity refers to the power to enter into a valid marriage. Two forms of impediments are provided in the Family Code: (a) absolute disqualification; and, (b) relative disqualification. The

[43] Family Code, Art 31.
[44] Family Code, Art 32.
[45] Family Code, Art 4, para 1.
[46] Family Code, Art 35(2).
[47] *Tenchavez v Escaño* GR No L-19671 (1965).
[48] Family Code, Art 6.
[49] *Morigo v People of the Philippines* GR No 145226 (2004).
[50] Family Code, Art 26, para 1 in relation to Civil Code, Art 17, para 1.
[51] *Yao Kee v Sy-Gonzales* GR No L-55960 (1988).
[52] Civil Code, Art 15.
[53] Family Code, Art 2.
[54] Family Code, Art 4, paras 1 and 2.

former pertains to the sex and age requirements, while the latter is due to the civil or natural relationship of the parties.

For a marriage to be valid, difference in the sex of the contracting parties is clearly required in the definition of marriage under Article 1, *that is*, a special contract of permanent union between a man and a woman. So, too, in the definition of the essential requisites under Articles 2 and 5 – legal capacity of the contracting parties who must be a male and female, and any male or female aged 18 years or more not under any impediments. A person's sex is an essential factor in marriage and family relations.[55] Sex, however, is the one assigned at birth and that which conforms to the person's biological composition. Hence, no legal change in sex may be permitted simply by undergoing sex reassignment surgery.[56] But an intersex person, when medically diagnosed with congenital adrenal hyperplasia, and when no unnatural steps were undertaken to interfere with what one is born with, may be allowed to determine his sex and have the entry in the birth certificate corrected.[57]

Any person of at least 18 years of age may validly contract marriage,[58] otherwise, the marriage shall be void even if the parents or guardians consented.[59] If either of the contracting parties is below 21 years, parental consent shall be required and must be submitted when applying for a marriage licence.[60] The absence of parental consent may be a ground for annulling a marriage, unless after attaining the age of 21, the party freely cohabited with the other and they both lived together as husband and wife.[61] When either of the contracting parties is between 21 and 25 years, they shall be obliged to ask for parental advice,[62] however the absence of this shall not affect the validity of the marriage.

The relative disqualifications provided under the Family Code are the following:

(1) those considered incestuous, when the marriage is between ascendants and descendants, or brothers and sisters;[63]
(2) an offence against public policy, such as a marriage between step-parents and step-children, adopter and adopted, or collateral blood relatives up to fourth civil degree;[64]
(3) bigamous or polygamous marriage;[65]
(4) commission of a crime, specifically killing one's spouse or the other person's spouse in order to marry the other;[66]
(5) psychological incapacity, which causes a party to be truly without knowledge of the basic marital covenants that concomitantly must be assumed and discharged by the parties to the marriage;[67]
(6) physical incapacity to consummate the marriage, or sexual impotence which must be permanent and appears to be incurable;[68] and,
(7) affliction of a serious sexually-transmissible disease, which appears to be incurable.[69]

[55] *Silverio v Republic of the Philippines* GR No 174689 (2007).
[56] *Republic of the Philippines v Cagandahan* GR No 166676 (2008).
[57] ibid.
[58] Family Code, Art 5.
[59] Family Code, Art 35(1).
[60] Family Code, Art 14.
[61] Family Code, Art 45(1).
[62] Family Code, Art 15.
[63] Family Code, Art 37.
[64] Family Code, Art 38.
[65] Family Code, Art 35(4).
[66] Family Code, Art 38(9).
[67] Family Code, Art 36; *Santos v Court of Appeals* GR No 112019 (1995); *Tan-Andal v Andal* GR No 193659 (2021).
[68] Family Code, Art 45(5).
[69] Family Code, Art 45(6).

The first five disqualifications render the marriage void from the beginning, while the latter two may render the marriage voidable or annullable. However, it must be noted that a marriage may only be declared void *ab initio* based on psychological incapacity if the impediment had already existed at the time of the marriage ceremony.

ii. Consent

Marriage, although special in nature, is a contract. The requisite of consent is the same as in any other contract. It must be intelligent; hence, consent cannot be given through mistake as to the identity,[70] or during a state of insanity,[71] of either party. It must be free, not secured through force, intimidation or undue influence.[72] It must also be spontaneous. Therefore, the presence of fraud, the exclusive grounds of which have been provided, vitiates consent.[73] Moreover, it is a crime for a contracting party to secure the consent of the other by means of violence, intimidation or fraud.[74]

C. Polygamous Marriages

Marriage in the Philippines is only between *a* man and *a* woman.[75] At any given moment, one person can only be validly married to another. Bigamy and polygamy are proscribed under statutory laws. Under the Family Code, bigamous marriages are considered void *ab initio*,[76] and bigamy is a crime under the Revised Penal Code.[77] Furthermore, notwithstanding the fact that the previous marriage is void from the beginning, contracting a subsequent marriage without a final judgment declaring the nullity of the former marriage is also considered void and bigamous.[78]

Nonetheless, there are instances where bigamy in fact appears to be permitted. First, in case of a reappearing prior spouse under Articles 41 and 42 of the Family Code. The law allows a present spouse, who has a well-founded belief that the prior spouse was already dead, to contract marriage with another during the subsistence of the previous marriage after instituting a summary proceeding for the declaration of presumptive death of the prior spouse who became absent. If the absentee reappears, the subsequent marriage shall automatically be terminated by the recording of an affidavit of reappearance of the absent spouse. However, if the reappearing spouse undertook no legal steps, either by the filing of such affidavit or other court action, such reappearance will not terminate the subsequent marriage. By legal fiction, the reappearing spouse is deemed an absentee married to the present spouse. The subsequent marriage continues to be valid.

Second, a Muslim male can have up to four wives if and only if he can deal with them with equal companionship and just treatment as enjoined by Islamic law.[79] Nevertheless, even if the male is Muslim at the time of the celebration of the marriage, the Family Code shall apply if the

[70] Family Code, Art 35(5).
[71] Family Code, Art 45(2).
[72] Family Code, Art 45(4).
[73] Family Code, Arts 45(3) and 46.
[74] Revised Penal Code, Art 350.
[75] Family Code, Arts 1 and 2(1).
[76] Family Code, Arts 35(4) and 41.
[77] Revised Penal Code, Art 349.
[78] *Wiegel v Sempio-Dy* GR No L-53703 (1986), which was adopted by Family Code, Art 40.
[79] Code of Muslim Personal Laws of the Philippines (PD No 1083), Art 27.

marriage is not solemnised in accordance with Islamic law or the Code of Muslim Personal Laws (Muslim Code).[80] In fact, the Supreme Court recently held that converting to Islam and contracting another marriage despite a subsisting prior marriage is a crime of bigamy. The Muslim Code requires a formal process such as securing the consent of the prior wife or wives or, in case of objection, the permission of the *Shari'a* Circuit Court.[81]

D. Same Sex Marriages and Civil Unions

Marriage in the Philippines can only be contracted by a *man* and a *woman*.[82] In fact, the Supreme Court observed that this definition serves as the foundation of many other gendered provisions of the Family Code and other laws.[83] It is to be noted that the definition is only statutory, not constitutional. The Philippine Constitution does not provide a definition of marriage, but only a description of its role and function in the society.[84]

While the Supreme Court appears to be sympathetic to the advocates of same-sex marriage, it nevertheless dismissed a case challenging the constitutionality of Articles 1 and 2 of the Family Code for violating the rights to equal protection, due process, and privacy.[85] However, it limited the holding to the lack of an actual controversy; no actual application for a marriage licence was submitted by the petitioner to the local civil registrar. Regarding the absence of legal standing: mere open and self-identification as homosexual, having a stake in the outcome of the case, and the law's normative impact, do not sufficiently clothe the petitioner with the requisite standing.

Nonetheless, in the absence of a comprehensive national law, major cities and municipalities have already passed local ordinances providing protection for members of the lesbian, gay, bisexual and transgender community against some forms of discrimination.[86] Bills were also filed in the Philippine Senate and House of Representatives recognising civil unions[87] or partnerships.[88]

E. Recognition of Same Sex Marriages Contracted Abroad

Possible recognition issues may arise if Filipino citizens who carry dual citizenship engage in a same-sex marriage in a country where such union is allowed. It may also be a concern if a Filipino marries a foreigner of the same gender in a country which allows same-sex unions. Article 15 of the Civil Code provides that laws relating to family rights and duties, or to the status, condition and legal capacity of persons are binding upon citizens of the Philippines, even those living abroad.[89] However, it is stated in the Philippine jurisdiction under Article 26 of the Family Code that:

> All marriages solemnized outside the Philippines in accordance with the laws in force in the country where they were solemnized, and valid there as such, shall also be valid in this country, except those prohibited under Articles 35(1), (4), (5) and (6), 36, 37 and 38.

[80] *Nollora v People of the Philippines* GR No 191425 (2011).
[81] *Malaki v People of the Philippines* GR No 221075 (2021).
[82] Family Code, Arts 1 and 2(1).
[83] *Falcis v Civil Registrar General* GR No 217910 (2019).
[84] Constitution, Art XV, s 2.
[85] *Falcis v Civil Registrar General* GR No 217910 (2019).
[86] ibid.
[87] Senate Bill No 449 (2022).
[88] House Bill No 1015 (2022).
[89] Civil Code, Art 15.

These articles cited under Article 26 are the void marriages by reason of 'those contracted by any party below eighteen years of age even with the consent of parents or guardians';[90] those bigamous or polygamous marriages not failing under Article 41';[91] 'those contracted through mistake of one contracting party as to the identity of the other';[92] 'and those subsequent marriages that are void under Article 53'.[93] Article 36 addresses psychological incapacity, while Articles 37 and 38 cover incestuous marriages and those void due to public policy.

While none of the enumerated causes in Article 26 explicitly ban same-sex marriage, it must be noted that the prohibition against same-sex marriage in the Philippines is not couched in negative terms. It is understood that the definition of marriage is a union between a man and a woman, as explicitly stated in Article 1 of the Family Code. It took effect in 1988, when same-sex unions were still widely considered as culturally unacceptable even in present-day progressive countries. There was therefore no need to explicitly prohibit same-sex unions in express negative terms since to do so in the 1980s would be linguistically and legally superfluous.

Same sex marriage, while valid abroad particularly where the law of such country recognised the same, cannot qualify as valid marriage in the Philippines because the source of marriage law, the Family Code, does not provide for same sex marriage. Primarily, the definition of marriage, which is not an ordinary contract, is between 'man and woman' as specified in Article 1 of the Family Code and reiterated as between 'male and female' in Article 2 of the Family Code. These Articles leave no doubt that marriage should be between members of the opposite sex. Hence, by reason of public policy and consistent with the terminologies used in the Family Code, same sex marriage between Filipinos contracted abroad cannot be considered as valid despite the recognition of the laws on marriage of the country where the marriage was contracted under Article 26 of the Family Code. The non-recognition of same sex marriage between Filipinos, whether in the Philippines or abroad, is also supported under private international law.

Legal luminary and former Senate President Jovita Salonga, as cited in a Department of Justice (DOJ) opinion, mentioned that: 'In private international law, there is universal recognition of the proposition that the legal position of an individual should normally be determined by the law of the state with which s/he is connected to in a permanent way, instead of the divergent laws of states in which he or she may be physically present, to act or engage in various transactions. This proposition includes two parts: (a) that a person is attributed certain legal characteristics of a comparatively permanent character; and (b) that these permanent characteristics should be determined by one law for all purposes rather than on a case-to-case basis by different laws.'[94] There is no extant ruling of the Supreme Court on the validity of same sex marriage. In fact, on 6 January 2020, the Philippines' Supreme Court announced that it had dismissed a motion to reconsider its September 2019 ruling in *Falcis v Civil Registrar General*, denying a petition to approve same-sex marriage in the country, effectively concluding this case 'with finality.'[95] The case of *Falcis v Civil Regsirar General*[96] involved a petition to declare the aforementioned articles

[90] Family Code, Art 35(1).
[91] Family Code, Art 35(4).
[92] Family Code, Art 35(5).
[93] Family Code, Art35(6).
[94] J Salonga, *Private International Law* (Rex Book Store, 1995) 153 as cited in JE Malaya and ACR Iglesias, 'Recognizing The Effects of Same Sex Marriage: An Examination of DOJ Opinion No. 11, Series of 2019 On The Issuance of 9(E-1) Visas to Same Sex Spouses of Foreign Diplomats', law.upd.edu.ph/wp-content/uploads/2021/11/Recognizing-the-Effect s-of-Same-Sex-Marriages.pdf.
[95] www.loc.gov/item/global-legal-monitor/2020-01-24/philippines-supreme-court-rules-on-same-sex-marriage/.
[96] *Falcis v Civil Registrar General* GR No 217910 (2019).

of the Family Code unconstitutional in order to allow Filipinos to contract same-sex marriage in the Philippines. However, it did not involve a situation wherein a Filipino enters a same-sex union abroad based on the local laws of the country where the marriage was solemnised. It was dismissed primarily on procedural grounds.

Eventually, Filipino magistrates and lawmakers have to deal with the reality that same-sex unions are now allowed in many countries which host millions of overseas Filipinos. Policy decisions have to be made on whether it is necessary to introduce legislation to address same-sex unions contracted abroad on matters such as marital property regimes, purchase of real estate in the Philippines, the determination of compulsory heirs in succession, inter-country and local adoption, and the designation of a spouse as a beneficiary in both state-run and private insurance systems.

F. Same Sex Couples and Foreign Adoption

Under the Inter-Country Adoption Act[97] and the more recent Domestic Administrative Adoption and Alternative Child Care Act of 2022,[98] adoption in the Philippines is open only to legal spouses, which in the Philippines may only be a man and woman, or to individuals who qualify as adopters. The statutes do not contemplate adoption by same-sex couples. Hence, even if a same-sex couple validly adopts a child under foreign law, such adoption may not produce the full effects of legitimate filiation in the Philippines. The adoptive child's status as a 'legitimate child' of the adoptive parents may be denied recognition, particularly in respect of parental authority[99] and compulsory succession.[100]

This non-recognition, however, does not leave the child without rights.[101] Philippine courts, applying the doctrine of comity[102] and the best interests of the child, may still acknowledge the legal parent-child relationship for limited purposes, such as custody[103] and support. Yet, in the absence of explicit legislative reform, recognition for purposes of succession and parental authority remains uncertain.

III. Matrimonial Cause

A. Divorce, Nullity, and Separation

i. Permanence of Marriage

Marriage, as an inviolable social institution, is a contract of permanent union. When the contracting parties expressed their consent, such consent becomes immutable and irrevocable.[104] The Philippines, therefore, joins the Vatican City as the only states that prohibit divorce. However, to say that divorce is absolutely prohibited in the Philippines is inaccurate.

[97] Inter-Country Adoption Act (RA 8043).
[98] Domestic Administrative Adoption and Alternative Child Care Act of 2022 (RA 11642).
[99] Family Code, Art 189.
[100] Family Code, Art 190.
[101] 1987 Constitution, Art XV, s 3(2).
[102] Rules of Court, Rule 39, s 48.
[103] Family Code, Art 213. j.
[104] *Malcampo-Sin v Sin* GR No 137590 (2001).

First, divorce is allowed among Muslim Filipinos. In fact, Article 45 of the Muslim Code allows seven forms of divorce:

(1) repudiation of the wife by the husband (*talaq*);
(2) vow of continence by the husband (*ila*);
(3) injurious assimilation of the wife by the husband (*zihar*);
(4) acts of imprecation (*li'an*);
(5) redemption by the wife (*khul'*);
(6) exercise by the wife of the delegated right to repudiate (*tafwid*); or
(7) judicial decree (*faskh*).

Second, a divorce decree obtained abroad may be recognised under Philippine laws. The second paragraph of Article 26 of the Family Code states that: 'Where a marriage between a Filipino citizen and a foreigner is validly celebrated and a divorce is thereafter validly obtained abroad by the alien spouse capacitating him or her to remarry, the Filipino spouse shall have capacity to remarry under Philippine law.'

The rule encapsulated therein has been subject to a long line of interpretation and reinterpretation. Originally, the following requisites must be present for a foreign divorce decree to be recognised in the Philippines: (a) a valid marriage between a Filipino and a foreigner; and (b) a foreigner obtained a valid divorce abroad. Hence, Philippine courts are prohibited from recognising a divorce decree if the Filipino travelled abroad for the sole purpose of obtaining such divorce.[105] The rule holds true even if the person who obtained the divorce subsequently became a foreign national, but at the time the decree was issued the person was still a Filipino.[106] The rule was gradually relaxed by the Supreme Court in *Van Dorn v Judge Romillo*. Since by virtue of the nationality principle only Filipino nationals are covered by the policy against absolute divorces, it would be unjust for them to still be considered as married to a foreigner who, in obtaining a divorce decree, becomes capacitated to remarry. Filipino citizens should not be discriminated using Philippine law in their very country.[107] The rule was further relaxed: *Van Dorn* will apply if a Filipino became a foreign national at the time of the divorce.[108] The reckoning point is the citizenship of the parties at the time of the issuance of the divorce decree that capacitate the alien spouse to remarry, not their citizenship at the time of the celebration of the marriage.[109]

In *Republic of the Philippines v Manalo* (2018), the Supreme Court presented a more liberal reading of the provision: 'Based on a clear and plain reading of the provision, it only requires that there be a divorce validly obtained abroad. The letter of the law does not demand that the alien spouse should be the one who initiated the proceeding wherein the divorce decree was granted. It does not distinguish whether the Filipino spouse is the petitioner or the respondent in the foreign divorce proceeding.'[110] Even if the foreign divorce decree was obtained jointly, by mutual agreement of the foreigner and Filipino spouse, Philippine courts may recognise such decree.[111] Nonetheless, Philippine courts may only recognise a foreign divorce decree only upon filing of a petition for such recognition, and proof of the existence of such decree and whether the same was obtained in accordance with applicable foreign law.[112] Just recently, the Supreme Court in

[105] *Gorayeb v Hashim* GR No L-25577 (1927).
[106] *Tenchavez v Escaño* GR No L-19671 (1965).
[107] *Van Dorn v Judge Romillo* GR No L-68470 (1985).
[108] *Quita v Court of Appeals* GR No 154380 (2005).
[109] *Republic of the Philippines v Orbecido* GR No L-68470 (1985).
[110] *Republic of the Philippines v Manalo* GR No 221029 (2018).
[111] *Galapon v Republic of the Philippines* GR No 243722 (2020). (AM No 11-3-6-SC).
[112] *Republic of the Philippines v Kikuchi* GR No 243646 (2022).

Republic of the Philippines v Ng (2024) ruled that foreign divorce decrees resulting from administrative process or by mutual consent may be recognised.[113] A legal or judicial proceeding is not required.

Notably, the permanence and inviolability of marriage depend on whether it exists and is valid.[114] If the marriage is inexistent or illegal for being void,[115] or defective for being voidable,[116] then such may be dissolved through a declaration of nullity or decree of annulment, respectively.

A marriage is void when any of the essential or formal requisites is absent, when contracted through the mistake of one contracting party as to the identity of the other, when incestuous, when it violates public policy, when either party is psychologically incapacitated, when bigamous, or where there was failure to comply with the requirement to record certain information in the appropriate registries. While a void contract generally produces no legal effect, a void marriage has the following consequences, among others: (a) children conceived or born before a declaration of nullity under Articles 36 or 53 of the Family Code are considered legitimate, while the rest are illegitimate; (b) the property relation shall be dissolved, with the spouse in bad faith disqualified from inheriting from the innocent spouse and forfeiting the net profits in favour of certain individuals, and any donations by reason of marriage given to such spouse shall be revoked by operation of law; (c) the family home shall be adjudicated to the spouse with whom the majority of the common children choose to remain; and, (d) the wife must revert to her birth name or that which she used prior to the marriage.[117]

A marriage is voidable when the consent given is defective, such as when no parental consent was given if the age of either of the contracting parties is between 18 and 21 years, or either party was of unsound mind, or when the consent was obtained by fraud, force, intimidation or undue influence, or when either party was impotent or is afflicted with a serious sexually-transmissible disease. The defect may still be cured through ratification or convalidation, usually in the form of free cohabitation after the ground disappeared or ceased to exist.[118] Being binding unless annulled within a certain period,[119] a voidable marriage shall have the following consequences: (a) children born or conceived before the decree of annulment are considered legitimate; (b) the wife may choose to continue employing her former husband's surname, unless she is the guilty spouse, or a court decrees otherwise, or she or her former husband has married another person;[120] and, (c) generally, the effects of a void marriage with respect to the properties and family home.

ii. Extent of Permanence

Parties who contract a valid marriage have certain marital obligations. As such, the husband and wife are obliged to live together, observe mutual love, respect and fidelity, and render mutual help and support.[121]

The permanence of a valid marriage extends only to the matrimonial bond, not the performance of the marital obligations. It is true that a matrimonial bond may not be severed if the marriage was validly contracted. It is equally true that neglect or failure to comply with the

[113] *Republic of the Philippines v Ng* GR No 249238 (2024).
[114] *Malcampo-Sin v Sin* GR No 137590 (2001).
[115] Family Code, Arts 35–38, 40–41, 53.
[116] Family Code, Arts 45–46.
[117] *Yasin v The Honorable Judge Shari'a District Court Third Shari'a Judicial District* GR No 94986 (1995).
[118] Family Code, Art 45.
[119] Family Code, Art 47.
[120] Civil Code, Art 371.
[121] Family Code, Art 68.

essential marital obligations may result in penalties. However, it does not permit Philippine courts to compel contracting parties to perform these obligations, such as continued cohabitation.[122] Philippine law, therefore, admits separation of spouses; but either of them remains prohibited from remarrying.

Without filing any action with the court, spouses may separate in fact or abandon one another. There is a *prima facie* case of abandonment when a spouse left the conjugal dwelling for a period of three months or has failed within the same period to give any information as to his or her whereabouts.[123] In such cases, Articles 100, 101, 127, 128 and 239 of the Family Code penalise the abandoning spouse and empower the present spouse to perform certain actions, such as the withholding of support, or filing of a petition for receivership, judicial separation of property, administration of the specific separate property of the abandoning spouse or sole administration of the community property.

An innocent spouse may file for an action for legal separation entitling him or her to live separately and to the custody of the children, and disqualifying the guilty spouse from any inheritance by intestate succession.[124] The following are the grounds for legal separation:[125]

(1) repeated physical violence or grossly abusive conduct directed against the petitioner, a common child, or a child of the petitioner;
(2) physical violence or moral pressure to compel change in religious or political affiliation;
(3) attempt of respondent to corrupt or induce the petitioner, a common child, or a child of the petitioner, to engage in prostitution, or connivance in such corruption or inducement;
(4) final judgment sentencing the respondent to imprisonment of more than six years, even if pardoned;
(5) drug addiction or habitual alcoholism
(6) lesbianism or homosexuality;
(7) contracting a subsequent bigamous marriage, whether in the Philippines or abroad;
(8) sexual infidelity or perversion;
(9) attempt by the respondent against the life of the petitioner; or
(10) abandonment without justifiable cause for more than one year.

Some of the above grounds may also be separately penalised as a crime under the Anti-Violence Against Women and their Children Act (RA No 9262) and the Special Protection of Children Against Abuse, Exploitation and Discrimination Act (RA No 7610).

An action for legal separation must be filed within five years of the time of the occurrence of the ground, and cannot be tried until after a mandatory cooling-off period of six months where the court must take steps to reconcile the spouses. A decree of legal separation may only be issued when a court is fully satisfied that reconciliation is highly improbable.[126]

B. Absence and Presumption of Death

The Family Code did not totally repeal the Civil Code with respect to the rules on absence and presumptive death. What the former did was to introduce an exception for purposes of remarriage.

[122] *Arroyo v Vasquez de Arroyo* GR No L-17014 (1921).
[123] Family Code, Art 101.
[124] Family Code, Art 64.
[125] Family Code, Art 55.
[126] Family Code, Arts 57–59.

The following rules govern the various reliefs for absence, which is a special legal status of persons not in their domicile, and their whereabouts being unknown:[127]

i. Provisional Declaration

Articles 381–383 of the Civil Code provide for the requisites for a judge to declare provisional absence: (a) absence for a considerable period; (b) a specific urgent matter necessitating immediate representation; and, (c) the absentee left no agent or the agency has expired. The declaration, which may be at the instance of any interested party, a relative, or even a friend, shall indicate specific purpose and powers which a representative may undertake on behalf of the absentee, including the necessary measures to safeguard the absentee's rights and interest. The judge may appoint any competent person as a representative, unless the absentee has left a spouse who is not legally separated from the absentee.

Note that in the Family Code, abandonment is *prima facie* presumed when a spouse left the conjugal dwelling for a period of three months or has failed to give any information as to his or her whereabouts within the same period. The present spouse shall be authorised to perform certain actions.

ii. Declaration

When an absentee left a property requiring administration, a declaration of absence may be obtained only at the instance of the persons enumerated in the exclusive list under Article 385 of the Civil Code. The petition may only be filed after two years or, if the person left an agent, after five years from the date of disappearance. If there was news about the absentee, the applicable period shall be reckoned from the time the absentee was referred to in the most recent news. As in provisional absence, the court may appoint any competent person to represent the absentee unless a present spouse is left. However, such spouse cannot alienate or encumber the properties being administered without judicial authority.[128]

iii. Presumption of Death

Articles 390 and 391 of the Civil Code provide for the periods when a person may be presumed dead for certain purposes, depending on the age of the absentee and the circumstances that may have attended prior to the absence.

Ordinarily, a person shall be presumed dead after an absence of seven years. This presumption is applicable for all purposes, except succession and remarriage. For purposes of succession, if the absentee at the time of disappearance is 75 years or below, he or she shall be presumed dead after an absence of ten years. But if older than 75 years, an absence of five years shall suffice. However, for purposes of remarriage, Article 41 of the Family Code requires only four years.

In case of disappearance where there is danger of death under Article 392, such as when a person was on board a vessel lost during a sea voyage or a missing airplane, a person in the armed forces who has taken part in war, or a person who has been in danger of death under other circumstances and his or her existence is not known, the person shall be presumed dead for all

[127] Civil Code, Art 381.
[128] Civil Code, Art 388.

purposes, except for remarriage, after an absence of four years. The Family Code requires only two years for purposes of remarriage based on the aforementioned circumstances.

While the periods provided under the Family Code are shorter, a summary proceeding for the declaration of presumptive death must be instituted. On the other hand, under the Civil Code, no court declaration is required; the mere running of the period triggers the presumption.

C. Financial Relief

If the marriage is dissolved either by a declaration of nullity or decree of annulment, the rights and obligations between spouses are likewise terminated. This includes the duty to render mutual support. Support comprises everything indispensable for sustenance, dwelling, clothing, medical attendance, education and transportation, in keeping with the financial capacity of the family.[129] But the spouse in bad faith shall: (a) forfeit net profits in the community or conjugal properties in favour of the common children or, if none, his or her other children, or when there are none, the innocent spouse; (b) any donation *propter nuptias* given to the spouse in bad faith is automatically revoked; and, (c) he or she shall be disqualified to inherit from the innocent spouse.[130]

If the marriage was validly celebrated, divorce is not permitted. This means that the essential marital obligations, including mutual support, are not terminated unless there are grounds for legal separation.

If the parties are legally separated, the above consequences of a void or voidable marriage shall ensue. However, the court may order the guilty spouse to provide continued support to the innocent spouse.[131]

Nonetheless, regardless of the status of the marriage, whether valid, dissolved or legally separated, children must be supported at all times. This duty includes an unborn child.[132] Notably, the right to receive educational support extends even beyond the age of majority.[133] Furthermore, the Revised Penal Code considers a crime the indifference of parents, as when parents who neglect their children by not giving them the education which their station in life requires and financial conditions permit.[134]

When a husband fails to give legal support to his wife or their children, he may be criminally charged for committing psychological or economic abuse, pursuant to the Anti-Violence Against Women and their Children Act. The Supreme Court, however, clarified that it should not be mere failure but a deliberate one.[135]

IV. Unions without Marriage

The Family Code does not recognise the concept of common-law marriage but it acknowledges the circumstance where persons live together without the benefit of a valid marriage. Nonetheless,

[129] Family Code, Art 194, para 1.
[130] Family Code, Arts 50 and 43.
[131] Family Code, Art 198.
[132] *Quimiging v Icao* GR No26795 (1970).
[133] Family Code, Art 194, para 2.
[134] Revised Penal Code, Art 277, para 2.
[135] *Calingasan v People of the Philippines* GR No 239313 (2022).

a distinction must first be made whether either party is incapacitated to marry and whether the parties are cohabiting exclusively.

If the parties, a man and woman, are unmarried but do not suffer from any legal impediment to marry one another and are cohabiting exclusively, the Family Code applies the regime of special co-ownership.[136] Here, the parties' salaries and wages as well as the properties acquired by them through their work or industry are co-owned by them. All properties acquired while the parties are cohabiting are presumed to have been obtained by their joint effort and owned by them in equal shares. Properties purchased during the cohabitation, even by way of installment, are covered; although the equal share thereto shall pertain only to the paid portion.[137] Nonetheless, either party shall be deemed to have made a joint contribution in the acquisition of properties, even in the absence of actual participation, if such person exerted efforts toward the care and maintenance of the family and the household.

On the other hand, if a man and woman, when one or both of them are incapacitated, are living together but not exclusively, the rule on limited co-ownership applies.[138] The Family Code provides that only the properties acquired by them through their actual joint contribution of money, property, or industry shall be included. The benefit given to homemakers is not available.[139]

V. Children

Republic Act No. 6809 amended Article 4 of the Family Code and lowered the age of majority from 21 to 18 years. Upon attainment of this age, the person becomes qualified for all acts of civil life, except for the restrictions and limitations provided by law.

A. Filiation

i. Legitimate

A legitimate child is a product of, and, therefore requires, a valid and subsisting marriage. Without a lawful marriage, there can be no legitimate filiation between parents and child.[140] Nonetheless, the Family Code does not strictly require that the child be conceived *and* born during a valid marriage, for it considers other forms of legitimate filiation when:

(1) conceived or born during a valid marriage (Art 164, para 1);
(2) conceived prior to the automatic termination of a subsequent marriage upon the filing of an affidavit of reappearance of the absentee (Art 43);
(3) conceived or born before the decree of annulment (Art 54);
(4) conceived or born before the declaration of nullity due to psychological incapacity or failure to comply with the requirement to record certain information in the appropriate registries (Art 54);
(5) conceived by artificial insemination of the wife with the sperm of the husband or a donor, provided that the husband and wife both authorised or ratified the act (Art 164, para 2);

[136] Family Code, Art 147.
[137] *Paterno v Paterno* GR No 213687 (2020).
[138] Family Code, Art 148.
[139] *Tumlos v Spouses Fernandez* GR No 137650 (2000).
[140] *Continental Steel Manufacturing Corporation v Montano*, GR No 182836 (2009).

(6) born to a mother convicted of adultery (Art 167);
(7) legitimated (Art 179); and,
(8) legally adopted.

Legitimation takes place by the subsequent valid marriage between the parents of a child conceived *and* born outside of wedlock. The parents must, at the time of the child's conception, not be disqualified by any impediment to marry each other, except if such impediment pertains only to being underaged.[141]

All the above forms of legitimate filiation are by nature. The law also recognises legitimate filiation by legal fiction or through adoption. Adoption refers to the socio-legal process of providing a permanent family to a child whose parents had voluntarily or involuntarily given up their parental rights, permanently transferring all rights and responsibilities, along with filiation, making the child a legitimate child of the adoptive parents.[142] Previously, domestic adoption requires a judicial decree. But with the recent enactment of the Domestic Administrative Adoption and Alternative Child Care Act in 2022, petitions for domestic adoption shall be adjudicated by the National Authority for Child Care. Notably, if the prospective adopters are spouses, they should adopt jointly, unless they are legally separated, or one of them seeks to adopt the legitimate child of the other, or his own illegitimate child as long as the other consented.[143]

All legitimate children have the following right:

(1) To bear the surnames of the father. In a recent case, the Supreme Court allowed the use of the surname of the mother since Article 364 of the Civil Code merely states that legitimate children shall *principally* use the surname of the father.[144] However, the law does not allow a legitimate child to use the surname of the mother's new husband or the step-father as confusion might arise as to the correct parentage;[145]
(2) To receive support from their parents, ascendants, and even brothers and sisters;[146]
(3) To be entitled to the legitime and other successional rights;[147]
(4) To be under the joint parental authority of their father and mother;[148] and,
(5) To prove filiation during their lifetime.[149]

ii. Illegitimate or Nonmarital

Generally, those conceived *and* born outside a valid marriage are considered illegitimate children.[150] However, Article 54 of the Family Code provides for an exception – those conceived or born before the decree of annulment, or declaration of nullity based on psychological incapacity or failure to comply with the requirement to record certain information in the appropriate registries. Children whose legitimacy was successfully impugned under Article 166 are likewise considered illegitimate.

[141] Family Code, Arts 177–178.
[142] Domestic Administrative Adoption and Alternative Child Care Act (RA No 11642), s 4(d).
[143] Domestic Administrative Adoption and Alternative Child Care Act, s 21.
[144] *Alanis v Court of Appeals* GR No 216425 (2020).
[145] *Republic of the Philippines v Court of Appeals* GR No 88202 (1998).
[146] Family Code, Arts 194–196.
[147] Civil Code, Art 888.
[148] Family Code, Art 211.
[149] Family Code, Art 165.
[150] *Heirs of Maramag v Maramag* GR No 181132 (2009).

Article 176 of the Family Code accords illegitimate children with certain rights:

(1) To use the surname of their mother. However, they can use the surname of their father if filiation was proven[151] or when the father has expressly recognised their filiation;[152]
(2) To be under the parental authority of their mother, the latter being the only legally known parent. Therefore, a putative father cannot register an illegitimate child on his own;[153]
(3) To be entitled to one-half of the legitime of a legitimate child;
(4) To be entitled to successional rights. The Supreme Court recently struck down Article 992 of the Civil Code which bars illegitimate children from inheriting by intestacy from the legitimate children and relatives of their father or mother;[154]
(5) To prove filiation during their lifetime, except when the supporting proof consists of open and continuous possession of the status or other means allowed by the Rules of Court and special laws. In the latter, the action to recognise filiation must be filed during the lifetime of the putative parent;[155] and
(6) To be beneficiaries in an insurance policy taken by their father.[156]

B. Parental Responsibility and Authority

The Family Code recognises parental authority and responsibility as a natural right and duty of parents over the person and property of their unemancipated children. These include the caring for and rearing of children for civic consciousness and efficiency and the development of their moral, mental and physical character and well-being.[157]

Parental authority and responsibility may neither be renounced nor transferred,[158] except in the cases authorised by law such as legal adoption or entrusting disadvantaged children to orphanages.

Generally, parental authority is exercised jointly by the father and mother.[159] However, in their default, substitute parental authority shall be exercised by the: (a) surviving grandparent; (b) oldest brother or sister, over 21 years of age, unless unfit or disqualified; or, (c) the child's actual custodian, over 21 years of age, unless unfit or disqualified. Under the Foster Care Act (RA No 10165), foster parents also exercise substitute parental authority over the child under their foster care, but they cannot inflict corporal punishment. On the other hand, special parental authority and responsibility shall be exercised by the school, its administrators and teachers over the child while under their supervision, instruction, or custody.[160] Parents and other persons exercising parental authority shall be civilly liable for the injuries and damages caused by the acts or omissions of their children living in their company and under their parental authority subject to the appropriate defences provided by law.[161]

It is a fundamental principle that in all questions on the care, custody, education and property of children, the latter's welfare shall be paramount.[162] The court shall consider, in addition

[151] *Dela Cruz v Gracia* GR No 177728 (2009).
[152] RA No 9255.
[153] *Barcelote v Republic of the Philippines* GR No 222095 (2017).
[154] *Aquino v Aquino* GR No 209018 (2021).
[155] Family Code, Art 175.
[156] *Heirs of Maramag v Maramag* GR No 181132 (2009).
[157] Family Code, Art 209.
[158] Family Code, Art 210.
[159] Family Code, Art 211.
[160] Family Code, Art 218.
[161] Family Code, Art 221.
[162] *Medina v Makabali* GR No L-26953 (1969).

to the child's choice of parents, the minor's moral and material welfare in deciding actions on declaration of nullity or annulment. Any property acquired by the child through work or industry or by onerous or gratuitous title shall belong to the child, and shall be exclusively devoted to his or her support and education.[163]

C. Guardianship

Article 225 of the Family Code states that the father and mother shall jointly exercise legal guardianship over the property of their child without the necessity of a court appointment. Where the market value of the property or the annual income of the child is more than P50,000, the parent concerned shall be required to post a bond fixed by the court. The parents' rights over the fruits and income of the child's property shall be limited primarily to support the child, and secondarily to the collective daily needs of the family.[164] The child labour law (RA No 9231) supplements this rule by setting a ceiling: only up to 20 per cent of the child's property may be used for the collective needs of the family, while requiring parents to set-up a trust fund for the child by setting aside 30 per cent of the property.

Since parents exercise parental authority over their children, the ordinary rules on guardianship shall only apply suppletorily. However, ordinary guardianship rules shall apply when the child is under substitute parental authority, or the guardian is a stranger, or a parent has remarried.[165]

Nevertheless, the Family Code allows courts to appoint a guardian of the child's property or guardian *ad litem*. Under the Rules on Guardianship of Minors (AM No 03-02-05-SC), a petition for guardianship over the person or property of a minor may be filed upon:

(1) death, continued absence, or incapacity of the parents;
(2) suspension, deprivation or termination of parental authority;
(3) remarriage of the surviving parent, if the latter is found unsuitable to exercise parental authority; or,
(4) when the best interests of the minor so require.

The rules also require the court to order a social worker to conduct a case study of the minor and all prospective guardians. The social worker must prepare a recommendation which shall be submitted to the court for its consideration.

Guardians may be criminally liable if they, having charge of the rearing or education of a minor, shall deliver said minor to a public institution or other persons, without the consent of the one who entrusted such child to their care or in the absence of the latter, without the consent of the proper authorities.[166]

D. Custody and Removal of Children

The right of custody accorded to parents springs from the exercise of parental authority.[167] As a rule, this right must be exercised and enjoyed jointly by the father and mother. But when the parents are unmarried, or when their marriage has been dissolved, or when they legally separate

[163] Family Code, Art 226.
[164] ibid.
[165] Family Code, Art 225.
[166] Revised Penal Code, Art 277, para 1.
[167] *Santos v Court of Appeals* GR No 113054 (1995).

from one another, the determination of who among the parents is entitled to exercise such right shall be made considering the best interest of the child. The best interests of the minor refer to the totality of the circumstances and conditions as are most congenial to the survival, protection, and feelings of security of the minor encouraging to his or her physical, psychological and emotional development. It also means the least detrimental available alternative for safeguarding the growth and development of the minor.[168]

Accordingly, while the Family Code provides for a tender-age presumption that children below the age of seven are deemed to have chosen the mother, if there are compelling reasons, such child may be ordered separated from the mother.[169] For instance, the Supreme Court deemed that it is in the best interest of the child to be freed from the mother when psychological and case study reports show that the child's feelings of insecurity and anxiety had been traced to strong conflicts with the mother,[170] or when the mother is cohabiting with the child's uncle-in-law.[171] However, it must be noted that 'sexual preference [like lesbianism] or moral laxity alone does not prove parental neglect or incompetence. Not even the fact that a mother is a prostitute or has been unfaithful to her husband would render her unfit to have custody of her minor child. To deprive the wife of custody, the husband must clearly establish that her moral lapses have had an adverse effect on the welfare of the child or have distracted the offending spouse from exercising proper parental care.'[172]

The writ of *habeas corpus* may be availed of as a remedy when a child is wrongfully removed from the parent with the right to custody or the appropriate guardian. It can also be availed of even against the parents themselves: '[t]he general rule is that parents should have custody over their minor children. But the State has the right to intervene where the parents, rather than care for such children, treat them cruelly and abusively, impairing their growth and well-being and leaving them emotional scars that they carry throughout their lives unless they are liberated from such parents and properly counseled.'[173] Furthermore, the Revised Penal Code provide for the following criminal offences for wrongful removal:

(1) kidnapping and failure to return a minor, against any person who, being entrusted with the custody of a minor person, shall deliberately fail to restore the latter to his or her parents or guardians (Art 270);
(2) inducing a minor to abandon his or her home (Art 271), against anyone who shall induce a minor to abandon the home of his or her parent or guardians or the persons entrusted with custody; and,
(3) abandoning a minor (Art 275), anyone who shall abandon a minor under seven years of age, the custody of which is incumbent upon the person who abandoned the minor.

VI. Surrogacy

Another emerging issue in Philippine family law is the legal status of children born through surrogacy arrangements abroad. Surrogacy agreements are not recognised under existing Philippine

[168] Rule on Custody of Minors and Writ of Habeas Corpus in Relation to Custody of Minors (AM-03-03-04-SC), s 14, para 2.
[169] *Medina v Makabali* GR No L-26953 (1969).
[170] *Espiritu v Court of Appeals* GR No 115640 (1995).
[171] *Unson v Navarro* GR No L-52242 (1980).
[172] *Gulaberto v Gualberto* GR No 154994 (2005).
[173] *Vingson v Cabcaban* UDK No 14817 (2014).

statutes, and no legislation currently regulates such practice. The status of children conceived via surrogacy is fraught with uncertainties in respect of filiation, citizenship, and inheritance rights.

If a Filipino couple enters into a surrogacy arrangement abroad, the determination of the child's filiation[174] will depend on the applicable foreign law. Upon a return to the Philippines, however, the recognition of such parentage may be challenged, as Philippine law adheres strictly to the rules on maternity and paternity established in the Family Code.[175] The woman who gives birth is deemed the mother, and paternity is established through marriage[176] or voluntary recognition.[177] Thus, intended parents may be compelled to resort to adoption proceedings to establish full parental authority.

For succession purposes, if the surrogacy-born child is not recognised as the legitimate or legally adopted child of the Filipino intended parents,[178] he or she will not qualify as a compulsory heir.[179] Nonetheless, courts may take into account international developments and the constitutional mandate to protect the best interests of the child in resolving such cases. This area of law remains unsettled and will likely continue to develop as more Filipino families participate in assisted reproductive arrangements abroad.

There are also other matters that may complicate how surrogacy is legally treated in the Philippines. The manner by which the surrogacy was pursued may cause division among policy makers on how to regulate the practice. For example, traditional surrogacy involves the use of the sperm of the father and the egg of the surrogate mother, while gestative surrogacy takes the sperm of the biological father and combines it artificially with the egg of the mother. In both cases, a surrogate mother carries the fetus in her womb. However, in traditional surrogacy, the surrogate mother contributes her genetic material. This could complicate possible custody cases in the future since the surrogate is technically the biological mother of the child. However, in gestational pregnancy, the biological mother is also the wife/partner of the biological father.[180]

The Family Code provides that children conceived as a result of artificial insemination of the wife with the sperm of the husband or that of a donor, or both, are legitimate children of the husband and wife. However, they must both authorise or ratify the artificial insemination in a written instrument before the birth of the child. This instrument is to be recorded together with the child's birth certificate.[181] It must be noted that the Family Code expressly provides that the wife must be the one artificially inseminated. It does not cover surrogacy and it does not apply to artificial insemination procedures involving non-married couples.

VII. Mental Incapacity

Not all forms of mental health conditions may be considered as restrictions or limitations to a person's capacity to act. In fact, discrimination against a person with a mental health condition is a criminal offence under the Mental Health Act (RA No 11036); but special measures meant solely to protect the rights or secure the advancement of persons with decision-making

[174] Family Code, Art 172.
[175] Civil Code, Art 15.
[176] Family Code, Art 164.
[177] Family Code, Art 172.
[178] Family Code, Art 179.
[179] Civil Code, Art 887.
[180] CAE Ang and LLE Villamor, 'Changing the Status Quo: An Examination of the Legal and Social Considerations for Determining the Legitimacy of Surrogate Children' (Bachelor, De La Salle University, Animo Repository, 2023).
[181] Family Code, Art. 164.

impairment capacity are not discriminatory. What the Civil Code and Family Code consider as incapacity, and what the Revised Penal Code treats as an exempting circumstance, is insanity.

Insanity is more of a legal concept than a medical one. For instance, while the Mental Health Act may consider schizophrenia as a mental health condition, it being a neurologic or psychiatric condition based on scientifically-accepted medical nomenclature and best available scientific and medical evidence,[182] it may not fall under insanity referred to in the Revised Penal Code.[183] Insanity demands complete loss of intelligence of the subject prior to or during the act itself.[184] A lower threshold appears in the Civil Code. Under the law on succession, the testator must be of sound mind, which simply means that at the time of making the will, he or she must know the nature of the estate to be disposed of, the proper objects of the bounty, and the character of the testamentary act.[185] Soundness of mind need not require full possession of reasoning facilities or wholly broken or impaired mind. That is why a will may still be allowed even if the testator was insane but the will was proved to be made during a lucid interval.[186] In contract law, while insanity incapacitates a person from giving valid consent, contracts entered into during lucid intervals are valid.[187]

A person's capacity to act, which is the power to commit acts with legal effects, is restricted when he or she is afflicted with insanity.[188] Insanity renders ineffective the offer in an ordinary contract,[189] dissolves the contract of partnership,[190] extinguishes the contract of agency,[191] and extinguishes the officious management.[192] In family law, insanity is a ground of voidable marriage since it makes consent defective, although the insane may ratify such marriage after coming to reason.[193] The action to claim legitimacy, while belonging to the child, may be transferred to the heirs should the child die in a state of insanity.[194] It may even be a ground justifying the separation of children from their mother.

[182] Mental Health Act (RA No 11036), s 4(k).
[183] *People of the Philippines v Madarang* GR No 132319 (2000).
[184] *People of the Philippines v Rafanan* GR No L-54135 (1991).
[185] Civil Code, Art 799.
[186] Civil Code, Art 800.
[187] Civil Code, Art 1328.
[188] Civil Code, Arts 37–39.
[189] Civil Code, Art 1323.
[190] Civil Code, Art 1860.
[191] Civil Code, Art 1919(3).
[192] Civil Code, Art 2153(3).
[193] Family Code, Art 45(2).
[194] Family Code, Art 173.

6

Overview of Intellectual Property in the Philippines

CHRISTOPHER E CRUZ, PETER IMMANUEL DL TENIDO, AND PAMELA RAYE M TADEO

I. Introduction

A. The Concept of Intellectual Property

Intellectual property refers to 'creations of the mind – everything from works of art to inventions, computer programs to trademarks and other commercial signs.'[1] Unlike the traditional form of property, which is tangible, like a parcel of land or a ten-story building, intellectual property is intangible. This means that intellectual property generally cannot be perceived by the senses but can be represented as a product of an idea or concept. 'Intellectual' refers to things related to the mind, while 'Property' refers to something that can be possessed or owned. Combining the two words means that intellectual property is created, related to, or produced by the mind, which can be the source of property rights.

According to Mark Getty, 'intellectual property is the oil of the 21st century.' Throughout economic development, there has been a shift from the agrarian economy, where people 'grow things,' to the industrial economy, where people 'make things,' and now to the current technological economy, where people 'invent things.' The fourth stage is sometimes called the digital economy, where people 'transform things from analog to digital.' Intellectual property becomes increasingly important during these third and fourth stages. In the twenty-first-century digital economy, intellectual property has become the new oil – a new currency used to determine the wealth of nations.

Based on the World Intellectual Property Office (WIPO) definition, intellectual property can be divided into two main categories: (1) industrial property (such as inventions, designs, symbols, and names used in commerce) and (2) copyright and related rights (covering literary and artistic works). Under section 4.1 of the Intellectual Property Code of the Philippines (R.A. 8293), intellectual property includes 'a) Copyright and Related Rights; (b) Trademarks and Service Marks; (c) Geographic Indications; (d) Industrial Designs; (e) Patents; (f) Topographies of Integrated Circuits; and (g) Protection of Undisclosed Information.' This list is not exhaustive, as other types like trade secrets and data are also considered intellectual property. The scope of what can be protected as intellectual property has expanded with more creations being covered. However, the

[1] 'What is intellectual property?' *World Intellectual Property Organization* (2020) 3.

law also limits protection for certain types, especially those in the public domain, such as 'ideas as such,' natural laws (for patents), or anything against public order and morality. In this chapter, the three main types of intellectual property – patents, trademarks, and copyright – will be discussed.

In the Philippines, the legal foundation for protecting intellectual property rights is outlined in Article XIV, section 13 of the 1987 Constitution, which states: 'The State shall protect and secure the exclusive rights of scientists, inventors, artists, and other gifted citizens to their intellectual property and creations, particularly when beneficial to the people, for such period as may be provided by law.'[2]

This is supported by section 2 of the Intellectual Property Code of the Philippines, which provides that the 'State recognizes that an effective intellectual and industrial property system is vital to the development of domestic and creative activity, facilitates transfer of technology, attracts foreign investments, and ensures market access for our products. It shall protect and secure the exclusive rights of scientists, inventors, artists, and other gifted citizens to their intellectual property and creations, particularly when beneficial to the people, for such periods as provided in this Act. The use of intellectual property bears a social function. To this end, the State shall promote the diffusion of knowledge and information for the promotion of national development and progress and the common good.'[3]

B. The Characteristics of Intellectual Property

Many people are confused by the term 'intellectual property' because of its highly technical and legal nature. Some even call it 'obscure' and believe it should be left to scientists and lawyers. Although intellectual property definitely relates to law and legal rights, it was also created to encourage creativity and innovation. It also aims to help turn ideas into products and services that benefit the public. Besides being intangible, as mentioned, here are the main characteristics of intellectual property:

(1) Private: Like land or a car, intellectual property can be owned and held by individuals who create it. This right allows them to permit or prevent others from exercising these rights. For example, a patent holder of a machine can prevent others from using the patented technology, similar to a person who builds a fence around their house to keep others from entering their property. However, like all private property, intellectual property rights (IPRs) are not absolute and are limited by law.
(2) Negative: IPRs grant the owner the right to exclude, prohibit, or restrict others from using the protected work. It is considered a negative right because it is usually exercised by prohibiting or restraining others from exercising the rights provided by law. For example, the copyright owner of a movie has the right to prohibit others from making duplicate copies of the film.
(3) Territorial: The rights over intellectual property can only be exercised in the country or jurisdiction where it is registered. This means that work protected in one country is not necessarily protected in another. There is no such thing as 'international protection' for intellectual property. However, cross-border protection is possible when countries enter into treaties or international agreements.

[2] 1987 Constitution, Art XIV, s 13.
[3] Intellectual Property Code of the Philippines (RA No 8293), s 2.

While intellectual property (IP) rights are inherently territorial, they can still have effects beyond borders, which warrant discussion in private international law. For example, Philippine copyright law extends protection to foreign works based on the country's treaty commitments or international agreements like the Berne Convention for the Protection of Literary and Artistic Works. This convention ensures that copyrighted works are protected not only in the Philippines but also in all member states, based on the principle of reciprocity. Similarly, although trademark protection is territorial, it also recognises 'well-known marks,' which are protected even if not registered in the Philippines. Additionally, disputes involving trademarks often have cross-border elements, such as the use of confusingly similar marks in international trade or online commerce. Patent rights, while granted at the national level, also intersect with foreign jurisdictions in cases involving licensing, infringement, and technology transfer. These examples demonstrate that, although the principle of territoriality is fundamental, Philippine IP law interacts with and influences international borders, establishing connections with private international law and conflict of laws analysis.

(4) Time-bound: IPRs, being private rights, are protected only for a limited period. For patents, the term is 20 years from filing. For copyrights, it is 50 years (Philippines) after the author's death. For trademarks, the term is 10 years, subject to renewal. This is consistent with the policy of the intellectual property system that, ultimately, the intellectual property system of protection was established to reward the inventor or author and benefit society.[4] According to the WIPO, 'The IP system is designed to help society as a whole, striking a delicate balance to ensure the needs of both the creator and the user are satisfied. IPRs usually allow their owner to exercise rights over the use of their work for a limited period. In return for granting such rights, the IP system provides benefits to society in several ways by enriching the pool of public knowledge and culture; maintaining fair competition and encouraging the production of a wide range of quality goods and services; underpinning social, cultural, and economic growth and employment; sustaining innovation and creation; and promoting technological advances and cultural expression.'[5]

(5) Statutory: IPRs are created by law and are therefore purely statutory rights. IPRs exist because of the law. However, some argue that IPRs should be respected because they also have a moral aspect. These include various philosophical justifications for the existence of IPR, such as natural law theory, reward theory, personality theory, and utilitarian theory. The main law protecting intellectual property in the Philippines is the Intellectual Property Code (R.A. 8293) and its amendments.

(6) Tool: Intellectual property is not an end but a means to an end. It is an instrument or tool to pursue higher goals. Being a tool, it remains neutral. When used properly, it can offer significant benefits to the economy and society. When misused, it can be exploited to limit innovation and creativity. The existence of patent trolls and non-practicing entities (NPEs) illustrates the improper use of IPRs. Therefore, the role of government is to find a balance that serves both individual and societal interests. Specifically, IPRs are utilised as tools in business transactions and are now included in a company's balance sheet. As an economic tool, they generate value for both the IP owner and society. In his book 'Intellectual Property Strategy,' John Palfrey suggests that organisations 'consider intellectual property an asset class.'[6]

[4] *Manzano v Court of Appeals* GR No 113388 (1997).

[5] World Intellectual Property Organization. (2011). Making Intellectual Property Work for Business, WIPO Pub. No. 956-E. Geneva, Switzerland.

[6] J Palfrey, *Intellectual Property Strategy* (The MIT Press Knowledge Series, 2012).

(7) International: While the enforcement of intellectual property rights is national, its impact can have international implications. There is a consensus among countries that protecting the intellectual creations of inventors and creators is essential. Although intellectual property protection varies across nations, there is a continuous effort to harmonise IP laws to reduce inconsistencies. This is why many treaties and international agreements related to IPRs, such as TRIPS (Trade-Related Aspects of Intellectual Property Rights), are managed by the WIPO. In this context, IP is considered international because it depends on maintaining good relationships among countries. The principle of National Treatment under Article 3 of TRIPS sets the international standard that IPRs should be applied equally and without discrimination to citizens of all signatory states, with some exceptions.

II. Patents

A patent is a government-granted intellectual property right that gives the owner a limited-time exclusive right to an invention. An invention can be a product or a process that provides a technical solution to a problem in any area of human activity. Patents are thus closely linked to technological innovation. Philippine patents are issued by the Intellectual Property Office, which reviews patent applications and decides whether to grant a patent based on specific requirements. A patent document includes a description of the invention, sometimes drawings necessary for understanding it, at least one claim, and an abstract. When submitting a patent application, all these elements are included along with a request for the patent and information identifying the inventor(s) and the applicant(s).

A. The Functions of Patents

A patent serves two main functions. First, it protects an inventor's exclusive rights over the outputs of their inventive efforts. A patent owner, or patentee, has the right to prevent (ie, it is a negative right) unauthorised third parties from making, using, offering for sale, selling, or importing a product that embodies the invention claimed in the patent. If a patent covers a process, the owner has the right to prevent others from using the process or from making, offering for sale, selling, or importing a product obtained from that process. A patentee may assign or sell their patent to a third party, relinquishing their exclusive rights to the invention and transferring them. They also have the positive right to license their patent to a third party, where they maintain ownership but allow the licensee to use the invention in exchange for various benefits. These benefits typically include payments such as an upfront fee or royalties based on the licensee's earnings from the patented invention. The rights granted by a patent enable the inventor or their assigns to commercially develop their invention while restricting competitors from doing the same without a licence for a limited time.

The second function of patents is disclosure. In exchange for the patent, the invention must be clearly and completely disclosed in a patent document so that a person with the necessary skill to carry out the invention could do so. The patent office then publishes the patent application after a certain period: for patent applications filed in the Philippines, after 18 months from the filing date. A patent document effectively teaches the invention to the public, allowing others to build upon or design around the technology described, or to implement the technology once the patentee's temporary monopoly on the invention has expired.

A patent's two main functions are to achieve socially beneficial effects. Granting exclusive rights to inventors or their assigns encourages further inventive activity and motivates investment in technology development and the introduction of new and innovative products to the market. Additionally, because patents can be sold, assigned, or licensed, they promote collaboration, knowledge sharing, and technology transfer. Meanwhile, the public can access technical information from published patent documents or use detailed technical data to develop alternative or improved technologies, which can then become the subject of their own patents. Overall, a well-functioning patent system is designed to support innovation, stimulate socioeconomic growth, and advance the arts and sciences. Consequently, it is a national policy goal to foster an environment conducive to invention. Inventors of patented inventions in the Philippines may receive cash rewards, enjoy tax incentives related to developing their inventions, and obtain tax exemptions for income derived from commercialising their patented technology. Moreover, the Inventions Development Assistance Fund, managed by the Technology Application and Promotion Institute of the Department of Science and Technology, is available to support inventors in prototype development and experimentation during inventive activities. At the same time, the Invention Guarantee Fund, deposited with the Development Bank of the Philippines, offers financing and guarantees for loan assistance, cash rewards, incentives, and other special programs for Filipino inventions.

i. Patent Principles under the Paris Convention and the TRIPS Agreement

Patents are a form of industrial property protected under the Paris Convention for the Protection of Industrial Property. Members of the World Trade Organization (WTO), as signatories to the WTO Agreement on Trade-Related Aspects of Intellectual Property Rights (TRIPS) – the most comprehensive multilateral agreement on intellectual property – are required to provide patent protection for any inventions in any technological field, as long as they are new, involve an inventive step, and are industrially applicable. The Philippines, a WTO member and a signatory to the Paris Convention, must grant patents.

The key patent principles outlined in the Paris Convention are shown below. These provisions are incorporated by reference into the TRIPS Agreement.

(a) National Treatment. A contracting state to the Paris Convention must grant nationals of other contracting states the same protection over industrial property rights as it would to its own nationals. Nationals of states not part of the Paris Convention can also receive this national treatment if they are domiciled or have a genuine and effective industrial or commercial establishment in the territory of a contracting state. National treatment is confirmed in the Intellectual Property Code of the Philippines.[7]

(b) Independence and Territoriality. An applicant seeking patent protection for an invention in multiple territories must file a patent application in each relevant jurisdiction. Whether a patent will be granted in a specific country depends on that country's national patent laws and procedures. A state is not obligated to grant a patent for an invention if the same invention has already been patented in another state by the same applicant. Similarly, a state cannot refuse, annul, or terminate a patent solely because a patent for the same invention filed elsewhere by the same applicant has been refused, annulled, or terminated.

[7] Intellectual Property Code of the Philippines (RA No 8293), s 3.

(c) Right of Priority. The right of priority allows a patent applicant to seek patent protection in multiple countries while maintaining an earlier filing date.[8] The following example illustrates how the right of priority works. Suppose an inventor wants to obtain patent protection for an invention in the Philippines and Singapore and files their first patent application in the Philippines on 1 February 2023. Within 12 months, the inventor can claim the right of priority by filing a second patent application in Singapore for the same invention, claiming priority from the first application. Even if this second application was filed with the Intellectual Property Office of Singapore on 1 April 2023, it would have an effective filing date of 1 February 2023, the priority date. Therefore, if the inventor had published details of their invention or started selling a product covered by the patent application between 1 February and 1 April 2023, or if another inventor independently filed a similar patent during that time, these activities and disclosures would not affect the second patent application – it retains priority over these events. The right of priority is established by the Intellectual Property Code of the Philippines.

B. The Requirements of Patentability

For a patent to be granted for an invention, it must satisfy patentability requirements. These requirements are strict to ensure that ideas already in the public domain stay free for public use. The minimum standards for patentability are outlined in the TRIPS Agreement. As a member of the WTO and a signatory to the TRIPS Agreement, the Philippines adheres to these standards and establishes the following patentability requirements.

(1) Patent-Eligible Subject Matter. The invention must fall within the statutory categories of patentable inventions. The TRIPS Agreement requires Member States to make patents available 'for any inventions … in all fields of technology ….' In the Philippines, a patentable invention must relate to a product, a process, a computer-related invention, or an improvement of any of these. Subject matter outside of these classes and therefore ineligible for patent protection includes, but is not limited to, mere discoveries, scientific theories, mathematical models, laws of nature, scientific truths, abstract ideas or theories, and aesthetic creations. Section 23 of the Intellectual Property Code provides the 'negative list' of items that cannot be patented. The Philippines also excludes from patentability surgical, therapeutic, and diagnostic methods performed on the human or animal body, plant varieties, animal breeds, essentially biological processes for producing plants and animals, and anything that is contrary to public order, health, welfare, or morality.

(2) Novelty. The invention must be new to the world or different from what exists in the prior art, meaning it must not be part of the existing knowledge made available to the public before the filing or priority date of the application.[9] Prior art includes everything disclosed to the public before that date, such as earlier-filed and later-published patent applications, sometimes called 'secret prior art.' An example illustrates how much prior art may exist: Suppose a first patent is filed on 1 February 2024. After about 18 months, or 1 August 2025, that patent application is published. Before its publication, the document remains secret, and its contents are unknown to the public (assuming no other disclosures were made). Consequently, if a second patents applications is filed on 1 April 2024, for an invention

[8] Intellectual Property Code of the Philippines (RA No 8293), s 29.
[9] Intellectual Property Code of the Philippines (RA No 8293), s 23.

related to the first, the second applicant would not be aware of the first application despite it potentially being relevant prior art. In the Philippines, such 'secret prior art' would only affect the novelty of a new Philippine patent application if it had an earlier filing or priority date in the Philippines, if it has been published, and if the applicant or inventor of the new application is different from that in the 'secret prior art' reference.

In evaluating novelty, a claimed invention undergoes a strict identity test: to fail the novelty requirement, a single prior art reference must teach every element of the invention. Only one prior art reference is considered at a time for assessing novelty, and equivalents of features are not taken into account. Consider the following hypothetical example. Suppose an inventor has created an office chair with a seat, a backrest, two armrests, legs, and wheels. Would this office chair be novel compared to a prior art reference disclosing a classroom chair with a seat, a backrest, and two armrests, where one armrest has an extended writing surface and legs? Likely, yes, since the classroom chair does not teach a chair with wheels. The fact that one armrest on the classroom chair has an extended writing surface does not affect this novelty assessment.

Would the same office chair be considered new in light of prior art references describing a cafe stool with a seat, legs, and wheels? Likely, since the cafe stool does not teach a chair with a backrest and armrests. One may observe that combining the features of a classroom chair and those of a cafe stool would result in an object with all the characteristics of the office chair. However, such a combination would not be considered when evaluating novelty if only one prior art reference is used. Now, consider a prior art reference describing a hotel chair with a seat, backrest, two armrests, legs, and wheels, where the height of the seat and the angle of the backrest are both adjustable. Would the office chair be considered new over this hotel chair? Likely not, since the hotel chair already includes all the features of the office chair. The fact that the hotel chair has additional adjustability features does not affect the novelty assessment.

The novelty requirement means inventors and patent applicants must be careful about publicly disclosing an invention before filing a patent application. However, the patent laws of some jurisdictions include provisions for non-prejudicial disclosures. Such provisions typically involve a grace period during which certain disclosures do not jeopardise a patent application due to lack of novelty. In the Philippines, a prior art reference cannot be used to reject an application for lack of novelty if the reference was published no more than 12 months before the filing or priority date of the application, and if one of the following is true: the disclosure was made by the inventor; the disclosure was made by a third party who obtained the information directly or indirectly from the inventor; the disclosure was made through another published patent application filed by the inventor, which should not have been disclosed by the patent office; or, the disclosure was made through another published patent application filed by a third party, based on information obtained from the inventor without the inventor's knowledge or consent. Therefore, if a Philippine patent application is filed for an invention developed by a university researcher, and the researcher had already shared details of the invention at a conference held one month prior to filing, that conference presentation would not harm the application's novelty. Likewise, if an audience member wrote an internet blog about the invention and published it one week after the conference, the blog would also not be prejudicial to the invention's novelty, as it contains information obtained from the inventor. However, if the invention was disclosed in a peer-reviewed journal article published 12 months prior to the conference (about 13 months before the patent application was filed), the invention is likely to be considered lacking in novelty, as it is already part of the prior art, especially in the journal article.

(3) Inventive Step. The invention must involve an inventive step, meaning it must not, at the filing date or priority date of the application and considering the prior art, be obvious to a person skilled in the art or the technical field to which the invention pertains. The Implementing Rules and Regulations for Patents state that, when assessing the inventive step, only prior art made available to the public before the filing date or priority date of the claimed invention is considered, suggesting that 'secret prior art' is not cited in evaluating inventive step.

Philippine patent examiners assess inventive step using the problem and solution approach, a method also used by the European Patent Office that aims to ensure objective and predictable evaluations of inventive step. The problem and solution approach involves four steps: (1) determine the closest prior art; (2) identify the differences between the claimed invention and the closest prior art; (3) form the technical problem based on the differences found in step 2; and, (4) given the objective technical problem from step 3 and the closest prior art from step 1, look for any indications in the prior art that would lead a person skilled in the field to combine documents to solve the technical problem. The following hypothetical example demonstrates how the problem and solution approach is used to assess inventive step. An inventor files a patent application for an insulated tumbler with an integrated display showing the liquid's temperature inside the tumbler. Assume that in step 1, the closest prior art is a standard insulated tumbler. In step 2, the novel feature of the invention is the integrated display, which is absent in the closest prior art. For step 3, the technical problem is formulated; in this case, it might be the lack of a means for a user of a standard insulated tumbler to know the liquid's temperature without contact. In the final step, the question could be: Is there anything in the prior art that would motivate a skilled person to combine prior art references to solve the problem of not knowing the liquid's temperature by including an integrated display? In answering this, an examiner might consult additional references and consider whether a skilled person would combine them with the closest prior art to reach the invention. For example, the examiner might find another reference teaching a patch that displays temperature on a surface and argue that it would be obvious to combine this patch with a standard insulated tumbler. If so, the examiner might conclude that the invention lacks inventive step. During patent prosecution, the applicant can argue for inventive step, such as by claiming that integrating the display into the tumbler involves inventive effort and is not obvious compared to simply attaching a patch.

The US approach employs the same analysis but also considers secondary and ancillary factors. These include elements like 'long-felt need,' commercial success, and teaching against the advice of experts in the field. While the Philippines mainly uses the EU approach, it occasionally considers the US approach to support its arguments for or against inventive step.

In the interest of public health, the inventive step requirement is especially strict for drugs and medicines. Such inventions would be considered to lack an inventive step if they only involve a new form or property of a known substance without improving its known efficacy, or if they only relate to a new use for a known substance. Additionally, they would also lack inventive step if they involve a new use of a known process without resulting in a new product that uses at least one new reactant.

(4) Industrial Applicability. The invention must be suitable for industrial use, meaning it can be manufactured and utilised in any industry or capable of industrial exploitation.[10] It is uncommon for patent applications to be rejected for lack of industrial applicability, as the

[10] Intellectual Property Code of the Philippines (RA No 8293), s 27.

term 'industry' is broadly interpreted to include useful, practical, or physical activities of a 'technical character,' as opposed to activities in the aesthetic arts. Although not explicitly stated, it is implied that inventions should have beneficial utility to be patentable. This implication is supported by the IP Code, which states that it is meant to: '... protect and secure the exclusive rights of scientists, inventors, artists, and other gifted citizens to their intellectual property and creations, particularly when beneficial to the people ....'[11]

(5) Enablement. A patent application must provide an enabling disclosure,[12] meaning a clear and detailed description of at least one embodiment of the invention that is enough for a person skilled in the art to practice the invention. The enablement requirement ensures that the disclosure function of the patent system is fulfilled.

C. Ownership of a Patent

Patent ownership begins with the inventor and can be transferred to the inventor's heirs or assigns. When multiple inventors co-develop an invention, they share joint ownership of the patent. However, if several inventors or groups of co-inventors develop an invention independently and separately, the ownership of the patent is determined by the first-to-file rule, meaning the patent is owned by the applicant with the earliest filing or priority date. It is important to note that ownership of patent rights may not always lie with the inventor. Various factors, including national laws, institutional policies, and contractual agreements related to the inventive process – such as employment contracts, grant funding agreements, or collaborative research agreements – may lead to the patent rights belonging to parties other than the inventor or impose an obligation for the inventor to assign their patent rights to others.

If the inventor is commissioned to develop an invention, the owner of the patent would typically be the one who commissioned the invention unless there is a different agreement.[13] If the inventor develops the invention as an employee, their employer generally owns the patent for inventions created as part of their usual job duties, unless there is a contrary agreement. However, the inventor-employee retains ownership of patent rights for inventions they develop outside their regular duties, even if they use the employer's time and resources.[14] For example, a scientist hired to develop new paints and coatings in a paint manufacturing company's laboratory created a series of paints that change colour based on environmental conditions like temperature and humidity. These paints were created using company facilities, and while most of the inventive work happened during work hours, some ideas for the paints were conceived on weekends, recorded in the scientist's notebook, and later developed in the lab when the workweek resumed. Patents were filed for these paints. Outside of work, the scientist enjoys backpacking in the mountains. On several occasions, they used company lab equipment to design and develop a prototype of a device that improves the weight distribution in a backpack, making it easier to carry heavy loads over long distances. Some experiments to test the device were also conducted during work hours, and a patent was filed for this device. Who owns the patents for the paints and the backpack device? It is likely that the paint company's patents for the paints remain with the company, which hired the scientist precisely to develop such paints. It is irrelevant that the scientist may have developed some of the paints outside of working hours. On the other hand, the patent for the

[11] Intellectual Property Code of the Philippines (RA No 8293), s 2.
[12] Intellectual Property Code of the Philippines (RA No. 8293), s 35.
[13] Intellectual Property Code of the Philippines (RA No 8293), s 30.
[14] Intellectual Property Code of the Philippines (RA No 8293), s 30.2.

backpack device will likely belong to the scientist because developing the device was outside his regular duties, notwithstanding any reprimands the scientist will receive for working on personal matters on company time and using company resources.

The Philippines has a technology transfer law (R.A. No. 10055) that governs the ownership of IP (including patents) generated from projects funded by a government agency. Specifically, when a government agency provides full or partial funding to a research and development institution for a project, the IP created during that project – and any rights obtained over that IP – belongs to the institution. The IP can also be co-owned by multiple institutions collaborating on a government-funded project, according to a collaborative research agreement among them. The institution is responsible for disclosing potential IP to the funding agency and for initiating protection of that IP; failing to do so, the agency will assume ownership. IP ownership may also transfer to the government agency if the research institution voluntarily assigns the IP to the agency in the interest of national security, nutrition, health, or the development of vital sectors, or if the institution ceases to be a Filipino corporation. The Philippine Technology Transfer Act of 2009 (R.A. 10055) was inspired by similar laws in the United States (Bayh-Dole Act) and recognises the important role that research and development institutions – mostly universities – play in national innovation. By granting these institutions ownership and responsibility for IP from government-funded projects, they are encouraged to participate more actively in IP commercialisation through licensing deals and the creation of new ventures where IP can be licensed.

D. Patent Infringement

A party commits infringement when, without authorisation from the patent owner, it makes, uses, offers for sale, sells, or imports a product that embodies an invention claimed in the patent.[15] It also commits infringement if it uses a patented process and deals in, uses, sells, offers for sale, or imports a product obtained from that process. A party can also contribute to infringement and be held liable alongside the infringer. Examples of contributory infringement include actively inducing another person to infringe a patent and providing an infringer with the means to infringe, knowing those means are specifically designed for infringing and lack a suitable or substantial non-infringing use. The owner of a patent that has been infringed may file a civil lawsuit against the alleged infringer to recover damages and seek an injunction. Additionally, repeat infringers can be held criminally liable. A court may order the removal of infringing materials from commercial channels or even have them destroyed.

For a product or process to infringe on a patent, it must fall within the scope of the patent claims. The patent claims specifically identify and distinctly define the invention that the patent owner claims as theirs; they are interpreted together with the patent description and drawings. To determine whether an alleged infringing item falls within the literal meaning of the patent claims, a court compares the patent claims with the accused item within the context of the entire patent document to see if they are essentially the same. This test for literal infringement can be seen as the opposite of the strict identity test used to assess novelty. This is also known as the 'All elements rule,' where every element of the invention outlined in the claims must match the allegedly infringing invention. It also highlights the importance of carefully drafted claims that cover the actual invention rather than just specific embodiments or examples.

[15] Intellectual Property Code of the Philippines (RA No 8293), s 76.

An accused item can still infringe a patent even if it falls outside the literal scope of the claims. For example, by replacing at least one element with an alternative feature not explicitly claimed. Under the 'doctrine of equivalents,' if an accused item is a version of a patented invention that has been modified or changed but 'performs substantially the same function in substantially the same way to achieve substantially the same result' and still includes the same inventive concept as described in the patent, it would infringe on that patent. When claiming infringement under the 'doctrine of equivalents,' the patent owner must prove that this function-means-result test is satisfied.

One defence an accused infringer can use is to show that the patent being enforced against them, or any of its claims, is invalid.[16] The defendant might, for instance, argue that when the patent was filed, the invention was no longer new or lacked inventive step and provide supporting evidence, such as prior art references that may not have been found during prosecution. A patent or patent claim deemed invalid will be cancelled.

E. Licensing

As discussed above, a patent owner may voluntarily license their patent to a third party, which may then exploit the claimed invention to develop products or offer services.[17] Voluntary patent licences facilitate the transfer and dissemination of technology but must be regulated to ensure that they do not negatively affect competition and trade.[18] As such, the Philippine patent law prohibits specific clauses from being included in voluntary licensing agreements.[19] Such clauses include those that require the licensee to obtain goods, intermediate products, raw materials, and other technologies from a source specified by the licensor;[20] those that require the licensee to surrender to the licensor without compensation its rights to inventions or improvements that may be obtained through the use of the licensed technology;[21] and, those which require payments for patents after their expiration.[22] Meanwhile, specific provisions are mandatory in voluntary licensing agreements,[23] including those that require licences to be interpreted under Philippine laws,[24] those that make improvements related to the licensed technology available for the period of the licensing arrangement,[25] and those that place the responsibility of tax payments related to the licence on the licensor.[26] Voluntary licences that do not comply with the law, eg, they include at least one of the prohibited clauses or lack at least one of the mandatory clauses, are automatically unenforceable,[27] but could be made valid in exceptional cases and with approval from the Intellectual Property Office of the Philippines.[28]

Patent licences, however, can be granted even without the consent of the patent owner. Such compulsory licences may be issued by the Director General of the Intellectual Property

[16] Intellectual Property Code of the Philippines (RA No 8293), s 81.
[17] Intellectual Property Code of the Philippines (RA No 8293), s 90.
[18] Intellectual Property Code of the Philippines (RA No 8293), s 85.
[19] Intellectual Property Code of the Philippines (RA No 8293), s 87.
[20] Intellectual Property Code of the Philippines (RA No 8293), s 87.1.
[21] Intellectual Property Code of the Philippines (RA No 8293), s 87.6.
[22] Intellectual Property Code of the Philippines (RA No 8293), s 87.10.
[23] Intellectual Property Code of the Philippines (RA No 8293), s 88.
[24] Intellectual Property Code of the Philippines (RA No 8293), s 88.1.
[25] Intellectual Property Code of the Philippines (RA No 8293), s 88.2.
[26] Intellectual Property Code of the Philippines (RA No 8293), s 88.4.
[27] Intellectual Property Code of the Philippines (RA No 8293), s 92.
[28] Intellectual Property Code of the Philippines (RA No 8293), s 91.

Office of the Philippines to anyone capable of exploiting the claimed invention under specific circumstances, including national emergencies, preservation of national security and public health, and when a judicial or administrative body finds that the patent owner or its licensees are engaging in anti-competitive practices. When the supply of a patented product is limited because only a few manufacturers can produce it, compulsory licences can ensure that the public has access to that product in necessary quantities. These licences can be especially useful during emergencies like pandemics, when only a few companies control the supply of patented drugs and vaccines. Indeed, Philippine patent law includes provisions related to compulsory licences for the manufacture, import, and export of drugs and medicines. Additionally, a compulsory licence helps prevent the development of monopolies.

F. Limitations of Patent Rights and Flexibilities

To balance innovation and the rights of patent owners with the public interest, patent rights have specific limitations. These limitations serve as defences that an alleged infringer may invoke. For instance, patent owners cannot prevent third parties from privately and non-commercially using a patent invention (unless such use causes economic harm to the patent owner) or from conducting experimental use of a patented invention for educational and research purposes. Patent limitations are especially important in the pharmaceutical industry, where enforcing patent rights could negatively affect public health. For example, patent owners cannot stop third parties from testing, using, making, or selling a patented drug or medicine when these actions are solely for purposes reasonably related to obtaining regulatory approval, as required under the law of the Philippines or other countries regulating the manufacture, use, or sale of such products. This 'Bolar provision' enables generic drug manufacturers to seek regulatory approval even before a patent for the original drug expires, allowing them to enter the market promptly after patent expiration at prices more accessible to the public.

III. Trademarks

A. Introduction to Trademarks

As defined in the IP Code, a 'mark' is a 'visible sign capable of distinguishing the goods (trademark) or services (service mark) of an enterprise.'[29] A mark can be a symbol, a term, a phrase, a design, or a combination of these that can identify, differentiate, and indicate the source of a company's goods and services from those of other businesses.

Part III of the Intellectual Property Code of the Philippines governs trademark law in the country. Trademarks, service marks, trade names, and other unique signs used in commerce can be registered and protected under the law. Trademark owners have the exclusive right to use their marks in connection with their products and services, and they can enforce their rights legally in case of infringement. The task of managing and assisting in enforcing trademark rights in the Philippines falls to the Intellectual Property Office of the Philippines (IPOPHL).

[29] Intellectual Property Code of the Philippines (RA No 8293), s 121.

A trademark can be protected and renewed indefinitely if it is managed properly and monitored regularly. The protection period of a trademark is 10 years from the registration date; it can be extended for additional 10-year periods at a time.[30]

B. Requirements for Registration of Trademarks

Any symbol that identifies a company's products (trademark) or services (service mark) can be registered as a trademark. In the Philippines, only visible marks are protected, unlike in other countries where sound or scent marks can also be registered. The distinctiveness of a mark determines its registrability. The more distinctive a mark, the greater the chance of registration. The 'Spectrum of Distinctiveness' helps describe the strength of marks and their likelihood of registration. It categorises marks into five levels from least to most distinctive: (1) Generic, (2) Descriptive, (3) Suggestive, (4) Arbitrary, and (5) Fanciful, with 'Fanciful' marks being inherently distinctive and automatically protected, while 'Generic' marks are never distinctive and are unlikely to be protected. The spectrum also affects the level of protection for a mark. Generally, the stronger a mark's ability to defend its rights against unauthorised third-party uses of similar marks, the higher it ranks on the spectrum. Here is a description of each type:

(1) Fanciful marks: These are made-up words, symbols, or devices that have no connection to the product or service being offered. They are used solely to distinguish the product in the market and set it apart from competitors. Also called 'coined marks,' fanciful marks are specifically created to serve as trademarks and nothing else. Examples include 'Rolex' for watches, 'Adidas' for shoes, and 'Google' for online services. These marks are not found in the dictionary. Fanciful marks possess the strongest level of distinctiveness and are most likely to be registered with IPOPHL.

(2) Arbitrary marks: As the word implies, arbitrary marks are marks made up of common terms used to identify unrelated products or services. The most common example of an arbitrary mark is 'Apple,' where the word commonly used to describe a fruit was used to identify products and services of a company on computers, software, and mobile devices. Another example would be 'Starbucks,' where common words 'star' and 'bucks' are put together to identify a company offering coffee, which is not connected to both words. A local example is the trademark 'Bench,' which is a 'long seat' associated with clothing in the context of the trademark of a popular Philippine apparel retailer. Arbitrary marks follow fanciful marks in terms of strength.

(3) Suggestive marks: Suggestive marks hint at the identity of a product or service without explicitly describing it. A well-known example of a suggestive mark is 'Netflix.' Someone encountering the mark for the first time might think it relates to movies or 'flicks' on the internet, implying that the company offers movies accessible online. Another example is the trademark 'Burger King.' The term suggests that the company 'rules' when it comes to 'burgers.' 'Safeguard' can also be considered a suggestive mark. The word hints at 'protection' without specifically describing a soap that kills 99.9 per cent of germs. Connecting a suggestive mark to a product or service requires imagination, thought, and perception. Classification as a suggestive mark is the minimum level needed for a mark to be unconditionally registrable without requiring a secondary meaning or acquired distinctiveness.

[30] Intellectual Property Code of the Philippines (RA No 8293), s 145.

As Judge Learned Hand stated: 'The validity of the mark ends where suggestion ends, and description begins.' Suggestive marks have less protection than arbitrary marks but more than descriptive marks.

(4) Descriptive marks: It provides details about a product or service's characteristics, purpose, and features. As mentioned earlier, descriptive marks are not 'inherently descriptive' and are therefore often less easily registered. They are less likely to be protected than the first three classifications discussed above. However, marks in this category can gain distinctiveness over time through use and promotion, making them protectable or registrable. Distinctiveness can be acquired when the public associates the mark with a particular idea due to its use (secondary meaning). The trademark 'Cartoon Network' is a prime example of a descriptive mark, as it describes a television network with cartoon programmes. Another example is 'Play-Doh,' which describes a dough-based product intended for recreation. Generally, descriptive marks are less likely to be registered unless there is evidence of secondary meaning.
(5) Generic marks: These marks are common product or service names used to identify them. For example, a pasta restaurant might use 'Pasta' as a trademark. Another example is a bicycle company that uses the word 'Bicycle' to identify their products and services. Words like 'wallet,' 'basket,' 'coin,' or other common terms cannot be registered as trademarks. A generic mark is the least distinctive type of mark on the spectrum and cannot be registered, even if the applicant proves secondary meaning has been acquired.

C. Function of Trademarks

Trademarks have four main functions. They are:

(1) Distinguishing: This is the most important function of a mark. It is used to differentiate between the goods and services of one company and those of another. For example, the 'Jollibee' mark distinguishes their products from those of other fast-food restaurants like McDonald's or Burger King.
(2) Marketing and Advertising: Trademarks help promote goods and services they identify. They are closely tied to brand and trade dress, helping to create the overall customer perception of the product. For example, the KFC slogan 'Finger-lickin' good' helps build an image of delicious food in customers' minds, and their trademark for that slogan allows them to prevent other companies from using similar phrases that could cause confusion.
(3) Origin: It helps identify where products or services come from and can show the geographic location of the source. For example, the trademark 'Ilocos Delicacies' indicates that the goods originate from the Ilocos province in Luzon.
(4) Quality: Consumers associate trademarks with the quality and reliability of a specific product or service, helping them make purchasing decisions. A firm's reputation and brand identity are built and maintained through trademarks, which are linked to the quality and dependability of its products and services. For example, premium brands like Rolex for watches or Mercedes Benz for cars signal high quality for the products bearing the marks.

Trademarks can be licensed or franchised, bringing in extra revenue for the owner and increasing consumer awareness of the brand. They also serve as symbols of quality and reliability. Because they represent a company's reputation and brand recognition, trademarks can enhance the value of a business and its assets. Trademarks are considered the company's most valuable intangible asset. Generally, trademarks act as indicators of the source of goods or services. They are vital to businesses because they promote products and services, strengthen their reputation and brand identity, and provide legal protection.

D. Registrable and Non-Registrable Marks

In the Philippines, registrable marks are classified as (1) word marks, (2) figurative marks, (3) figurative marks with words, (4) three-dimensional marks, and (5) stamped or marked containers of goods. The distinctiveness of the mark is usually the main factor considered for approval of registration in any of these categories. It should be noted that other types of marks, such as colour marks and sound marks, must still be registered with the IPOPHL under the current IP Code (RA 8293).

Under Section 123.1 of the IP Code of the Philippines, marks that cannot be registered are those that (1) are immoral, deceptive, scandalous, or any matter that may falsely suggest a connection with persons, (2) consist of the flag, coat of arms, or other insignia of the Philippines, (3) contain the name, portrait, or signature identifying a particular living individual, (4) are identical with a registered mark that follows the first-to-file rule in trademark registration, (5) are identical with famous marks or well-known marks, (6) are generic, (7) are descriptively misleading, (8) consist of shapes that describe the technical factors of the product, (9) consist of colours alone, and (10) are contrary to public order or morality.[31]

E. Trademark Infringement and Remedies

Infringement is defined as the 'use in commerce any reproduction, counterfeit, copy, or colourable imitation of registered mark or the same container or a dominant feature thereof' of goods or services where such use 'is likely to cause confusion, or to cause mistake, or to deceive'; or 'reproduce, counterfeit or copy or colorably imitate a registered mark or a dominant feature thereof' without consent of the registered owner of the mark.[32] In the case of *McDonald's Corporation v L.C. Big Mak, Inc.*,[33] the Supreme Court of the Philippines provided the following elements of trademark infringement: (1) the plaintiff's ownership of the mark; (2) the validity of the plaintiff's mark; and, (3) the use of the mark by the alleged infringer will cause 'likelihood of confusion.' Actual confusion is not required as the mere likelihood of confusion is sufficient to prove infringement.

There are two tests used to determine the 'likelihood of confusion': (1) the dominancy test and (2) the holistic test. In the case of *Kolin Electronics Co. Inc. v Kolin Philippines International, Inc.*, the Supreme Court distinguished these two tests in the following way:

> The Dominancy Test focuses on the similarity of the prevalent features of the competing trademarks, which might cause confusion or deception and, thus, infringement. If the competing trademark contains the main, essential, or dominant features of another, and confusion or deception is likely to result, infringement takes place. Duplication or imitation is not necessary, nor is it necessary that the infringing label should suggest an effort to imitate. The question is whether the use of the marks involved is likely to cause confusion or mistake in the mind of the public or deceive purchasers.
>
> On the other hand, the Holistic Test requires that the entirety of the marks in question be considered in resolving confusing similarity. Comparison of words is not the only determining factor. The trademarks in their entirety as they appear in their respective labels or hang tags must also be considered in relation

[31] Intellectual Property Code of the Philippines (RA No 8293), s 123.1.
[32] Intellectual Property Code of the Philippines (RA No 8293), s 155.
[33] *McDonald's Corporation v L C Big Mak Burger Inc* GR No 143993 (2004).

> to the goods to which they are attached. The discerning eye of the observer must focus not only on the predominant words but also on the other features appearing in both labels in order that he may draw his conclusion whether one is confusingly similar to the other.

The Supreme Court has, in many cases, applied either the dominancy test or the holistic test separately or both at the same time. Of the two, only the dominancy test was specifically stated in section 155.1 of the Intellectual Property Code. However, in the same Kolin case, the Supreme Court said that it recommends adopting the dominancy test and that the holistic test has been discontinued.

The registered owner of a mark can file a civil action for infringement against anyone who uses the mark without permission. The owner can seek damages and request an injunction to stop the infringing activity. They may also ask the court to order the destruction of the infringing materials. Additionally, the owner can pursue criminal charges for infringement.[34]

IV. Copyright

Philippine law does not categorically define the concept of copyright but outlines a list of works that may be protected by copyright. Generally, copyright is a part of intellectual property that safeguards authors of artistic and literary works. It is the legal protection granted to the rights holder for an original work they created. What are the conditions for protection? According to the Berne Convention for the protection of literary and artistic works, the two requirements for protection are (1) originality and (2) expression, regardless of the form or mode of expression. 'Originality' does not mean 'new' or 'novel' as it does in patents. It simply means that the work originates from the author and is not copied from another source. 'Expression' indicates that the work is derived from an idea and presented in a literary, scientific, or artistic manner. It is important to note that under Philippine law, 'creativity' is not a requirement for the protection of any work. It is sufficient that the author expressed their idea and that it was not copied from others.

A. Copyright Principles

The Berne Convention and the Intellectual Property Code of the Philippines establish the following copyright principles:

(1) National Treatment: Copyrighted works from one contracting state should receive the same protection in other contracting states. In other words, the local state must grant the same copyright protections to works by foreign nationals from other contracting states that are signatories to the Berne Convention for the Protection of Literary and Artistic Works. There is an international consensus that all member states should recognise copyright.

(2) Non-formality Rule: Copyright protection is automatic and does not require formal registration. Unlike in patents or trademarks, there is no need to register the work to obtain protection. This means protection cannot be based on compliance with any formalities.

(3) Independence of Copyright: Each contracting party is sovereign and independent of the others. Therefore, protection in one country is separate from protection in other countries, subject to variations based on treaties and international agreements.

[34] Intellectual Property Code of the Philippines, s 170.

(4) Bundle of Rights: Copyright protection consists of several rights the copyright owner can exercise. These rights are separate and independent of each other. Under section 177 of the IP Code, the copyright or economic rights include the right to reproduce, translate, publish, rent, public display, public performance, and communication to the public.[35] This means one can assign the publication rights to one entity and the rental rights to another.

(5) Idea-Expression Dichotomy: Mere ideas and concepts are not protected by copyright. Only ideas expressed in literary or artistic form can be protected. For example, the idea of a boy walking along a beach cannot be copyrighted. However, a painting or picture of a boy walking along the coast, as artistically expressed in a painting or song, can be protected by copyright. 'Ideas are cheap' in the context of copyright. It needs to be expressed.

B. Works Protected

Under sections 172 and 173 of the Intellectual Property Code of the Philippines, the following are the original and derivative works protected by copyright:

(a) Books, pamphlets, articles, and other writings;
(b) Periodicals and newspapers;
(c) Lectures, sermons, addresses, and dissertations prepared for oral delivery, whether or not reduced in writing or other material form;
(d) Letters;
(e) Dramatic or dramatico-musical compositions; choreographic works or entertainment in dumb shows;
(f) Musical compositions, with or without words;
(g) Works of drawing, painting, architecture, sculpture, engraving, lithography, or other works of art; models or designs for works of art;
(h) Original ornamental designs or models for articles of manufacture, whether or not registrable as an industrial design, and other works of applied art;
(i) Illustrations, maps, plans, sketches, charts, and three-dimensional works relative to geography, topography, architecture, or science;
(j) Drawings or plastic works of a scientific or technical character;
(k) Photographic works, including works produced by a process analogous to photography, lantern slides;
(l) Audiovisual works and cinematographic works and works produced by a process analogous to cinematography or any process for making audio-visual recordings;
(m) Pictorial illustrations and advertisements;
(n) Computer programs; and
(o) Other literary, scholarly, scientific, and artistic works.[36]

The following are the derivative works:

(a) Dramatizations, translations, adaptations, abridgments, arrangements, and other alterations of literary or artistic works; and
(b) Collections of literary, scholarly, or artistic works and compilations of data and other materials that are original by reason of the selection coordination or arrangement of their contents. (Sec. 2, [P] and [Q], P.D. No. 49).[37]

[35] Intellectual Property Code of the Philippines, s 177.
[36] Intellectual Property Code of the Philippines, s 172.
[37] Intellectual Property Code of the Philippines, s 173.

Original works are those independently created by the author and not copied from another source. They do not have to be new, similar to the concept of novelty in patents. Conversely, derivative works are based on original works, either through transformation, adaptation, or as a collection of works. As indicated in the list, they include artistic or written works, including computer programs. Essentially, derivative works are variations of the original in a different form or expression. This means that creating or using derivative works without the original author's permission constitutes copyright infringement.

C. Limitations to Copyright Protection

Copyright protection is not absolute but subject to certain limitations. These limitations can be categorised into (1) subject matter, and (2) manner of use. Limitations concerning subject matter include those outside the scope of protection due to their nature or public policy. In the IP code, they are listed under sections 175 and 176.

> Section 175. Unprotected Subject Matter. – Notwithstanding the provisions of Sections 172 and 173, no protection shall extend, under this law, to any idea, procedure, system, method or operation, concept, principle, discovery or mere data as such, even if they are expressed, explained, illustrated or embodied in a work; news of the day and other miscellaneous facts having the character of mere items of press information; or any official text of a legislative, administrative or legal nature, as well as any official translation thereof.
>
> Section 176. Works of the Government. – 176.1. No copyright shall subsist in any work of the Government of the Philippines. However, prior approval of the government agency or office wherein the work is created shall be necessary for exploitation of such work for profit. Such agency or office may, among other things, impose the payment of royalties as a condition. No prior approval or conditions shall be required for the use of any purpose of statutes, rules and regulations, and speeches, lectures, sermons, addresses, and dissertations, pronounced, read or rendered in courts of justice, before administrative agencies, in deliberative assemblies and in meetings of public character. (Sec. 9, first par., P.D. No. 49)
>
> 176.2. The author of speeches, lectures, sermons, addresses, and dissertations mentioned in the preceding paragraphs shall have the exclusive right of making a collection of his works. (n)
>
> 176.3. Notwithstanding the foregoing provisions, the Government is not precluded from receiving and holding copyrights transferred to it by assignment, bequest or otherwise; nor shall publication or republication by the Government in a public document of any work in which copyright is subsisting be taken to cause any abridgment or annulment of the copyright or to authorize any use or appropriation of such work without the consent of the copyright owner. (Sec. 9, third par., P.D. No. 49).

Limitations as to the manner of use are those mentioned in sections 184 and Fair Use under section 185 of the IP Code, respectively:

> Section 184. Limitations on Copyright. – 184.1. Notwithstanding the provisions of Chapter V, the following acts shall not constitute infringement of copyright:
>
> (a) The recitation or performance of a work, once it has been lawfully made accessible to the public, if done privately and free of charge or if made strictly for a charitable or religious institution or society; (Sec. 10(1), P.D. No. 49)
>
> (b) The making of quotations from a published work if they are compatible with fair use and only to the extent justified for the purpose, including quotations from newspaper articles and periodicals in the form of press summaries: Provided, That the source and the name of the author, if appearing on the work, are mentioned; (Sec. 11, third par., P.D. No. 49)
>
> (c) The reproduction or communication to the public by mass media of articles on current political, social, economic, scientific or religious topic, lectures, addresses and other works of the same

nature, which are delivered in public if such use is for information purposes and has not been expressly reserved: Provided, That the source is clearly indicated; (Sec. 11, P.D. No. 49)

(d) The reproduction and communication to the public of literary, scientific or artistic works as part of reports of current events by means of photography, cinematography or broadcasting to the extent necessary for the purpose; (Sec. 12, P.D. No. 49)

(e) The inclusion of a work in a publication, broadcast, or other communication to the public, sound recording or film, if such inclusion is made by way of illustration for teaching purposes and is compatible with fair use: Provided, That the source and of *(sic)* the name of the author, if appearing in the work, are mentioned;

(f) The recording made in schools, universities, or educational institutions of a work included in a broadcast for the use of such schools, universities or educational institutions: Provided, That such recording must be deleted within a reasonable period after they were first broadcast: Provided, further, That such recording may not be made from audiovisual works which are part of the general cinema repertoire of feature films except for brief excerpts of the work;

(g) The making of ephemeral recordings by a broadcasting organization by means of its own facilities and for use in its own broadcast;

(h) The use made of a work by or under the direction or control of the Government, by the National Library or by educational, scientific or professional institutions where such use is in the public interest and is compatible with fair use;

(i) The public performance or the communication to the public of a work, in a place where no admission fee is charged in respect of such public performance or communication, by a club or institution for charitable or educational purpose only, whose aim is not profit-making, subject to such other limitations as may be provided in the Regulations; (n)

(j) Public display of the original or a copy of the work not made by means of a film, slide, television image or otherwise on screen or by means of any other device or process: Provided, That either the work has been published, or, that the original or the copy displayed has been sold, given away or otherwise transferred to another person by the author or his successor in title; and

(k) Any use made of a work for the purpose of any judicial proceedings or for the giving of professional advice by a legal practitioner.

184.2. The provisions of this section shall be interpreted in such a way as to allow the work to be used in a manner which does not conflict with the normal exploitation of the work and does not unreasonably prejudice the right holder's legitimate interests.

Section 185. Fair Use of a Copyrighted Work. – 185.1. The fair use of a copyrighted work for criticism, comment, news reporting, teaching including multiple copies for classroom use, scholarship, research, and similar purposes is not an infringement of copyright. Decompilation, which is understood here to be the reproduction of the code and translation of the forms of the computer program to achieve the inter-operability of an independently created computer program with other programs may also constitute fair use. In determining whether the use made of a work in any particular case is fair use, the factors to be considered shall include the following:

(a) The purpose and character of use, including whether such use is of commercial nature or is for non-profit educational purposes;

(b) The nature of the copyrighted work;

(c) The amount and substantiality of the portion used in relation to the copyrighted work as a whole; and

(d) The effect of the use upon the potential market for or value of the copyrighted work.

185.2. The fact that a work is unpublished shall not by itself bar a finding of fair use if such finding is made upon consideration of all the above factors.

Limitations on subject matter under sections 175 and 176 of the IP Code consist of works that are outside the scope of copyright protection by law. They can be summarised as follows: (1) mere ideas or concepts as such; (2) news of the day or press information; (3) official legislative, legal, or administrative texts; and, (4) works of the government. These works are not protected because they are considered part of the public domain and can be used as resource materials for further work. Protecting these works would restrict the free flow of ideas and creativity.

Limitations on the manner of use under section 184 of the IP Code refer to works that are protected by copyright but can be used without permission under specific conditions. In other words, using these works without adhering to the limitations provided by law is technically copyright infringement. Section 184 of the IP Code lists acts that are not considered copyright infringement. These acts mainly include (1) those that are done privately and without charge or for charitable or civic purposes; (2) quotations from published works consistent with fair use; (3) reproduction, communication, performance, or exhibition to the public under certain conditions; and, (4) use for judicial or legal proceedings.

Section 185 provides the limitation based on 'Fair Use' to supplement these restrictions. An act qualifies as 'fair use' (or 'fair dealing') if it passes the four-factor test: (1) purpose and character of use; (2) nature of the work; (3) amount of work used; and, (4) effect on potential market. This is commonly called the 'four-factor test.' Indicators of fair use according to this test include: (1) the work is educational and not for profit; (2) the work is based on factual events and is already published; (3) the amount used is small and not essential to the work; and, (4) the use will not impact the potential revenue or market value of the copyrighted work. The opposite of these indicators suggests unfair use. Using the work as a parody is also considered 'fair use,' as it involves making fun of, satirizing, or creating a humorous account of the original work. Such use is regarded as fair because it's impossible to create humor or satire of another work without using it. It also counts as fair criticism, observation, or commentary.

The IP code does not clarify the application of the four-factor test, but it is reasonable to believe that the more indicators of the four-factor test that are met, the more likely it is to be considered fair use. The concept of fair use is evolving and is determined on a case-by-case basis based on the specific facts. To decide what constitutes fair use, reliance is placed on case law or jurisprudence. Due to differing rulings on fair use, there is considerable debate about its application. It is the most commonly used principle in defending against copyright infringement.

In the recent case of *FILSCAP v Anrey, Inc.*,[38] the Supreme Court gave a comprehensive discussion on the concept of fair use as applied in the Philippine context. It ruled that a restaurant is liable for infringement if it plays a radio broadcast inside its premises without a licence from the copyright owners, in violation of the economic right of the owner for public performance of the work in section 177.6 of the Intellectual Property Code. Using the four-factor test, the Supreme Court ruled that there is infringement as it is not considered fair use:

> *First*, the purpose and character of the use of the copyrighted songs are undeniably commercial, being played throughout the restaurants of Anrey, which are open to the public, for the entertainment of Anrey's customers. Commercial use excludes fair use and should be weighed against it.
>
> *Second*, the nature of the copyrighted songs is creative rather than factual, and thus fair use is weighed against the user, Anrey.
>
> *Third*, an exact reproduction of the copyrighted songs are made when they are played by means of radio-over-loudspeakers, and not just small portions thereof, supporting the conclusion that their use is not fair. The fact that some customers may not hear or listen to the entire copyrighted music played -in the radio reception is not significant. The fact remains that the copyrighted music from the radio- reception

[38] *Filipino Society of Composers, Authors and Publishers v Anrey Inc* GR No 233918 (2022).

transmitted through the loudspeakers is exactly reproduced or played in whole, and not just portions thereof.

Fourth, the use of the copyrighted songs in this case could 'result in a substantially adverse impact on the potential market for the subject copyrighted songs The unrestricted and widespread conduct of playing copyrighted music by means of radio-over-loudspeakers in public commercial places for entertainment of the public would substantially impact restaurants, bars, clubs, and other commercial establishments, which are potential market for the subject copyrighted songs. Such use should thus be deemed unfair.

D. Ownership of Copyright

Section 178 of the IP Code outlines the rules on copyright ownership. Usually, the original literary and artistic works belong to the creator of the work. In cases of joint authorship, the co-authors are regarded as co-owners of the work. However, if the work can be divided and the creator of each part can be identified, then each creator is deemed the owner of that specific part.

In an employer-employee relationship, the employee owns the rights to work if it is not part of their regular duties, even if they use the employer's time and resources. Conversely, the employer owns the work if it results from the employee's regular duties.[39] For example, a biology teacher who writes a poem will own the copyright for that work. However, the school employee shall own the lesson plan created by the same biology teacher, as this is part of their regular duties. What constitutes regular duties should be defined in the institution's intellectual property policy to prevent confusion and misunderstanding. The reason for granting ownership to the employer is that the work is produced under the employer's direction and the employee's salary is considered compensation.

In cases of commissioned work where no employer-employee relationship exists, the person who commissions the work owns it. However, the copyright remains with the creator unless there is a written agreement otherwise.[40] For example, if A commissions B to create a painting, the physical painting belongs to A, but the copyright remains with B unless there is a written agreement stating otherwise.

In the case of audiovisual works, copyright belongs to each creator involved in the production process.[41] This means that the script's author, the movie's cinematographer, and the music's composer each own their respective works individually. However, for the work to be exhibited, the producer holds the copyright for the exhibition. To clarify, each author of an audiovisual work is usually required to assign the exhibition rights to the producer so they can display the work.

Regarding letters, the copyright shall belong to the author in accordance with Article 723 of the Civil Code. It should be noted that R.A. 10372, or the latest amendments to the IP Code under section 181, states that 'the copyright is distinct from the property in the material object subject to it. Consequently, the transfer, assignment, or licensing of the copyright shall not constitute a transfer of the material object.'

Ownership issues related to intellectual property, especially in copyright, are among the most debated topics in academia. It is crucial to establish clear IP ownership rules in policies to prevent confusion and disputes. Keeping documented evidence of IP ownership is always recommended.

[39] Intellectual Property Code of the Philippines, s 178.2.
[40] Intellectual Property Code of the Philippines, s 178.4.
[41] Intellectual Property Code of the Philippines, s 178.5.

E. Related Rights of Copyright

Related rights of copyright, also known as neighbouring rights, are another form of copyright protection besides copyrighted works. These related rights give life to the copyrighted work. They include the rights of actors, dancers, performers, and producers of phonograms and broadcasting organisations in the case of radio or television programmes. The purpose of protecting these related rights is to recognise the contributions of those who bring the work to life. Without them, the work would just be a piece of paper. Can you imagine a song without a singer? Or a script without an actor?

Section 203 of the IP Code outlines the scope of performers' rights. Performers hold exclusive rights to authorise (1) the exhibition of their performances; (2) the fixation of the performance (recording); (3) the reproduction of their performances; (4) the right of first public distribution; (5) the right to rent copies of their performances commercially; and, (6) the right to authorise making their performances available to the public via wire or wireless means. Section 205 of the IP Code states that once a performer authorises broadcasting or fixation of the performance, those performance rights no longer apply.

Section 212 of the IP Code further outlines the limitations on related copyright rights, such as (1) the use of a natural person exclusively for personal purposes; (2) the use of short excerpts for reporting current events; (3) use solely for teaching or scientific research; and, (4) fair use under section 185 of the IP Code.

For example, with a popular K-pop band holding a live concert, the band itself holds related rights of copyright over its performance during the concert, separate from the rights over the music, production, or storyline. This prevents bootlegging or recording of live performances for commercial use, subject to the limitations under section 212 mentioned above.

F. Copyright Infringement

Like other forms of intellectual property, copyright grants the owner the right to prevent others from using their rights without permission. Someone who violates these rights is considered to have infringed. In the case of *Columbia Pictures Inc. v Court of Appeals* (G.R. No. 110318, 28 August 1996), the Supreme Court described infringement as 'a trespass on a private domain owned and occupied by the owner, and therefore, protected by law, and infringement of copyright xxx consists of doing by any person, without consent of the owner of the copyright, of anything the sole right to do which is conferred by statute on the owner of the copyright.' It is important to understand that damage or malicious intent are not part of copyright infringement. Therefore, ignorance or acting in good faith are not defences against infringement.

There are two main types of infringement: (1) direct and (2) indirect. Direct infringement happens when someone uses copyrighted material without the owner's permission. For example, photocopying a large part of a book without authorisation constitutes direct infringement. Indirect infringement involves activities related to the infringing work, such as selling, showing, or importing it. It's important to note that since copyright protects the expression of ideas, the concept itself is not protected. In the case of *Joaquin v Drilon* (G.R. No. 108946, 28 January 1999), it was held that the format of a game show is not protected by copyright because it is just an idea.

Copyright infringement is different from plagiarism, although they are related ideas. Infringement involves copying without permission, while plagiarism involves copying without citing the source. Copyright is a legal concept, whereas plagiarism is an ethical one. For example, a person who copies three paragraphs from a book but provides the original source may be guilty of infringement but not plagiarism. Conversely, someone who copies three paragraphs without citing the source but has permission from the copyright owner is liable for plagiarism but not infringement. Of course, someone who neither asks for permission nor cites the source is liable for both plagiarism and infringement.

Section 216 of the IP Code outlines remedies for infringement, which include: (1) injunction; (2) damages and costs; (3) impounding of the infringing materials; (4) destruction of the infringing materials; and, (4) other terms such as payment of moral and exemplary damages. The court also has the authority to seize the infringing materials, which can serve as evidence during the trial.

In the case of *Habana v Robles* (GR No.131522, 19 July 1999), the Supreme Court held that 'to constitute infringement, it is not necessary that the whole or even a large portion of the work shall have been copied. If so much is taken that the value of the original is sensibly diminished, or the labors of the original author are substantially and to an injurious extent appropriated by another, that is sufficient in point of law to constitute piracy.'

The common defences against copyright infringement in the IP Code include those related to limitations on subject matter (sections 174 and 175), limitations on use (section 184), and fair use (section 185).

V. Conclusion

This chapter aims to provide an introduction and overview of intellectual property in the Philippine context. The first part discusses the concept and features of intellectual property in general. This is followed by a discussion of the three main types of intellectual property: patent, trademark, and copyright in the Philippine context. Although there are other types of intellectual property, such as industrial designs, trade secrets, and geographical indications, these three are the primary focus of the discussion.

The importance and significance of intellectual property in society, business, and the economy have increased at the turn of the century with the rise of artificial intelligence, data science, and digital transformation. Protecting and enforcing intellectual property is crucial for encouraging innovation and creativity. In the Philippines, intellectual property is essential in providing a platform for innovation and setting businesses apart from their competitors. It benefits both large corporations and small to medium-sized enterprises by allowing them to safeguard their inventions, trademarks, and creative works. Overall, it supports the economy by attracting local and foreign investments, which help create jobs, promote economic growth, and facilitate technology transfer.

Despite recent progress, challenges in raising awareness of intellectual property in the Philippines still exist. There is a need to increase awareness and understanding of intellectual property among all stakeholders – government, industry, and academia. May this humble work contribute to this goal and help make the Philippines a global leader in innovation, creativity, and respect for intellectual property.

7

Law of Corporations and Insolvency

LAMBERT YANCY B GARGANTA

This chapter discusses the fundamentals of corporation law and insolvency law in the Philippines in relation to Private International Law. This is important in the present-day corporate landscape as business entities in the Philippines may seek cross-border insolvency wherein assistance is sought in a foreign state in connection with a parallel insolvency proceeding governed by the Philippine law. An example of this is when a Philippine corporation that lodged an insolvency proceeding in a foreign state initiates the filing for a petition for recognition in a Philippine court through a foreign representative. Furthermore, cross-border insolvency proceedings of a Philippine corporation must also consider the principle of reciprocity between the two states. Hence, this outlines the relevance of the Philippine law on corporations and insolvency in an international context.

I. Corporations: Capacity, Agency and Internal Management

In the Philippines, corporations are entities created by operation of law and are organised under the provisions of the Revised Corporation Code of the Philippines (hereinafter referred to as 'RCC').[1] Foreign entities previously doing business in the Philippines should take note that the RCC, which became effective in 2019, repealed the 1980 Corporation Code of the Philippines. The changes in Philippine corporate law are discussed in this chapter. A corporation's existence is dependent on the state as it is a creature without any existence until it has received the *imprimatur* of the state according to law.[2] This is done by the filing of the Articles of Incorporation and By-laws with the Securities and Exchange Commission (hereinafter referred to as the 'SEC').

This kind of filing is now done through an online facility introduced by the SEC: Electronic Simplified Processing of Application for Registration of Company (eSPARC). The system allows the applicants or their duly appointed representative to submit the proposed company name and input details of the Articles for review of the SEC.[3] However, submission of four sets of the required documents to the SEC processing office shall still be done within 30 calendar days from date of payment of registration.[4]

The substantive requirements of forming a corporation have been revised with the passage of the RCC. The incorporators who originally composed the body corporate and act as signatories

[1] Republic Act No. 11232 effectively repealed The Corporation Code of the Philippines (Batas Pambansa Blg. 68).
[2] *Tayag v Benguet Consolidated Inc.* GR No L-23145 (1968).
[3] Regular Processing of SEC-ESPARC (with uploading of documents) User Guide, Securities and Exchange Commission, see esparc.sec.gov.ph/docs/UserGuide-esparc.pdf.
[4] ibid.

of the Articles now have no minimum prescribed number.[5] Furthermore, juridical entities such as other corporations can now become incorporators, and the majority can be non-Philippine residents, provided they own at least one share of the capital stock.[6] Along with the retained provision that there shall be no minimum authorised capital stock or the maximum amount of capital of the corporation fixed in the Articles, the RCC has no minimum subscribed capital stock or committed amount of capital the corporation will receive from its existing subscribers, and paid-up capital.[7]

In addition to this, corporations in the Philippines shall now enjoy a perpetual term, unless the Articles provide a limit to their term of existence.[8] The old requirement for a corporate name is that it should not be identical or deceptively or confusingly similar to another. The RCC amended this by requiring that the corporate name should be distinguishable from that already reserved or registered for the use of another corporation.[9] There was no change with regards to the requirement to indicate the purpose of the corporation or the main business it shall undertake in the Philippines. Finally, on the matter of principal office address, it must be located within the Philippines and must be specifically indicated in the Articles as it will determine the proper venue for a petition for voluntary insolvency on the insolvent debtor corporation.[10] As previously discussed, incorporation is now done through electronic means. Upon submission of the Articles and By-Laws through eSPARC, the SEC shall review the same and shall notify the applicant that the documents are ready for signing and notarisation. After such execution, the scanned copies will be uploaded for review, and if the same is deemed sufficient, the applicant will be directed to payment of registration. Thereafter, the Certificate of Incorporation shall be issued by the SEC.

Only until the SEC issues a Certificate of Incorporation can a corporation exercise its capacity as a juridical person with personality separate and distinct from the shareholders forming it.[11] The certificate is an indispensable requirement for the corporation to acquire capacity to acquire and possess property, as well as incur obligations.[12] This Doctrine of Separate Personality, along with the Limited Liability Rule,[13] make a corporation the most desirable business organisation for many businessmen.[14] The separate and distinct personality allows a corporation to own and acquire properties, enter into contractual obligation, and bring criminal or civil actions.

However, the said separate juridical personality can be disregarded, and the corporate fiction may be pierced, attaching personal liability to the responsible persons, if the corporate personality is used to defeat public convenience, justify wrong, protect fraud, or defend crime.[15] One such application of piercing the veil is in 'fraud piercing' where there is a fraudulent transaction, and the corporate entity has been used in the perpetration of the fraud resulting in damage and

[5] N.B. Notwithstanding, a single incorporator shall be deemed as an incorporator of a One Person Corporation (OPC).

[6] Revised Corporation Code, s 10.

[7] TJ Herbosa and ER Recalde, *The Revised Corporation Code of the Philippines (Its Theories and Applications)* (Quezon City, Rex Printing Company Inc, 2020) 69.

[8] Revised Corporation Code, s 10.

[9] Revised Corporation Code, s 17.

[10] Herbosa and Recalde (n 7) 77.

[11] Revised Corporation Code, s 18; Civil Code, Art 44.

[12] Civil Code, Art 46.

[13] A stockholder is personally liable for the financial obligations only to the extent of his unpaid subscription.

[14] TB Aquino and MAA Aquino, *Commentaries and Jurisprudence on the Revised Corporation Code of the Philippines* (Quezon City, Rex Printing Company Inc, 2020) 30.

[15] *Dutch Movers, Inc. v Lequin*, GR No. 210032 (2017).

prejudice towards third persons.[16] The Supreme Court, in *Maricalum Mining Co. v Florentino*, discussed another type of piercing the veil known as 'alter-ego piercing':

> xxx where the corporation is merely a farce since it is a mere alter ego or business conduit of a person, or where the corporation is so organized and controlled and its affairs are so conducted as to make it merely an instrumentality, agency, conduit, or adjunct of another corporation xxx.[17]

It was expounded in the same case that for alter-ego piercing, there should be complete control or dominion of the corporate entity as to render it without a separate mind, will or existence of its own, and such control must have been used to commit fraud or wrongdoing which results in damage and injury.[18] Hence, when the corporate veil is pierced, the two corporations shall be treated as one with regards to their liability.

It is also settled in Philippine corporate law that as juridical persons, corporations shall exercise corporate powers, conduct all business, and control all properties through the Board of Directors or Trustees elected by their stockholders or members.[19] This is consistent with the Agency Theory which posits that all powers reside in the stockholders and are just delegated to the directors as agents. The Board of Directors is thus a creation of the stockholders and derives its power to control and direct the affairs of the corporation from those who have been actually elected on an annual basis.[20] Hence, the board should exercise utmost good faith in managing corporate affairs.

The adherence to the agency theory follows that the board is now able to administer the internal affairs and management of the corporation as well as its assets. The Doctrine of Centralised Management is a well-entrenched rule in Philippine jurisprudence where a corporation exercises all its powers through the board and/or its duly authorised officers, except in instances where the Corporation Code (presently RCC) requires stockholders' approval for certain specific acts.[21] This doctrine is necessary to promote efficiency in such an organisation where the stockholders are too numerous and unfamiliar with the business of a corporation.

In order to facilitate the effective management of the board, Philippine jurisprudence observes the Business Judgement Rule, which recognises that questions of policy or of management of corporate affairs must be left solely to the honest decisions of officers and directors of a corporation, and so long as they act in good faith, their orders are not reviewable by the courts.[22] With this rule in place, the courts cannot undertake to control the discretion of the board regarding administrative matters where the board has legitimate powers.[23] The board of directors are also not liable to the stockholders in making decisions using their business judgements, even in cases of mismanagement resulting in corporate damages and/or business losses, if there is no showing of bad faith in committing the acts.[24]

The requisites for the applicability of the business judgment rule are as follows: (1) the presence of a business decision including decisions on policy, management and administration, (2) the decision must be *intra vires* or within the powers of the corporation and must comply

[16] *Concept Builders, Inc. v NLRC* GR No. 108734 (1996).
[17] GR No. 221813 (2018).
[18] *Maricalum Mining Corp. v Florentino*, GR No. 221813 (2018).
[19] Revised Corporation Code, s 22.
[20] *Valle Verde Country Club Inc. v Africa*, GR No. 151969 (2009).
[21] *Tom v Rodriguez*, GR No 215764 (2016).
[22] *Saber v Court of Appeals* GR No. 132981 (2004).
[23] *Gamboa v Victoriano* GR No. L-40620 (1979).
[24] *Montelibano v Bacolod-Murcia Milling Co.* GR No. L-15092 (1962).

with the law, (3) good faith, (4) due care in making the decision, and (5) the director must not have personal interest or must not be self-dealing[25] or must not otherwise be in breach of the duty of loyalty.[26] This duty of loyalty prevents directors from engaging in business opportunities that should have been directed to the corporation. This is otherwise known as the Doctrine of Corporate Opportunity where a director, by their office, acquires a business opportunity which should belong to the corporation thereby obtaining profits therefrom. Hence, the observance of the business judgement rule is a recognised advantage in pursuing a corporate form of business organisation.

Directors shall enjoy a term of one year, while trustees have a term not exceeding three years. However, in instances where a new director or trustee was not elected after the provided term, Philippine law allows the application of the 'hold-over principle' which allows the incumbent to remain as such until a successor is elected and qualified. It is now necessary to discuss the minimum qualifications which are as follows: directors need to have at least one share of the capital stock, should be a natural person, and of legal age.[27] The director and trustee must not also be convicted by final judgment of an offence punishable by imprisonment for a period exceeding six years, a violation of the RCC or the Securities Regulation Code, must not be found administratively liable for offences involving fraudulent acts, or convicted by a foreign court or equivalent foreign regulation authority regarding similar offences to the ones stated above.[28]

The RCC also provides a revision in the composition of the board of a corporation vested with public interest wherein it is required to elect independent directors who shall constitute at least 20 per cent of the board.[29] A corporation is vested with public interest if it is: (a) a corporation with assets amounting to 50 million pesos, (b) a corporation whose securities are registered in an exchange, (c) financial intermediaries such as banks and quasi-banks, and those engaged in money service business, or (d) corporations engaged in business vested with public interest similar to the above.[30] Hence, the nature of these corporations requires a safeguard in the person of the independent director who is independent of management and free from any business or other relationship which could, or could reasonably be perceived to, materially interfere with the exercise of independent judgement in carrying out the responsibilities of a director.[31]

Philippine law also identifies the officers of the corporation, namely: the president, treasurer, corporate secretary, and compliance officer for corporations vested with public interest. The president must be a director and shall handle the day-to-day operations of the corporation, while the treasurer handles the funds and other assets of the corporation and has authority to receive in the name of and for the benefit of the corporation all subscriptions, contributions and donations paid or given by the subscribers or members, and one of the main signatories of the financial statements of the corporation. Hence, to exercise these duties, the treasurer must be a resident of the Philippines. On the other hand, the corporate secretary is the one tasked to maintain corporate housekeeping, send notices for meetings, take the minutes of the meeting, attest to board resolutions by issuing a secretary's certificate, and sign the General Information Sheet (GIS) as a reportorial requirement to the SEC. The corporate secretary should be both a citizen and resident of the Philippines.

[25] Revised Corporation Code, s 31 states that self-dealing directors, trustees or officers are those who personally contract with the corporation in which they are directors, trustees or officers.

[26] Aquino and Aquino (n 14) 291.

[27] Revised Corporation Code, s 22.

[28] ibid s 26.

[29] ibid s 22.

[30] Herbosa and Recalde (n 7) 103.

[31] Revised Corporation Code, s 22.

The board of directors or trustees exercise corporate powers which include those expressly authorised by the RCC or its Articles, those incidental to the existence of the corporation, and those implied or necessary for the exercise of its business. Notwithstanding this, the corporation, through its board, also has the capacity to exercise special powers which can result in fundamental changes in the corporation. Hence, apart from board approval, approval of the stockholders or members is required in certain instances. This includes the power to increase or decrease the authorised capital stock.[32] With regards to increase of authorised capital stock, it is necessary that there shall also be a 25 per cent increase on both the subscribed and paid-up capital stock. It should be certified by the corporation's treasurer.[33]

A corporation is also allowed, by a majority vote of its board, to sell, lease, exchange, mortgage, pledge or otherwise dispose of its property and assets. However, by way of exception, if the sale involves all or substantially all of its assets and properties, this should be first approved by the board and then ratified by the vote of the stockholders representing at least two-thirds of the outstanding capital stock or the members with or without voting rights.[34] Furthermore, as a general rule, board approval is only necessary if the investment of the corporation is to reasonably accomplish its primary purpose. Nonetheless, if the investment will be directed towards the secondary purpose enumerated in the Articles, it shall follow the same procedure with regards to stockholder approval or member approval. Otherwise, it shall be deemed as an *ultra vires* act, or one committed outside the approved purposes of the corporation and therefore voidable.[35]

Philippine law also allows corporations to distribute dividends or corporate profits allocated, lawfully declared, and ordered by the directors to be paid to the stockholders, when there are unrestricted retained earnings (URE).[36] If there are UREs, a board resolution is required to distribute cash and property dividends, but if stock dividends are to be declared, it is necessary to also have the approval of two-thirds of the outstanding capital stock prior to the distribution. Stockholder concurrence is necessary because by declaring stock dividends, a corporation ploughs back a portion of its entire unrestricted retained earnings either into its working capital or for capital asset acquisitions or investments.[37] It is likewise important to understand the common purposes of the corporation for declaring stock dividends which are as follows: (1) the corporation simply desires a larger permanent capitalisation, (2) the market price may have increased above a desirable trading range and stock dividends will generally reduce the per share market value of the company's stocks, (3) the corporation may wish to have more stockholders and expects to eventually increase the number of outstanding shares, and (4) stock dividends may be used to satisfy stockholders' demands for cash dividends when the corporation may not be willing to pay cash dividends but may have enough unrestricted retained earnings.[38]

Corporations can also merge or consolidate. A merger is one where a corporation absorbs another corporation, where the former remains in existence while the latter is dissolved. On the other hand, consolidation is one where a new corporation is created and the consolidating

[32] Revised Corporation Code, s 37.

[33] ibid.

[34] ibid s 39.

[35] *Pirovana, et al v The Dela Rama Steamship Co.* GR No. L-5377 (1954).

[36] Unrestricted Retained Earnings are the amount of accumulated profits and gains realised out of a normal and continuous operation of the company after deducting therefrom distributions to stockholders and transfers to capital stock or other accounts and not appropriated by its Board for corporate expansion projects, not covered by a restriction for dividend declaration, and not required to be retained under special circumstances. See SEC Memorandum Circular No. 11, Series of 2008, s 2.

[37] *PLDT v NTC*, GR No. 152685 (2007).

[38] Aquino and Aquino (n 14) 497–98.

corporations are extinguished.[39] In order to effect a merger or consolidation, the board of each corporation shall draw up a plan which should be approved by the majority of the vote of each entity. Afterwards, the plan shall be approved by two-thirds of the outstanding capital stock or members of the constituent corporations in separate meetings. The Articles of Merger or Consolidation shall be executed by each of the constituent corporations, signed by the President or Vice-President and certified by the Corporate Secretary or Assistant Secretary.[40] Afterwards, four copies of the Articles shall be submitted to the SEC along with the favourable recommendation of the pertinent government agency in applicable cases. If necessary, the SEC shall set a hearing if, upon investigation, the Commission believes that the proposed merger or consolidation is contrary to or inconsistent with the RCC or existing laws. Otherwise, it shall issue a Certificate of Merger or Consolidation which shall render its effectivity.

The effects of merger and consolidation of corporations are as follows: (1) the constituent corporations shall become a single corporation, (2) the separate existence of the constituent corporations shall cease except that of the surviving or consolidated one, (3) the surviving or consolidated corporation shall possess all rights, privileges, immunities and powers and shall be subject to all duties of a corporation, (4) the surviving or consolidated corporation shall possess all rights, privileges and franchises of each constituent and properties shall be deemed transferred to the surviving or consolidated one, and (5) all liabilities of the constituent shall pertain to the surviving or consolidated corporation.[41] As to the existing employment contracts affected by the merger or consolidation, the surviving corporation shall assume the employees of the dissolved corporation, while the consolidated corporation shall absorb the employees of its constituents.

If a stockholder disagrees with the corporate action mentioned above, the stockholder may demand payment of the fair value of their shares after dissenting from the proposed corporate action involving a fundamental change in the corporation.[42] This is available in the following instances: (1) in case any amendment of the Articles of Incorporation has the effect of changing or restricting the rights of any stockholder or class of shares, (2) in case of any amendment to the Articles authorising preferences in any respect superior to those outstanding shares of any class, (3) in case of amendment to the Articles extending the corporate term, (4) in case of amendment of the Articles shortening the corporate term, (5) in case of sale, lease, exchange, transfer, mortgage, pledge or other disposition of all or substantially all of the corporate property and assets, (6) merger or consolidation, and (7) investment of corporate funds in another corporation or business for any purpose other than the corporation's primary purpose. The list of grounds is exclusive.[43]

Close corporations, otherwise known as 'incorporated partnerships,' are also feasible in the Philippines where the stockholders enjoy limited liability but provide restrictions on the ownership of shares and management of the corporation.[44] A close corporation is beneficial to those maintaining a close-knit corporation who view their stockholders as partners, but is deemed prejudicial to those who want to maximise the free transferability of shares due to its restrictions.[45] This entails that a close corporation, aside from the substantial and indispensable provisions in the Articles of Incorporation, shall likewise contain the following: (1) all the corporation's

[39] Aquino and Aquino (n 14) 697.
[40] Revised Corporation Code, s 77.
[41] Revised Corporation Code, s 79.
[42] Aquino and Aquino (n 14) 718.
[43] Revised Corporation Code, s 80.
[44] Herbosa and Recalde (n 7) 334.
[45] ibid 336.

issued stock of all classes, exclusive of treasury shares, shall be held of record by not more than a specified number of persons, not exceeding 20, (2) all the issued stock of all classes shall be subject to specified restrictions on transfer, and (3) the corporation shall not be listed in any stock exchange.[46] The restriction of transfer has a right of first refusal in favour of the stockholders of the close corporation.[47]

It is interesting to note that stockholders of a close corporation may act as directors without need of election and shall therefore be liable in the same manner as directors. This also provides an exception to the rule that a resolution of the board of directors is necessary in enacting corporate acts. Notwithstanding this, any action by the directors of the close corporation without a meeting shall still be valid if: (1) before or after such action is taken, written consent is signed by all the directors, (2) the directors are accustomed to take informal action with the express or implied acquiescence of all stockholders, (3) all the stockholders have actual or implied knowledge of the action and make no prompt objection in writing, or (4) all the directors have express or implied knowledge of the action in question and none of them makes a prompt objection in writing.[48]

Due to its nature, deadlocks can also occur in a close corporation when the directors or stockholders are so divided on the management of the business and affairs of the corporation that the votes required for any corporate action cannot be obtained and, as a result, business could no longer be conducted to the advantage of the stockholders.[49] As a remedy in case of a deadlock, the SEC, upon written petition by any stockholder, shall have the power to arbitrate the dispute. The SEC can exercise the following orders: (1) cancelling or altering any provision contained in the Articles of Incorporation, by-laws, or any stockholders' agreement; (2) cancelling, altering or enjoining a resolution or act of the corporation, or its board of directors, stockholders, or officer; (3) directing or prohibiting any act of the corporation or its board of directors, stockholders, officers, or other persons party to the action; (4) requiring the purchase at their fair value of shares of any stockholder, either by the corporation regardless of the availability of unrestricted retained earnings in its books, or by the other stockholders; (5) appointing a provisional director who shall be an impartial person who is neither a stockholder nor creditor of the corporation; (6) dissolving the corporation; or (7) granting such other relief as the circumstances may warrant.[50]

The RCC also provides for the establishment of One Person Corporations (hereinafter referred to as 'OPC'). These are otherwise known as 'incorporated sole proprietorships' wherein a single person owns the corporation.[51] By incorporating an OPC, the single stockholder will also enjoy limited liability and separate juridical personality. A natural person, trust, or an estate may form an OPC, with the exception of banks and quasi-banks, and other financial intermediaries. In the same manner as a close corporation, an OPC must also include specific provisions in its Articles such as: (1) if the single stockholder is a trust or an estate, the name, nationality, and residence of the trustee, administrator, executor, guardian, conservator, custodian, or another person exercising fiduciary duties together with the proof of such authority to act on behalf of the trust or estate; and (2) the name, nationality, residence of the nominee and alternative nominee, and the extent, coverage and limitation of the authority.[52] Furthermore, it is also required that the corporate name expressly indicates 'OPC' either below or at the end of the corporate name.[53]

[46] Revised Corporation Code, s 95.
[47] Aquino and Aquino (n 14) 769.
[48] Revised Corporation Code, s 100.
[49] ibid s 103.
[50] ibid.
[51] Herbosa and Recalde (n 7) 362.
[52] Revised Corporation Code, s 118.
[53] ibid s 120.

In an OPC, the single stockholder shall concurrently serve as the sole director and president. Furthermore, the single stockholder shall also be self-appointed as the treasurer, unlike in an ordinary stock corporation where this is one of the restrictions. What is necessary is that these appointments should be effected within 15 days from the issuance of the Certificate of Incorporation of the OPC. However, the single stockholder is not allowed to concurrently act as the corporate secretary, since the position is entrusted with the following responsibilities: (1) be responsible for maintaining the minutes book and/or records of the corporation, (2) notify the nominee or alternate nominee of the death or incapacity of the single stockholder, which notice shall be given no later than five days from such occurrence, (3) notify the SEC of the death of the single stockholder within five days as well, and (4) call the nominee or alternate nominee and the known legal heirs to a meeting regarding the election of a new director, the amendment of the Articles, and other consequential matters.[54] A single stockholder, upon acquiring all the stocks of an ordinary stock corporation, may convert it to an OPC. Upon the approval of the SEC, the OPC shall own all the properties and assume all rights, privileges, obligations, and liabilities of the converted corporation. On the other hand, an OPC may be converted into an ordinary corporation following compliance of the single stockholder with the requirements and the approval of the SEC.[55]

Foreign corporations may also be allowed the privilege of doing business in the Philippines, provided that they are formed, organised, or exist under any laws other than those of the Philippines and the laws of the country where the corporation was organized, allowing Filipino citizens and corporations to do business in their own country or state.[56] The foreign corporations are provided with several ways to be involved in doing business in the Philippines. They can incorporate a domestic subsidiary, which is a corporation where more than 50 per cent of the voting stock is owned or controlled, directly or indirectly, through one or more intermediaries by another corporation, which thereby becomes the parent company.[57] However, the domestic subsidiary corporation must still comply with the capitalisation requirement of US$ 200,000.00 if it chooses to pursue a domestic market enterprise with 40 per cent foreign equity.

A branch office may also be created. It is not a legally independent unit as it has no separate juridical personality from the parent company. It shall simply obtain a licence to do business in the Philippines.[58] Alternatively, a representative office may also be established to cater to the clients of the foreign parent company, but it cannot derive income from the Philippines and may only undertake information dissemination and promotion of products. Both shall be deemed as operational upon issuance of a Licence to Transact Business by the SEC. Transacting or doing business in the Philippines is the actual performance of specific commercial acts within the territory of the country on a continuing basis in its own name and account.[59] In these corporations a resident agent, who must be a Philippine resident, is required to be appointed in order for Philippine courts to acquire jurisdiction over it. The appointment is merely for the receiving of summons or other legal process served to the corporation.

It should be further understood that no foreign corporation transacting business in the Philippines without a licence shall be permitted to maintain any suit or proceeding in the country. However, if the foreign corporation acted in good faith in what it believed was an isolated

[54] Revised Corporation Code, s 122.
[55] ibid ss 131–32.
[56] ibid s 140.
[57] Rules of Procedure on Corporate Rehabilitation (A.M. No. 00-8-10-SC), s 1, Rule 2.
[58] *Philippine Deposit insurance Corporation v. Citibank* GR No. 170290 (2012).
[59] *B. Van Zuiden Bros., Ltd. v GTVL Mfg. Industries, Inc.* GR No. 147905 (2007).

transaction, the doctrine of estoppel shall apply as the law never intended to prevent foreign corporations from performing single or isolated acts, or to favour domestic corporations who renege in solitary transaction with them.[60] The Philippine Supreme Court ruled that the law was intended to bar foreign corporations from acquiring a domicile for the purpose of doing business in the country without first taking the steps necessary to allow them to sue in the local courts.[61]

Corporations can have their separate juridical personality extinguished through dissolution of the entity and termination of the corporate existence.[62] It follows that since the corporation is created by operation of law, it is also the same law that may take it away. Hence, dissolution may take effect only by the act or with the consent of the state by which it was established.[63] The dissolution results in the corporation's cessation as an entity to continue the business it was incorporated for. There are two methods of corporate dissolution in the Philippines: voluntary and involuntary. Voluntary dissolution can be initiated through a vote of the board of directors or trustees and stockholders or members if no corporate creditors shall be affected. The board needs to file a request for dissolution with the SEC. However, if the corporation has outstanding debts and creditors, the proper action is to file a petition with the SEC to ascertain that no creditors will be prejudiced by its immediate dissolution. Dissolution may also be done by amending the Articles of Incorporation to shorten the corporate term.

Dissolution may also be involuntary, such as a dissolution initiated by the SEC *motu proprio*, after proper notice or hearing, on the grounds of: (1) fraud or misrepresentation, and (2) non-use of corporate charter. This can also be effected upon receipt of a lawful order dissolving the corporation on the ground of insolvency, where the proper course of action is the liquidation of the assets of the corporation and the transfer of legal title to remaining corporate properties to the stockholders.[64,65] Nonetheless, a corporation in financial distress may seek rehabilitation rather than filing a petition for dissolution leading to liquidation.

II. Insolvency: Rehabilitation, Liquidation, Assignment of Property and Discharge of Debts

Insolvency under the Financial Rehabilitation and Insolvency Act (hereinafter referred to as 'FRIA')[66] covers the financial condition of debtors who are generally unable to pay liabilities as they fall due in the ordinary course of business or has liabilities that are greater than their assets.[67] In conjunction with the so-called 'balance sheet test,' insolvency is the relative condition of a person's assets and liabilities that the former, if all made immediately available, would not be sufficient to discharge the latter.[68] As applied in a corporation, the determination of a corporation's

[60] *Steelcase, Inc. v Design International Selections, Inc.* GR No. 171995 (2012).

[61] Ibid.

[62] 16 Fletcher 655.

[63] ibid 659.

[64] Aquino and Aquino (n 14) 827.

[65] There is also an alternative option of rehabilitation for corporations in distress but the board and shareholders believe that it can still continue. ibid 840.

[66] Republic Act No. 10142 effectively repealed the Insolvency Law (Act 1956) and is accompanied by procedural rules such as Financial Rehabilitation Rules of Procedure, FRR (A.M. No. 12-12-11-SC), and Financial Liquidation and Suspension of Payments Rules of Procedure for Insolvent Debtors, FLSPR (A.M. No. 15-04-06-SC).

[67] FRIA, s 4.

[68] HS De Leon and HM De Leon Jr., *Comments and Cases on Credit Transactions* (Quezon City, Rex Printing Company Inc, 2016) 689.

insolvency is whether or not its assets, fairly valued as of that date, are not sufficient to cover its liabilities, disregarding liability to stockholders, either preferred or common, as insufficiency of assets presupposes that nothing is left to the stockholders.[69,70]

The remedies of an insolvent juridical debtor (ie, a corporation) may be availed judicially or extrajudicially. Judicial remedies available include corporate rehabilitation or continuance of corporate life and activities in an effort to restore and reinstate the corporation to its former position of successful operation and solvency, the purpose of which is to gain a new lease on life and allow its creditors to be paid their claims out of their earnings.[71] Extrajudicial remedies include infusing additional equity, selling core assets of its business to raise funds, implementing debt-to-equity conversion, or assigning assets as payment of its debts, otherwise known as *dacion en pago*.[72]

It is provided in local jurisprudence that rehabilitation proceedings have a two-pronged purpose, namely: (1) to efficiently and equitably distribute the assets of the insolvent debtor to its creditors, and (2) to provide the debtor with a fresh start.[73] The Philippine Supreme Court discussed that rehabilitation proceedings have equitable and rehabilitative purposes. On the one hand, they attempt to provide for the efficient and equitable distribution of an insolvent debtor's remaining assets to its creditors. On the other hand, it provides debtors with a fresh start by relieving them of the weight of their outstanding debts and permitting them to reorganise their affairs as it enables them to have a new lease on life and thereby allows creditors to be paid their claims from its earnings.[74]

There are three available modes of corporate rehabilitation: (1) court-supervised which can be either voluntary or involuntary, (2) pre-negotiated, and (3) out-of court or informal restructuring.

For voluntary proceedings, a petition for voluntary rehabilitation may be initiated by the corporation through the majority of the board of directors or trustees and authorised by a two-thirds vote of the stockholders holding outstanding capital stock or members of a non-stock corporation. Alternatively, a voluntary petition can also be filed by a group of debtors when one or more of its members foresee the impossibility of meeting debts when they respectively fall due, and the financial distress would likely adversely affect the financial condition and/or operations of the other members of the group or the participation of the other members of the group.[75] Involuntary proceedings, on the other hand, is when a creditor or group of creditors file a petition with the proper court if the claim is at least one million pesos (Php1,000,000.00) or at least 25 per cent of the subscribed capital stock or partners' contributions, whichever is higher. This is initiated through the filing of a petition for rehabilitation based on the following grounds: (1) there is no genuine issue of fact or law on the claim of the petitioner and that the due and demandable payments thereon have not been made for at least 60 days or the debtor has failed generally to meet its liabilities as they fall due, or (2) a creditor, other than the petitioner, has initiated foreclosure proceedings against the debtor that will prevent the debtor from paying its debts as they become due or will render it insolvent.[76]

After filing the petition, and if the court finds that the petition for rehabilitation is sufficient, a Commencement Order shall be issued by the court within five working days which shall: (1) declare that the debtor is under rehabilitation, (2) appoint a rehabilitation receiver who may

[69] ibid 691.
[70] There is no distinction as to insolvency and bankruptcy in Philippine law and jurisprudence.
[71] *Town and Country Enterprises, Inc. v Quisumbing* GR No. 173610 (2012).
[72] De Leon and De Leon Jr. (n 68) 695.
[73] *Philippine Bank of Communications v Basic Polyprinters and Packaging Corp.* GR No. 187581 (2014).
[74] ibid.
[75] FRIA, s 12.
[76] ibid s 13.

or may not be from among the nominees of the petitioner, (3) prohibit the debtor's suppliers of goods or services from withholding the supply of goods and services in the ordinary course of business for as long as the debtor makes payments after the issuance of the Commencement Order, (4) authorise the payment of administrative expenses, and (5) set the case for initial hearing, which will not be more than 40 days from the date of filing.[77] Upon issuance, the Commencement Order shall vest the rehabilitation receiver with all the powers and functions provided in the FRIA such as the right to review and obtain all records to which the debtor's management and directors have access to, including bank accounts of whatever nature of the debtor, subject to the approval by the court of the performance bond filed by the rehabilitation receiver.[78]

The court may also issue a Stay or Suspension Order in conjunction with the Commencement Order which shall: (1) suspend all actions or proceedings, in court or otherwise, for the enforcement of claims against the debtor; (2) suspend all actions to enforce any judgment, attachment or other provisional remedies against the debtor; (3) prohibit the debtor from selling, encumbering, transferring or disposing in any manner any of its properties; and (4) prohibit the debtor from making any payment of its liabilities outstanding as of the commencement date except as may be provided. Both orders are effective for the duration of the rehabilitation proceedings. The Stay or Suspension Order is effected in order to enable the rehabilitation receiver to effectively exercise their powers free from or unburdened by any judicial or extrajudicial interference that might unduly hinder or prevent the 'rescue' of the debtor company.[79]

A rehabilitation plan is a necessary requirement for both voluntary and involuntary rehabilitation. It is a plan by which the financial well-being and viability of an insolvent debtor can be restored using various means including debt forgiveness, debt rescheduling or other similar arrangement as may be approved by the creditors and confirmed by the court after approval of the creditors or even without such approval or over objection from the creditor.[80] The Philippine Supreme Court held that:

> Successful rehabilitation of a distressed corporation will benefit its debtors, creditors, employees, and the economy in general. The court may approve a rehabilitation plan even over the opposition of creditors holding a majority of the total liabilities of the debtor, if, in its judgment, the rehabilitation of the debtors is feasible, and the opposition of the creditors is manifestly unreasonable. The rehabilitation plan, once approved, is binding upon the debtor and all persons who may be affected by it, including the creditors, whether or not such persons have participated in the proceedings or have opposed the plan or whether or not their claims have been scheduled.[81]

In order for a rehabilitation plan to be approved, it must be economically feasible wherein: (1) the debtor has assets that can generate more cash if used in its daily operations than if sold, (2) liquidity issues can be addressed by a practicable business plan that will generate enough cash to sustain daily operations, and (3) the debtor has a definite source of financing for the proper and full implementation of the rehabilitation plan that is anchored on realistic assumptions and goals.[82] As stated above, the court shall have the power to approve or implement the rehabilitation plan despite the lack of approval or objection from the owners, partners, or stockholders of an insolvent debtor when the same is necessary to restore the well-being and viability

[77] ibid s 18.
[78] FRR, Rule 2, s 9.
[79] *PAL v Spouses Sadic and Aisha Kurangking* GR No. 146698 (2002).
[80] ibid s 64.
[81] *Pacific Wide Realty and Development Corp. v Puerto Azul Land, Inc.* GR Nos. 178768 & 180893 (2009).
[82] *Viva Shipping Lines, Inc. v Keppel Philippines Mining, Inc.* GR No. 177382 (2016).

of the insolvent debts.[83] This is known as the Cram-Down Principle which consists of two things: (1) approval despite opposition, and (2) binding effect of the approved plan, which is necessary to force the creditors to accept the terms and conditions of the rehabilitation plan, preferring long-term viability over immediate but incomplete recovery.[84]

Philippine courts can terminate the proceedings if at any time from the filing of the petition, any interested party or the rehabilitation receiver file a motion for the termination of the proceedings. Upon hearing, the court may declare the termination of the proceedings either due to a successful implementation of the Rehabilitation Plan or failure of rehabilitation. The Supreme Court laid down two factors to determine a successful rehabilitation which are as follows: (1) a positive change in the business fortunes of the debtor, and (2) the willingness of the creditors and shareholders to arrive at a compromise agreement on repayment of burdens and extent of dilution.[85] On the other hand, there is failure of rehabilitation when: (a) there is a failure of the debtor to comply, conform, or achieve the objectives of the approved Rehabilitation Plan, (b) there is a finding that fraud was committed in securing the approval of the Rehabilitation Plan, or (c) the Rehabilitation Plan is not confirmed by the court.[86] This shall result in the discharge of the rehabilitation receiver and the lifting of the Stay or Suspension Order.

The insolvent debtor, by itself or jointly with any of its creditors, may also file a verified petition with the court for the approval of a pre-negotiated Rehabilitation Plan. The filing of the petition must be authorised by the majority of the board of directors or trustees, and by at least two-thirds of the outstanding capital stock or the members. This must be approved by creditors holding at least two-thirds of the total liabilities of the debtor, including secured creditors holding more than 50 per cent of the secured claims, and unsecured creditors holding more than 50 per cent of the unsecured claims.[87] This shall then be filed with the Regional Trial Court which has jurisdiction over the principal office of the corporation as registered in the SEC.

Another option for corporations is to undergo Out-of-Court Rehabilitation (hereinafter referred as 'OCRA'), otherwise known as undertaking an Informal Restructuring Agreement wherein the insolvent corporation, instead of filing a petition for a court-supervised rehabilitation, will proceed with an OCRA plan agreed upon by the debtor and approved by the following: (1) creditors representing at least 67 per cent of the secured obligations of the debtor, (2) creditors representing at least 75 per cent of the unsecured obligations of the debtor, and (3) creditors holding at least 85 per cent of the total liabilities, secured and unsecured, of the debtor.[88] Notice of the OCRA must be published once a week for at least three consecutive weeks in a newspaper of general circulation in the Philippines, and will take effect upon the lapse of 15 days from the date of the last publication thereof.[89]

A standstill period or the period agreed upon by the debtor and its creditors to enable them to negotiate and enter into an OCRA can also be utilised and may include provisions identical or similar to the legal effects of a Commencement Order in a court-supervised rehabilitation.[90] A standstill pending negotiation and finalisation shall be effective not only to the contracting parties but also against the other creditors provided that: (1) the standstill agreement is approved

[83] FRR, Rule 2, s 67(a).
[84] *Bank of the Philippine Islands v Sarabia Manor Hotel Corporation*, GR No. 175844 (2013).
[85] *San Jose Timber Corporation v SEC* GR No. 162196 (2012).
[86] FRR, Rule 2, s 73.
[87] FRR, Rule 3, s 1.
[88] FRR, Rule 4, s 1.
[89] ibid.
[90] FRIA, s 85; FRR, Rule 4, s 2.

by creditors representing more than 50 per cent of the total liabilities of the creditor, (2) publication of the notice of the agreement is in a newspaper of general circulation in the Philippines once a week for at least two consecutive weeks, and (3) the standstill period is not made to exceed 120 days from the date of its effectivity.[91] The standstill period shall expire upon the lapse of 120 days from the effectivity of the standstill agreement, the effectivity of the OCRA, or the termination of the negotiations for the OCRA as declared by creditors representing more than 50 per cent of the total liabilities of the debtor.[92]

If an OCRA or standstill agreement is not filed with or approved by the court, the insolvent debtor or a creditor may seek assistance from the court to execute or implement a standstill agreement or OCRA which may be in the form of a writ of execution to enforce said agreement, or any other form of assistance as may be necessary to execute the same.[93] Furthermore, a debtor or creditor may also file a petition to annul the standstill agreement or OCRA based on the ground of non-compliance with the requirements for the said agreements, or caused by vitiation of consent due to fraud, intimidation or violence, if committed against the creditors whose consent is required for the approval of the OCRA or the agreement. This should be filed not later than 30 days from the effectivity thereof.[94] Finally, the judgment in any action in the standstill agreement involving the assistance or annulment by the court is final and immediately executory. On the other hand, judgment involving the OCRA shall be final within 10 days from receipt of decision.[95]

The FRIA provides that if rehabilitation is not feasible, the appropriate proceeding would be a liquidation proceeding to facilitate the liquidation of the debtor's assets and the settlement of the obligations. Rehabilitation proceedings, whether court-supervised or pre-negotiated, can also be converted to one for liquidation, through the filing of a motion, in the following instances: (1) upon finding that the debtor is insolvent and that there is no substantial likelihood for the debtor to be successfully rehabilitated, or (2) upon failure to rehabilitate.[96]

There can also be a direct liquidation of an insolvent corporation wherein an insolvent juridical debtor may voluntarily file a petition for liquidation in the Regional Trial Court which has jurisdiction over its principal office as duly specified in its articles of incorporation.[97] Alternatively, involuntary liquidation of a juridical person may also be facilitated when three or more creditors with an aggregate claim of at least either one million pesos (P1,000,000), or at least 25 per cent of the subscribed capital stock or partner's contribution of the debtors, whichever is higher, may apply for and seek liquidation by filing a petition with the court.[98]

For voluntary liquidation, if the court finds the petition is sufficient in form and substance, it will issue a Liquidation Order.[99] In cases involving involuntary liquidation of a juridical debtor, if the petition or motion is sufficient in form and substance, the court will issue an Order: (1) directing the publication of the petition or motion in a newspaper of general circulation, and (2) directing the debtor and all creditors who are not the petitioners to file their

[91] FRR, Rule 4, s 2.
[92] ibid, s 3.
[93] ibid s 10.
[94] ibid s 11.
[95] ibid s 16.
[96] FRR, Rule 2, s 73.
[97] FLSPR, Rule 2, s 1.
[98] FRIA, s 91; FLSPR, Rule 2, s 4.
[99] ibid s 90.

comment within 15 days from the date of last publication. After considering the comments filed, and if the court determines that the petition is meritorious, it will issue a Liquidation Order.[100]

The Liquidation Order shall: (1) declare the debtor insolvent, (2) order the liquidation of the debtor and, in the case of a juridical debtor, declare it as dissolved, (3) order the court sheriff to take possession and control of all the property of the debtor, except those that may be exempt from execution, (4) order the publication of the Liquidation Order, together with the petition or motion in a newspaper of general circulation once a week for two consecutive weeks, (5) direct payments of any claims and conveyance of any property due the debtor to the liquidator, (6) prohibit payments by the debtor and the transfer of any property by the debtor, and (7) direct all creditors to file their claims with the liquidator not later than five days from the time the liquidator takes their oath of office.[101]

The Liquidation Order shall have the following effects: (1) the juridical debtor shall be deemed dissolved and its corporate or juridical existence terminated, (2) the legal title to and control of all the assets of the debtor, except those exempt from execution, shall be deemed vested in the liquidator or, pending their election or appointment, with the court, (3) all contracts of the debtor shall be deemed terminated and/or breached, unless the liquidator, within 90 days from the date of assumption, declares otherwise and the contracting party agrees, (4) no separate action for the collection of an unsecured claim shall be allowed, and (5) no foreclosure proceeding shall be allowed for a period of 180 days.[102]

It should be understood that the Liquidation Order shall not affect the right of secured creditors to enforce their liens in accordance with the applicable contract or law.[103] They can either waive their right under the security or lien, prove their claim in the liquidation proceedings, and share in the distribution of the assets of the debtor; or maintain their rights under the security or lien.[104] If the secured creditors choose to maintain their right, the value of the secured property may be fixed in a manner agreed upon by the creditors and the liquidator, as approved by the court. However, if the value of the property is less than the claim it secures, the liquidator may convey the property to the secured creditor and the latter will be admitted in the proceedings as a creditor for the balance. On the other hand, if the value exceeds the claim secured, the liquidator may convey the property to the secured creditor and waive the debtor's right of redemption upon receiving the excess from the creditor. In both instances, the liquidator may sell the property and satisfy the secured creditor's entire claim from the proceeds of the sale.[105]

The liquidator shall then submit the Liquidation Plan for approval of the court which shall enumerate all the assets of the debtor not exempt from execution, list all creditors and their claims which have been duly proved, and include a proposed mode and schedule of liquidation of the assets and payment of the claims.[106] The provisions on concurrence and preference of credit shall be applied in the Liquidation Plan. The special preferred credits are secured as liens or encumbrances on the specific real or personal property and shall enjoy the highest priority.[107] On the other hand, ordinary preferred credits are created in respect of the

[100] ibid s 91.
[101] ibid s 112.
[102] FRIA, s 113.
[103] N.B. A secured creditor is one which holds a lien on the debtor's property, whether real or personal.
[104] FLSPR, Rule 4, s 5.
[105] ibid Rule 4, s 7.
[106] FRIA, s 133.
[107] Civil Code, Art 2241.

insolvent's 'free property.'[108] Finally, common credits enjoy no preference and shall be paid pro rata regardless of dates.[109]

The Trust Fund Doctrine, another settled rule in Philippine jurisdiction, also applies in cases of an insolvent corporation. Ordinarily, the doctrine provides that the subscribed capital stock of a corporation constitute a fund to which the creditors have a right to look for the satisfaction of their claims.[110] However, as mentioned above, in case of an insolvent corporation, the doctrine does not only encompass the capital stock, but also other property and assets generally regarded in equity as a trust fund for the payment of corporate debts. All assets and property belonging to the corporation held in trust for the benefit of the creditors that were distributed or in the possession of the stockholders, regardless of full payment of their subscriptions, may be reached by the creditors in satisfaction of their claim.[111]

Further to this and with the approval of the court, the liquidator may sell the unencumbered assets of the debtor and convert the same into money at a public auction. Nonetheless, a private sale may be allowed with the approval of the court if: (1) the goods to be sold are of a perishable nature, or are liable to quickly deteriorate in value, or are disproportionately expensive to keep or maintain; or, (2) it is for the best interest of the debtor and their creditors.[112]

Any transaction occurring prior to the issuance of the Liquidation Order, or in the case of conversion of the rehabilitation to liquidation proceedings prior commencement, entered into by the debtor or involving its assets, may be rescinded or declared null and void on the ground that the same was executed with intent to defraud a creditor or creditors or which constitute undue preference of creditors.[113] This can be initiated by the liquidator or, with their conformity, a creditor. Notwithstanding, if the creditor does not consent to the filing of such action, any creditor may seek leave of the court to commence said action.[114]

Liquidation can also be applied to a securities market participant who is a broker, dealer, underwriter, transfer agent or other juridical person transacting securities in the capital market. The provisions of the FRIA are without prejudice to the power of a regulatory agency or self-regulatory organisation to liquidate trade-related claims of clients or customers of a securities market participant which, for purposes of investor protection, are deemed to have absolute priority over all other claims of whatever nature or kind insofar as trade-related assets, which include cash, securities, trading right and other assets, are concerned.[115]

After all the properties of the juridical debtor not exempt from execution have been sold and after their proceeds are distributed to the creditors in accordance with the Liquidation Plan, the liquidator shall submit a final report to the court, together with the final accounting of the administration and a recommendation for the termination of the proceedings.[116] If after notice and hearing the court is satisfied with the final report, it shall issue an order approving the same and directing the removal of the name of the juridical debtor from the register of legal entities of the SEC and other government agencies. Upon receipt of evidence showing that the juridical debtor has been removed from the registry of legal entities of the SEC, the court shall then issue an order terminating the proceedings.[117]

[108] ibid Art 2244.
[109] ibid Art 2245.
[110] *Ong Yong v Tiu* GR No. 144476 (2003).
[111] *Halley v Printwell, Inc.* GR No. 157549 (2011).
[112] FLSPR, Rule 4, s 26.
[113] FRIA, s 128.
[114] ibid.
[115] FRIA, s 136.
[116] FLSPR, Rule 4, s 28.
[117] ibid s 29.

III. Cross-Border Insolvency

The FRIA adopted the United National Center for International Trade and Development Model Law on Cross-Border Insolvency (hereinafter referred to as 'UNCITRAL Model Law').[118] It should be understood that the UNCITRAL Model Law's goal is to provide effective mechanisms for instances of insolvency occurring across international borders. The proceedings shall apply in the following circumstances: (1) assistance is sought in a Philippine court by a foreign court or a foreign representative in connection with a foreign proceeding, (2) assistance is sought in a foreign state in connection with a proceeding governed by the FRIA and the Financial Rehabilitation Rules of Procedure (FRR), (3) a foreign proceeding and a proceeding governed by the FRIA and FRR are concurrently taking place, or (4) creditors in a foreign state have an interest in requesting the commencement of, or participating in, a proceeding under the FRR.[119]

However, the court shall refuse to take any action in any cross-border insolvency proceeding if the action is manifestly contrary to the public policy of the Philippines and the court finds the country where the foreign rehabilitation is taking place does not extend recognition to a Philippine rehabilitation proceeding, or the court of which the petitioner-foreign creditor is a national does not grant the same right to a Philippine creditor.[120] To initiate proceedings, the Regional Trial Court which has jurisdiction over the place where the debtor resides or hold principal office, shall set a hearing on an insolvency or rehabilitation proceeding taking place in a foreign jurisdiction, upon the submission of a petition by the representative of the foreign entity that is subject to the foreign proceeding.[121] The petition must be accompanied by a certified copy of the order commencing the foreign proceeding and appointing the foreign representative, or a certificate from the foreign court affirming the existence of the foreign proceeding and the appointment of the foreign representative.[122]

The court, by way of provisional relief, may issue orders either to suspend any action to enforce claims against the entity or otherwise seize or foreclose on property of the foreign entity in the Philippines, or to require the surrender of property of the foreign entity to the foreign representative, or to provide other necessary reliefs.[123] In determining whether to grant relief, the court shall consider the following: (1) the protection of creditors in the Philippines and the inconvenience to be caused in pursuing their claims in a foreign proceeding, (2) the just treatment of all creditors through resort to a unified insolvency proceeding, (3) whether other jurisdictions have given recognition to the foreign proceeding, (4) the extent that the foreign proceeding recognises the rights of creditors and other interested parties, and (5) the extent that the foreign proceeding has recognised and shown deference to the proceedings under the FRIA.[124]

If the court recognises the foreign proceeding, it shall result in the commencement or continuation of individual proceedings concerning the debtor's assets, and the foreign representative is entitled to participate, through counsel, in any proceeding involving the debtor. This recognition does not affect the right of Philippine creditors to commence or continue a rehabilitation or liquidation proceeding against the debtor.[125] Furthermore, upon recognition of foreign proceedings, and when necessary to protect the assets of the debtor or interests of

[118] FRIA, s 139.
[119] FRR, Rule 5, s 1.
[120] FRR Rule 5, s 4.
[121] FRIA, s 140, ibid Rule 5, s 5.
[122] ibid Rule 5, s 5.
[123] ibid s 141.
[124] ibid s 142.
[125] FRR Rule 5, s 12.

the creditor, the court may, upon motion of the foreign representative, issue an order granting additional reliefs such as: (1) staying the commencement or continuation of the individual proceedings concerning the debtor's assets, (2) staying execution against the debtor's assets, (3) suspending the rights to transfer, encumber or otherwise dispose of any asset of the debtor, (4) providing the examination of witnesses, the taking of evidence or any delivery of information concerning the debtor's assets, affairs, rights, obligation or liabilities, (5) entrusting the administration or realisation of all or part of the debtor's assets located in the Philippines to the foreign representative or another person designated by the court, and (6) granting any additional relief that may be provided to the rehabilitation receiver.[126] Finally, upon recognition of such foreign proceeding, the court may, at the request of the foreign representative, entrust the distribution of all or part of the debtor's assets located in the Philippines to the foreign representative or another person designated by the court; provided that the court is satisfied that the interests of local creditors are adequately protected.[127]

The foreign representative is allowed to intervene, through local counsel, in any action or proceeding in the Philippines, provided that the foreign proceeding has been recognised. The foreign representative acquires legal personality to initiate actions, through legal counsel, to either avoid or render ineffective acts detrimental to creditors. With this, recognition is deemed a condition *sine qua non* before a foreign representative may officially intervene.[128] Philippine courts can likewise cooperate to the maximum extent possible with foreign courts for court-to-court communications concerning information or assistance, as well as reciprocate the same relief provided by the foreign courts.[129]

The objective is to promote cooperation between the Philippine courts and other competent authorities of states involved in cases of cross-border insolvency.[130] This cooperation may be implemented through any appropriate means, including, but not limited to, the following: (1) appointment of a person or body to act at the discretion of the court, (2) coordination of the administration and supervision of the debtor's assets and affairs, (3) coordination of concurrent proceedings regarding the same debtor, (4) suspension of proceedings against the debtor, and (5) limiting the relief of assets that should be administered in a foreign proceeding pending in a jurisdiction other than the place where the debtor has its principal place of business.[131] Furthermore, after the recognition of a foreign proceeding, a local proceeding for liquidation may be commenced only if the debtor is doing business in the Philippines. The effects of the proceedings are restricted only to the assets of the debtor located in the country and shall be enforced to the extent necessary to implement cooperation coordination with foreign courts or foreign representatives with respect to the assets of the debtor.[132] Finally, if local and foreign proceedings are taking place concurrently, the Philippine court shall seek to coordinate and cooperate on the matter, and any relief granted to the foreign proceeding must be consistent with the relief granted by Philippine courts in the local proceeding.[133]

[126] FRR Rule 5, s 13.
[127] ibid.
[128] DRC Aquino, *Financial Rehabilitation Rules of Procedure Annotated* (Quezon City, Rex Printing Company Inc, 2018) 193.
[129] ibid.
[130] De Leon and De Leon Jr. (n 68) 799.
[131] FRR Rule 5, s 20.
[132] ibid s 21.
[133] ibid s 22.

8

Law on Bankruptcy

EMILIANO S BANTOG

I. Introduction

This chapter covers the pertinent laws on insolvency in the Philippines. Insolvency proceedings are no longer limited to just local stakeholders, considering that transactions, property ownership, and debtor-creditor relationships have to account for countless cross-border transactions with possible private international law concerns. This was considered by the Philippine Congress in passing the Financial Rehabilitation and Insolvency Act of 2010, which includes pertinent provisions on cross-border insolvency proceedings and the adoption of the United Nations Commission on International Trade Law (UNCITRAL) Model Law on Cross-Border Insolvency.[1] The Financial Rehabilitation Rules of Procedure issued by the Philippine Supreme Court provides the necessary procedural guidelines on cross-border insolvency cases.[2]

The first Philippine law relating to bankruptcy was enacted in 1909. Entitled An Act Providing for the Suspension of Payments, the Relief of Insolvent Debtors, the Protection of Creditors, and the Punishment of Fraudulent Debtors, Act No. 1956 is also simply known as The Insolvency Law. It provided for the suspension of payments and protection of creditors.[3] It was derived from the Insolvency Act of California (1895), with a few provisions taken from the United States Federal Bankruptcy Act of 1898.[4] Remedies under the law were through a suspension of payment (for a debtor who was solvent but illiquid) or a discharge from debts and liabilities through the voluntary or involuntary insolvency proceedings (for a debtor who was insolvent).[5] Act No. 1956 was meant to be a complete law on insolvency, and debts were to be liquidated in accordance with the order of priority set forth in the classification and preference of creditors.[6]

It is the policy of Act No. 1956 to place all the assets and liabilities of the insolvent debtor completely within the jurisdiction and control of the insolvency court without the intervention of any other court in the insolvent debtor's concerns or in the administration of the estate.[7] It was considered to be of prime importance that the insolvency proceedings follow their course as speedily as possible in order that a discharge, if the insolvent debtor is entitled to it, should be decreed without unreasonable delay. Proceedings of this nature cannot function properly or with

[1] Republic Act No. 10142, ss 138–142.
[2] Financial Rehabilitation Rules of Procedure (2013), Rule 5. Administrative Matter No. 12-12-11-SC.
[3] Act No 1956 (1909).
[4] *Sun Life Assurance Company of Canada v Ingersoll*, GR No 16475 (1921).
[5] *Metropolitan Bank and Trust Company v S.F. Naguiat Enterprises* GR No 178407 (2015).
[6] ibid.
[7] ibid.

due dispatch unless they are absolutely controlled by the court having charge thereof.[8] Act No. 1956 will remain the primary law on Bankruptcy or Insolvency, both legal terms are synonymous in this jurisdiction,[9] for over a century. It was repealed by Republic Act No. 10142, or the Financial Rehabilitation and Insolvency Act (FRIA) of 2010.[10]

The purpose of insolvency proceedings is to encourage debtors and their creditors to collectively and realistically resolve and adjust competing claims and property rights while maintaining certainty and predictability in commercial affairs, preserving and maximising the value of the assets of these debtors, recognising creditor rights and respecting priority of claims, and ensuring equitable treatment of creditors who are similarly situated.[11] FRIA provides a broader definition of the term, 'insolvent' as referring to 'the financial condition of a debtor that is generally unable to pay its or his liabilities as they fall due in the ordinary course of business or has liabilities that are greater than its or his assets.[12] 'FRIA also expressly categorises different forms of debt relief available to a corporate debtor in financial distress: these are out-of-court restructuring agreements; pre-negotiated rehabilitation; court-supervised rehabilitation; and liquidation (voluntary and involuntary). Insolvent individual debtors can avail of suspension of payments, or liquidation.[13]

The declaration of bankruptcy is a legal process. Bankruptcy or insolvency are legal and technical terms that will not simply refer to one who is out of money, or not liquid and unable to fend off his creditors or is just incapable of making ends meet. It is the proper court which will declare a person or entity bankrupt or insolvent. One who is declared as such is not necessarily a pauper, to the effect that his creditors should well enough leave him alone. Rather, it is a process where the goal is to protect creditors and still find ways on how the down on his luck debtor can pay them off. It could be a liquidity issue and the debtor may have assets to satisfy his obligations.

Under Philippine law, an entity is considered insolvent if it is generally unable to pay its liabilities as they fall due in the ordinary course of business or has liabilities that are greater than its assets.[14] In the event of insolvency, a principal objective should be to effect an equitable distribution of the insolvent's property among his creditors. To accomplish this, there must first be some proceeding where notice to all of the insolvent's creditors may be given and where the claims of preferred creditors may be bindingly adjudicated.[15] The debtor may still be able to recover and in the near predictable future, be able to meet his debts or it could also be that his liabilities already outweigh his assets. It is then incumbent upon the debtor to meet such obligations through the management of his remaining properties or assets or his expected income. To do this, he must seek relief through the appropriate court by filing either a petition for rehabilitation, liquidation, or suspension of payments. At times though, the creditors themselves may initiate the legal process against an unwilling debtor.[16]

For purposes of jurisdiction, the debtor or his creditors must file the insolvency proceedings with the appropriate court where the debtor is a resident. It must be in the exact city and not just within the same region. As held by the Supreme Court:

> Despite being in the same region, Makati and Manila are treated as two distinct venues. To deem them as interchangeable venues for being in the same region has no basis in law.

[8] ibid.
[9] *Development Bank of the Philippines v National Labor Relations Commission* GR No 108031 (1995).
[10] RA No 10142 (2010).
[11] *Metropolitan Bank and Trust Company v S.F. Naguiat Enterprises* GR No 178407 (2015).
[12] FRIA, Ch I, s 4 (p).
[13] *Metropolitan Bank and Trust Company v S.F. Naguiat Enterprises* GR No 178407 (2015).
[14] FRIA, Ch I, s 4 (p).
[15] *Development Bank of the Philippines v Santos* GR Nos 82763-64 (1990).
[16] FRIA, Ch II, ss 13 and 14; FRIA, Ch V, s 91.

> Respondent is a resident of Manila. The law should be read to lay the venue of the insolvency proceeding in the actual location of the debtor's activities ....[17]

FRIA allows a corporate debtor to either undergo rehabilitation or liquidation proceedings.[18] Natural persons or individual debtors, in turn, may avail of suspension of payments, or liquidation which may be voluntary or involuntary.[19] The debtor, who still possess property, but cannot by any means timely pay his debts to one or several creditors may file a petition for him to be placed in a state of suspension of payments or voluntary insolvency. Such court, which is in a city where the debtor resides, will restructure the debt payments to allow for a longer period of repayment or require the debtor to be divested of his properties as payment for his debts.

II. Rehabilitation

As defined by law, rehabilitation is the restoration of the debtor to a condition of successful operation and solvency, if it is shown that its continuance of operation is economically feasible and its creditors can recover by way of the present value of payments projected in the plan, more if the debtor continues as a going concern than if it is immediately liquidated.[20] If rehabilitation is still viable, creditors may be able to recover the full value of the credit. If the assets are immediately liquidated even when rehabilitation is viable, creditors run the risk of sharing in the losses of the corporation, especially if the book value of its assets is less than its outstanding credits. Rehabilitation goes beyond deferment of payments, it involves the development of a rehabilitation plan to revive a financially distressed corporation to a state of liquidity.[21] The rationale in corporate rehabilitation is to resuscitate businesses in financial distress because assets are often more valuable when so maintained than they would be when liquidated. Rehabilitation assumes that assets are still serviceable to meet the purposes of the business.[22]

Rehabilitation may be voluntary or involuntary. It is voluntary when the petition for rehabilitation is filed by the debtor itself, of course requiring a majority vote of its controlling interest;[23] or involuntary, as when it is initiated by the creditor/s, who has or have an aggregate claim of at least One Million Pesos (Php1,000,000.00) or at least 25 per cent of the subscribed capital stock or partners' contributions, whichever is higher, and there is no issue of fact or law on their claims against the debtor, and the debtor has not paid to them his due and demandable debts for at least sixty (60) days; or, that a creditor who did not initiate or join the other creditors in the petition but has actually initiated foreclosure proceedings against the debtor that will prevent the debtor from paying his or its debts.[24]

Corporate rehabilitation is one of many statutorily provided remedies for businesses that experience a downturn and it allows a court-supervised process to rejuvenate a corporation.[25]

[17] *Pilipinas Shell Petroleum Corporation v Royal Ferry Services, Inc.* GR No. 188146 (2017).
[18] FRIA, Chs II–V; FRIA, ss 12–93.
[19] FRIA, Ch VI, ss 94–11.
[20] FRIA, Ch 1, s 4(gg).
[21] *Metropolitan Bank and Trust Company v Fortuna Paper Mill and Packaging Corporation* GR No 190800 (2018).
[22] ibid.
[23] FRIA, Ch 22, s 12.
[24] FRIA, Ch II, s 13.
[25] *Pryce Corporation v China Banking Corporation* GR No 172302 (2014).

It provides a corporation's owners a sound chance to reengage the market, hopefully with more vigour and enlightened services, having learned from a painful experience.[26] Necessarily, a business in the red and about to incur tremendous losses may not be able to pay all its creditors. Rather than leave it to the strongest or most resourceful amongst all of them, the state steps in to equitably distribute the corporation's limited resources.[27]

A rehabilitation plan is a plan by which the financial well-being and viability of an insolvent debtor can be restored using various means including, but not limited to, debt forgiveness, debt rescheduling, reorganisation or quasi-reorganisation, *dacion en pago*,[28] debt-equity conversion and sale of the business, or parts of it, as a going concern, or setting-up of new business entity, or other similar arrangements as may be approved by the court or creditors.[29] Rather than let struggling corporations slip and vanish, the better option is to allow commercial courts to come in and apply the process for corporate rehabilitation.[30]

Creditors may oppose the voluntary filing of a petition of rehabilitation by a debtor, but the rehabilitation plan submitted by the debtor can still be approved by the court if it may be shown that it is feasible and the opposition of the creditors has no basis at all. This is referred to as the cram-down principle, when the court permits the approval of a rehabilitation plan even over the opposition of creditors, or when it imposes a binding effect of the approved plan on all parties including those who did not participate in the proceedings, and the burden of loss is shifted to the creditors to allow the corporation to rehabilitate itself from insolvency.[31]

The effect on the creditors of the court-approved rehabilitation plan of the debtor or the issuance of a Commencement Order will be: (a) the suspension of all actions, in court or any other tribunal seeking to enforce a claim against the debtor; (b) suspension of the enforcement of any judgment against the creditor, including attachment or provisional remedies against the debtor and his/its assets; and, (c) at the same time, the debtor is prohibited from selling, encumbering, transferring or disposing in any manner any of its properties except in the ordinary course of business; or, from (d) making any payment of its liabilities outstanding as of the commencement date.[32]

In addition, the imposition of all taxes and fees including penalties, interests and charges thereof due to the national government or to local government units shall be considered waived, in furtherance of the objectives of rehabilitation.[33] The Commencement Order can also nullify any: (a) extrajudicial activity or process to seize property, sell encumbered property, or otherwise attempt to collect or enforce a claim against the debtor after commencement date; (b) set off after the commencement date of any debt owed to the debtor by any of the debtor's creditors; and, (c) the perfection of any lien against the debtor's property after the commencement date.[34]

All creditors must be included in the petition for rehabilitation. They are not only to be informed of the fact of its filing but are actual parties to the case for rehabilitation. A corporate rehabilitation case cannot be decided without the creditors' participation.[35] The court's

[26] ibid.
[27] ibid.
[28] Civil Code, Art 1245.
[29] FRIA, Ch 1, s 4.
[30] *Pryce Corporation v China Banking Corporation* GR No 172302 (2014).
[31] ibid.
[32] FRIA, Ch II, s 17.
[33] FRIA, Ch II, s 19.
[34] FRIA, Ch II, s 17.
[35] *Viva Shipping Lines, Inc. v Keppel Philippines Mining, Inc.*, GR No 177382 (2016).

role is to balance the interests of the corporation, the creditors, and the general public.[36] The courts will not be able to balance these interests if the creditors are not parties to a case.[37] The importance of rendering a true and complete statement of the matters called for in the schedule cannot be over-emphasised; if the name of a creditor is omitted, he stands to be deprived of personal notice of the proceedings, apart from publication, and of his right to vote in the election of an assignee.[38] The purpose for which the Insolvency Law was enacted is to effect an equitable distribution of the bankrupt's properties among his creditors and to benefit the debtor by discharging him from his liabilities and enabling him to start afresh with the property set apart for him as exempt.[39]

Rehabilitation is designed to benefit the debtor and its creditors, as well as the public because any closure of a company, regardless of its size, affects the economy greatly. The public's interest lies in the court's ability to effectively ensure that the obligations of the debtor, who has experienced severe economic difficulties, are fairly and equitably served.[40] The alternative might be a chaotic rush by all creditors to file separate cases with the possibility of different trial courts issuing various writs competing for the same assets. Rehabilitation is a means to temper the effect of a business downturn experienced for whatever reason. In the process, it gives entrepreneurs a second chance.[41] Not only is it a humane and equitable relief, it encourages efficiency and maximises welfare in the economy.

There was a concern by the Supreme Court that courts outside of the rehabilitation court where actions are filed against the debtor and his properties are ongoing may not be made aware of the filing by the debtor of a petition for rehabilitation. That such courts may fail to suspend its proceedings and render judgment against the debtor to the detriment of the creditors participating in the rehabilitation proceedings. Hence, the promulgation of the Supreme Court Guidelines on Actual Notice to Concerned Courts in Financial Rehabilitation Proceedings.[42]

Courts are not always informed of the issuance of commencement orders involving party litigants in financial rehabilitation proceedings. The purpose of these Guidelines is to avoid delay in the consolidation of all legal proceedings in rehabilitation courts, and avoid the possibility of separate suits or appeals questioning orders or judgments rendered in violation of a commencement/stay order, which will only delay the consolidation of all legal proceedings in the rehabilitation court.[43]

Aside from the discussed voluntary and involuntary rehabilitation of the debtor, the debtor and the creditor may also come together prior to any court action and jointly file a verified petition with the appropriate court for the approval of a Pre-Negotiated Rehabilitation Plan which has been endorsed or approved by creditors holding at least two-thirds of the total liabilities of the debtor, including secured creditors holding more than 50 per cent of the total secured claims of the debtor and unsecured creditors holding more than 50 per cent of the total unsecured claims of the debtor.[44] The joint petitioners shall cause the publication in a newspaper of general circulation for at least two consecutive weeks of the Order of the court stating the fact of the filing of the

[36] ibid.
[37] ibid.
[38] *In the Matter of the Estate of Mindanao Motor Line, Inc. v Alforque* GR No L-27944 (1974).
[39] ibid.
[40] *Securities and Exchange Commission v College Assurance Plan Philippines, Inc.* GR No 213130 (2020).
[41] ibid.
[42] *Pacific Cement Company v Oil and Natural Gas Commission* GR No 229471 (2023).
[43] ibid.
[44] FRIA, Ch III, ss 76–82.

petition for rehabilitation and for any creditor or other interested parties to file their objections or comments thereto within a period of not later than 20 days from the second publication of the Order, and within ten days from the date of the second publication of the Order, the court shall approve the Rehabilitation Plan, unless a creditor or other interested party submits a verified objection to the petition not later than eight days from the date of the second publication of the Order.[45]

The debtor and his creditors can also agree to have the matter settled between or among themselves without seeking any court intervention. The debtor can voluntarily enter into a rehabilitation plan with his creditor/s. An out-of-court or informal restructuring agreement or Rehabilitation Plan is recognised under FRIA.[46] Provided that the said plan or agreement meets the minimum requirements set by FRIA. The agreed plan must have the creditors hold at least 67 per cent of the secured obligations of the debtor, or at least 75 per cent of the unsecured obligations of the debtor, or at least 85 per cent of the total liabilities, secured and unsecured, of the debtor.[47] A Rehabilitation Plan shall be effective and enforceable not only against the contracting parties but also against the other creditors,[48] provided it is published once a week for at least three consecutive weeks in a newspaper of general circulation.[49] The contracting parties are also not precluded from resorting to court action as they may seek court assistance for the execution or implementation of the Rehabilitation Plan.[50]

In order to determine the feasibility of a proposed rehabilitation plan, it is imperative that a thorough examination and analysis of the debtor's financial data is done. If the results of such examination and analysis show that there is a real opportunity to rehabilitate the corporation in view of the assumptions made and financial goals stated in the proposed rehabilitation plan, it may be determined that a rehabilitation is feasible and the court should not hesitate to allow the corporation to operate as an on-going concern under the terms and conditions stated in the approved rehabilitation plan.[51] On the other hand, if the results of the financial examination and analysis clearly indicate that there lies no reasonable probability that the distressed corporation could be revived and that liquidation would, in fact, better subserve the interests of its stakeholders, then it may be said that a rehabilitation would not be feasible. In such case, the rehabilitation court may convert the proceedings into one for liquidation.[52]

To reiterate, courts must endeavour to balance the interests of all the parties that have a stake in the success of rehabilitating the debtors and these include the debtor, its creditors, and the public in general. However, there are instances when corporate rehabilitation can no longer be achieved and when rehabilitation will not result in a better present value recovery for the creditors, the more appropriate remedy is liquidation.[53] It does not make sense to hold, suspend, or continue to devalue outstanding credits of a business that has no chance of recovery and in such cases, the optimum economic welfare will be achieved if the corporation is allowed to wind up its affairs in an orderly manner as liquidation allows the corporation to wind up its affairs and equitably distribute its assets among its creditors.[54]

[45] ibid.
[46] FRIA, Ch IV, s 83.
[47] FRIA, Ch IV, s 84.
[48] FRIA, Ch IV, s 85.
[49] FRIA, Ch IV, s 86.
[50] FRIA, Ch IV, s 88.
[51] *Phil. Asset Growth Two, Inc. v Fastech Synergy Phils., Inc.* GR No 206528 (2016).
[52] ibid.
[53] *Philippine Bank of Communications v Basic Polyprinters and Packaging Corporation* GR No 187581 (2014).
[54] *Metropolitan Bank and Trust Company v Fortuna Paper Mill and Packaging Corporation* GR No 190800 (2018).

III. Liquidation

Liquidation is diametrically opposed to rehabilitation. Both cannot be undertaken at the same time. In rehabilitation, corporations have to maintain their assets to continue business operations. In liquidation, on the other hand, corporations preserve their assets in order to sell them. Without these assets, business operations are effectively discontinued. The proceeds of the sale are distributed equitably among creditors, and surplus is divided or losses are re-allocated.[55]

A juridical entity debtor may resort to, or be made to undergo, liquidation if it can no longer meet its obligations through any plan of rehabilitation or recovery. As with rehabilitation, liquidation is also voluntary or involuntary. It is voluntary when the debtor files a verified petition in court,[56] after acquiring at least the majority vote of the board of directors or trustees and the vote of its shareholders holding at least two thirds of the outstanding capital stock or members if it be a stock or non-stock corporations,[57] or at least two-thirds vote of the partners, if the debtor is a partnership.[58] A petition for liquidation may be filed with the court by either an insolvent debtor or voluntary liquidation, or by his or its creditors or involuntary liquidation. Again, at any time during the pendency of or after a rehabilitation through a court-supervised or pre-negotiated rehabilitation, the court may order the conversion of rehabilitation proceedings to liquidation proceedings.[59]

In involuntary liquidation, three or more creditors having monetary claims of at least Pnp1,000,000.00, or 25 per cent of the subscribed capital stock or partner's contributions, whichever is higher, may file a verified petition in court, seeking the liquidation of the corporate or partnership debtor.[60] If the court where either the voluntary or involuntary petition for liquidation of the juridical debtor is filed, finds it to be sufficient in form and substance, having also determined that there is no substantial likelihood that the debtor may be rehabilitated, it will direct the petitioner to cause the publication of the petition in a newspaper of general circulation once a week for two consecutive weeks, which also directs either the debtor (in involuntary) and all creditors (in voluntary) who are not the petitioners to file their comment on the petition 15 days from the date of last publication.[61]

After consideration of the comments, if any are filed, and finding the petition meritorious,[62] the court shall then issue a Liquidation Order, which will declare the debtor insolvent and order its liquidation; order the court sheriff to take possession and control of all the properties of the debtor and direct all creditors to file their claims with the court-appointed liquidator; and the debtor is also prohibited from making payments and transfers of any of its property.[63] No separate action for the collection of any unsecured claim against the debtor is allowed, and any action that is already pending will be transferred to the liquidator for consideration. Foreclosure proceeding against any property of the debtor is prohibited for 180 days from the issuance of the Liquidation Order.[64]

[55] *Metropolitan Bank and Trust Company v S.F. Naguiat Enterprises* GR No 178407 (2015).
[56] FRIA, Ch V, s 90.
[57] Revised Corporation Code (RA No 11232), title XIV, ss 133–139.
[58] Civil Code, Arts 1828–1842.
[59] FRIA, Ch V, s 93.
[60] FRIA, Ch V, s 91.
[61] ibid.
[62] ibid.
[63] FRIA, Ch XII, s 112.
[64] FRIA, Ch XII, s 113.

Even if the debtor was allowed to undergo rehabilitation, voluntary or otherwise, the court may order the conversion of the court-supervised or pre-negotiated rehabilitation proceedings if the rehabilitation of the debtor is no longer feasible pursuant to the approved Rehabilitation Plan, and that there is no substantial likelihood for the debtor to be successfully rehabilitated, or if the said plan was disallowed by the court, or the debtor exhibits bad faith in its compliance to such plan. In such cases, the court shall instead issue a Liquidation Order against the insolvent juridical debtor and bringing with it the effects of dissolution or liquidation as discussed above.[65]

IV. Suspension of Payments

An individual or personal debtor, who is not yet on the verge of liquidation, can opt to file a petition in court for the suspension of payments of his debts. The objective of suspension of payments is the deferment of the payment of debts until such time as the debtor, who possesses sufficient property to cover all debts, is able to convert such assets into cash or otherwise acquires the cash necessary to pay his debts.[66] An individual debtor who, possessing sufficient property to cover all his debts but foreseeing the impossibility of meeting them when they respectively fall due, may file a verified petition that he be declared in the state of suspension of payments by the court of the city in which he reside. Attached to his petition shall be a schedule of debts and liabilities, inventory of his assets, and a proposed agreement with his creditors.[67] The court shall call for a meeting of the creditors, who at such time must have submitted their claims against the debtor in court. Publication of the court order taking cognizance of the petition shall also be published in a newspaper of general circulation once a week for two consecutive weeks.[68]

As with the rehabilitation or liquidation, the debtor in a state of suspension of payments is prohibited from selling, transferring, encumbering, or disposing in any manner of his property or from making any payment outside of the necessary or legitimate expenses of his business or industry.[69] Any pending execution against the properties of the debtor may also be suspended by the court. Such suspension will lapse after three months without any proposed agreement accepted by the creditors. At the same time, no creditor shall institute proceedings to collect the claim from the debtor as long as the suspension of payments proceedings remain pending. Such suspension however, does not apply against claimants for payments of personal labour, maintenance, expense of last illness and funeral of the wife or children of the debtor incurred in the 60 days immediately prior to the filing of the petition.[70]

The meeting of the creditors set by the court must be attended by creditors representing at least three-fifths of the petitioner debtor's debts for there to be a quorum, and they must vote on the proposed agreement of payment by a vote of at least two-thirds of the creditors present. Only creditors who have incurred their credits more than 90 days prior to the filing of the petition shall be entitled to vote. Failure to reach a quorum or a favourable vote shall lead to the termination of the proceedings.[71] If there will be any objection to the agreement, such as allegations of a defect in the call for meeting or connivance between or among the debtor and one or more creditors,

[65] FRIA, Ch V, s 93.
[66] *Metropolitan Bank and Trust Company v S.F. Naguiat Enterprises* GR No 178407 (2015).
[67] FRIA, Ch VI, s 94.
[68] FRIA, Ch VI, s 95.
[69] ibid.
[70] FRIA, Ch VI, s 96.
[71] FRIA, Ch VI, s 97.

the court shall declare the proceedings terminated and the creditors shall be at liberty to exercise the rights which may correspond to them.[72]

V. Effect of Bankruptcy on Assignments of Property

The objective in insolvency proceedings is to effect an equitable distribution of the bankrupt's properties among his creditors and to benefit the debtor by discharging him from his liabilities and enabling him to start afresh with the property set apart for him as exempt.[73] Whenever rehabilitation is no longer feasible, it is in the interest of the state to facilitate a speedy and orderly liquidation of the debtors' assets and the settlement of their obligations.[74] An obligation is extinguished by payment or performance.[75] There is payment when there is delivery of money or performance of an obligation.[76]

As discussed, being in a state of bankruptcy or insolvency will allow the debtor to either suspend payments to creditors, undergo rehabilitation, or go through voluntary or involuntary dissolution. The crux of bankruptcy is liquidity, the debtor is not in any position to pay his creditors as his debts become due and demandable. Being under this state of insolvency allows the debtor to hang on to his assets, either to the little money he still has but is insufficient to pay all his creditors, or to his other assets that remain beneficial to him and/or his business interests. However, such does not mean that the debtor has free disposal over his assets.[77] He may still enjoy possession over his properties and they remain in his name but being in a state of bankruptcy prevents the debtor from disposing of his property on his own, even if it is for the purpose of raising funds to pay his creditors.

To reiterate, being declared bankrupt is a legal process and when the debtor undergoes such process, even voluntarily, he loses control over such assets and business interests. Receivers are appointed by the court where the bankruptcy is filed, to exercise control over the remaining assets of an insolvent debtor. With the declaration of insolvency of the debtor, insolvency courts obtain full and complete jurisdiction over all property of the insolvent and of all claims by and against it.[78] It follows that the insolvency court has exclusive jurisdiction to deal with the property of the insolvent.[79]

Creditors, secured or otherwise, may eagerly want to get a hold of such assets but being under a state of insolvency, they are to submit to the process and follow a payment schedule that may be laid out under a rehabilitation plan or the dissolution of the juridical debtor. This is common in either dissolution, rehabilitation or suspension of payments. All creditors must submit their claims with the court where such rehabilitation, dissolution, or suspension of payments is pending. Only those who make their claims in such courts or were already included by the debtor in filing his petition with the court will be recognised as such and included in the payment plan to be established and approved by the court. The creditors who have submitted their claims against the debtor will get paid under a preference of credits.

[72] FRIA, Ch VI, s 100.
[73] *Metropolitan Bank and Trust Company v S.F. Naguiat Enterprises* GR No 178407 (2015).
[74] ibid.
[75] Civil Code, Art 1231.
[76] Civil Code, Art 1232.
[77] FRIA, Ch VII, ss 127–128.
[78] *Metropolitan Bank and Trust Company v S.F. Naguiat Enterprises* GR No 178407 (2015).
[79] ibid.

A. Application of Payments

Bankruptcy connotes that not all creditors will get paid, even if all of them duly submitted and made their lawful claims against the debtor. Therefore, not all creditors are equal. Under Philippine Law, there is an Order of Preference of Credits within which all liabilities of a debtor are paid or satisfied. So which debts enjoy preference over another, is it priority in time, amount of the debt, or relationship with the creditor? The answer is provided by Book IV of the New Civil Code of the Philippines. Before looking at said preference, it is also important to note, that at this juncture, it is already established that all the liabilities of the insolvent debtor are due and demandable.

In the law on application of payments, it states that a debtor having multiple debts of the same kind with one and the same creditor has the choice of which debt to apply his payment, if he is unable to pay all such debts, provided such debts are due.[80] But if all his debts with such creditor are all due, the debtor may then choose to settle that which is most burdensome, or onerous such as secured debts or those that bear interest. However, if all debts are equally onerous, and the debtor is unable to pay them all, then the payment shall be made to all such debts proportionately.[81] Such situation of course, is not limited to having a single creditor. A debtor may have similar obligations with multiple creditors, having the same due dates, and equally onerous. That is when preference of credits come to play.

B. Preference of Credits

Concurrence of credits occurs when the same specific property of the debtor or all of his property is subjected to the claims of several creditors. The concurrence of credits raises no questions of consequence where the value of the property or the value of all assets of the debtor is sufficient to pay in full all the creditors. However, it becomes material when said assets are insufficient, causing some creditors to not be paid or some creditors to not obtain the full satisfaction of their claims. In this situation, the question of preference will then arise, that is to say who of the creditors will be paid ahead of the others.[82]

As the New Civil Code of the Philippines provides, those creditors who extended credit to the debtor which are secured or covered by a collateral under chattel or real estate mortgages enjoy preference with respect to the value of such personal or real properties as payment for the debts, in exclusion of other creditors.[83] But if the debtor used the same property as security for two or more creditors, then such liabilities shall be satisfied *pro rata*.[84] However, such payments to the secured creditors through the concerned personal or real property may be done only after payment of taxes and duties still due from such personal and/or real property involved.

Also, if the insolvent debtor is an employer, certain preference is enjoyed by his workers under Philippines Labor Law. 'In the event of bankruptcy or liquidation of an employer's business, his workers shall enjoy first preference as regards wages due them for services rendered during the period prior to the bankruptcy or liquidation, any provision to the contrary notwithstanding. Unpaid wages shall be paid in full before other creditors may establish any claim to a share in

[80] Civil Code, Art 1252.
[81] Civil Code, Arts 1252 and 1254.
[82] EP Caguioa, *Comments and Cases on Civil Law* (Quezon City, Central Law Book Publishing, 1970) 472.
[83] Civil Code, Arts 2246 and 2248.
[84] Civil Code, Arts 2247 and 2249.

the assets of the employer.[85] 'Unpaid wages earned by the employees before the declaration of bankruptcy or judicial liquidation of the employer's business shall be given first preference and shall be paid in full before other creditors may establish any claim to a share in the assets of the employer.[86]

As held by the Supreme Court: 'a preference of credit bestows upon the preferred creditor an advantage of having his credit satisfied first ahead of other claims which may be established against the debtor. Logically, it becomes material only when the properties and assets of the debtors are insufficient to pay his debts in full; for if the debtor is amply able to pay his various creditors in full, how can the necessity exist to determine which of his creditors shall be paid first or whether they shall be paid out of the proceeds of the sale of the debtor's specific property.'[87] Indubitably, the preferential right of credit attains significance only after the properties of the debtor have been inventoried and liquidated, and the claims held by his various creditors have been established.[88]

When after all the liabilities with the preferred secured creditors are settled, and excess property or properties of the debtor still remain, either from the excess in the value of the mortgaged property or other properties not used as collateral, such excess shall be added to the free property which the debtor may have, for the payment of the other credits.[89]

For creditors without any security or preference, or even those preferred secured creditors but were not fully paid out of the value of the mortgaged property, they shall be satisfied following the order provided by law. First to be settled shall be the debtor's employees, labourers, or household helpers for services rendered the insolvent one year preceding the commencement of the proceedings in insolvency; second, expenses related to the treatment of any illness of the individual debtor, his spouse or his children under his parental authority and do not have property of their own; third, compensation for damages due the debtor's labourers from work related accident or illness; fourth, fines and civil indemnification arising from a criminal offence; fifth, legal expenses, and expenses incurred in the administration of the insolvent individual's estate; sixth, taxes and assessments due the national government, other than those due from the personal or real property used to secure his liabilities; and seventh, payment of damages arising from a quasi-delict or tort.[90] FRIA provides that a Liquidation Plan and its implementation must ensure the concurrence and preference of credits as enumerated in the New Civil Code of the Philippines and other relevant laws shall be observed, unless a preferred creditor voluntarily waives his preferred right.[91]

C. Dation in Payment

But why is property of the debtor being applied to the payment of his liabilities, secured or otherwise? The Philippine Constitution guarantees that 'No person shall be imprisoned for debt or non-payment of a poll tax.[92] 'If a debtor cannot pay his debts, he cannot be subjected to criminal prosecution but he is not excused from civil accountability for his liabilities. A common mode of

[85] Labor Code, Art 110.
[86] Revised Rules and Regulations Implementing the Labor Code of the Philippines, book III, Rule VIII, s 10.
[87] *Development Bank of the Philippines v Secretary of Labor*, GR No 79351 (1989).
[88] ibid.
[89] Civil Code, Art 2250.
[90] Civil Code, Art 2244.
[91] FRIA, s 133.
[92] Constitution, Art III, s 20.

payment presented to an insolvent or bankrupt debtor who is either undergoing rehabilitation, liquidation or is in a state of suspension of payments under the Laws of Bankruptcy is the disposition of his or its properties. Such payment of property for a monetary debt or '*dacion en pago*' (dation in payment) is recognised in this jurisdiction under the New Civil Code of the Philippines.[93] The New Civil Code provides that the debtor is liable with all his property, present and future, for the fulfillment of his obligations, subject to the exemptions provided by law.[94] Bankruptcy will not excuse an insolvent debtor from the settlement of his obligations as the law protects the creditors up to the extent that the debtor is bled dried and no asset may be squeezed out of him. Creditors may proceed against their debtors, so long as the debt has not been fully collected.[95]

The law sets different standards for the payment of debts through properties for a natural and juridical insolvent debtor. For the juridical debtor, all its assets may be liquidated, seized and applied as payment for its liabilities while such is not the case for the natural debtor. The properties mentioned that are exempt to be applied as payment for the debtor's liabilities are: (1) his family home, as duly constituted,[96] except if the liabilities consist of non-payment of taxes on the family home,[97] debts incurred prior to its constitution,[98] debts secured by mortgages on the premises before or after such constitution,[99] or payment due to those who built or supplied materials for its construction;[100] (2) money or property obtained as support;[101] (3) salaries, wages or earnings of the individual debtor for his personal services within the four months preceding the levy or judgment against him as are necessary for the support of his family,[102] except if the debt was incurred for the purchase of food, shelter, clothing and medical attendance;[103] and, (4) tools of the trade for an individual debtor.[104]

These are for individual or natural debtors; such protection is not available to juridical or corporate debtors. Properties of individual debtors necessary for trade such as a dentist's dental chair, are protected, but corporate assets even if connected to the business such as a dump truck for a hauling company will be the subject of execution or payment for existing liabilities. As held by the Supreme Court, 'if properties used in business are exempt from execution, there can hardly be an instance when a judgment claim can be enforced against the business entity.'[105] It stands to reason that only natural persons whose salaries, wages and earnings are indispensable for his own and that of his family's support are exempted under section 13(i) of Rule 39 of the Rules of Court. Undeniably, a corporate entity such as a security agency is not covered by the exemption. Properties of a natural debtor that belong to either a conjugal partnership or absolute community shall not be among the assets to be taken off by the assignee for payment of the insolvent debtor's obligations, except insofar as the latter have redounded to the benefit of the family.[106]

[93] Civil Code, Art 1245.
[94] Civil Code, Art 2236.
[95] Civil Code, Art 1216.
[96] Family Code, Art 155.
[97] Family Code, Art 155 (1).
[98] Family Code, Art 155 (2).
[99] Family Code, Art 155 (3).
[100] Family Code, Art 155 (4).
[101] Family Code, Art 194.
[102] Rules of Civil Procedure (AM No 19-10-20-SC), Rule 39, s 13(i).
[103] Civil Code, Art 1708.
[104] ibid.
[105] *Pentagon Security and Investigation Agency vs. Jimenez*, GR No 88114 (1990).
[106] Civil Code, Art 2238.

Dation in payment must be distinguished from *pactum commissorium*, which is null and void under the New Civil Code.[107] In the latter, the creditor automatically appropriates the things given by way of pledge or mortgage, or dispose of them. It is a guaranty for the fulfillment of the obligation in the event the obligor fails to live up to his undertakings, without further formality, such as foreclosure proceedings, and a public sale.[108] In the former, the parties actually novate the earlier contract. Instead of the monetary debt owed by the debtor, he offers a property to pay for the debt. That is why the Civil Code provides that such form of payment shall be governed by the law on sales,[109] because in reality the thing offered by the debtor as payment becomes the object of the contract of sale, while the debt is treated as the purchase price.[110] If the parties entered into a separate contract, like a deed of absolute sale, it proves that there was no automatic transfer of ownership, and therefore, no *pactum commissorium*, only *dacion en pago*.[111]

D. Payment by Cession

The debtor, even outside of bankruptcy proceedings, may offer to use his properties as payment if he comes to an agreement with his creditors. As the Civil Code provides, '(W)hen only one prestation has been agreed upon, but the obligor may render another in substitution, the obligation is called facultative.'[112] The debtor can present another means to settle his obligations, such as offering his properties instead of the sum of money he owes his creditors. The creditor must give his consent in order for such facultative obligation to take place. If the parties are in agreement, then '(T)he debtor may cede or assign his property to his creditors in payment of his debts'.

Compared to *dacion en pago*, which in reality is a contract of sale as it requires transfer of ownership of specific property, cession involves the conveyance of all properties of the debtor for the purpose of being sold, with the proceeds to be used as payment of his debts. As such, it does not extinguish the debt in full and shall only release the debtor from responsibility for the net proceeds of the thing assigned, unless there is stipulation to the contrary.[113]

E. Assignment of Properties

The effect of using his or its properties as payment for debts, whether this be voluntary or involuntary, in general, releases the debtor from his or its obligations. An insolvent debtor, with nothing more to offer than his existing properties or its assets is considered to have already paid and performed. The properties or its value is meant to satisfy the creditors and for them to no longer pursue any action against the insolvent debtor. As discussed above, the creditors can proceed against their debtors until the debts are fully collected. Inasmuch as forfeiting his properties or its assets should already provide the debtor with a sigh of relief, the creditors must ultimately be satisfied with the properties or the net proceeds thereof that they acquire to put an end to their desire for complete collection or satisfaction of the debt. As held by the Supreme Court, '[t]he dation in payment extinguishes the obligation to the extent of the value of the thing delivered,

[107] Civil Code, Art 2088.
[108] *Ruby Shelter Builders and Realty Development Corporation v Tan* GR No 217368 (2004).
[109] Civil Code, Art 1245.
[110] *Filinvest Credit Corporation v Philippine Acetylene, Co., Inc.* GR No L-50449 (1982).
[111] *Ruby Shelter Builders and Realty Development Corporation v Tan* GR No 217368 (2004).
[112] Civil Code, Art 1255.
[113] ibid.

either as agreed upon by the parties or as may be proved, unless the parties by agreement, express or implied, or by their silence, consider the thing as equivalent to the obligation, in which case the obligation is totally extinguished.'[114]

A dation in payment does not necessarily mean total extinguishment of the obligation. The obligation is totally extinguished only when the parties, by agreement, express or implied, or by their silence, consider the thing as equivalent to the obligation.[115] In *dacion en pago*, property is alienated to the creditor in satisfaction of a debt in money. The debtor delivers and transmits to the creditor the former's ownership over a thing as an accepted equivalent of the payment or performance of an outstanding debt.[116] As applied to an insolvent debtor, the creditors are left without any real choice. The debtor having been declared as bankrupt is without any other means to satisfy his debts. The transfer of ownership or the receipt of the net proceeds of the properties of the debtor serves as payment and performance and extinguishes the obligation of the debtor.

VI. Effect of Bankruptcy as a Discharge of Debts

Obligations are extinguished, among others, by payment or performance. An insolvent debtor is not in any position to make payments. The New Civil Code provides the other modes of extinguishment of obligations, namely: loss of the thing due, condonation, compensation, confusion, novation, the fulfillment or happening of a resolutory condition or period, prescription, and annulment of a contract.[117] Bankruptcy or insolvency is not among the modes of extinguishing an obligation. The insolvent debtor is not excused from paying his obligations by reason of his would-be inability to pay. As discussed, being in a state of insolvency is a problem of liquidity with the debtor unable to meet all his obligations as they fall due. Insolvency, at most changes the form of payment by the debtor and instead of sum of money, payment is made through the assignment of his properties or the net proceeds thereof.

Such, however, is the general rule, as when not all obligations against all creditors are satisfied with the properties of the debtor. It may either not be enough or some creditors, such as unsecured creditors, do not even get to have a slice of the pie from the property of the debtor as payment. Bankruptcy is intended to both allow the debtor to settle his obligations and be free of all his debts incurred prior to the declaration of bankruptcy. Bankruptcy is meant to end the obligations of the insolvent debtor, one way or another, in fact, in one case, the Supreme Court even held that a debtor is considered to be legally dead after being declared insolvent, thus 'when a petition is filed by creditors to have a person declared an involuntary insolvent where, in the regular course of business, he is declared insolvent, and an assignee is elected, the title of the assignee to all of the estate and assets of the insolvent relates back and becomes vested in the assignee as of the date of the filing of the original petition by the creditors. In other words, as to his estate, the insolvent is then declared judicially dead as of the date of the filing of the petition.'[118]

As such, bankruptcy, through the seizing of the assets of the insolvent debtor, discharges his liabilities to his creditors. But if the assets and all the properties of the debtor is drained, then does being in a state of insolvency or being declared bankrupt absolve the debtor from performing his obligations or paying his liabilities? In rehabilitation, attempts are being made to allow the

[114] *Lopez v Court of Appeals* GR No L-33157 (1982).
[115] *Caltex (Philippines), Inc. v The Intermediate Appellate Court* GR No 72703 (1992).
[116] *Tan Shuy v Maulawin* GR No 190375 (2012).
[117] Civil Code, Art 1231.
[118] S. *W. O'Brien's v Del Rosario* GR No L-26320 (1926).

debtor to recover by conserving or administering his remaining assets in the most beneficial way in the hopes of restoring his financial well-being and viability. The hope is that there may still be a chance for the debtor to be liquid enough, profitable at that and meet all his obligations. But if the insolvent debtor has been made to undergo liquidation, voluntarily or otherwise, then such ends any attempt of liquidity and his creditors are forced to collect payment from what assets the debtor has.

In any case, whether the properties of the debtor have been exhausted or did not have any to begin with in the bankruptcy proceedings, being bankrupt will have the effect of discharging the debtor from the payment of his liabilities. From the standpoint of a personal debtor, only his estate will be liable and his debts, unless stipulated otherwise, will not be passed on to his heirs.[119] If the debtor were a juridical entity, then the situation will be different. If the debtor is a partnership, then it has a juridical personality separate and distinct from that of each of the partners that comprise it,[120] and if it were a corporation, then it also has a juridical personality separate and distinct from the stockholders or members that comprise it.[121]

Such is the general rule for juridical debtors, the partners or corporators do not share the assets and/or liabilities of the partnership or corporation and hence, are not made to answer for its obligations. However, general partners in a partnership are liable *pro rata* with all their property and after all the partnership assets have been exhausted, for the contracts which may be entered into in the name and for the account of the partnership, under its signature and by a person authorised to act for the partnership.[122] The insolvency of the juridical partnership debtor does not discharge its liabilities even if already under insolvency proceedings, as the creditors may still resort to go after the partners for payment of partnership debts even after the assets of the partnership were exhausted to answer for its liabilities if there is still a deficiency in such payment.

The same goes for the insolvency of a juridical corporation debtor, although not to the same extent. It also does not discharge such debtor from the payment of its liabilities despite being bankrupt as its creditors may still resort to go after the shareholders or members of the corporation for payments of its debts even after the assets of the partnership were exhausted to answer for its liabilities if there is still a deficiency in such payment. The obligations of a corporation, which only acts through its directors, officers or authorised representatives, as a general rule are its own obligations and such natural persons is not to be held liable for it.[123] Creditors may still proceed against the shareholders of the corporation, however unlike a general partner in a partnership, which is bound to answer for partnership liability with his own property, 'stockholders of a corporation are liable for the debts of the corporation up to the extent of their unpaid subscriptions.'[124] Stockholders are only liable up to their capital contribution, which means that they may not get a return on their capital investment. Will a bankrupt debtor be discharged of all debts and obligations after all his properties are seized to use as payment? The purpose for which the Insolvency Law was enacted is to effect an equitable distribution of the bankrupt's properties among his creditors and to benefit the debtor by discharging him from his liabilities and enabling him to start afresh with the property set apart for him as exempt.[125]

[119] *Hinlo v De Leon* GR No L-4860 (1911).
[120] Civil Code, Art 44.
[121] Civil Code, Art 44; Revised Corporation Code, s 2.
[122] Civil Code, Art 1816.
[123] *Bank of Commerce v Marilyn Nite* GR No 211535 (2015).
[124] *Halley v Printwell, Inc.* GR No 157549 (2011).
[125] *In the Matter of the Estate of Mindanao Motor Line, Inc. v Alforque* GR No L-27944 (1974).

Debts owed to the government in the form of taxes, both national or local, including the fees and penalties are considered waived for a debtor undergoing rehabilitation.[126] Except if such collection will be under a criminal prosecution for tax evasion. Criminal actions arising from debt payments filed against the debtor shall not be extinguished by insolvency. If a debtor is criminally prosecuted for estafa[127] or violation of the Bouncing Checks Law,[128] insolvency proceedings cannot stop exaction of criminal liability from such criminal prosecution. The most relief that the insolvent debtor may avail of is the staying of such criminal action against him pending the insolvency proceedings.

Lastly, the insolvency of the debtor and the proceedings must be genuine. It should not be a ploy to evade liability or an attempt by the debtor to dispose of his property or put it beyond reach of creditors. Aside from the granting of the insolvency proceedings being nullified, the debtor will be further subject to criminal proceedings. According to the Revised Penal Code, any person who shall abscond with his property to the prejudice of his creditors shall suffer imprisonment.[129] Such is referred to as fraudulent insolvency.

Also, any contract involving such fraudulent transfer of the debtor's properties, may be cancelled or rescinded by a court which will not just necessitate the return of the properties but both the debtor as seller and the supposed buyer will be liable for the payment of damages to the affected creditors.[130] FRIA provides a similar provision that any transaction occurring prior to the commencement date of insolvency proceedings entered into by the debtor or involving its funds or assets may be rescinded or declared null and void on the ground that the same was executed with intent to defraud a creditor or creditors or which constitute undue preference of creditors.[131] It further provides that the rehabilitation receiver or, with his conformity, any creditor may initiate and prosecute any action to rescind, or declare null and void any such fraudulent transaction.

[126] FRIA, Ch II, s 17.
[127] Revised Penal Code, Art 315.
[128] BP No 22.
[129] Revised Penal Code, Art 314.
[130] Civil Code, Arts 1387–1388.
[131] FRIA, Ch 2, s 58.

9

Competition Law in the Philippines

JAMES KEITH C HEFFRON

I. Introduction

This chapter covers the competition law in the Philippines. While the Philippine Competition Act is a domestic Philippine Law, it specifically provides that it is applicable to international trade which have direct, substantial, and foreseeable effects in the country. The law explicitly states that these effects may come as a result of acts done outside the Philippines. The extraterritorial application of this domestic law is consistent with the effects doctrine and protective principle of international law. It also acknowledges the reality that Philippine businesses are involved in numerous cross-border transactions. An example is the acquisition of Grab Holdings Inc., a Singapore-based firm, of the assets of Uber B.V. and Uber Systems Inc. in the Philippines. This acquisition allowed Grab to achieve market dominance in the four and six-door vehicle Transportation Network Vehicle Service (TNVS) industry in the country.

As a member of the free world, the Philippines has strived to inculcate policies that promote and protect the fundamental rights of its people. From basic human and political to consumer rights, the body of Philippine law continues to evolve to address its people's ever-developing needs and concerns. One of these primary concerns is the eradication of poverty, which the state hopes can be solved with the help of meaningful social legislation. For decades since the establishment of the Philippines as an independent republic, the state has enacted a myriad of legislations that are aimed at addressing poverty and wealth distribution at its very core. These laws usually promote social welfare, access to basic services, and economic development. Competition laws are at the heart of this struggle. For decades, the Philippine legislature has enacted numerous laws that attempt to prevent the evils of anti-competitive business practices in the marketplace. These acts of unfair competition, whether directly or indirectly, harm the economy and society by restricting market fairness, limiting consumer choice, and suppressing economic opportunities, thereby exacerbating poverty. Aside from higher prices of goods and services, undue concentration of wealth in the hands of a few that prevents fair distribution of income, job losses, and limited employment opportunities, one of the major impacts of these business practices is the suppression of small and medium size businesses and entrepreneurship, which according to the 2023 statistics of the Philippine Department of Trade and Industry composes of 99.63 per cent of the total businesses in the country.[1] Thus, being a real threat to national and economic development, it is no surprise that the Philippines finally enacted a comprehensive anti-competition law similar to that of the United States, European Union, and United Kingdom.

[1] www.dti.gov.ph/dti-knowledge-hub/dti-statistics.

II. The Constitutional Basis of Competition Laws in the Philippines

The 1987 Philippine Constitution provides for several provisions that serve as the fundamental basis of anti-competition laws. Article II, Section 9 provides that the '(t)he State shall promote a just and dynamic social order that will ensure the prosperity and independence of the nation and free the people from poverty through policies that provide adequate social services, promote full employment, a rising standard of living, and an improved quality of life for all.' It recognises that poverty and gross economic and social inequality are hurdles to the nation's prosperity that concern the very foundation of the dignity of the human person.[2] This provision is read in consonance with Section 10, which provides that '(t)he State shall promote social justice in all phases of national development.' Further, Article XIII, Section 1 provides that '(t)he Congress shall give highest priority to the enactment of measures that protect and enhance the right of all the people to human dignity, reduce social, economic, and political inequalities, and remove cultural inequities by equitably diffusing wealth and political power for the common good.' Social justice, in the context of constitutional law, pertains to the 'equalization of economic, political, and social opportunities with special emphasis on the duty of the state to tilt the balance of social forces by favoring the disadvantaged in life.'[3] Its promotion 'shall include the commitment to create economic opportunities based on freedom of initiative and self-reliance.'[4] The Philippines' adoption of economic justice as state policy is in line with the basic tenets of international law. Article 22 of the International Declaration of Human Rights provides that every person's 'economic, social and cultural rights (are) indispensable for his dignity and the free development of his personality.' Likewise, the International Covenants on Economic, Social and Cultural Rights, and of Civil and Political Rights affirm the indivisibility of these basic rights. Anti-competition laws promote economic and social justice by preventing business practices that ensnare people in poverty. It ensures that anti-competitive practices such as monopolies and cartels do not hinder economic opportunities, especially for the disadvantaged, such as small businesses and consumers.

Article II, Section 20 provides that '(t)he State recognizes the indispensable role of the private sector, encourages private enterprise, and provides incentives to needed investments.' In recognising the private sector as an indispensable keg in the wheel of economic and social development, the state is mandated to protect it from unfair and unreasonable business practices. Private sector growth will only be realised through a healthy economic environment brought about by fair competition. Therefore, anti-competition measures, among others, are justified to create a level playing field for businesses.

Article XII, Section 1 provides that '(t)he goals of the national economy are a more equitable distribution of opportunities, income, and wealth; a sustained increase in the amount of goods and services produced by the nation for the benefit of the people; and an expanding productivity as the key to raising the quality of life for all, especially the underprivileged.' It further states that 'the State shall protect Filipino enterprises against unfair foreign competition and trade practices.' These provisions are read in consonance with Article II, Section 19 which provides that '(the) State shall develop a self-reliant and independent national economy effectively controlled by Filipinos.' Thus, the state is mandated to ensure that Filipino enterprises adopt business

[2] J Bernas, *1987 Philippine Constitution: A Comprehensive Reviewer* (2011) 17.
[3] ibid.
[4] 1987 Philippine Constitution, Art XIII, s 2.

practices that not just promote but adhere to equitable distribution of opportunities, income, and wealth. These policies are likewise applicable to foreign enterprises that do business in the country. However, though these provisions prescribe a Filipino-first principle, especially against unfair foreign competition and trade practices, the intention is not to protect local enterprises in the event of their inadequacies or inefficiencies at the expense of the consuming public.[5] Public interest and welfare are still of paramount importance and the state shall act accordingly, under its police powers, to promote them even at the expense of Filipino enterprises.

Article XII, Section 19 provides that '(t)he State shall regulate or prohibit monopolies when the public interest so requires. No combinations in restraint of trade or unfair competition shall be allowed.' This provision directly prohibits core anti-competitive business practices such as combinations in restraint of trade or unfair competition. It likewise empowers the state to regulate industries to prevent economic abuse brought about by monopolies, even if the very government that is mandated to espouse its spirit shall create laws that violate it. Thus, in the landmark case of *Tatad v Secretary of the Department of Energy*,[6] where the constitutionality of Republic Act No. 8180 entitled 'An Act Deregulating the Downstream Oil Industry and For Other Purposes' was questioned, the Philippine Supreme Court, in shooting down the said law since its provisions on tariff differential, stocking of inventories, and predatory pricing violate the constitutional prohibition on unfair competition and restraint of trade, held:

> Section 19, Article XII of our Constitution is anti-trust in history and in spirit. It espouses competition. The desirability of competition is the reason for the prohibition against restraint of trade, the reason for the interdiction of unfair competition, and the reason for regulation of unmitigated monopolies. Competition is thus the underlying principle of section 19, Article XII of our Constitution which cannot be violated by R.A. No. 8180. We subscribe to the observation of Prof. *Gellhorn* that the objective of anti-trust law is 'to assure a competitive economy, based upon the belief that through competition producers will strive to satisfy consumer wants at the lowest price with the sacrifice of the fewest resources. Competition among producers allows consumers to bid for goods and services, and thus matches their desires with society's opportunity costs.' He adds with appropriateness that there is a reliance upon 'the operation of the 'market' system (free enterprise) to decide what shall be produced, how resources shall be allocated in the production process, and to whom the various products will be distributed. The market system relies on the consumer to decide what and how much shall be produced, and on competition, among producers to determine who will manufacture it.
>
> Again, we underline in scarlet that the fundamental principle espoused by section 19, Article XII of the Constitution is competition for it alone can release the creative forces of the market. But the competition that can unleash these creative forces is competition that is fighting yet is fair. Ideally, this kind of competition requires the presence of not one, not just a few but several players. A market controlled by one player (monopoly) or dominated by a handful of players (oligopoly) is hardly the market where honest-to-goodness competition will prevail. Monopolistic or oligopolistic markets deserve our careful scrutiny and laws which barricade the entry points of new players in the market should be viewed with suspicion.

Though the Constitution does not allow combinations of restraint of trade or unfair competition, the Supreme Court however is careful to adjudge what indeed constitutes as restraint of trade. In the case of *Avon Cosmetics, Inc. v Luna*,[7] where Luna questioned the validity of the exclusivity clause of her contract with Avon, arguing that the contract is a restraint in trade since it prohibits her from selling other cosmetic products, the Court held that '(w)hat is brought about to lay

[5] Bernas (n 2) 458.
[6] G.R. Nos. 124360 & 127867, (5 November 1997) 346 Phil 321–423.
[7] G.R. No. 153674, (20 December 2006), 540 Phil 389–409.

the test on whether a given agreement constitutes an unlawful machination or combination in restraint of trade is whether under the particular circumstances of the case and the nature of the particular contract involved, such contract is, or is not, against public interest.' Contracts that require exclusivity are therefore not per se void as all the surrounding circumstances must be taken into account in determining whether a restrictive business practice does indeed result in unreasonable restraint on trade.[8]

Monopolies on the other hand are not totally prohibited. It is only when these monopolies affect – and as may be are required by – public interest, that the state mandates its regulation or total prohibition. In the case of *Eastern Assurance & Surety Corp. v LTFRB*,[9] Eastern Assurance & Surety Corporation (EASCO) questioned the legality of Memorandum Circular No. 2001-001 issued by the Land Transportation Franchising and Regulatory Board (LTFRB) that required that before a certificate of public convenience be issued to any public utility vehicle, the public utility must acquire an insurance policy from any member of the two groups of insurance monopolies accredited by the LTFRB pursuant to the said memorandum circular. In supporting its position, EASCO argued that creating this policy violates their right to engage in the insurance business and thereby violates the constitutional prohibition against monopolies, combination in restraint of trade, and unfair competition. The Philippine Supreme Court, in upholding the legality of the memorandum circular, held that the LTFRB is well within its power to regulate the two insurance monopolies as public utility vehicles are common carriers that engage in a business that affects the public interest. Thus, '(w)hile embracing free enterprise as an economic creed, the Constitution does not totally prohibit the operation of monopolies, … (h)owever, it mandates the State to regulate them when public interest so requires.'[10]

III. Competition Laws Prior to the Philippine Competition Act

In 2015, the Philippines enacted Republic Act No. 10667, or the Philippine Competition Act. It is the current primary comprehensive legislation that governs competition policy in the Philippines. However, prior to the enactment of this law, the Philippines has adapted several anti-competition laws that address monopolies, restraint of trade, and unfair competition. The following are the more pertinent legislative acts:

A. An Act to Prohibit Monopolies and Combinations in Restraint of Trade

Taking inspiration from the Sherman Act, which is the primary antitrust law of the United States, Act 3247, or 'An Act to Prohibit Monopolies and Combinations in Restraint of Trade' was enacted in 1923 and was the earliest major law that addressed anti-competitive practices. It declared as illegal those agreements in restraint of trade or those that prevent free competition.

[8] ibid.
[9] G.R. No. 149717, (07 October 2003), 459 Phil 395–416.
[10] ibid.

It also prohibited monopolistic practices. Those who were found to be engaged in said business practices were punished by fine and/or imprisonment.[11]

B. The Revised Penal Code

Similar to Act 3247, Article 186 of the Philippine Revised Penal Code prohibited and made punishable certain anti-competitive acts. Persons, both natural and juridical, who enter into agreements in restraint of trade or to prevent free competition in the market, and those who shall monopolise any object of trade with the intent of restraining free competition shall be punished by fine and/or imprisonment. Additionally, the manufacturer, producer, processor, or importer of any object of commerce who shall combine or agree with any person to make transactions that are prejudicial to lawful commerce or to increase its market price shall likewise be punished by fine and/or imprisonment.

Further, Article 189 punishes persons who 'in unfair competition, and for the purpose of deceiving or defrauding another of his legitimate trade or the public in general, shall sell his goods giving them the general appearance of goods of another manufacturer or dealer, either as to the goods themselves, or in the wrapping of the packages in which they are contained, or the device or words thereon, or in any other feature of their appearance which would be likely to induce the public to believe that the goods offered are those of a manufacturer or dealer other than the actual manufacturer or dealer, or shall give other persons a chance or opportunity to do the same with a like purpose.'

C. The Civil Code of the Philippines

Article 28 of the Civil Code of the Philippines provides that '(u)nfair competition in agricultural, commercial or industrial enterprises or in labor through the use of force, intimidation, deceit, machination or any other unjust, oppressive or highhanded method shall give rise to a right of action by the person who thereby suffers damage.' Thus, any business practice that tends to cause unfair competition, especially if accompanied by force, intimidation, deceit, or any unjust and oppressive act, thereby leading to injury or harm to another shall not just be punishable under criminal law but shall likewise be a basis for a tort action.

D. The Price Act

Republic Act No. 7581 or the Price Act was enacted in 1992 'to ensure the availability of basic necessities and prime commodities at reasonable prices at all times without denying

[11] Act 3247 provides: **Section 1.** Every agreement, contract, conspiracy, or combination in the form of trust or otherwise, in restraint of trade or commerce or intended to prevent or preventing by artificial means free competition in the market, is hereby declared to be illegal, and any person who shall make any such contract or engage in any such combination or conspiracy shall be punished by fine not exceeding five thousand pesos, or by imprisonment not exceeding one year, or by both such fine and imprisonment, in the discretion of the court.

Section 2. Every person who shall monopolize, or attempt to monopolize, or combine or conspire with any other person or persons, to monopolize by artificial means restraining' free competition in the market, any part of trade or commerce, shall be punished by fine not exceeding five thousand pesos, or by imprisonment not exceeding one year, or by both such fine and imprisonment, in the discretion of the court.

legitimate business a fair return on investment.' The law protects consumers against illegal acts that result in price manipulation such as hoarding, profiteering, and cartels concerning the supply, distribution, marketing, and pricing of goods. It likewise provided for automatic price controls and gave the President the power to impose price ceilings in the event of calamities and emergencies.

E. The Public Telecommunications Policy Act

Republic Act No. 7925 or the Public Telecommunications Policy Act was enacted in 1995 and one of its policies ensures that 'a healthy competitive environment shall be fostered, one in which telecommunications carriers are free to make business decisions and to interact with one another in providing telecommunications services, with the end in view of encouraging their financial viability while maintaining affordable rates'[12] To realise this, it empowers the National Telecommunication Commission (NTC) to establish rates and tariffs to be imposed on telecommunications entities while authorising it to exempt entities from said regulation if it has sufficient competition that would ensure fair and reasonable prices. However, despite the exemption, the NTC may still 'regulate rates or tariffs when ruinous competition results or when a monopoly or a cartel or combination in restraint of free competition exists and the rates or tariffs are distorted or unable to function freely and the public is adversely affected.'

F. The Intellectual Property Code

Republic Act No. 8293 or the Intellectual Property Code of the Philippines was enacted in 1997 and encourages the transfer and dissemination of technology while regulating practices that may lead to the abuse of intellectual property rights which in turn would have adverse effects on competition. One of the policies of the law is to 'streamline administrative procedures of registering patents, trademarks and copyright, to liberalize the registration on the transfer of technology, and to enhance the enforcement of intellectual property rights in the Philippines.'[13] Specifically, it mandates that agreements such as technology transfer arrangements[14] should comply with the limitations and clauses provided for in Chapter IX of the law, which include a list of prohibited anti-competitive acts.[15]

[12] Republic Act 7925, Public Telecommunications Policy Act, s 4(f).

[13] Republic Act No. 8293, Intellectual Property Code of the Philippines, s 2.

[14] N.B. Per s 4.2 of the Intellectual Property Code, the term 'technology transfer arrangements' refers to contracts or agreements involving the transfer of systematic knowledge for the manufacture of a product, the application of a process, or rendering of a service including management contracts; and the transfer, assignment or licensing of all forms of intellectual property rights, including licensing of computer software except computer software developed for mass market.

[15] Republic Act No. 8293, Intellectual Property Code of the Philippines, s 87. *Prohibited Clauses.* – Except in cases under Section 91, the following provisions shall be deemed prima facie to have an adverse effect on competition and trade:

87.1. Those which impose upon the licensee the obligation to acquire from a specific source capital goods, intermediate products, raw materials, and other technologies, or of permanently employing personnel indicated by the licensor;

87.2. Those pursuant to which the licensor reserves the right to fix the sale or resale prices of the products manufactured on the basis of the license;

87.3. Those that contain restrictions regarding the volume and structure of production;

87.4. Those that prohibit the use of competitive technologies in a non-exclusive technology transfer agreement;

G. The Generics Act of 1998

Republic Act No. 6675 or the Generics Act was enacted in 1998. It requires the use of generic terminology in the importation, manufacture, distribution, marketing, advertising and promotion, prescription, and dispensing of drugs. It also ensures the adequate supply of drugs with generic names at the lowest possible cost. Section 8 also empowers the Department of Health to require drug manufacturing companies 'to produce, distribute and make available to the general public the medicine it produces, in the form of generic drugs.' This ensures that drug companies will also produce generic counterparts of their branded products and make them accessible to the public.

H. The Downstream Oil Deregulation Act of 1998

Republic Act No. 8479 or the Downstream Oil Deregulation Act was enacted in 1998 to liberalise the downstream oil industry in the Philippines, promoting competition, enhancing efficiency, and ensuring fair pricing in the oil sector. This law aimed to break the monopoly in the oil industry by allowing for greater market participation, ensuring that the oil market operates under competitive conditions. It provided for anti-trust safeguards by prohibiting and penalising acts that create *cartelisation*, which is defined as 'any agreement, combination or concerted action by refiners, importers and/or dealers, or their representatives, to fix prices, restrict outputs or divide markets, either by products or by areas, or allocate markets, either by products or by areas, in restraint of trade or free competition, including any contractual stipulation which prescribes pricing levels and profit margins' and *predatory pricing* which means 'selling or offering to sell any oil product at a price below the seller's or offeror's average variable cost for the purpose of destroying competition, eliminating a competitor or discouraging a potential competitor from entering the market.'[16]

87.5. Those that establish a full or partial purchase option in favor of the licensor;
87.6. Those that obligate the licensee to transfer for free to the licensor the inventions or improvements that may be obtained through the use of the licensed technology;
87.7. Those that require payment of royalties to the owners of patents for patents which are not used;
87.8. Those that prohibit the licensee to export the licensed product unless justified for the protection of the legitimate interest of the licensor such as exports to countries where exclusive licenses to manufacture and/or distribute the licensed product(s) have already been granted;
87.9. Those which restrict the use of the technology supplied after the expiration of the technology transfer arrangement, except in cases of early termination of the technology transfer arrangement due to reason(s) attributable to the licensee;
87.10. Those which require payments for patents and other industrial property rights after their expiration, termination arrangement;
87.11. Those which require that the technology recipient shall not contest the validity of any of the patents of the technology supplier;
87.12. Those which restrict the research and development activities of the licensee designed to absorb and adapt the transferred technology to local conditions or to initiate research and development programs in connection with new products, processes or equipment;
87.13. Those which prevent the licensee from adapting the imported technology to local conditions, or introducing innovation to it, as long as it does not impair the quality standards prescribed by the licensor;
87.14. Those which exempt the licensor for liability for non-fulfilment of his responsibilities under the technology transfer arrangement and/or liability arising from third party suits brought about by the use of the licensed product or the licensed technology; and
87.15. Other clauses with equivalent effects.

[16] Republic Act No. 8479, Downstream Oil Deregulation Act of 1998, s 11.

I. General Banking Law of 2000

Republic Act No. 8791 or the General Banking Law was enacted in 2000 and is the primary legislation that governs the operations of banks and other financial institutions in the Philippines. It establishes the regulatory framework for the banking system and ensures that it is globally competitive, dynamic and responsive to the demands of a developing economy.[17] To allow fairness, transparency, and healthy market competition within the sector, the Monetary Board, pursuant to the law, has provided for limitations on ownership by related interests or a family group in a domestic bank.[18]

J. Electric Power Industry Reform Act of 2001 (EPIRA Law)

Republic Act No. 9136 or the Electric Power Industry Reform Act was enacted in 2001 and regulates the electric power industry in the Philippines. Section 45 of the law prohibits any person from engaging in anti-competitive behaviour which includes, but is not limited to, cross-subsidisation, price or market manipulation, or other unfair trade practices detrimental to the encouragement and protection of contestable markets. Further, the law promotes market competition and prevent harmful monopoly and market power abuse by empowering the Energy Regulatory Commission (ERC) to ensure ownership and control regulations of the national installed generating capacity and prohibiting distribution utilities to source from bilateral power supply contracts more than 50 per cent of its total demand from an associated firm engaged in generation.

K. Universally Accessible Cheaper and Quality Medicines Act (Cheaper Medicines Act)

Republic Act No. 9502 or the Cheaper Medicines Act was enacted in 2007 and ensures access to quality affordable drugs and medicines for all regardless of social status. To carry out this objective, it promotes and prioritises an effective competition policy in the supply and demand of quality affordable drugs and medicines. Section 24 provides that 'it shall be unlawful for any manufacturer, importer, trader, distributor, wholesaler, retailer, or any person engaged in any

[17] Republic Act No. 8791, General Banking Law of 2000, s 2.

[18] BSP Circular No. 332, May 13, 2002, provides that pursuant to Monetary Board Resolution No. 567 dated 25 April 2002, the following rules and regulations are hereby issued to implement ss 12, 13 and 14 of Republic Act No. 8791, known as 'The General Banking Law of 2000:

SECTION 1. Stockholdings of Family Groups or Related Interest. – Individuals related to each other within the fourth degree of consanguinity or affinity, whether legitimate, illegitimate or common-law, shall be considered family groups or related interests but may each own up to forty percent (40%) of the voting stock of a domestic bank: Provided, That said relationship must be fully disclosed in all transactions by such individual or family group with the bank.

SECTION 2. Corporate Stockholdings. – Two or more corporations owned or controlled by the same family group or same group of persons shall be considered related interests but may each own up to forty percent (40%) of the voting stock of a domestic bank: Provided, that said relationship must be fully disclosed in all transactions by such corporations or related groups of persons with the bank.

SECTION 3. A natural person and a corporation or corporations which are wholly-owned, or a majority of the voting stock of which is owned, by him may own only up to a combined forty percent (40%) of the voting stock of a domestic bank.

method of disposition of drugs and medicines to engage in acts of price manipulation such as hoarding, profiteering, or illegal combination or forming cartel … and all other acts committed in restraint of trade.'

IV. The Philippine Competition Act

On 28 July 2014, the Philippine Congress passed Republic Act No. 10667 entitled An Act Providing for a National Competition Policy Prohibiting Anti-competitive Agreements, Abuse of Dominant Position and Anti-Competitive Mergers and Acquisitions, Establishing the Philippine Competition Commission and Appropriating Funds therefor or simply the Philippine Competition Act. Rooted under the constitutional mandate of social justice, the ultimate objective of this arguably piece of social legislation is to ensure the efficient and equitable distribution of opportunity, wealth, and income. The framers of the law believe that it is only by eliminating the inefficiencies of the market brought about by anti-competitive acts that the constitutional mandate would be truly realised. Section 2 of the Act provides:

> Declaration of Policy. – The efficiency of market competition as a mechanism for allocating goods and services is a generally accepted precept. The State recognizes that past measures undertaken to liberalize key sectors in the economy need to be reinforced by measures that safeguard competitive conditions. The State also recognizes that the provision of equal opportunities to all promotes entrepreneurial spirit, encourages private investments, facilitates technology development and transfer and enhances resource productivity. Unencumbered market competition also serves the interest of consumers by allowing them to exercise their right of choice over goods and services offered in the market.

Being the current premier piece of anti-trust legislation in the Philippines, it has effectively repealed some of the anti-competitive laws scattered throughout the nation's legislative landscape. Some of these laws include Article 186 of the Revised Penal Code penalising acts that constitute monopolies and restraint of trade; all relevant provisions in the EPIRA law including Section 43(u) thereof on the exercise of original jurisdiction on anti-competitive issues in the electric power industry; Section 24 on Illegal Acts of Price Manipulation and Section 25 on Penalty for Illegal Acts of Price Manipulation of the Cheaper Medicines Act; and, Executive Order No. 45, Series of 2011, Designating the Department of Justice as the Competition Authority, Department of Justice Circular No. 005 Series of 2015, and other related issuances. The Philippine Competition Act also consolidated some of the previous laws that address specific anti-competitive acts and declared that 'all other laws, decrees, executive orders and regulations, or part or parts thereof inconsistent with any provision of (the) Act, are hereby repealed, amended or otherwise modified accordingly.'

The law essentially provides for several salient features. It defines what are considered prohibited and/or regulated anti-competitive acts, it provides for the penalties for these prohibited acts, and it sets a mechanism for its regulation and/or enforcement.

A. Prohibited Anti-Competitive Acts

Under the law, there are two categories of prohibited anti-competitive acts. One is those that are defined as anti-competitive agreements and another is those considered as abuse of dominant position.

B. Anti-Competitive Agreements

Section 4 of the Act defines an agreement as 'those that refers to any type or form of contract, arrangement, understanding, collective recommendation, or concerted action, whether formal or informal, explicit or tacit, written or oral.' It does not limit itself to formal contracts as defined under the Philippine Civil Code but can refer to any kind of arrangement or understanding between competitors or any other party even without any clear cause or consideration. It can even refer to any collaborative action even without any express agreement. As long as these actions are collectively and collusively done to achieve anti-competitive acts, they fall within the purview of the definition.

There are two kinds of anti-competitive agreements. Those that are prohibited per se and those that are prohibited because they have an anti-competitive object or effect.

Anti-competitive agreements that are prohibited per se are those that are inherently illegal for simply existing. These are agreements that provide for price fixing and bid rigging between or among competitors. Thus, Section 14 (a) provides that 'the following agreements, between or among competitors, are *per se* prohibited: (1) Restricting competition as to price, or components thereof, or other terms of trade; (2) Fixing price at an auction or in any form of bidding including cover bidding, bid suppression, bid rotation and market allocation and other analogous practices of bid manipulation.' Price-fixing is not expressly defined but can be reasonably inferred under the law. The United States Federal Trade Commission essentially defines price-fixing as a naked agreement between competitors, also called a horizontal agreement, to fix prices, whether it is to lower, raise, maintain, or stabilise them.[19] Price-fixing regardless of the reason is illegal. Thus, colluding competitors cannot argue benefit and reasonableness as a defence. These agreements are inherently void *ab initio* under the law. Price-fixing is not just limited to agreements that fix prices of goods and services, it may also be related to any component that determines prices, such as discounts, costs, terms of credit, interest rates for financing, and the like. The idea is to manipulate prices artificially through any collusive means instead of letting natural market and economic forces dictate them. Bid-rigging on the other hand is when competitors employ coordinated means to control the outcome of the bidding process of any kind of procurement, whether private or public. It is inherently illegal as it destroys the competitive nature and integrity of the bidding process, thereby depriving consumers of the opportunity to obtain the best possible value for their money. The law defines several forms of bid-rigging: price-fixing at auctions or in any form of bidding which includes cover bidding, bid suppression, bid rotation and market allocation. The Philippine Competition Commission (PCC) defines cover bidding as when competitors agree to submit bids that are higher than the designated winning lowest bidder or to specifically set the terms of their bid to be unacceptable to the purchaser in order to benefit the designated winner.[20] There is bid suppression when the competitors agree that one or more will not submit a bid or when they withdraw an existing one.[21] Bid rotation happens when competitors agree that they will take turns on who will be the winning bidder.[22] Market allocation is when competitors agree to allocate or divide the market among themselves and not compete

[19] U.S. Federal Trade Commission, Price Fixing, www.ftc.gov/advice-guidance/competition-guidance/guide-antitrust-laws/dealings-competitors/price-fixing.

[20] Philippine Competition Commission, 'Bid-Rigging: What it is and How to Detect', www.phcc.gov.ph/enforcement/bid-rigging-what-it-is-and-how-to-detect#:~:text=BID%20RIGGING%20occurs%20when%20competitors, Philippine%20Competition%20Act%20(PCA).

[21] ibid.

[22] ibid.

with each other on these defined allocated markets.[23] Both price-fixing and bid-rigging are forms of anti-competitive agreements that unjustly benefit competitors and directly harm consumers. No form of justification or reason can immune anyone who commits these acts from criminal, civil, and administrative liability.

Another prohibited anti-competitive agreement is one that has an anti-competitive object or effect. These agreements are not illegal per se because they do not involve price-fixing or bid-rigging, but their implementation will lead to an unjust anti-competitive effect that ultimately harms the public. There are two categories of these types of agreements. One is an agreement between and among competitors under Section 14(b) 'which have the object or effect of substantially preventing, restricting or lessening competition … (namely) … (1) Setting, limiting, or controlling production, markets, technical development, or investment; (2) Dividing or sharing the market, whether by volume of sales or purchases, territory, type of goods or services, buyers or sellers or any other means.' Another is any vertical agreement made by any party, such as those between a producer and a distributor or the like, other than those specified in Sections 14(a) and (b) which have the object or effect of substantially preventing, restricting or lessening competition.[24] Since these agreements are not inherently illegal, they can be entered into by and among competitors (horizontal agreements) or by and between other parties such as between producers, suppliers, and distributors (vertical agreements) as long as these parties can justify the reasonableness of these agreements – that is, they do not substantially prevent, restrict or lessen competition. This is called the *rule of reason* in American jurisprudence.

C. The Rule of Reason

The rule of reason doctrine evaluates whether a business practice unreasonably restrains trade. Instead of deeming an agreement or business practice as illegal *per se*, the law empowers the courts to determine whether the act is beneficial or harmful to competition. Though this doctrine was first introduced in *Addyston Pipe and Steel Co. v United States*,[25] it was in the landmark case of *Standard Oil Co. of New Jersey v United States*[26] where it was significantly expounded. In this case, Standard Oil Co. of New Jersey was a conglomerate owned by the Rockefeller family that then controlled almost 90 percent of the petroleum industry in the United States by creating holding companies and acquiring almost all the oil refining companies in the country. Due to its sheer size, Standard Oil allegedly committed anti-competitive acts such as underpricing, threats to suppliers and distributors of competitors, etc., to solidify its control over the market and the industry itself. The United States Justice Department brought an antitrust suit against the company for violating the Sherman Act. In its defence, Standard Oil questioned the power of Congress to prohibit companies from acquiring others, arguing that this should be within the principles of freedom to contract. In upholding the validity of the power of Congress to pass the Sherman Act under the Commerce Clause of the United States Constitution, the US Supreme Court ruled that though monopolistic acts may be considered as 'restraint of trade,' those that are deemed *unduly* shall be considered illegal. Unduly restrained trade happens when the questioned acts lead to one of the following possible consequences: higher prices, reduced output, and reduced quality. In this

[23] ibid.
[24] Republic Act 10667, Philippine Competition Act, s 14(c).
[25] 175 U.S. 211 (1899).
[26] 221 U.S. 1 (1911).

case, the US Supreme Court held that the actions of Standard Oil led to these consequences and therefore violated the Sherman Act.

The rule of reason as adopted from American jurisprudence and the Sherman Act is the basis of Sections 14(b) and (c) of the Philippine Competition Act. Section 14(b), which pertains to horizontal agreements, sets the parameters of the doctrine strictly within the purview of those that have the object or effect of substantially preventing, restricting, or lessening competition. Section 14(c) on the other hand, which pertains to vertical agreements, expands the rule of reason by providing that these agreements, though having an object or effect of substantially preventing, restricting, or lessening competition, may not necessarily violate the Act if it can be reasonably shown that they contribute to improving the production or distribution of goods and services or to promoting technical or economic progress, while allowing consumers a fair share of the resulting benefits.

The last paragraph of Section 14 further provided that, 'an entity that controls, is controlled by, or is under common control with another entity or entities, have common economic interests, and are not otherwise able to decide or act independently of each other, shall not be considered competitors.' This provision is known as the single economic entity doctrine and is significant in determining whether an agreement may be considered anti-competitive and if so, whether it will fall within Sections 14(a) and (b) or (c). This is important as a violation of Sections 14(a) and (b) carries with it criminal sanctions while a breach of Section 14(c) is merely administrative and civil in nature.[27]

D. Abuse of Dominant Position

The Philippine Competition Act defines dominant position as 'a position of economic strength that an entity or entities hold which makes it capable of controlling the relevant market independently from any or a combination of the following: competitors, customers, suppliers, or consumers.'[28] There is control when an entity has 'the ability to substantially influence or direct the actions or decisions of an entity, whether by contract, agency or otherwise.'[29]

It is not illegal per se for an entity to have a dominant position in the market or industry. The Philippine Competition Act provides that if an entity maintains or increases its market share through legitimate means and this does not substantially prevent, restrict, or lessen competition, then its dominance is not anti-competitive. Likewise, the Act recognises that efforts employed by entities that help improve the production or distribution of goods and services or promote economic progress, though dominant, may not necessarily be

[27] Republic Act No. 10067 – Philippine Competition Act, 'SEC. 29. Administrative Penalties. (a) Administrative Fines. – In any investigation under Chapter III, Sections 14 and 15, and Chapter IV, Sections 17 and 20 of this Act, after due notice and hearing, the Commission may impose the following schedule of administrative fines on any entity found to have violated the said sections: First offense: Fine of up to one hundred million pesos (P100,000,000.00); Second offense: Fine of not less than one hundred million pesos (P100,000,000.00) but not more than two hundred fifty million pesos (P250,000,000.00).

SEC. 30. Criminal Penalties. An entity that enters into any anti-competitive agreement as covered by Chapter III, Section 14(a) and 14(b) under this Act shall, for each and every violation, be penalized by imprisonment from two (2) to seven (7) years, and a fine of not less than f fifty million pesos (P50,000,000.00) but not more than two hundred fifty million pesos (P250,000,000.00). The penalty of imprisonment shall be imposed upon the responsible officers, and directors of the entity. When the entities involved are juridical persons, the penalty of imprisonment shall be imposed on its officers, directors, or employees holding managerial positions, who are knowingly and willfully responsible for such violation.'

[28] Philippine Competition Act, s 4(g).

[29] ibid s 4(f).

prohibited.[30] However, if it abuses its dominant position by engaging in acts that intentionally and substantially prevent, restrict, or lessen competition, then this is considered to be anti-competitive and therefore prohibited.[31]

Under the law, several acts are considered as abuse of dominance. These include selling goods or services below cost with the intention, in bad faith, of driving out competition; engaging in acts with the intention of preventing competitors from entering or from growing within the market; requiring the approval of unrelated entities before one accepts a transaction; setting prices or terms that unreasonably discriminate between customers or sellers of the same goods or services with the intent of lessening competition substantially; imposing restrictions on the lease or sale or trade of goods or services where the intent is to prevent, restrict or lessen competition substantially; tying agreements or practices where the supply of particular goods or services are dependent upon the purchase of unrelated goods or services from the same supplier; unfair or predatory pricing practices such as imposing unfairly low purchase prices for the goods or services of marginalised producers, and imposing unfair purchase or selling price on competitors, customers, suppliers or consumers; and restricting the supply of goods or services, blocking market access, or stifling innovation in a way that harms consumer welfare.[32] In essence, these acts allow an entity to misuse its market dominance in ways that exploit consumers, restrict or distort competition, or suppress the efficient functioning of the market. The law aims to ensure that businesses with significant market power do not use that power to engage in anti-competitive behaviour that harms the competitive process, and ultimately, the interests of consumers. The primary goal is to protect consumer welfare by ensuring that markets remain open, competitive, and fair, which in turn leads to better choices, lower prices, and innovation for consumers.

E. Anti-Competitive Mergers and Acquisitions

Under the Revised Corporation Code of the Philippines, an entity such as a corporation has the express power to merge or acquire other corporations subject to the processes and approvals as outlined under the law.[33] However, under the Philippine Competition Act, merger or acquisition agreements that substantially prevent, restrict, or lessen competition in the relevant market or in the market for goods or services shall be prohibited.[34] A merger is defined as 'the joining of two (2) or more entities into an existing entity or to form a new entity' while acquisition 'refers to the purchase of securities or assets, through contract or other means, for the purpose of obtaining control by: (1) One entity of the whole or part of another; (2) Two or more entities over another; or (3) One or more entities over one or more entities'.[35] These entities are not just limited to artificial or juridical persons such as corporations but also include 'any person, natural or juridical, sole proprietorship, partnership, combination or association in any form, whether incorporated or not, domestic or foreign, including those owned or controlled by the government, engaged directly or indirectly in any economic activity'.[36]

Though mergers or acquisitions that prevent, restrict, or lessen competition are generally prohibited, the Act provides for certain exceptions: those that bring about gains in efficiencies

[30] ibid s 15.
[31] Republic Act 10667, Philippine Competition Act, s 15.
[32] ibid.
[33] Republic Act No. 11232, Revised Corporation Code of the Philippines, s 35(h).
[34] ibid s 20.
[35] ibid, s 4(a) and (b).
[36] ibid, s 4(h).

that are greater than the effects of any limitation on competition that result or are likely to result from the merger or acquisition agreement; or those involving financially distressed entities where the agreement is the least anti-competitive arrangement among the known alternative uses for the assets of such distressed entity.[37] Thus, merger or acquisition agreements that provide economic benefits or efficiencies that outweigh the anti-competitive effects of the consolidation will most likely be allowed. These economic benefits should nonetheless promote the ultimate objectives of the Act – that is they ensure an enhanced consumer welfare due to lower prices and improved quality of services and products, and that they increase or strengthen competition in the market.

F. Enforcement of the Act and the Philippine Competition Commission

The scope of the Philippine Competition Act is not just limited to persons and entities that engage in trade or commerce in the Philippines, but it has extra-territorial applicability over persons and entities that likewise engage in international trade that directly and substantially affect trade and commerce in the Philippines. However, the law does not apply to labour agreements and arrangements for the purpose of collective bargaining as these are exclusively subject to labour laws and regulations.[38] To enforce and implement the provisions of the Act, the law created the Philippine Competition Commission (PCC) under Section 5.[39] In implementing and enforcing the policies of the Act, the PCC's ultimate mandate is to promote and preserve competitive markets and consumer welfare. Being a collegial and independent quasi-judicial body, the PCC has powers and functions that can be categorised as follows: regulatory, investigative and enforcement, adjudicatory, advocacy, and advisory. It is an attached agency of the head organ of the Executive Branch of the Government of the Philippines, the Office of the President, which is constitutionally tasked with the enforcement of all domestic laws.

G. Regulatory Powers

The Act mandates and enables the PCC to oversee, review, and regulate market transactions and activities that may affect competition. Under Section 12(b), the PCC has the 'power to review proposed mergers and acquisitions, determine thresholds for notification, determine the requirements and procedures for notification, and upon exercise of its powers to review, prohibit

[37] ibid, s 21.

[38] 'SEC. 3. Scope and Application. – This Act shall be enforceable against any person or entity engaged in any trade, industry and commerce in the Republic of the Philippines. It shall likewise be applicable to international trade having direct, substantial, and reasonably foreseeable effects in trade, industry, or commerce in the Republic of the Philippines, including those that result from acts done outside the Republic of the Philippines. This Act shall not apply to the combinations or activities of workers or employees nor to agreements or arrangements with their employers when such combinations, activities, agreements, or arrangements are designed solely to facilitate collective bargaining in respect of conditions of employment.'

[39] 'SEC. 5. Philippine Competition Commission. – To implement the national competition policy and attain the objectives and purposes of this Act, an independent quasi-judicial body is hereby created, which shall be known as the Philippine Competition Commission (PCC), hereinafter referred to as the Commission, and which shall be organized within sixty (60) days after the effectivity of this Act. Upon establishment of the Commission, Executive Order No. 45 designating the Department of Justice as the Competition Authority is hereby amended. The Office for Competition (OFC) under the Office of the Secretary of Justice shall however be retained, with its powers and functions modified pursuant to Section 13 of this Chapter. The Commission shall be an attached agency to the Office of the President.'

mergers and acquisitions that will substantially prevent, restrict, or lessen competition in the relevant market.'

Per Section 17, the PCC may *motu propio* or via notification to the said agency by the concerned entities, initiate the review of a proposed merger or acquisition. This notification requirement before proceeding is obligatory on entities and transactions that meet the minimum thresholds as determined by the PCC. Any merger or acquisition agreement that fails to comply with the notification requirement shall be void. Usually, these thresholds are adjusted every two years and as of 2024, mergers and acquisitions in the Philippines that have at least a Size of Party (SOP) of Php 7.8 billion and a Size of Transaction (SOT) of Php 3.2 billion are subject to compulsory notification.[40] According to the PCC, 'SOP pertains to the aggregate value of assets or revenues of the ultimate parent entity of either party involved in the transaction, while SOT refers to the total value of assets or revenues of the acquired entity and all its controlled entities.'[41] In assessing the proposed merger or acquisition, the PCC is mandated to determine whether the transaction will likely substantially prevent, restrict, or lessen competition in the relevant market and it shall take into account any substantiated efficiencies that are likely to arise as a result thereof.[42] In doing so, the law provides the PCC with certain parameters to guide it in its review, allowing it to do so in phases, with the end goal of determining whether the transaction will stifle and restrict competition in the market.[43] After its review, the Act grants the PCC the power to absolutely prohibit the merger or acquisition or in the alternative impose certain legal conditions, whether structural or behavioural, before its approval of the transaction.[44] As the Act likewise provides that a party may seek exemption, despite the prohibition, in case the transaction results in net efficiency gains brought about by the merger or acquisition or in cases of financially distressed parties, the burden of proof in establishing these grounds will be on the party seeking the exemption.[45] Significantly, if the PCC renders a ruling granting the merger or acquisition, the decision is deemed final and executory unless the ruling was based on fraud or misrepresentation by any of the parties in the transaction.[46]

As a testament to its preemptive regulatory powers, the PCC imposed price monitoring, quality standards, and transparency conditions to ensure consumer protection and competitive market outcomes in the *Grab Holdings, Inc. (Grab) and Uber B.V. and Uber Systems, Inc. (Uber)* acquisition case. In this 2018 case, Singapore-based Grab sought to acquire the business and

[40] Philippine Competition Commission Resolution 01-2024, Adjusting the Merger Notification Thresholds pursuant to Memorandum Circular 18-001, 21 February 2024.

[41] 'Computing Merger Thresholds', Philippine Competition Commission, phcc.gov.ph/mergers-and-acquisitions/computing-merger-thresholds.

[42] Implementing Rules and Regulations of Republic Act No. 10667, Rule 4, s 1.

[43] ibid Rule 4, s 1 of the Implementing Rules and Regulations of Republic Act No. 10667, provide: '(b) In evaluating the competitive effects of a merger or acquisition, the Commission shall endeavor to compare the competitive conditions that would likely result from the merger or acquisition with the conditions that would likely have prevailed without the merger or acquisition. (c) In its evaluation, the Commission may consider, on a case to-case basis, the broad range of possible factual contexts and the specific competitive effects that may arise in different transactions, such as: (1) the structure of the relevant markets concerned; (2) the market position of the entities concerned; (3) the actual or potential competition from entities within or outside of the relevant market; (4) the alternatives available to suppliers and users, and their access to supplies or markets; (5) any legal or other barriers to entry.'

[44] ibid 'SEC. 6. Effect of Notification. – If within the relevant periods stipulated in the preceding section, the Commission determines that such agreement is prohibited under Section 20 and does not qualify for exemption under Section 21 of this Chapter, the Commission may: (a) Prohibit the implementation of the agreement; (b) Prohibit the implementation of the agreement unless and until it is modified by changes specified by the Commission; (c) Prohibit the implementation of the agreement unless and until the pertinent party or parties enter into legally enforceable agreements specified by the Commission.'

[45] ibid s 10.

[46] ibid s 23.

assets of Uber in the Philippines in exchange for substantial shares equivalent to 27.5 per cent ownership in Grab. The PCC found that the acquisition would result in negative effects resulting in lessening of competition in the market but instead of outright prohibiting the transaction, it imposed certain voluntary conditions to prevent these negative effects. Upon compliance of the parties, the PCC approved the transaction agreement and allowed the acquisition.[47] This however was not the case in the proposed merger of Universal Robina Corporation (URC) with Central Azucarera Don Pedro Inc (CADPI) and Roxas Holdings Inc (RHI) in 2018. In this case, URC, a company engaged in a wide array of food-related businesses, proposed to acquire the assets and equipment of RHI, a sugar refinery and milling company, in their plant in Batangas, Philippines. As the PCC investigated the transaction and notified the parties of its findings, the parties proposed certain voluntary commitments such as increasing sugar recovery rates, performing capital upgrades, maintaining trucking allowances, providing planter assistance, sharing ratios, and obtaining feedback from stakeholders.[48] However, despite the proposed commitments, the PCC disapproved the merger as this would create a monopoly in the sugar milling industry that would substantially lessen competition, which would ultimately be detrimental to the farmers since they stand to lose the benefits of that competition. Unlike in the *Grab* case, here, the PCC found that the proposed commitments failed to negate and eliminate the negative effects of the merger.[49]

H. Investigative and Enforcement Powers

As the premier anti-trust authority in the Philippines, the PCC is mandated to ensure compliance, investigate violations, and enforce competition laws in the country. Section 12(a) mandates that the PCC shall have the power to 'conduct inquiry, investigate, and hear and decide on cases involving any violation of this Act and other existing competition laws *motu proprio* or upon receipt of a verified complaint from an interested party or upon referral by the concerned regulatory agency, and institute the appropriate civil or criminal proceedings.' Its power to investigate and conduct inquiry for purposes of determining criminal or civil violations of the Act though is limited to fact-finding as the power to prosecute these cases is lodged with the Office of Competition under the Department of Justice (OFC-DOJ).[50] The appropriate Regional Trial Court shall have original and exclusive jurisdiction of all criminal and civil cases involving violations of the Act and other competition-related laws.[51]

Significantly, the PCC has the power to issue adjustment or divestiture orders including orders for corporate reorganisation or divestment in the manner and under such terms and conditions as may be prescribed in the rules and regulations of the Act.[52] The PCC, after observing procedural due process, can require businesses found in violation of the Act to divest or sell specific assets or business units to restore market competition. It can also order corporate reorganisation, including structural changes to dismantle monopolies or eliminate anti-competitive arrangements, or

[47] Philippine Competition Commission, Decision No. 26-M-12/2018, *Acquisition by Grab Holdings, Inc. and MyTaxi. PH Inc., of Assets of Uber B.V. and Uber Systems, Inc.*, PCC Case No. M-2018-001. 10 August 2018.

[48] 'Philippine Commission Blocks Merger' (2019) *Asia Business Law Journal*, law.asia/philippine-commission-blocks-merger/.

[49] Philippine Competition Commission, Decision No. 03-M-021/2019, *In the Matter of the Proposed Acquisition by Universal Robina Corporation of Assets of Central Azucarera Don Pedro, Inc. and Roxas Holdings, Inc. Universal Robina Corporation, Central Azucarera Don Pedro, Inc. and Roxas Holdings, Inc.*, PCC Case No. M-2018-006, 12 February 2019.

[50] ibid ss 13 and 31.

[51] ibid s 44.

[52] ibid s 12(h).

impose terms and conditions on the divestment or reorganisation process to ensure effectiveness and fairness in remedying anti-competitive effects. This power is significant as it allows the PCC to impose structural remedies, considered among the strongest tools in competition law enforcement, that can effectively restore or maintain competition, particularly when behavioural remedies are inadequate.

Further, in the exercise of its enforcement powers, the PCC can impose administrative fines for violations of the Act which include failure to comply with its orders. It can also have the power of *forbearance*, where it can exempt an entity from the application and enforcement of certain provisions of the Act provided certain conditions are met.[53]

I. Adjudicatory Powers

The PCC is not just an administrative agency but is likewise a quasi-judicial body. Under the Act, the PCC has the power, whether motu *propio* or via a verified complaint, to conduct preliminary fact-finding inquiries for violations of the law.[54] This authority is exclusive, and non-compliance is a jurisdictional issue and can cause the dismissal of the complaint. Pursuant to its exercise of administrative inquiry, the PCC, upon due notice and hearing, may issue orders to temporarily restrain acts that may adversely affect consumers and competition in the market.[55] After its inquiry, the PCC can file the corresponding criminal charges before the OFC-DOJ, which in turn would have the power to prosecute criminal violations of the Act before the regular courts.[56] In the exercise of its adjudicatory functions, the PCC shall have the power to issue subpoenas to summon the appearance of witnesses and to require the production of evidence. It also has the power to punish for contempt and impose fines for failure to comply with such orders.[57]

J. Advocacy and Advisory Powers

As the PCC is primarily mandated to promote and protect market competition for the benefit of consumer welfare, its powers are not just limited to enforcement but are likewise broadened to include advocacy and advisory powers. The PCC's advocacy objectives are intrinsically carried out through competent and careful research and analysis of the competition practices not just in the Philippine markets but also abroad.[58] The PCC also advocates pro-competitive policies

[53] 'SEC. 28. Forbearance. – The Commission may forbear from applying the provisions of this Act, for a limited time, in whole or in part, in all or specific cases, on an entity or group of entities, if in its determination: (a) Enforcement is not necessary to the attainment of the policy objectives of this Act; (b) Forbearance will neither impede competition in the market where the entity or group of entities seeking exemption operates nor in related markets; and (c) Forbearance is consistent with public interest and the benefit and welfare of the consumers. A public hearing shall be held to assist the Commission in making this determination. The Commission's order exempting the relevant entity or group of entities under this section shall be made public. Conditions may be attached to the forbearance if the Commission deems it appropriate to ensure the long-term interest of consumers. In the event that the basis for the issuance of the exemption order ceases to be valid, the order may be withdrawn by the Commission.'

[54] ibid s 31.

[55] ibid.

[56] ibid.

[57] ibid s 33.

[58] Sections 12(l) and (m) provides that the PCC has the power to monitor and analyse the practice of competition in markets that affect the Philippine economy; implement and oversee measures to promote transparency and accountability; and ensure that prohibitions and requirements of competition laws are adhered to; and conduct, publish, and disseminate studies and reports on anti-competitive conduct and agreements to inform and guide the industry and consumers.

of the government by: '(1) reviewing economic and administrative regulations, *motu proprio* or upon request, as to whether or not they adversely affect relevant market competition, and advising the concerned agencies against such regulations; and (2) advising the Executive Branch on the competitive implications of government actions, policies and programs.'[59] Further, the PCC has the power to issue advisory opinions and guidelines on matters relating to the effective enforcement of competition laws, including providing special reports to Congress and proposed legislation for the regulation of commerce, trade, or industry.[60] It assists the National Economic and Development Authority (NEDA) in the preparation and formulation of a national competition policy and also acts as the official representative of the Philippine government in competition matters.[61]

K. Philippine Competition Commission and its Role in the Future of Enforcement

In sum, the PCC wields a comprehensive array of regulatory, investigative, adjudicatory, and advocacy powers essential for maintaining robust competition in Philippine markets. The PCC's authority to review and control mergers, investigate anti-competitive agreements, and penalise abuses of market dominance empowers it to act decisively against practices detrimental to consumer welfare and economic efficiency. Particularly significant is its authority to order structural remedies, such as corporate reorganisations, divestitures, and asset adjustments, which underscores its ability to address the root causes of anti-competitive market conditions rather than merely mitigating their effects. These extensive powers, however, must be consistently complemented by institutional support, sufficient resources, clear legal frameworks, and strong judicial backing to overcome inherent enforcement challenges and powerful commercial interests. Moving forward, strengthening these institutional foundations and enhancing public awareness of competition principles will be pivotal. A fully empowered and effectively functioning PCC does not merely correct market distortions; it establishes the necessary conditions for vibrant competition, consumer protection, innovation, and sustained economic growth, thereby promoting the nation's long-term economic resilience and prosperity.

[59] ibid s 12(r).
[60] ibid s 12(k).
[61] ibid s 12(o) and (p).

10

Recognition and Enforcement of Foreign Judgments

SEVERO C MADRONA JR AND ANDREI V ELINZANO

I. Applicable Laws Concerning Recognition and Enforcement of Foreign Judgment

Philippine domestic law plays a vital role in the recognition and enforcement of foreign judgments. While judicial decisions and legal doctrines addressing this matter are abundant in Philippine law, there exists no unified and comprehensive code governing this important aspect of private international law. There are no comprehensive set of rules that actually provides guidelines as to the recognition and enforcement of foreign judgments.

As this chapter will demonstrate, despite the existence of international conventions aimed at resolving issues related to domestic recognition and enforcement of foreign judgments, the Philippines has only limited engagement with such instruments. Particularly, the Philippines has never entered into any major international conventions that standardise rules in recognition and enforcement of foreign judgments. At best, the Philippines only has entered into a few bilateral agreements that, in some way, address this issue.

Thus, whenever confronted with issues concerning the recognition and enforcement of foreign judgments, domestic courts in the Philippines rely primarily on domestic laws for guidance. Fortunately, albeit not as extensive and as sophisticated as international frameworks, existing Philippine laws provide sufficient guidance for domestic courts to adjudicate matters concerning the recognition and enforcement of foreign judgments.

A. Recognition under Bilateral, Multilateral Treaties, and Conventions

i. Philippines' Limited Participation in International Conventions

The Philippines has not acceded to major international conventions that standardise the recognition and enforcement of foreign judgments. For instance, the country is not a party to the Hague Convention on the Recognition and Enforcement of Foreign Judgments in Civil and Commercial Matters (1971) or its successor, the Hague Judgments Convention (2019).

The absence of the Philippines in such multilateral conventions reflects its cautious approach to binding international agreements that may affect its sovereignty over legal disputes. Instead, the recognition and enforcement of foreign judgments in the Philippines are primarily governed by domestic law and jurisprudence, which are grounded in principles of comity of nations rather than reciprocal treaty obligations.

The Hague Judgments Convention, which has garnered increasing international attention, seeks to promote certainty and efficiency in cross-border legal disputes by creating uniform rules for enforcement. However, the Philippines has yet to ratify or even signal its intention to accede to this framework. This non-participation limits the country's ability to benefit from streamlined enforcement mechanisms available to convention members.

ii. Limited Bilateral Agreements

While the Philippines lacks comprehensive multilateral treaty participation, it has entered into limited bilateral agreements that address reciprocal recognition of judgments. However, these agreements are often narrow in scope and do not provide a robust and comprehensive framework for the enforcement of all types of foreign judgments.

Presently, the Philippines has agreements with certain countries that facilitate cooperation in specific areas, such as trade, investment, or family law. However, these agreements typically do not include detailed provisions on the recognition and enforcement of civil or commercial judgments.

Good examples of bilateral treaties that the Philippines has entered into can be found in the Philippine-Spain Treaty on Civil and Commercial Matters, which provides for mutual legal assistance, and the Convention Between the Republic of the Philippines and Spain for the Avoidance of Double Taxation and the Prevention of Fiscal Evasion with Respect to Taxes on Income. However, both bilateral agreements do not comprehensively address the enforcement of judgments. Such treaties are often limited to facilitating procedural cooperation rather than guaranteeing the enforcement of substantive rulings.

The limited scope of bilateral agreements leaves significant gaps in the legal framework, compelling Philippine courts to fall back on domestic laws and principles of equity when dealing with foreign judgments.

B. Application of Philippine Domestic Laws

Despite the Philippines not acceding to any comprehensive international conventions on recognition and enforcement of foreign judgments, the general principles, such as the principle of comity of nations, embodied under these conventions are nevertheless recognised by Philippine law. The fundamental law, the 1987 Constitution of the Republic of the Philippines (the 1987 Constitution), contains an incorporation clause, which dictates that the general principles of international law are adopted in Philippine domestic law even in the absence of a treaty obligation, thus:[1]

> The Philippines renounces war as an instrument of national policy, adopts the generally accepted principles of international law as part of the law of the land and adheres to the policy of peace, equality, justice, freedom, cooperation, and amity with all nations.

In addition to the Philippines' fundamental law – the 1987 Constitution – Republic Act No. 386, as amended, or the New Civil Code of the Philippines (the Civil Code) also embodies the

[1] 1987 Constitution, s 2, Art II.

principle of comity among nations. While the Civil Code is not as comprehensive and detailed as the Hague Judgments Convention, it offers clear and sufficient guidelines for Philippine courts in dealing with foreign judgments. It comprehensively covers key areas of private international law, including family law, legal status and capacity of persons, property, wills and succession, and contract law. Particularly, as will be briefly discussed below, there are three provisions under the Civil Code that address these matters.

First, Article 15 of the Civil Code addresses issues concerning family rights and duties, as well as the status, condition, and legal capacity of persons. It establishes the extraterritorial application of Philippine personal and family laws to its citizens, regardless of where they may be situated, stating that '[l]aws relating to family rights and duties, or to the status, condition and legal capacity of persons are binding upon citizens of the Philippines, even though living abroad.'

Second, Article 16 of the Civil Code governs maters of property relations and succession. It draws a clear distinction between the application of the lex situs rule, which refers to the law of the place where the property is situated, in matters of property relations, and the application of a decedent's national law in matters of succession, as follows:

> Real property as well as personal property is subject to the law of the country where it is situated.
>
> However, intestate and testamentary successions, both with respect to the order of succession and to the amount of successional rights and to the intrinsic validity of testamentary provisions, shall be regulated by the national law of the person whose succession is under consideration, whatever may be the nature of the property and regardless of the country wherein said property may be found.

Finally, Article 17 of the Civil Code deals with the formal validity of instruments and other juridical acts, including contracts, wills, and other public instruments executed abroad. It further affirms the primacy of Philippine public policy and mandatory provisions of law, which remain inviolable regardless of foreign elements, thus:

> The forms and solemnities of contracts, wills, and other public instruments shall be governed by the laws of the country in which they are executed.
>
> When the acts referred to are executed before the diplomatic or consular officials of the Republic of the Philippines in a foreign country, the solemnities established by Philippine laws shall be observed in their execution.
>
> Prohibitive laws concerning persons, their acts or property, and those which have for their object public order, public policy and good customs shall not be rendered ineffective by laws or judgments promulgated, or by determinations or conventions agreed upon in a foreign country.

The provisions cited above embody a concise yet effective guideline in resolving cross-border legal issues. Although the said provisions are less extensive than multilateral conventions like the Hague Judgments Convention, the Civil Code still enshrines the general principle of comity among nations, while respecting its own legal sovereignty.

As will be shown in the succeeding discussions, Philippine jurisprudence has heavily relied on the aforementioned provisions in addressing issues concerning the recognition and enforcement of foreign judgments. In this light, before a foreign judgment is recognised, Philippine courts ensure that such judgments comply with procedural and substantive safeguards, such as determining whether the foreign court exercised proper jurisdiction, complied with due process requirements, and rendered a decision consistent with Philippine public policy.

The principle of comity is not a legal obligation but a discretionary act of deference to foreign courts. Philippine courts exercise significant discretion in determining whether a foreign judgment should be recognised or enforced. This reliance on domestic rules and jurisprudence underscores the importance of judicial interpretation in bridging the gaps left by the absence of international agreements.

C. Importance of Philippine Jurisprudence

In the Philippine legal system, jurisprudence serves as a central instrument in the development of rules governing the recognition and enforcement of foreign judgments. Owing to the absence of a dedicated statutory regime or binding multilateral treaty – such as the Hague Judgments Convention – judicial decisions, particularly those promulgated by the Supreme Court of the Philippines, function as sources of law in addressing issues on recognition and enforcement of foreign judgments.

The landmark case of *Mijares v Ranada*[2] provides a detailed framework for the recognition and enforcement of foreign judgments in the Philippines. The Supreme Court of the Philippines in this case articulated that foreign judgments are presumed valid and binding, unless proven otherwise.

> It is clear then that it is usually necessary for an action to be filed in order to enforce a foreign judgment, even if such judgment has conclusive effect as in the case of *in rem* actions, if only for the purpose of allowing the losing party an opportunity to challenge the foreign judgment, and in order for the court to properly determine its efficacy. Consequently, the party attacking a foreign judgment has the burden of overcoming the presumption of its validity.

However, as will be discussed extensively in this chapter, the presumption of validity established in the aforementioned case does not mean that foreign judgments are automatically enforceable. Philippine courts still retain the authority to examine whether the foreign court possessed proper jurisdiction, whether due process was observed, and whether the foreign judgment conflicts or offends Philippine public policy.

In the earlier case of *Asiavest Merchant Bankers (M) Berhad v Court of Appeals*,[3] the Supreme Court ruled that foreign judgments are not automatically enforceable in the Philippines. It states that a foreign judgment must be filed as an independent action for enforcement, during which the Philippine court must examine its validity based on jurisdiction, due process, and public policy considerations. In this case, the Supreme Court stated that foreign judgments are factual matters requiring the reception of evidence, and Philippine courts, prior to recognising foreign judgments, must be convinced that the foreign court acted with jurisdiction and observed due process. Thus:

> In this case, it is the procedural law of Malaysia where the judgment was rendered that determines the validity of the service of court process on private respondent as well as other matters raised by it. As to what the Malaysian procedural law is, remains a question of fact, not of law. It may not be taken judicial notice of and must be pleaded and proved like any other fact. Sections 24 and 25 of Rule 132 of the Revised Rules of Court provide that it may be evidenced by an official publication or by a duly attested or authenticated copy thereof. It was then incumbent upon private respondent to present evidence as to what that Malaysian procedural law is and to show that under it, the assailed service of summons upon a financial officer of a corporation, as alleged by it, is invalid. It did not. Accordingly, the presumption

[2] G.R. No. 139325, 12 April 2005, 495 Phil 372–399, citing J Salonga, *Private International Law*, 3rd edn (Central Lawbook Publishing Company, 1967) 500; further citing Goodrich, 600, 601; Chesire, 628; II Beale, 1377; also citing E Scoles and P Hay, *Conflict of Laws*, 2nd edn (West Publishing Company, 1982) 969; the *Mijares v Ranada* case also cited *Philsec Investment Corp. v Court of Appeals*, G.R. No. 103493, 19 June 1997, 274 SCRA 102, 110 and *Northwest Orient Airlines v Court of Appeals*, G.R. No. 112573, 9 February 1995, 241 SCRA 192, 199.

[3] G.R. No. 110263, 20 July 2001, 414 Phil 13-32, citing *Northwest Orient Airlines, Inc. v Court of Appeals*, 241 SCRA 192, 199 [1995].

of validity and regularity of service of summons and the decision thereafter rendered by the High Court of Malaya must stand.

Given the limited the application of international conventions in the Philippines, jurisprudence plays a pivotal role in shaping the rules for foreign judgment recognition. The Supreme Court has crafted doctrines to address issues such as establishing the requirement that foreign judgments must be proven as facts, typically through the presentation of authenticated copies of the judgment sought to be recognised and proof of finality. The High Court also require lower courts to evaluate the compatibility of the foreign judgment with Philippine laws and principles.

In sum, the recognition and enforcement of foreign judgments in the Philippines are characterised by the country's limited participation in international conventions, reliance on domestic rules like Articles 15, 16, and 17 of the Civil Code, and the importance of judicial pronouncements in filling legal gaps. While the principle of comity allows for flexibility, the absence of comprehensive treaty obligations creates uncertainty for parties seeking to enforce foreign judgments. Consequently, Philippine courts must carefully balance respect for foreign judicial decisions with the need to safeguard domestic legal principles and public policy.

II. Doctrines and Rules Observed by Philippine Courts in Foreign Judgment Recognition and Enforcement

A. Doctrine of Indirect Jurisdiction

As a result of the above doctrines crafted by the Supreme Court, the principle of indirect jurisdiction takes a central role in the recognition and enforcement of foreign judgments in the Philippines. As mentioned earlier, Philippine courts do not automatically recognise foreign judgments; the courts first evaluate whether the foreign court, in issuing the judgment sought to be recognised, had proper jurisdiction over the case. This evaluation ensures that the judgment respects fundamental principles of justice, such as due process and fairness, before it is given legal effect domestically.

i. The Power of Philippine Courts to Evaluate Foreign Court Jurisdiction

Philippine courts assess the jurisdiction of the foreign court as a preliminary step before recognising or enforcing a foreign judgment. This evaluation involves analysing both personal jurisdiction and subject matter jurisdiction, in line with domestic rules and principles established in jurisprudence.

Under the Philippine legal system, courts are required to have personal and subject matter jurisdictions over a case before proceeding to hearing and deciding them. In fact, personal and subject matter jurisdictions are basic requirements before a Philippine court can resolve justiciable controversies. The absence of personal and subject matter jurisdiction are grounds for the dismissal of cases.

a. Personal Jurisdiction

Personal jurisdiction refers to the authority of the foreign court to bind parties to the case, particularly the defendant. Stated otherwise, it is the power of the court to render judgments and issue rulings that are legally enforceable upon the parties involved in the action. Personal jurisdiction was sufficiently defined by the Supreme Court in the recent case of *Estate of Williams v Percy*,[4] stating:

> On the other hand, jurisdiction over the person or the parties, or jurisdiction *in personam*, refers to the power of the court to render a personal judgment or to subject the parties in a particular action to the judgment and other rulings rendered in the action. It is the power of the court to make decisions that are binding on persons. It is an element of due process that is essential in all actions, civil as well as criminal, except in actions *in rem* or *quasi in rem*.

Similarly, for a foreign judgment to be recognised in the Philippines, it must be shown that the defendant must have been properly subjected to the jurisdiction of the foreign court. One essential ingredient for establishing personal jurisdiction is the proper service of summons. The foreign court must have ensured that the defendant was properly notified of the proceedings, in a manner consistent with the foreign country's procedural rules. This requirement includes providing the defendant with sufficient time and opportunity to respond to the claims made against them. If this requirement is not met, then the Philippine courts are reluctant and may deny recognition of the judgment in the Philippines on the ground that due process was not followed.

The requirement of personal jurisdiction was discussed in the case of *Asiavest Merchant Bankers (M) Berhad v Court of Appeals*,[5] where the Supreme Court emphasised that proper jurisdiction by the foreign court is a prerequisite for recognition of its judgment. The Supreme Court held that there exists a burden of proof, by clear and convincing evidence, to show a lack of personal jurisdiction to warrant the denial of an action for the recognition and enforcement of a foreign judgment, thus:

> Private respondent failed to sufficiently discharge the burden that fell upon it – to prove by clear and convincing evidence the grounds which it relied upon to prevent enforcement of the Malaysian High Court judgment, namely, (a) that jurisdiction was not acquired by the Malaysian Court over the person of private respondent due to alleged improper service of summons upon private respondent and the alleged lack of authority of its counsel to appear and represent private respondent in the suit; (b) the foreign judgment is allegedly tainted by evident collusion, fraud and clear mistake of fact or law; and (c) not only were the requisites for enforcement or recognition allegedly not complied with but also that the Malaysian judgment is allegedly contrary to the Constitutional prescription that the 'every decision must state the facts and law on which it is based.'

A good example where the requirement of personal jurisdiction by a foreign court was extensively discussed is the case of *Northwest Orient Airlines, Inc. v Court of Appeals*.[6]

The petitioner in this case, Northwest Orient Airlines (Northwest), a corporation organised under the laws of the United States of America (US), sought to enforce in the Philippines a judgment rendered in its favour by a Japanese Court against private respondent C.F. Sharp & Company, Inc. (Sharp), a corporation incorporated under Philippine law. Sharp opposed the enforcement of the Japanese court's judgment on the ground that the same was rendered without due and proper notice to Sharp. Sharp argued that there was improper notice because the Japanese court effected the service of summons in Sharp's Manila office, which is outside the territorial boundaries of Japan.

The Supreme Court, in this case, ruled in favour of recognising the Japanese court's judgment on the ground that there was proper extraterritorial service of summons on the ground that

[4] G.R. No. 249681, 31 August 2022, citing *Macasaet v Co, Jr.*, 710 Phil 167, 177 (2013); also citing *De Pedro v Romasan Development Corporation*, 748 Phil 706, 724 (2014); further citing *Guy v Gacott*, 778 Phil 308, 318 (2016).

[5] See n 3, 414 Phil 13–22, citing 1987 Constitution, s 14, Art VIII.

[6] G.R. No. 112573, 09 February 1995, 311 Phil 203–227.

Sharp failed to overcome the presumption of regularity of the said service. The Supreme Court was convinced that the manner by which the summons was served is consistent with the requirements under Philippine law. Thus:

> As found by the Court of Appeals, it was the Tokyo District Court which ordered that summons for SHARP be served at its head office in the Philippines after the two attempts of service had failed. The Tokyo District Court requested the Supreme Court of Japan to cause the delivery of the summons and other legal documents to the Philippines. Acting on that request, the Supreme Court of Japan sent the summons together with the other legal documents to the Ministry of Foreign Affairs of Japan which, in turn forwarded the same to the Japanese Embassy in Manila. Thereafter, the court processes were delivered to the Ministry (now Department) of Foreign Affairs of the Philippines, then to the executive Judge of the Court of First Instance (now Regional Trial Court) of Manila, who forthwith ordered Deputy Sheriff Rolando Balingit to serve the same on SHARP at its principal office in Manila. This service is equivalent to service on the proper government official under Section 14, Rule 14 of the Rules of Court, in relation to Section 128 of the Corporation Code. Hence, SHARP's contention that such manner of service is not valid under Philippine laws holds no water.

Since the Supreme Court was convinced that personal jurisdiction over Sharp was properly acquired by the Japanese court, the presumption of validity of the foreign judgment stands. Thus, it was proper to recognise and enforce the judgment of the Japanese court.

Another requirement is that the defendant must have a connection to the foreign jurisdiction. In other words, Philippine courts require that the defendant must have had sufficient ties or a meaningful connection to the foreign jurisdiction, such as having a residence or domicile in the country where the foreign judgment was issued, conducting business in the said state, and entering into a contract or committing an act within the foreign state that gave rise to the legal dispute. Without such a connection, the foreign court may be deemed to have improperly exercised jurisdiction over the defendant.

b. Subject Matter Jurisdiction

Subject matter jurisdiction refers to the authority of a court to hear and decide cases of a particular nature. This foundational principle was affirmed by the Supreme Court in *Bilag v Ay-ay*,[7] where the Court reiterated it as a well-established definition consistently upheld in a long line of judicial precedents. Thus:

> Jurisprudence has consistently held that '[j]urisdiction is defined as the power and authority of a court to hear, try, and decide a case. In order for the court or an adjudicative body to have authority to dispose of the case on the merits, it must acquire, among others, jurisdiction over the subject matter. It is axiomatic that jurisdiction over the subject matter is the power to hear and determine the general class to which the proceedings in question belong; it is conferred by law and not by the consent or acquiescence of any or all of the parties or by erroneous belief of the court that it exists. Thus, when a court has no jurisdiction over the subject matter, the only power it has is to dismiss the action.'

In cases for recognition of foreign judgments, Philippine courts must evaluate whether the foreign court had the legal authority to rule on the specific issue that was adjudicated. Thus, in determining subject matter jurisdiction, Philippine courts first determine whether a foreign court, in issuing the judgment sought to be recognised, had legal authority to do so under the foreign jurisdiction. In other words, Philippine courts assess, based on the evidence provided by

[7] G.R. No. 189950, (24 April 2017), 809 Phil 236–248, citing *Mitsubishi Motors Philippines Corporation v Bureau of Customs*, G.R. No. 209830, 17 June 2015, 759 SCRA 306, 311–312.

the petitioning litigant, whether the foreign court had jurisdiction over the subject matter under its own laws.

Furthermore, in some cases, Philippine courts also take into account whether the foreign court had properly exercised extraterritorial jurisdiction. This threshold finds relevance in cases where foreign judgments involved the disposition of properties situated or located outside the foreign state's territorial jurisdiction. Applying this scenario in the Philippines, in reference to Article 16 of the Civil Code, as discussed above, foreign courts generally lack jurisdiction over immovable property situated in the Philippines or other matters exclusively governed by Philippine law. Specifically, disputes involving real property located in the Philippines are governed by the principle of *lex situs* rule, which provides that the law of the place where the property is located applies. Furthermore, in accordance with Article 15 of the Civil Code, family law matters, such as annulment of marriages, are often considered within the exclusive jurisdiction of Philippine courts.

Accordingly, in view of the Supreme Court's ruling in *Northwest Orient Airlines, Inc. v Court of Appeals*,[8] Philippine courts do not automatically enforce foreign judgments, even if the judgment is final and executory in the foreign jurisdiction. Philippine courts still retain the authority to independently evaluate whether the foreign court had proper jurisdiction, both in terms of personal jurisdiction – whether the defendant was properly subject to the foreign court's authority – and even in terms of subject matter jurisdiction – whether the foreign court had the legal authority to decide on the specific issue.

In sum, the recognition and enforcement of foreign judgments in the Philippines hinge on the evaluation of the foreign court's jurisdiction. Philippine courts assess whether the foreign court had personal jurisdiction, ensuring the defendant had sufficient connection to the foreign court and was properly notified. Philippine courts also determine whether the foreign court had subject matter jurisdiction, confirming that the foreign court had legal authority to adjudicate the dispute.

B. The Principle of Reciprocity

In the recognition and enforcement of foreign judgments, the principle of reciprocity plays an influential but non-mandatory role in Philippine law. While Philippine courts do not require strict reciprocity for the enforcement of foreign judgments, it may be considered as a factor in determining whether a foreign judgment should be recognised. This principle is closely tied to the broader doctrine of comity of nations, which emphasises mutual respect and cooperation between sovereign states.

i. Definition and Role in Philippine Law

Reciprocity refers to the mutual recognition and enforcement of judgments between two jurisdictions. Under this principle, a court in one jurisdiction is more likely to recognise a foreign judgment if the foreign jurisdiction would likewise recognise a judgment from the enforcing court's jurisdiction.

In the Philippines, reciprocity is not a strict legal requirement, but it may influence judicial discretion when deciding whether to enforce a foreign judgment. This approach is consistent with the overarching principle of comity.

[8] See n 6 above.

ii. *Reciprocity* In Practice

Reciprocity is often assessed by Philippine courts on a case-by-case basis. Courts may inquire whether the foreign jurisdiction has a legal framework or established practice of recognising Philippine judgments. However, the absence of reciprocity does not automatically preclude enforcement, as long as the foreign judgment satisfies the other requirements under Philippine law, including the jurisdiction of the foreign court over the case and the parties involved, compliance with due process requirements, and the absence of fraud or public policy violations.

C. Comity of Nations

i. Definition and Application in Philippine Jurisprudence

The principle of comity of nations serves as the foundation for recognising and enforcing foreign judgments in the Philippines. Comity refers to the mutual respect and deference that sovereign states accord to each other's legal systems, provided that such deference does not compromise public policy or the rights of citizens.

The Philippine Supreme Court has consistently upheld the principle of comity as a guiding doctrine in cases involving foreign judgments. Recognition and enforcement are granted as a matter of judicial courtesy and international cooperation, subject to procedural and substantive safeguards. This principle aligns with the global trend of promoting cross-border legal harmony without compromising domestic sovereignty. True enough, sans any multilateral or bilateral conventions, foreign judgments are given recognition based on the rules of comity. This was discussed by the Supreme Court in the case of *Asiavest Merchant Bankers (M) Berhad v Court of Appeals*,[9] stating that:

> Generally, in the absence of a special compact, no sovereign is bound to give effect within its dominion to a judgment rendered by a tribunal of another country; however, the rules of comity, utility and convenience of nations have established a usage among civilized states by which final judgments of foreign courts of competent jurisdiction are reciprocally respected and rendered efficacious under certain conditions that may vary in different countries.

However, despite the clear recognition by Philippine jurisprudence on the principles of comity and reciprocity, the application of these principles still has to go side-by-side with the authority of Philippine courts to determine if the foreign court had personal and subject matter jurisdiction in rendering the judgment sought to be enforced.

ii. Requirements for Recognition under Comity

Thus, consolidating all the foregoing principles, the following requirements must be met in order for a foreign judgment to be recognised under the principle of comity:

(1) The foreign court had proper jurisdiction in rendering the judgment sought to be recognised and enforced. Philippine courts must be convinced that the foreign court had jurisdiction over the parties and subject matter of the case before rendering the judgment sought to be recognised and enforced.

[9] See n 3 above.

(2) The foreign court observed due process. The proceedings before the foreign court must have adhered to fundamental principles of fairness and justice, and the parties were given the opportunity to be heard.
(3) The foreign judgment is consistent with Philippine public policy. The foreign judgment must not contravene Philippine public policy or laws.
(4) Finality and executory nature of the foreign judgment sought to be recognised. The foreign judgment must be final and executory in the issuing jurisdiction.

The principle of comity ensures that Philippine courts respect foreign judgments while safeguarding the rights and interests of its citizens and maintaining the integrity of its legal system.

Pertinent to the principle of comity, the landmark case of *Mijares v Ranada*[10] is instructive. The case involved attempts of the petitioners to enforce a US judgment against the estate of the former Philippine President, Ferdinand E Marcos, in view of the human rights abuses committed during his presidency. The petitioners obtained a judgment from a US District Court in Hawaii awarding damages to the victims. The petitioners sought to enforce the judgment in the Philippines.

The Philippine Supreme Court ruled in favour of recognising the US judgment, emphasising the principle of comity and the non-essential role of reciprocity. In so ruling, the Philippine High Court laid down the following principles.

First, the Supreme Court clarified that reciprocity is not a strict requirement for the enforcement of foreign judgments in the Philippines. Instead, it is merely a factor that courts may consider when exercising discretion. The High Court also acknowledged that the existence of reciprocal enforcement mechanisms in the foreign jurisdiction could bolster the case for recognition, but its absence would not be determinative.

Second, the Supreme Court ruled that the enforcement of the US judgment was grounded in the principle of comity, provided that the judgment met the procedural and substantive requirements under Philippine law.

Finally, the Supreme Court emphasised that the recognition of foreign judgments is subject to public policy considerations. In this case, enforcing the US judgment aligned with the Philippines' commitment to human rights and justice.

The *Mijares v Ranada* ruling established several important principles regarding the recognition and enforcement of foreign judgments. In the said case, it was made clear that Philippine courts recognise foreign judgments on the basis of comity, even in the absence of reciprocity. The Supreme Court also upheld the fundamental rule that courts must ensure that foreign judgments do not violate public policy or due process. Finally, as a procedural matter, the Philippine Supreme Court ruled that the burden of proof lies with the party opposing the recognition of the foreign judgment to demonstrate why it should not be enforced.

The decision in *Mijares v Ranada* has become a cornerstone of Philippine jurisprudence on foreign judgment enforcement. It reinforced the idea that the Philippines, as part of the international community, should respect foreign judicial processes while safeguarding its domestic legal values. The case also clarified the discretionary role of reciprocity, thereby providing flexibility in handling cross-border disputes.

The principle of reciprocity, while not mandatory, plays a supplementary role in the recognition and enforcement of foreign judgments in the Philippines. Philippine courts primarily rely on the doctrine of comity of nations, which ensures respect for foreign judicial decisions while adhering to domestic legal principles such as jurisdiction, due process, and public policy.

[10] See n 2 above.

The landmark case of *Mijares v Ranada* exemplifies how Philippine courts balance international cooperation with the protection of domestic sovereignty. The decision underscores that recognition of foreign judgments is not contingent on strict reciprocity but is instead guided by fairness, justice, and mutual respect between nations.

III. Grounds for Refusing Recognition of Foreign Judgments

The recognition and enforcement of foreign judgments in the Philippines are subject to stringent scrutiny based on specific legal grounds. While Philippine courts generally seek to uphold the principle of comity of nations by recognising foreign judgments, they may refuse recognition or enforcement in certain circumstances. These grounds are codified under Rule 39, Section 48 of the Philippine Rules of Court, which governs the enforcement of foreign judgments and specifies conditions under which recognition may be denied.

Rule 39, Section 48 of the Rules of Court provides the framework for the recognition and enforcement of foreign judgments in the Philippines. It states:

> The effect of a judgment or final order of a tribunal of a foreign country, having jurisdiction to render the judgment or final order is as follows:
>
> (a) In case of a judgment or final order upon a specific thing, the judgment or final order is conclusive upon the title to the thing; and
>
> (b) In case of a judgment or final order against a person, the judgment or final order is presumptive evidence of a right as between the parties and their successors in interest by a subsequent title.
>
> In either case, the judgment or final order may be repelled by evidence of a want of jurisdiction, want of notice to the party, collusion, fraud, or clear mistake of law or fact.

This rule codifies the principle that foreign judgments are not automatically enforceable in the Philippines. Instead, they are treated as presumptive evidence of rights between the parties and are subject to challenge under specific defences, such as want of jurisdiction, want of notice to the party, evidence of collusion, fraud, or clear mistake of law or fact.

A. Lack of Jurisdiction

Philippine courts will refuse to recognise or enforce a foreign judgment if the foreign court lacked jurisdiction over the case or the parties. Jurisdiction is a basic requirement for the validity of any judgment, whether domestic or foreign. As a recap, before a foreign judgment is recognised and enforced, Philippine courts will assess whether the foreign court has subject matter jurisdiction or the legal authority to rule on the specific issue involved in the case. Philippine courts will also determine if the foreign court had jurisdiction over the parties, as established through proof of proper service of summons or the voluntary submission of the defendant to the jurisdiction of the foreign court.

In the case of *Asiavest Merchant Bankers (M) Berhad v Court of Appeals*,[11] the Supreme Court emphasised that a foreign judgment may be challenged by presenting evidence of want of

[11] See n 3 above.

jurisdiction. Philippine courts must independently evaluate whether the foreign court had jurisdiction over the parties and subject matter, regardless of the foreign court's determination.

B. Lack of Due Process

Recognition of a foreign judgment will be denied if the defendant was not given proper notice of the proceedings or was deprived of the opportunity to present their case. Philippine courts prioritise procedural fairness and will not enforce judgments that violate fundamental principles of due process. Again, Philippine courts must ensure that the defendant must have been served with summons in a manner that complies with the procedural rules of the foreign court and ensures that the defendant is aware of the proceedings. Ultimately, it must be established that the defendant must have been given a fair chance to defend himself or herself, or an opportunity to be heard.

This matter is precisely the issue in the case of *St. Aviation Services Co., Pte., Ltd. v Grand International Airways*.[12] The Supreme Court reiterated the basic rule that foreign judgments are considered merely as a presumptive evidence of right between parties. Thus, being presumptive, the recognition of the said judgment may be repelled by evidence of want of jurisdiction. Thus:

> [A] foreign judgment or order against a person is merely presumptive evidence of a right as between the parties. It may be repelled, among others, by want of jurisdiction of the issuing authority or by want of notice to the party against whom it is enforced. The party attacking a foreign judgment has the burden of overcoming the presumption of its validity.

Accordingly, in this case, the Philippine Supreme Court ruled that the Singapore High Court had jurisdiction over the person of the respondent, Grand International Airways (Grand). The Court said that there was personal jurisdiction considering that summons was served properly despite it being completely ignored by Grand. Consider the following:

> In the Philippines, jurisdiction over a party is acquired by service of summons by the sheriff, his deputy or other proper court officer either personally by handing a copy thereof to the defendant or by substituted service. In this case, the Writ of Summons issued by the Singapore High Court was served upon respondent at its office located at Mercure Hotel (formerly Village Hotel), MIA Road, Pasay City. The Sheriff's Return shows that it was received on May 2, 1998 by Joyce T. Austria, Secretary of the General Manager of respondent company. But respondent completely ignored the summons, hence, it was declared in default.

As a result, convinced that due process was properly given to Grand by the Singapore High Court, the Philippine Supreme Court allowed the proceedings for the recognition of the Singapore Judgment to continue.

C. Violation of Public Policy

Philippine courts will refuse to recognise a foreign judgment if it is contrary to public policy or the fundamental principles of Philippine law. Public policy pertains to legal principles and moral standards that the state seeks to uphold for the common good.

[12] G.R. No. 140288, 23 October 2006, 535 Phil 757–765, citing *Mijares v Ranada* (n 2); further citing *Northwest Orient Airlines, Inc. v Court of Appeals* (n 3).

Examples of public policy violations include foreign judgments that conflict with Philippine laws on family relations, such as those involving bigamy or same-sex marriages, which are not recognised under Philippine law. These violations may also consist of foreign judgments that impose obligations or penalties that are deemed unfair, excessive, or contrary to the moral standards of Philippine society.

The case of *Van Dorn v Romillo, Jr.*[13] is the most relevant in discussions on the recognition of foreign divorce decrees in the Philippines. In this case, the Supreme Court was confronted with the issue of whether a divorce decree obtained by an American husband in Nevada, US, can be recognised in the Philippines with respect to a Filipina spouse. While the Supreme Court acknowledged that divorce is not valid and binding in the Philippines, it nevertheless ruled that the Filipina spouse could invoke the divorce decree to her benefit. The Supreme Court explained that it would be unjust for the Filipina spouse to be subjected still to marital obligations, despite the absence and repudiation of the marriage by her American husband. As the Court held:

> Thus, pursuant to his national law, private respondent is no longer the husband of petitioner. He would have no standing to sue in the case below as petitioner's husband entitled to exercise control over conjugal assets. As he is bound by the Decision of his own country's Court, which validly exercised jurisdiction over him, and whose decision he does not repudiate, he is estopped by his own representation before said Court from asserting his right over the alleged conjugal property.

The Supreme Court further stressed the inequity in continuing to impose spousal duties on the Filipina:

> To maintain, as private respondent does, that, under our laws, petitioner has to be considered still married to private respondent and still subject to a wife's obligations under Article 109, *et. seq.* of the Civil Code cannot be just. Petitioner should not be obliged to live together with, observe respect and fidelity, and render support to private respondent. The latter should not continue to be one of her heirs with possible rights to conjugal property. She should not be discriminated against in her own country if the ends of justice are to be served.

This case illustrates a clear exception to the rule against foreign judgments that seemingly violate public policy, It shows a progressive application of justice over rigid adherence to statutory limitations.

D. Fraud

Philippine courts will not recognise a foreign judgment if it was procured through fraud. Fraud undermines the integrity of judicial proceedings and is considered a valid defence against the enforcement of foreign judgments. In Philippine law, there are two types of fraud: intrinsic and extrinsic.

Fraud is intrinsic if its commission relates to and affects the issues in the case and could have been addressed during the trial, such as when false testimony is given. Meanwhile, fraud is extrinsic if its commission prevented a party from fully participating in the case, such as when the summons, which is intended to notify the defendant of the pendency of the case and to require him or her to file a responsive pleading and submit evidence in his defence, was concealed by the other party.

[13] G.R. No. L-68470, 08 October 1985, 223 Phil 357–363.

In the landmark case of *Mijares v Ranada*,[14] the Supreme Court ruled that extrinsic fraud is a valid defence against the enforcement of foreign judgments. The burden of proving fraud lies with the party opposing the recognition of the judgment.

E. Clear Mistake of Law or Fact

Philippine courts may deny recognition of a foreign judgment if it contains a clear mistake of law or fact. While foreign judgments are presumptively valid, Philippine courts retain the authority to examine the judgment's substantive correctness.

On the one hand, mistake of law refers to instances when a foreign court misapplies its own laws or violates principles of justice. On the other hand, mistake of fact is when the judgment is based on factual findings that are demonstrably erroneous or unsupported by evidence.

In the case of *Asiavest Merchant Bankers (M) Berhad v Court of Appeals*,[15] the Supreme Court held that a foreign judgment may be repelled if it contains a clear mistake of law or fact. This safeguards against erroneous or unjust judgments being enforced in the Philippines.

Based on the foregoing premises, it cannot be emphasised enough that foreign judgments, albeit declared final and executory by a foreign court, are not automatically recognised and enforced under Philippine law. The recognition of a foreign judgment must still be coursed through Philippine courts by filing an action, in which case, Philippine courts shall first determine if the deciding foreign court had jurisdiction; due process was followed; and, the foreign judgment is consistent with Philippine law and public policy. Otherwise, upon showing of want of jurisdiction, lack of due process, violation of public policy, fraud, and clear mistake of fact or law, Philippine courts may refuse to recognise or enforce foreign judgments.

IV. Effects of Recognition and Enforcement of Foreign Judgments

Foreign judgments may be recognised in Philippine courts not only for enforcement purposes but also to serve as a basis for *res judicata* and issue estoppel. These doctrines prevent the re-litigation of matters that have already been adjudicated by a competent court, provided that the foreign judgment meets the requirements under Philippine law. This recognition ensures judicial efficiency, respects the finality of decisions, and upholds the principle of comity of nations.

A. Relevant Doctrines

i. Res Judicata

Res judicata is a Latin term meaning 'a matter already judged.' It bars the re-litigation of a matter that has been decided by a court with competent jurisdiction. In the context of foreign judgments,

[14] See n 2.
[15] See n 3.

Philippine courts may recognise the foreign judgment for its conclusiveness if it satisfies the requirements of *res judicata* under Philippine law.

The principle of *res judicata* as applied to foreign judgments is codified under Rule 39, Section 48 of the Rules of Court, which provides that a foreign judgment or final order is presumptive evidence of a right as between the parties. Thus, for the foreign judgment to have preclusive effect, it must meet the requirements of *res judicata.*

To better understand the concept of *res judicata* under Philippine law, reference must be made to the definition that the Supreme Court came up with. In *De Leon v Dela Llana,*[16] the Supreme Court defined *res judicata* as a rule of preclusion which bars parties from revisiting matters that had already been adjudged by the court through a prior and final judgment. Thus:

> *Res judicata (meaning, a 'matter adjudged')* is a fundamental principle of law which precludes parties from re-litigating issues actually litigated and determined by a prior and final judgment. It means that 'a final judgment or decree on the merits by a court of competent jurisdiction is conclusive of the rights of the parties or their privies in all later suits on all points and matters determined in the former suit.'

From the foregoing definition and in relation with the principles previously discussed in this article, there is *res judicata* under Philippine law when the following elements are present:

(1) The judgment sought to be recognised and enforced is final and executory in the jurisdiction where it was rendered.
(2) The foreign court must have jurisdiction over the subject matter and the parties.
(3) The judgment must have been rendered in compliance with procedural fairness.

Applying the foregoing elements to foreign judgments leads to the formulation of the triple identity rule. This rule requires the satisfaction of three essential identities for a foreign judgment to be recognised in the Philippines. First, the parties involved in the foreign case must be the same as those in the subsequent Philippine case. Second, the subject matter of the foreign judgment must be identical to the issue presented in the Philippine proceeding. Third, the cause of action in the foreign case must be the same as that raised in the Philippine case.

If all three identities are present, the foreign judgment may be recognised as conclusive and preclude re-litigation of the matter in Philippine courts.

ii. Issue Estoppel

Issue estoppel, also known as collateral estoppel, is a narrower doctrine compared to *res judicata.* It prevents the re-litigation of specific issues that have already been conclusively determined in a previous case, even if the subsequent case involves a different cause of action. While *res judicata* applies to entire claims or causes of action, issue estoppel applies to discrete issues that were essential to the judgment in the prior case.

For issue estoppel to apply to a foreign judgment, the following elements must be established:

(1) Identity of Issues: The specific issue in question must have been raised, litigated, and decided in the foreign court.
(2) Necessity of the Issue: The issue must have been essential to the foreign judgment. If the judgment could have been rendered without deciding the issue, it will not be binding.

[16] G.R. No. 212277, 11 February 2015, 753 Phil 692–706.

(3) Finality of Judgment: The foreign judgment must be final and executory with respect to the issue being invoked.

Philippine courts may apply issue estoppel to specific issues decided in foreign judgments. This doctrine ensures consistency in judicial decisions and avoids redundancy in litigation. For example, if a foreign court has conclusively determined the ownership of a property, Philippine courts may recognise that determination in subsequent cases, even if the cause of action differs (eg, enforcement of rights arising from ownership).

B. Legal Effect of Recognition

Once a foreign judgment is recognised for purposes of *res judicata* or issue estoppel, it is accorded the same effect as a domestic judgment. This means that the foreign judgment becomes conclusive and binding on the parties for the matters it adjudicated. As a result, the parties are barred from re-litigating the same claims or issues in Philippine courts.

The recognition of foreign judgments for *res judicata* and issue estoppel is likewise rooted in the principle of comity of nations, which promotes mutual respect and cooperation between jurisdictions. Philippine courts defer to the findings of foreign courts as long as the judgment complies with procedural fairness and does not violate Philippine public policy.

C. Limitations

Despite the legal effect of recognition, Philippine courts retain the discretion to refuse recognition if the foreign judgment violates public policy, the foreign court lacked jurisdiction, the judgment was obtained through fraud or collusion, and there is a clear mistake of law or fact in the judgment.

Foreign judgments may be recognised in Philippine courts for purposes of establishing *res judicata* and issue estoppel, provided they meet the following requirements:

(1) The foreign judgment is final and executory in the issuing jurisdiction.
(2) The foreign court had proper jurisdiction over the subject matter and the parties.
(3) Procedural fairness was observed in the foreign proceedings.
(4) For *res judicata*, the triple identity rule (identity of parties, subject matter, and cause of action) must be satisfied.
(5) For issue estoppel, the specific issue must have been raised, litigated, and conclusively decided in the foreign court.

Once recognised, the foreign judgment has the same effect as a domestic judgment, precluding the re-litigation of claims or issues previously adjudicated. This recognition reflects the principles of comity, judicial efficiency, and respect for the finality of decisions.

D. Interlocutory Judgments

In cross-border legal matters, Philippine courts generally distinguish between two types of foreign judgments: final judgments and interlocutory judgments. While the Philippines recognises and enforces final and executory foreign judgments subject to certain conditions, interlocutory judgments – those judgments that do not resolve the case on its merits and are only provisional in nature – are typically not given recognition. However, limited exceptions exist, particularly in urgent cases involving child custody or the preservation of property.

An interlocutory judgment is a provisional or interim court order issued during the pendency of a case to address temporary relief or procedural issues. These judgments do not settle the substantive rights of the parties and are not considered final. Examples include temporary restraining orders (TROs), preliminary injunctions, interim relief in child custody disputes, and orders preserving or securing assets pending resolution of a case.

In contrast, a final judgment is one that resolves the entire controversy on its merits, leaving nothing more for the court to do other than execute the judgment.

i. General Rule: Philippine Non-Recognition of Interlocutory Judgments

Under Philippine law, interlocutory judgments or provisional orders issued by foreign courts are generally not recognised or enforced. This principle reflects the following considerations:

(1) Lack of Finality: Interlocutory orders are provisional and subject to change by the issuing court. Philippine courts require that foreign judgments be final and executory before they can be recognised or enforced. Rule 39, Section 48 of the Rules of Court explicitly provides that foreign judgments must be final in the jurisdiction where they were rendered to be presumptive evidence of rights.
(2) Judicial Economy: Philippine courts aim to avoid duplicative or piecemeal litigation. Recognising interlocutory judgments may lead to unnecessary complications, especially if the foreign court subsequently modifies or overturns its provisional order.
(3) Limited Applicability: Interlocutory orders often involve procedural matters or temporary relief that may not align with the substantive or procedural laws of the Philippines. Recognising such orders could lead to conflicts with domestic legal principles, particularly when public policy or jurisdictional issues are involved.

ii. Exceptions: Limited Recognition of Interlocutory Judgments

While the general rule is non-recognition, Philippine courts may give limited recognition to interlocutory judgments in exceptional cases, particularly those involving urgent matters where immediate action is required to protect the rights or interests of the parties. These exceptions are grounded in principles of fairness, equity, and the need to address pressing concerns.

iii. Child Custody Cases

In cases involving child custody, provisional orders from foreign courts may be given limited recognition if they are necessary to protect the welfare and best interests of the child. Philippine courts recognise that custody disputes often involve urgent matters that cannot wait for a final judgment, such as preventing the unlawful removal of a child from the jurisdiction, or providing temporary custody arrangements to ensure the child's safety and well-being.

The Hague Convention on the Civil Aspects of International Child Abduction, to which the Philippines is a signatory, emphasises the need for urgent measures in cross-border custody disputes. This international context may influence Philippine courts to recognise provisional foreign custody orders under exceptional circumstances.

iv. Preservation of Property

Philippine courts may recognise provisional orders aimed at preserving or securing assets pending the resolution of a case, especially when there is a risk of irreparable harm or dissipation of property. Such recognition is typically limited to ensuring that the property remains available for enforcement of a final judgment. Examples of such orders include freezing orders or attachment orders to prevent the transfer or dissipation of assets, and orders securing property that is the subject of litigation.

Pertinently, Rule 39, Section 48 of the Rules of Court provides that foreign judgments involving specific property are conclusive upon the title to the property. By extension, provisional orders aimed at preserving the property may be given limited recognition, provided they do not conflict with Philippine public policy.

v. Urgent Matters

In exceptional cases involving urgent matters where immediate action is required to prevent harm, Philippine courts may recognise interlocutory judgments as a matter of equity. Examples include orders preventing the destruction of evidence, provisional measures to protect intellectual property rights, and injunctions to prevent imminent harm or injury.

vi. Legal and Policy Considerations

(1) Principle of Comity: Recognition of foreign interlocutory judgments in exceptional cases reflects the principle of comity of nations, which promotes mutual respect and cooperation between jurisdictions. However, such recognition is limited to situations where it does not conflict with Philippine laws or public policy.
(2) Public Policy: Philippine courts will not recognise interlocutory judgments that violate public policy or fundamental legal principles. For example, a provisional order enforcing a foreign law that is inconsistent with Philippine family law or property law would likely be denied recognition.
(3) Due Process: Recognition of interlocutory judgments is subject to the requirement that the parties were afforded due process in the foreign proceedings. Interlocutory orders issued without proper notice or an opportunity to be heard will not be recognised.

Philippine courts generally do not recognise or enforce interlocutory judgments or provisional orders from foreign jurisdictions, as such orders lack finality and may conflict with domestic legal principles. However, limited recognition may be granted in exceptional cases involving urgent matters, such as child custody disputes or the preservation of property. Such recognition is grounded in principles of equity, fairness, and the need to address pressing concerns while respecting the overarching framework of Philippine law.

The general rule and its exceptions reflect the balance Philippine courts maintain between respecting foreign judicial processes under the principle of comity and safeguarding domestic legal standards and public policy.

V. Application of the Principles on Recognition and Enforcement of Foreign Judgments to Specific Contracts

Recognition and enforcement of foreign judgments in disputes involving specific contracts vary depending on the nature of the contract, applicable laws, and public policy considerations in the Philippines. This discussion elaborates on the recognition of judgments arising out of commercial contracts, employment contracts, insurance contracts, and international sale of goods, highlighting the principles and limitations imposed by Philippine law.

A. Commercial Contracts

Foreign judgments arising from disputes over commercial contracts, particularly those involving international business transactions, are generally recognised and enforced by Philippine courts, subject to the conditions specified under Rule 39, Section 48 of the Rules of Court. These conditions include:

(1) Finality and Executory Nature: The foreign judgment must be final and executory in the jurisdiction where it was rendered.
(2) Jurisdiction: The foreign court must have had valid jurisdiction over the subject matter and the parties.
(3) Due Process: The parties must have been afforded notice and an opportunity to be heard.
(4) Public Policy Compliance: The foreign judgment must not violate Philippine public policy.

Commercial contracts often involve parties from different jurisdictions, and disputes are frequently adjudicated in foreign courts or through arbitration. Philippine courts generally respect and enforce judgments or arbitral awards in such disputes, provided that the above conditions are met.

In *Northwest Orient Airlines, Inc. v Court of Appeals*,[17] the Supreme Court recognised the importance of respecting foreign judgments, provided that they meet the requirements of jurisdiction, due process, and public policy compliance.

Philippine courts may refuse to recognise foreign judgments in commercial contract disputes if they violate domestic laws or public policy. For example, a judgment enforcing a contract with unconscionable terms or one involving illegal activities would be denied recognition.

In commercial transactions, parties often agree to arbitration as a means of dispute resolution. The Philippines is a signatory to the New York Convention on the Recognition and Enforcement of Foreign Arbitral Awards, which facilitates the enforcement of foreign arbitral awards. The Alternative Dispute Resolution Act of 2004 (Republic Act No. 9285) governs the enforcement of such awards in the Philippines.

B. Employment Contracts Involved in Cross-Border Labour Disputes

Judgments relating to employment contracts, particularly those involving cross-border labour disputes, are subject to special considerations under Philippine labour laws. The Philippines is

[17] See n 6 above.

highly protective of workers' rights, and foreign judgments must align with domestic labour standards and public policy.

The recognition of judgments in employment disputes typically involves the following considerations:

(1) Jurisdiction: The foreign court must have had proper jurisdiction over the labour dispute.
(2) Labour Rights Protection: The foreign judgment must not contravene Philippine labour law principles, including the constitutional mandate to provide full protection to labour.
(3) Public Policy: Judgments conflicting with Philippine labour policies, such as those denying minimum wage or imposing unfair labour practices, will not be recognised.

The Labour Code of the Philippines and related laws provide minimum standards for employment, including wages, working hours, and benefits. Foreign judgments that fail to meet these standards may be denied recognition.

Although there is limited jurisprudence specifically addressing cross-border labour disputes, Philippine courts have consistently upheld the principle that labour laws are infused with public policy considerations that cannot be waived or disregarded, even in international contexts.

These considerations are guaranteed by no less than Article XIII, Section 3 of the 1987 Constitution, which mandates full protection to labour. It serves as a guiding principle in recognising or rejecting foreign judgments in employment disputes.

C. Insurance Contracts

Foreign judgments involving insurance contracts are recognised and enforced in the Philippines, subject to the conditions under Rule 39, Section 48 of the Rules of Court. However, public policy plays a significant role in such cases, particularly where the foreign judgment affects the rights of Philippine residents or corporations.

Insurance is a heavily regulated industry in the Philippines under the Insurance Code.[18] Philippine courts are cautious in recognising foreign judgments involving insurance claims to ensure that they are consistent with mandatory domestic legal provisions. Public policy considerations include:

- Protecting policyholders against unfair practices.
- Ensuring compliance with the principle of utmost good faith in insurance contracts.
- Preventing the enforcement of insurance contracts that are deemed fraudulent or contrary to Philippine law.

Judgments that involve insurance claims related to events occurring in the Philippines or affecting Filipino policyholders are particularly scrutinised. For example:

- A foreign judgment denying a valid claim under an insurance policy might be refused recognition if it conflicts with Philippine insurance regulations.
- Conversely, a foreign judgment enforcing an insurance policy might be recognised if the insurer is a party to the contract and the judgment complies with due process and public policy requirements.

[18] Republic Act No 10607.

A foreign court's judgment involving a dispute over a life insurance policy covering a Filipino overseas worker could be recognised in the Philippines if it aligns with Philippine public policy and labour protections under the Migrant Workers and Overseas Filipinos Act.[19]

D. International Sale of Goods

The United Nations Convention on Contracts for the International Sale of Goods (CISG) provides a uniform legal framework for international sales transactions. However, the Philippines is not a signatory to the CISG, which limits its direct application to disputes adjudicated within Philippine courts. Nevertheless, foreign judgments arising from disputes involving the CISG may still be recognised in the Philippines under general rules on recognition and enforcement of foreign judgments.

Judgments involving international sales of goods are recognised and enforced in the Philippines if they meet the following conditions:

(1) Jurisdiction: The foreign court must have had proper jurisdiction over the dispute.
(2) Finality and Executory Nature: The judgment must be final and executory in the issuing jurisdiction.
(3) Compliance with Due Process: The parties must have been afforded notice and an opportunity to be heard.
(4) Public Policy Compliance: The judgment must not contravene Philippine public policy, including consumer protection laws.

While the CISG provides a framework for resolving disputes in international sales, Philippine courts apply domestic laws and principles when recognising foreign judgments. This is especially relevant in cases governed by consumer protection laws under the Consumer Act of the Philippines.[20] Also, Philippine courts refer to provisions of the Civil Code dealing with sales contracts, including warranties, remedies for breach, and obligations of the seller and buyer.

A foreign judgment awarding damages for breach of an international sales contract could be recognised in the Philippines if the judgment complies with the CISG, if applicable, or domestic laws on contracts and damages.

While there is limited jurisprudence directly addressing the CISG in the Philippine context, the principles of contract law under the Civil Code serve as the basis for recognising foreign judgments related to the sale of goods

The recognition and enforcement of foreign judgments relating to specific contracts in the Philippines involve a case-by-case analysis, guided by the following principles:

(1) Commercial Contracts: Foreign judgments in international business transactions are generally recognised if they meet the requirements under Rule 39, Section 48 of the Rules of Court and do not violate public policy.
(2) Employment Contracts: Philippine labour laws and public policy strongly influence the recognition of foreign judgments in labour disputes, ensuring the protection of workers' rights.
(3) Insurance Contracts: Public policy considerations under the Insurance Code play a critical role in determining the recognition of foreign judgments in insurance disputes.

[19] Republic Act No. 8042.
[20] Republic Act No. 7394.

(4) International Sale of Goods: While the Philippines is not a signatory to the CISG, foreign judgments in sales disputes are recognised under general rules of contract law, subject to public policy and consumer protection considerations.

These principles reflect the Philippines' commitment to upholding both international comity and domestic legal standards.

VI. Application of the Principles of Recognition and Enforcement of Foreign Judgments on Specific Torts

The recognition and enforcement of foreign judgments in tort cases by Philippine courts depend on the nature of the tort, the circumstances of the case, and the fulfilment of legal requirements under Philippine law. Tort-related judgments, such as those involving personal injury, product liability, professional negligence, and cross-border torts, raise unique issues, including public policy concerns, jurisdictional conflicts, and the need to balance the rights of parties.

This discussion addresses the recognition of foreign judgments in these categories of torts, highlighting the legal framework, limitations, and relevant jurisprudence.

A. Personal Injury

Foreign judgments awarding damages for personal injury are generally recognised by Philippine courts, provided they meet the criteria set forth under Rule 39, Section 48 of the Rules of Court:

(1) Finality and Executory Nature: The foreign judgment must be final and executory in the jurisdiction where it was issued.
(2) Jurisdiction: The foreign court must have valid jurisdiction over the parties and the subject matter.
(3) Compliance with Due Process: The defendant must have been given notice and an opportunity to be heard.
(4) Public Policy Compliance: The judgment must not contravene Philippine public policy.

Personal injury claims often involve the awarding of compensatory damages for physical harm, emotional distress, medical expenses, and lost income. Philippine courts recognise the importance of awarding just compensation to injured parties while ensuring that such judgments do not violate public policy or impose punitive damages that are excessive by Philippine standards.

While Philippine courts generally uphold the principle of comity, they may refuse to recognise foreign judgments for personal injury if the award includes punitive damages, which are not typically granted under Philippine tort law. Foreign judgments may also not be recognised if it conflicts with domestic principles of fairness, such as disproportionately high awards.

B. Product Liability

Foreign judgments involving product liability, which are claims for harm caused by defective or dangerous products sold across borders, may be recognised and enforced in the Philippines. These cases often involve manufacturers, distributors, or sellers who are held liable for injuries or damages caused by their defective products.

Philippine courts rely on general tort principles outlined in the Civil Code[21] to determine liability. Additionally, the Consumer Act of the Philippines[22] provides specific protections for consumers, including remedies for defective products. Foreign judgments in product liability cases must align with these laws to be enforceable.

One of the key challenges in product liability cases is determining whether the foreign court had jurisdiction over the defendant. For instance, if the defendant is a Philippine-based manufacturer, the foreign court must demonstrate proper jurisdiction over the company. Meanwhile, if the product was sold in multiple jurisdictions, the court must establish the connection between the product, the injury, and the defendant's activities.

Philippine courts may refuse to recognise foreign judgments in product liability cases if they impose liabilities that exceed what is reasonable under Philippine consumer protection laws. Philippine courts may also refrain from recognising foreign judgments if they conflict with domestic principles of fairness or equity.

While there is limited Philippine jurisprudence directly addressing foreign judgments in product liability cases, the recognition of such judgments would be consistent with the Consumer Act, which emphasises the protection of consumers and the accountability of manufacturers and sellers.

C. Professional Negligence

Foreign judgments involving professional negligence, such as malpractice by doctors, lawyers, engineers, or other professionals, are recognised by Philippine courts if they meet the requirements of Rule 39, Section 48. These cases often involve claims for damages arising from a breach of professional duty, carelessness, or incompetence.

Professional negligence cases raise unique issues because they involve specialised fields and often require expert testimony. In recognising foreign judgments, Philippine courts consider:

(1) Jurisdiction: Whether the foreign court had jurisdiction over the professional and whether the act of negligence occurred within the court's jurisdiction.
(2) Standard of Care: Whether the foreign court applied a standard of care consistent with Philippine professional standards.
(3) Due Process: Whether the defendant professional was given an opportunity to present a defence.

Philippine courts may refuse to recognise foreign judgments for professional negligence if the judgment imposes disproportionate penalties or damages. Also, a ground for refusal is when the judgment conflicts with domestic regulations governing professional practice, like the Medical Act of 1959 for doctors or the Code of Professional Responsibility and Accountability for lawyers.

[21] Art 2176-2194.
[22] Republic Act No. 7394.

Although there is no specific jurisprudence on foreign judgments for professional negligence, general principles of tort law and public policy would apply. For instance, a foreign judgment awarding excessive damages for medical malpractice might be denied recognition if it is inconsistent with Philippine standards for compensatory damages.

D. Cross-Border Torts

Cross-border torts involve wrongful acts committed in multiple jurisdictions, such as environmental damage, defamation, or cybercrime. Recognising foreign judgments in such cases requires careful analysis of jurisdictional issues and the applicability of Philippine public policy.

In cross-border torts, the primary issue is determining which court has jurisdiction over the case. Philippine courts may refuse to recognise a foreign judgment if the foreign court lacked jurisdiction over the defendant or the subject matter. A foreign judgment may also not be recognised if the acts giving rise to the tort occurred outside the foreign court's jurisdiction.

Philippine courts consider public policy when recognising foreign judgments in cross-border torts. For example, Philippine courts will not hesitate to refuse to recognise a foreign judgment for defamation if it violates the constitutional right to free speech under Article III, Section 4 of the 1987 Constitution. Meanwhile, a judgment awarding damages for environmental harm may be recognised if it aligns with the principles of environmental protection under Philippine law, such as the Clean Air Act[23] or the Clean Water Act.[24]

While no specific case addresses foreign judgments in cross-border torts, general principles of jurisdiction, due process, and public policy apply. For instance, Philippine courts have recognised their duty to protect human rights and the environment, which may influence their willingness to recognise foreign judgments in cross-border tort cases, especially those involving transnational corporations.

Rule 39, Section 48 of the Rules of Court governs the recognition and enforcement of foreign judgments in the Philippines. It provides that foreign judgments are presumptive evidence of a right between the parties, subject to the conditions of jurisdiction, due process, and public policy.

The Civil Code provides the foundation for tort law in the Philippines, including provisions on quasi-delicts,[25] which govern liability for wrongful acts or omissions. The Civil Code also establishes benchmarks for liability for damages under Articles 2195–2235, laying down the types and limits of damages recoverable in tort cases.

Public policy considerations play a vital role in determining whether foreign judgments in tort cases will be recognised. These considerations include protection of constitutional rights, consistency with Philippine laws and standards, and avoidance of excessive or punitive damages not recognised under Philippine law.

The recognition and enforcement of foreign judgments in tort cases depend on their compliance with the legal requirements under Rule 39, Section 48 of the Rules of Court, as well as their alignment with Philippine public policy. Specific considerations include:

(1) Personal Injury: Philippine courts recognise judgments awarding compensatory damages but may reject those imposing excessive punitive damages.

[23] Republic Act No 8749.
[24] Republic Act No 9275.
[25] Articles 2176–2194 of the Civil Code.

(2) Product Liability: Foreign judgments are recognised if they align with the Consumer Act and other domestic laws on product safety and consumer protection.
(3) Professional Negligence: Recognition depends on whether the foreign judgment adheres to Philippine standards of professional practice and the requirements of fairness.
(4) Cross-Border Torts: Jurisdiction and public policy play critical roles in determining whether foreign judgments in cross-border torts will be recognised.

Philippine courts strive to balance respect for foreign judgments with the need to uphold domestic legal principles and protect the rights of parties involved.

VII. Foreign Judgments Relating to Unjust Enrichment

The recognition and enforcement of foreign judgments in cases involving unjust enrichment by Philippine courts are governed by foundational legal principles, including equity, restitution, and the prevention of unjust retention of benefits. The doctrine of unjust enrichment is enshrined in the Civil Code of the Philippines, which prohibits one person from enriching themselves at the expense of another without a valid legal basis. Foreign judgments dealing with unjust enrichment, such as those involving restitution orders, recovery of payments, and constructive trusts, may be recognised and enforced subject to specific rules and limitations under Philippine law.

A. Restitution Orders

Foreign judgments requiring restitution – the return of benefits unjustly retained by one party at the expense of another – may be recognised in the Philippines if they meet the conditions set forth under Rule 39, Section 48 of the Rules of Court:

(1) Finality and Executory Nature: The foreign judgment must be final and executory in the jurisdiction where it was rendered.
(2) Jurisdiction: The foreign court must have had valid jurisdiction over the parties and the subject matter.
(3) Due Process: The parties must have been afforded notice and the opportunity to be heard.
(4) Public Policy Compliance: The foreign judgment must not contravene Philippine public policy.

The doctrine of unjust enrichment is codified in Article 22 of the Civil Code, which states:

> Every person who through an act of performance by another, or any other means, acquires or comes into possession of something at the expense of the latter without just or legal ground, shall return the same to him.

Restitution orders are consistent with this principle and are, therefore, generally recognised, provided they align with domestic legal and public policy standards.

Philippine courts may refuse to recognise restitution orders if they involve benefits retained under a valid contract or legal justification and the restitution is ordered under a foreign law that conflicts with Philippine legal principles.

Although there is limited jurisprudence directly addressing the recognition of foreign restitution orders, the principles of unjust enrichment under the Civil Code provide a clear basis for their recognition. For instance, a foreign judgment ordering the return of funds obtained through fraud or mistake would likely be enforceable in the Philippines, as such cases align with the principles of equity and fairness.

B. Recovery of Payments

Foreign judgments ordering the recovery of payments wrongfully received are recognised and enforced in the Philippines, provided they meet the criteria under Rule 39, Section 48. Such judgments typically involve situations where one party has been unjustly enriched by receiving payments to which they were not entitled, whether through mistake of fact or law, fraud or misrepresentation, or overpayment or duplicate payments.

Philippine law provides remedies for the recovery of payments made without legal justification. Article 2154 of the Civil Code governs the principle of *solutio indebiti*, which applies when persons receive something not due to them and are therefore obligated to return it. Additionally, Article 2155 states that any payment made by mistake in the construction or application of a law is likewise recoverable.

Thus, foreign judgments ordering the repayment of sums wrongfully received must meet certain conditions to be recognised in the Philippines. First, the foreign court must have had valid jurisdiction and must have complied with due process requirements. Second, the judgment must not contradict the principles of *solutio indebiti* or other relevant provisions of Philippine law governing unjust enrichment. Third, the ordered repayment must be consistent with Philippine public policy, particularly with respect to fairness and equity.

Philippine courts may deny recognition of such judgments in specific circumstances. These include cases where the repayment involves sums that were voluntarily given as a gift or provided under a valid compromise agreement. Recognition may also be withheld if enforcing the judgment would violate public policy or cause undue hardship to one of the parties.

For instance, a foreign judgment ordering the return of overpaid taxes to a Filipino taxpayer would likely be recognised, as it aligns with the doctrine of *solutio indebiti* under Philippine law. On the other hand, a judgment that orders repayment based on punitive damages or imposes excessive penalties may be denied recognition, as such awards are contrary to established Philippine public policy.

C. Foreign Judgments Related to Constructive Trusts

A constructive trust is an equitable remedy imposed to prevent unjust enrichment. It arises when a person holds property wrongfully or unfairly and is deemed, in equity, to be a trustee holding the property for the benefit of another. In the Philippines, foreign judgments imposing constructive trusts may be recognised, provided they are consistent with domestic legal standards, particularly those set out in Philippine trust law, as codified in Articles 1440 to 1457 of the Civil Code, and with prevailing principles of public policy and equity.

Under Philippine law, a constructive trust is recognised in specific circumstances. Article 1456 of the Civil Code establishes that a constructive trust arises when property is acquired through fraud, mistake, undue influence, or other wrongful means. Similarly, Article 1455 provides that a person who wrongfully retains property that rightfully belongs to another holds it in trust for the rightful owner.

Philippine courts may recognise foreign judgments imposing constructive trusts if certain conditions are met. These include the foreign court's valid jurisdiction over the property and the parties involved, the judgment's consistency with Philippine trust law and equitable principles, and the absence of any violation of public policy. However, recognition may be refused if the judgment conflicts with laws on property ownership – such as the constitutional prohibition against foreign ownership of land under Article XII, Section 7 of the Philippine Constitution – or imposes obligations inconsistent with Philippine trust or property laws.

For example, a foreign judgment imposing a constructive trust over property acquired through fraud would likely be recognised, as it upholds the principles of equity and unjust enrichment under Philippine law. Conversely, a judgment seeking to impose a constructive trust on land owned by a Filipino citizen in favour of a foreigner might be denied recognition due to constitutional restrictions on foreign land ownership.

The recognition and enforcement of foreign judgments in the Philippines are governed by Rule 39, Section 48 of the Rules of Court. This rule treats foreign judgments as presumptive evidence of a right between the parties, subject to compliance with requirements on jurisdiction, due process, and public policy. The Civil Code further provides the legal framework for unjust enrichment claims, including Article 22, which broadly prohibits unjust enrichment; Articles 2154 and 2155, which provide remedies for wrongful payments; and, Articles 1440 to 1457, which outline the rules on trusts, including constructive trusts.

Public policy plays a crucial role in determining whether foreign judgments related to unjust enrichment, such as those involving restitution, recovery of payments, or constructive trusts, will be recognised. Philippine courts will not enforce judgments that conflict with constitutional limitations, domestic contract and property law, or established principles of fairness and justice. To be recognised and enforced, foreign judgments must be final and executory, rendered by a court with proper jurisdiction, and consistent with Philippine principles of unjust enrichment, equity, and trust law. Most importantly, they must not contravene public policy or national interests.

VIII. Judgments Relating to Trusts and Charitable Foundations

Judgments relating to trusts and charitable foundations present unique challenges in recognition and enforcement, as they often involve principles of equity, fiduciary obligations, and public policy considerations. In the Philippines, the recognition of foreign judgments in such cases is governed by the Rules of Court, Civil Code of the Philippines, and other relevant laws. This discussion examines the recognition of foreign judgments in three key areas: foreign trust orders, charitable foundations, and trust administration, highlighting the legal framework, limitations, and relevant jurisprudence.

A. Foreign Trust Orders

Foreign judgments involving the administration of trusts may be recognised in the Philippines, provided they meet the conditions set out under Rule 39, Section 48 of the Rules of Court, which governs the enforcement of foreign judgments. A trust is a legal relationship in which one party, known as the trustee, holds property for the benefit of another, the beneficiary. When evaluating foreign trust orders, Philippine courts apply several key principles: the judgment must be final and executory in the jurisdiction where it was rendered; the foreign court must have had proper jurisdiction over the trust and the parties involved; due process must have been observed, ensuring all parties were given notice and an opportunity to be heard; and, the judgment must not violate Philippine trust law or public policy.

In the Philippines, the rules governing trusts are codified in Articles 1440 to 1457 of the Civil Code. These provisions recognise both express and implied trusts. Express trusts arise from the clear intent of the parties, typically through a written instrument. Implied trusts, on the other hand, arise by operation of law, often in cases involving fraud or mistake. For example, Article 1456 establishes a constructive trust when property is acquired through wrongful means, such as fraud or undue influence.

Despite the potential for recognition, Philippine courts may refuse to enforce a foreign judgment concerning a trust in certain situations. One such instance is when the trust involves property that cannot legally be owned or controlled by specific parties under Philippine law. For example, placing land owned by a Filipino citizen in trust for the benefit of a foreigner would violate the constitutional prohibition on foreign ownership of land, as stated in Article XII, Section 7 of the Philippine Constitution. Additionally, if the foreign judgment imposes obligations that are inconsistent with Philippine trust law or the principles of equity, it may be denied recognition.

To illustrate, a foreign judgment directing a trustee to sell trust property located outside the Philippines and to distribute the proceeds to the beneficiaries may be recognised, provided it complies with Philippine law. However, if the judgment orders the transfer of trust property located within the Philippines to a foreign national, it may be denied recognition due to constitutional restrictions on foreign land ownership. In all cases, Philippine courts seek to balance respect for foreign judgments with the imperative to uphold domestic legal principles and national interests.

B. Charitable Foundations

Foreign judgments involving charitable foundations, such as those addressing governance disputes, breaches of fiduciary duties, or dissolution, may be recognised in the Philippines under the general principles of comity, provided they comply with the requirements set forth in the Rules of Court. Although charitable foundations are typically governed by the laws of the jurisdiction where they are registered, their activities and assets may extend beyond national borders, including into the Philippines.

In the Philippines, charitable foundations are regulated by several legal frameworks. The Revised Corporation Code of the Philippines[26] governs the formation, governance, and dissolution of non-stock, non-profit corporations, which include charitable foundations. The Civil Code also applies, particularly its provisions on donations, obligations, and trusts, which are relevant in cases involving fiduciary responsibilities. Additionally, foundations engaged in specific activities, such as education or environmental advocacy, may be subject to special laws like the National Internal Revenue Code, which outlines the requirements for tax-exempt status.

Foreign judgments that address governance issues in charitable foundations, including disputes over board membership or allegations of mismanagement, may be recognised by Philippine courts if certain conditions are met. These include proper jurisdiction by the foreign court over the foundation and the parties involved, consistency with Philippine corporate governance laws and public policy, and the existence of operations or assets within the Philippines.

[26] Republic Act No. 11232.

The recognition of foreign judgments ordering the dissolution of charitable foundations presents additional complexities, especially when the foundation holds property or engages in activities within the Philippines. In such cases, courts will evaluate whether the dissolution aligns with the foundation's stated purpose and the terms of its charter or articles of incorporation. They will also assess whether the distribution of assets complies with Philippine laws governing trusts, donations, and property ownership.

Recognition may be denied if the judgment conflicts with the foundation's stated purpose, violates laws protecting public interest, or involves the transfer of property to individuals or entities not permitted to own or manage such assets under Philippine law.

For instance, a foreign judgment that seeks to address the mismanagement of a charitable foundation with assets in the Philippines may be recognised if it aims to protect beneficiaries and ensure the foundation operates according to its mission. On the other hand, a judgment ordering the transfer of assets to a foreign entity in violation of Philippine law would likely be refused. In all cases, recognition depends on the foreign judgment's compliance with Philippine legal standards and public policy considerations.

C. Trust Administration

Foreign judgments involving the administration of trusts with property located in the Philippines present jurisdictional and legal complexities. Although a trust may be governed by foreign law, Philippine courts retain jurisdiction over any property situated within the country. This is particularly significant when the trust involves immovable property, such as land, which falls under the exclusive jurisdiction of Philippine courts as established under Rule 4, Section 3 of the Rules of Court. Consequently, the enforcement of foreign judgments in such cases must account for jurisdiction over property, potential conflicts of laws, and compliance with public policy.

Jurisdictionally, Philippine courts exercise authority over immovable property located within the country regardless of the trust's origin or the governing foreign law. In cases where a foreign trust judgment seeks to affect Philippine property, courts evaluate whether the judgment respects constitutional and statutory limitations, such as those prohibiting foreign ownership of land. The principle of *lex situs* – where the law of the place where the property is situated governs – is strictly applied. Therefore, even if a trust is created and administered under foreign law, Philippine trust law takes precedence when the property in question is within national borders.

The Civil Code governs trusts involving domestic property and provides key provisions applicable to such cases. Article 1456 imposes constructive trusts when property is acquired through fraud, mistake, or other wrongful means, while Article 1452 addresses implied trusts arising from specific agreements. These rules apply regardless of whether the trust was formed under foreign or domestic law.

Philippine courts take particular care when reviewing foreign judgments involving trust property, especially land. For instance, the Philippine Constitution under Article XII, Section 7 prohibits foreign nationals from owning land. Therefore, a foreign judgment that orders the transfer of Philippine land to a foreign settlor or beneficiary will not be enforced. Additionally, courts prioritise the protection of trust beneficiaries, especially those who are minors or legally incapacitated.

An illustrative example would be a foreign judgment directing the sale of trust property located in the Philippines and the distribution of the proceeds to beneficiaries. This judgment may be recognised if it adheres to Philippine trust law and public policy. However, if the judgment involves transferring land to a foreign national or imposes obligations contrary to local law, it would likely be rejected.

The recognition and enforcement of foreign judgments in the Philippines are governed by Rule 39, Section 48 of the Rules of Court. This rule treats foreign judgments as presumptive evidence of a right between the parties but allows for their challenge on grounds such as lack of jurisdiction, denial of due process, or violation of public policy.

The Civil Code provides the legal foundation for trust law in the Philippines. Articles 1440 to 1457 govern express and implied trusts, while Articles 22 and 1456 address unjust enrichment and constructive trusts. Additionally, Articles 734 to 746 govern donations, which may be relevant to charitable trusts. The Corporation Code regulates the formation, governance, and dissolution of non-stock, non-profit corporations, including charitable foundations.

Public policy plays a vital role in determining the enforceability of foreign judgments relating to trusts and charitable foundations. Philippine courts will not enforce judgments that violate constitutional restrictions such as the prohibition on foreign land ownership, conflict with domestic trust law or corporate governance principles, or undermine public interest and the foundational purposes of charitable entities.

Ultimately, the recognition and enforcement of foreign judgments concerning trusts and charitable foundations depend on their conformity with Philippine law, observance of proper jurisdictional procedures, and alignment with public policy. Foreign trust orders are recognised if they comply with domestic trust law and do not involve unlawful transfers of property. Judgments involving charitable foundations are enforceable when consistent with the foundation's charter and Philippine corporate law. For trust administration, judgments affecting property in the Philippines must respect the country's jurisdictional authority and property ownership restrictions. Through this approach, Philippine courts uphold both the principle of comity and the supremacy of local legal and constitutional standards.

IX. Law of Property

The law of property governs the ownership, use, transfer, and succession of tangible and intangible assets. In the context of international law, disputes relating to property often involve cross-border elements, such as the ownership of immovable property (real estate) located in another country or issues concerning the transfer of rights under foreign laws. The recognition and enforcement of foreign judgments concerning property disputes in the Philippines are guided by principles of private international law, domestic statutes, and jurisprudence.

The Philippine legal system applies specific doctrines to address property-related cases, particularly the *lex situs* rule, which establishes that the law of the place where the property is situated governs disputes involving it. Philippine courts also exercise exclusive jurisdiction over immovable property located within the country, while carefully scrutinising foreign judgments that affect property rights.

A. Judgments Relating to Immovable Property

Foreign judgments involving immovable property are subject to special rules in the Philippines due to the sovereignty of domestic laws over land and real property. Immovable property is of significant importance in Philippine legal doctrine, and its treatment is governed by the *lex situs* rule, which provides that the law of the place where the property is located determines its legal status. Additionally, Philippine courts have strict jurisdictional rules regarding real estate within the country, and foreign judgments may be denied recognition if the foreign court lacked jurisdiction over such property.

This discussion explores the *lex situs* rule and the jurisdictional limitations on the recognition of foreign judgments involving Philippine real estate, along with the relevant legal framework and jurisprudence.

B. *Lex Situs* Rule

The *lex situs* rule is a foundational principle in private international law which holds that the law of the place where immovable property is situated governs its ownership, transfer, and administration. This rule ensures that the legal treatment of real property aligns with the specific laws and public policy of the jurisdiction where the property is located. In the Philippines, this principle is explicitly adopted in Article 16 of the Civil Code, which states that real and personal property are subject to the law of the country where they are situated. This is further supported by Article 415 of the Civil Code, which enumerates what constitutes immovable property under Philippine law, including land, buildings, and permanent fixtures.

The implications of the *lex situs* rule in the Philippine legal system are significant. First, the validity of ownership claims over real property located in the Philippines is determined solely by Philippine law. Second, any sale, donation, or other form of conveyance of such property must comply with the legal formalities and requirements set by Philippine law. Third, even in matters of succession, Philippine inheritance laws apply to real property located within the country, regardless of the nationality of the deceased.

Foreign judgments involving immovable property in the Philippines may be recognised, but only if they do not contravene the *lex situs* rule. For instance, a foreign judgment determining ownership of real property located outside the Philippines would generally be respected, in accordance with the principle that the law of the place where the property is situated governs. However, a foreign judgment that seeks to adjudicate ownership or rights over real property within the Philippines may not be recognised, as only Philippine courts have jurisdiction over such matters.

The *lex situs* rule is firmly rooted in Philippine public policy. It ensures that immovable property within the country is governed by local laws, which reflect the state's social, economic, and political priorities. As such, Philippine courts will refuse to recognise foreign judgments that conflict with these principles. For example, judgments that violate the constitutional prohibition on foreign ownership of land, as set out in Article XII, Section 7 of the Philippine Constitution, will be deemed unenforceable. Likewise, judgments that disregard requirements under laws such as the Property Registration Decree (Presidential Decree No. 1529) may also be denied recognition.

To illustrate, a foreign court ruling that attempts to transfer ownership of land in the Philippines to a foreigner would not be enforceable, as it violates constitutional restrictions. Similarly, a foreign judgment ordering the partition of Philippine real property without the involvement of Philippine courts would likely be rejected, as it circumvents the jurisdiction and legal processes required under Philippine law.

C. Jurisdiction Over Philippine Real Estate

Philippine courts have exclusive jurisdiction over immovable property located within the Philippines, a principle enshrined in Rule 4, Section 1 of the Rules of Court. This rule states that actions affecting title to, possession of, or interest in real property must be filed in the appropriate court within the area where the property is located. Forcible entry and detainer actions must be commenced and tried in the municipal trial court of the municipality or city where the property, or a portion of it, is situated. Foreign judgments involving real estate located in the Philippines may not be recognised if the foreign court lacks jurisdiction or fails to comply with Philippine law. Jurisdiction is inherently tied to the situs of the property, meaning foreign courts cannot adjudicate matters involving immovable property in the Philippines.

The case of *Mijares v Ranada*[27] emphasised the limitations on recognising foreign judgments affecting immovable property in the Philippines, stressing the necessity of complying with domestic laws.

Philippine courts may refuse to recognise foreign judgments involving real estate if they violate the constitutional prohibition on foreign ownership of land,[28] conflict with Philippine laws on property transfer (such as the requirement for contracts involving real property to be in writing under Article 1403 of the Civil Code), or undermine the integrity of the Torrens system of land registration, which guarantees the indefeasibility of land titles. For instance, a foreign judgment declaring a foreigner the rightful owner of land in the Philippines would be invalid due to the constitutional restriction on foreign ownership. Similarly, a foreign judgment ordering the sale of Philippine real property without complying with local laws on conveyance and registration would not be enforced.

Several legal provisions play a role in these matters. Rule 4, Section 1 of the Rules of Court defines real actions as those involving title to or possession of real property, setting venue requirements based on the property's location. The Civil Code, specifically Articles 16 and 415, defines real property and adopts the *lex situs* rule, while Article 1403 requires contracts for the sale of real property to be in writing. The Property Registration Decree governs the registration and transfer of real property under the Torrens system, ensuring that ownership and transfers comply with Philippine law.

The recognition of foreign judgments involving immovable property in the Philippines is strictly limited by the *lex situs* rule and the exclusive jurisdiction of Philippine courts over real estate within the country. The principles governing these matters ensure that ownership, transfer, and administration of immovable property are subject to Philippine law, preserving the integrity of property ownership and public interest. Foreign judgments affecting Philippine real property are not recognised if the foreign court lacked jurisdiction or if the judgment conflicts with Philippine laws or public policy. By adhering to these legal principles, Philippine courts ensure that property disputes are resolved in line with domestic laws and constitutional protections.

X. Judgments Relating to Succession to Property

Succession to property involves the process of transferring a decedent's estate to heirs or beneficiaries upon their death. Foreign judgments concerning succession, such as probate orders and distribution of estates, are recognised in the Philippines under specific conditions. However, these judgments are subject to Philippine laws on succession, procedural requirements under the Rules of Court, and public policy considerations.

This discussion examines the recognition and enforcement of foreign judgments in the context of succession, focusing on probate orders and estate distribution, and highlights the legal framework and jurisprudence governing these matters in the Philippines.

[27] G.R. No. 139325, April 12, 2005, 495 Phil 372–399.
[28] Philippine Constitution, Art XII, s 7.

A. Probate Orders

Probate is the judicial process of proving the validity of a will. It involves authenticating a deceased person's will, identifying heirs, and ensuring that the decedent's estate is distributed according to the will or, in its absence, the laws of succession.

Foreign probate orders (eg, orders recognising a will or appointing an executor) may be recognised in the Philippines, but only after complying with Philippine procedural rules. The recognition process is primarily governed by Rule 77 of the Rules of Court, which deals with probate of foreign wills.

Under Rule 77, Section 1 of the Rules of Court, a will that has been proven and allowed in a foreign country may be recognised and re-probated in the Philippines if certain conditions are met. First, the will must have been proven and allowed in accordance with the laws of the foreign country. Second, the will must be valid under Philippine laws on succession, particularly those outlined in the Civil Code of the Philippines. The process for recognising a foreign probate order involves filing a petition for reprobate in the Regional Trial Court (RTC) of the area where the decedent's property is located. The petitioner must present evidence that the foreign probate court had jurisdiction over both the decedent and the estate and demonstrate that the will complies with Philippine laws, especially with regard to formalities and testamentary capacity.

Several key considerations guide the recognition of foreign probate orders. First, Philippine courts require proof that the foreign court had jurisdiction over the probate proceedings. Jurisdiction becomes particularly important when the decedent owned property in the Philippines, as only Philippine courts have the authority to rule on the distribution of immovable property located within the country. Second, the validity of the will under Philippine law must be established. According to Article 816 of the Civil Code, wills executed by foreigners abroad are valid if they comply with the laws of the place where the will was executed, the laws of the decedent's nationality, or Philippine laws. However, wills involving immovable property in the Philippines must adhere to Philippine law, which governs issues such as reserved portions for compulsory heirs. Third, the foreign will and probate order must not conflict with Philippine public policy. Any provision in the will or probate order that violates Philippine laws on succession, such as the forced heirship rules outlined in Articles 887 and 904 of the Civil Code, will not be enforced.

For example, a foreign probate order recognising a will that disinherits a compulsory heir, such as a child, would not be fully enforceable in the Philippines, as it conflicts with the forced heirship provisions under Philippine law. Although the foreign will may still be reprobated, it would only be recognised to the extent that it aligns with domestic succession laws.

B. Distribution of Estates

Judgments concerning the distribution of estates rendered by foreign courts may be recognised in the Philippines under Rule 39, Section 48 of the Rules of Court, which governs the recognition and enforcement of foreign judgments. However, such judgments are not automatically enforceable and must comply with both substantive and procedural Philippine laws. To be recognised, foreign judgments must meet certain key requirements. First, the judgment must be final and executory in the jurisdiction where it was rendered. Second, the foreign court must have proper jurisdiction. For movable property, foreign judgments rendered by a court with jurisdiction over the decedent's estate are generally recognised. However, for immovable property located in the

Philippines, foreign judgments have no effect unless re-litigated in Philippine courts. Finally, the foreign judgment must not conflict with Philippine laws on succession, particularly the rules on forced heirship and legitime.

Philippine succession laws, codified in Articles 774 to 1105 of the Civil Code, govern both testate and intestate succession. Key principles include the protection of compulsory heirs and their legitimes. Article 887 identifies compulsory heirs, such as legitimate children, surviving spouses, and, in some cases, illegitimate children and ascendants. Article 904 guarantees that compulsory heirs are entitled to their legitimes, which cannot be impaired by a will or other acts of the decedent. If no valid will exists, intestate succession rules under Articles 960 to 1014 of the Civil Code apply. Additionally, the *lex situs* rule, as established in Articles 16 and 17, mandates that immovable property located in the Philippines is governed by Philippine law, regardless of the decedent's nationality.

For example, a foreign judgment that distributes the entire estate of a Filipino decedent to a single heir may not be recognised in the Philippines if it violates the legitime of compulsory heirs. Philippine courts will review the foreign judgment to ensure compliance with domestic succession laws before allowing its enforcement. Rule 77, Section 1 of the Rules of Court allows for ancillary probate of foreign wills, while Rule 39, Section 48 governs the recognition and enforcement of foreign judgments. Articles 816–817 of the Civil Code govern the validity of wills executed by foreigners, and Articles 887, 904, 960–1014 protect the rights of compulsory heirs and regulate intestate succession.

Foreign probate orders must undergo ancillary probate proceedings in Philippine courts under Rule 77. These wills must comply with Philippine succession laws, including formalities and forced heirship rules. Similarly, foreign judgments on estate distribution are recognised only if they are final, issued by a court with proper jurisdiction, and do not conflict with Philippine laws, particularly regarding legitimes and public policy. By requiring compliance with these principles, Philippine courts maintain the integrity of domestic succession laws while respecting valid foreign judgments to the extent that they align with local legal requirements.

XI. Intellectual Property

The recognition and enforcement of foreign judgments related to intellectual property (IP) disputes in the Philippines involve the interplay of domestic law, international treaties, and principles of private international law. Key considerations include the territoriality of intellectual property rights, compliance with the Intellectual Property Code of the Philippines (Republic Act No. 8293), and procedural requirements under the Rules of Court.

This discussion covers three primary areas of intellectual property: patents and trademarks, copyright disputes, and technology transfer agreements.

A. Patent and Trademark Judgments

Patents and trademarks, as forms of intellectual property, are territorial in nature, meaning they are granted and protected only within the jurisdiction where they are registered. Consequently, the recognition of foreign judgments on patent and trademark disputes in the Philippines is limited by the territorial scope of Philippine law. The Intellectual Property Code of the Philippines (Republic Act No. 8293) governs patents and trademarks. Sections 21 to 120 regulate the grant, management, and enforcement of patent rights in the Philippines, with protection applying only to patents registered with the Intellectual Property Office of the Philippines (IPOPHL). Meanwhile, Sections 121 to 170 cover trademarks, which must also be registered with IPOPHL to be protected under Philippine law.

The territoriality principle means that foreign judgments on patents or trademarks have no automatic effect in the Philippines unless they involve rights that are registered with IPOPHL. Rule 39, Section 48 of the Rules of Court governs the recognition of foreign judgments, stating that a foreign judgment on patents or trademarks may be recognised if it is final and executory in the foreign jurisdiction, does not conflict with Philippine law or public policy, and complies with Philippine procedural requirements.

Key considerations in the recognition of foreign judgments include jurisdiction, priority rights under international treaties, and public policy. A foreign court's ruling on patents or trademarks registered outside the Philippines has no bearing on Philippine registrations. Disputes involving patents or trademarks registered in the Philippines must be resolved under Philippine law. The Philippines is a party to international treaties such as the Paris Convention for the Protection of Industrial Property and the Agreement on Trade-Related Aspects of Intellectual Property Rights (TRIPS), which provide mechanisms for recognising priority rights in patent or trademark applications filed in other member states. However, foreign judgments that conflict with Philippine legal principles, such as the territoriality of IP rights, will not be enforced.

For example, a foreign judgment invalidating a trademark registered in another country will not affect a Philippine-registered trademark. However, a foreign judgment confirming the ownership of a trademark might be recognised if the trademark is also registered in the Philippines and the judgment does not conflict with Philippine law.

B. Copyright Disputes

Copyright protection differs from patents and trademarks in that it does not require registration for its enforcement. Under the Berne Convention for the Protection of Literary and Artistic Works, to which the Philippines is a signatory, copyright protection is automatically granted to original works. This international framework facilitates the recognition and enforcement of foreign judgments on copyright disputes. The Intellectual Property Code of the Philippines, specifically Sections 171 to 224, governs copyrights, and protection is automatically granted to original works such as literary, artistic, and musical works, without the need for registration. The Berne Convention ensures mutual recognition of copyright protection among member states, meaning that works originating in one member state are protected in other member states without requiring formalities.

Foreign judgments on copyright infringement may be recognised under Rule 39, Section 48 of the Rules of Court, provided they are final and executory in the foreign jurisdiction, do not conflict with Philippine law, and respect the rights granted under the Philippine Intellectual Property Code. Public policy considerations also play a significant role, as copyright protection in the Philippines includes moral rights and economic rights, which are protected under the IP Code. A foreign judgment affecting these rights must align with these protections.

Key considerations for the recognition of foreign judgments include jurisdiction, moral rights, and economic rights. Philippine courts require proof that the foreign court had jurisdiction over the copyright infringement dispute. Under Section 193 of the IP Code, authors have moral rights over their works, including the right to attribution and integrity. A foreign judgment that disregards these rights may not be enforced in the Philippines. Foreign judgments awarding damages for copyright infringement may be enforced if they comply with Philippine procedural rules and do not conflict with domestic copyright protections.

For example, a foreign judgment ordering damages for the unauthorised reproduction of a copyrighted film may be enforced in the Philippines if the film is protected under the Berne Convention and the judgment complies with Philippine rules on the enforcement of foreign judgments.

C. Technology Transfer Agreements

Technology transfer agreements (TTAs) involve the licensing of intellectual property rights, such as patents, trademarks, or copyrights, for use in another jurisdiction. These agreements often have international dimensions, and disputes may arise concerning their terms and enforcement. In the Philippines, TTAs are regulated by the Intellectual Property Code and must comply with specific provisions to be valid and enforceable. Sections 85 to 92 of the IP Code govern TTAs, which must adhere to mandatory provisions of the Code. For example, TTAs must not contain provisions that are anti-competitive or contrary to Philippine public policy, and they must be registered with the IPOPHL for enforcement.

Foreign judgments involving TTAs may be recognised under Rule 39, Section 48 of the Rules of Court, provided they are final and executory in the foreign jurisdiction, do not conflict with Philippine public policy, and comply with the mandatory provisions of the IP Code. The IP Code specifically prohibits certain clauses in TTAs, such as those that restrict competition or impose unreasonable conditions on licensees. Therefore, a foreign judgment enforcing such provisions may not be recognised. Additionally, the Philippines is part of the TRIPS Agreement, which provides a framework for the enforcement of TTAs and the protection of intellectual property rights in international licensing agreements.

Key considerations in the enforcement of TTAs include the mandatory provisions of the IP Code, the registration requirement, and jurisdiction. A TTA that violates Sections 87 and 88 of the IP Code, such as one requiring exclusive sourcing of raw materials, may be declared void. TTAs must be registered with IPOPHL to be enforceable, and a foreign judgment enforcing an unregistered TTA may not be recognised in the Philippines. Philippine courts also require proof that the foreign court had jurisdiction over the TTA dispute in order to recognise the foreign judgment.

For instance, a foreign judgment awarding damages for breach of a licensing agreement involving a patented technology may be recognised in the Philippines if the agreement complies with the mandatory provisions of the IP Code and is registered with IPOPHL.

The recognition and enforcement of foreign judgments in intellectual property disputes in the Philippines are subject to stringent requirements under domestic law, international treaties, and procedural rules. Key considerations include the territoriality of IP rights, compliance with the Intellectual Property Code of the Philippines, and alignment with Philippine public policy.

(1) Patent and Trademark Judgments: Foreign rulings on patents and trademarks are recognised only if they involve rights registered in the Philippines and comply with domestic laws.
(2) Copyright Disputes: Foreign judgments on copyright infringement are more readily enforceable due to the automatic protection under the Berne Convention, provided they align with Philippine copyright laws.
(3) Technology Transfer Agreements: Foreign judgments on TTAs must comply with the mandatory provisions of the IP Code and require registration with IPOPHL for enforcement.

By adhering to these principles, the Philippines ensures the protection of intellectual property rights while respecting valid foreign judgments to the extent that they are consistent with domestic legal requirements.

XII. Family Law

A. Decrees of Marriage

The recognition of foreign marriages in the Philippines is governed by principles of private international law, Executive Order No. 209, as amended, or the Family Code of the Philippines, and case law. Marriages validly celebrated abroad are generally recognised in the Philippines, subject to specific conditions under domestic law. This discussion focuses on the following aspects:

(1) Recognition of Foreign Marriages
(2) Requirements for Recognition

B. Recognition of Foreign Marriages

The Philippines follows the principle of *lex loci celebrationis*, meaning that the validity of a marriage is determined by the law of the place where it was solemnised. If a marriage is valid under the laws of the country where it was celebrated, it is generally recognised as valid in the Philippines, as provided under Article 26 of the Family Code. According to Article 26, '[a]ll marriages solemnised outside the Philippines, in accordance with the laws in force in the country where they were solemnised, and valid there as such, shall also be valid in this country, except those prohibited under Articles 35(1), (4), (5), and (6), 36, 37, and 38.'

However, there are exceptions to the recognition of foreign marriages. Foreign marriages are not recognised in the Philippines if they fall under the prohibited marriages listed in Articles 35(1), (4), (5), and (6), 36, 37, and 38 of the Family Code. These include void marriages under Article 35, such as those contracted without the legal capacity of the parties like marriages between minors, bigamous or polygamous marriages, or those where consent was obtained through fraud or force (unless ratified). Additionally, incestuous marriages under Article 37, such as those between ascendants and descendants of any degree or between siblings (whether full or half-blood), are also prohibited. Marriages that are void for public policy under Article 38, such as those between collateral relatives within the fourth civil degree (eg, first cousins) or between step-parents and step-children, or parents-in-law and children-in-law, are likewise not recognised.

While the Philippines recognises the principle of *lex loci celebrationis*, Filipino citizens are still bound by Philippine laws on marriage even if they marry abroad. For example, under Article 15 of the Civil Code, Filipinos are subject to Philippine laws relating to family rights and duties, including marriage, regardless of where they reside.

As an illustrative example, a Filipino citizen who marries a first cousin abroad in a country where such a marriage is valid (eg, some states in the United States) would not have their marriage recognised in the Philippines because it violates Article 38 of the Family Code.

C. Requirements for Recognition

For a foreign marriage to be recognised in the Philippines, it must be proven that the marriage was valid under the law of the place where it was solemnised. The party seeking recognition must present evidence to establish the validity of the marriage, in accordance with Rule 132, Section 24 of the Rules of Court, which is the applicable rule on the presentation of foreign laws and records in Philippine courts.

It must be noted that Philippine courts require proof of foreign law because they cannot take judicial notice of it without it being formally introduced as evidence. Accordingly, the documents required for recognition may include a certified copy of the marriage certificate or record issued by the country where the marriage was solemnised, and proof of the foreign law governing marriage, duly authenticated or certified by the foreign country's competent authorities. Additionally, the documents must be authenticated by the Philippine diplomatic or consular office in the country where the marriage was celebrated, or they must bear an apostille under the Apostille Convention, to which the Philippines is a party.

In the absence of evidence to the contrary, a marriage celebrated abroad is presumed valid. However, this presumption may be rebutted if it is shown that the marriage does not comply with the law of the place of celebration or violates Philippine laws or public policy. Case law on the recognition of foreign marriages includes *Republic v Orbecido III*[29] where the Supreme Court held that a foreign divorce obtained by a foreign spouse allows the Filipino spouse to remarry under Article 26, Paragraph 2 of the Family Code, reinforcing the principle that Philippine courts respect foreign marital laws as long as they do not violate Philippine public policy. In *Van Dorn v Romillo Jr.*,[30] the Court ruled that a marriage validly celebrated abroad under foreign law is binding on the Filipino spouse. In *Bayot v Court of Appeals*,[31] the case emphasised that documents proving the validity of a foreign marriage must be authenticated and comply with Philippine procedural laws.

The procedural steps for recognising foreign marriages in the Philippines include registration with the Philippine Civil Registry. A foreign marriage involving at least one Filipino citizen must be reported to the Philippine Embassy or Consulate in the country where the marriage was celebrated, and the marriage will then be recorded with the Philippine Civil Registry. If a foreign marriage needs to be recognised for specific purposes, such as remarriage, property settlement, or legal disputes, a petition for judicial recognition must be filed with the Regional Trial Court. The petitioner must present authenticated documents and proof of the foreign law governing the marriage.

The recognition of foreign marriages in the Philippines is governed by the principle of *lex loci celebrationis*, as codified in Article 26 of the Family Code. A marriage valid in the place where it was celebrated is generally recognised in the Philippines, provided it does not violate Philippine laws or public policy. Marriages celebrated abroad are recognised unless they fall under the void or prohibited marriages under Articles 35(1), (4), (5), and (6), 36, 37, and 38 of the Family Code. The requirements for recognition include proof of the marriage's validity under the laws of the place of celebration, including authenticated marriage records and proof of foreign law. Philippine courts respect foreign marital laws to the extent that they align with domestic legal principles, ensuring consistency with both international and local legal frameworks.

D. Decrees of Divorce, Nullity, and Separation

The recognition of decrees of divorce, nullity, and separation in the Philippines is a complex area of law governed by the Family Code, public policy, and jurisprudence. While the Philippines does not recognise divorce between Filipino citizens, certain exceptions exist, particularly in cases involving mixed marriages where a foreign divorce was obtained by a foreign spouse.

[29] G.R. No. 154380, 5 October 2005.
[30] G.R. No. L-68470, 8 October 1985.
[31] G.R. No. 155635, 7 November 2008.

Under the general rule, Filipino citizens are bound by Philippine family laws, regardless of where they reside, as stated in Article 15 of the Civil Code. Since the Family Code does not allow divorce for Filipino citizens married to other Filipino citizens, a divorce obtained abroad by two Filipino citizens is not recognised in the Philippines. However, Article 26, Paragraph 2 of the Family Code provides an exception for mixed marriages, which refers to marriages between a Filipino citizen and a foreigner. This provision allows a Filipino spouse to remarry under Philippine law if the foreign spouse has obtained a valid divorce abroad that capacitated them to remarry according to the laws of their nationality. The intent of this provision is to avoid situations where the Filipino spouse remains tied to the marriage while the foreign spouse is no longer bound by it.

The recognition of foreign divorces is generally limited to situations where one party is a foreigner. If both spouses are Filipino citizens, even if the divorce was validly obtained abroad, it will not be recognised. For a foreign divorce to be recognised, the validity of the divorce is determined by the law of the country where it was obtained. Proof of the foreign law and its application must be presented in Philippine courts for the divorce to be recognised. Furthermore, a foreign divorce decree must be judicially recognised in the Philippines before it can have legal effect. This is done by filing a petition for judicial recognition of the foreign divorce decree in the appropriate Regional Trial Court (RTC).

The landmark case of *Republic v Orbecido III*[32] clarified the application of Article 26, Paragraph 2 of the Family Code. The Supreme Court ruled that 'a Filipino citizen, who has been divorced by a spouse who had acquired foreign citizenship and remarried, also to remarry.' The Court emphasised a liberal interpretation of Article 26, Paragraph 2, to afford equal rights to the Filipino spouse, regardless of who initiated the divorce. This case solidified the idea that once the foreign spouse is capacitated to remarry under foreign law, the Filipino spouse should also be allowed to remarry to avoid inequity.

Regarding Filipino citizens, foreign divorce decrees are not recognised if both parties are Filipino citizens. This is because Philippine law prohibits divorce between Filipino citizens, reflecting the country's strong public policy favouring the permanence of marriage. Even if two Filipino citizens residing abroad obtain a divorce in a country where divorce is legal, such as the United States, the Philippine government will not recognise it. However, there are special cases where a Filipino citizen, after becoming a naturalised foreign citizen, may have their foreign divorce recognised under Article 26, Paragraph 2. Additionally, Filipino Muslims are governed by the Code of Muslim Personal Laws, which allows divorce under certain conditions.

To give legal effect to a foreign divorce decree in the Philippines, the Filipino spouse must file a petition for judicial recognition. The process involves filing a verified petition with the RTC, submitting authenticated copies of the foreign divorce decree, proof of foreign law, and proof of the foreign spouse's capacity to remarry. The court will then determine whether the foreign divorce complies with Philippine law, and if the decision becomes final, the Filipino spouse's civil status can be updated to reflect the recognition of the divorce.

In conclusion, while the Philippines generally does not recognise foreign divorces, exceptions exist for mixed marriages under Article 26, Paragraph 2 of the Family Code. However, as discussed above, the *Republic v Orbecido III* doctrine has clarified that a Filipino citizen may also contract a subsequent marriage if their Filipino spouse later becomes a foreign citizen and remarries. Yet, it should still be noted that foreign divorce decrees are not recognised between

[32] See n 30 above.

two Filipino citizens, reflecting the strong public policy in favour of marriage permanence in Philippine law.

XIII. Judgments on Matters Relating to the Well-being of the Child

Judgments on matters related to the well-being of a child, including custody, support, and welfare, in the Philippines are governed by the principle of the best interest of the child. This principle serves as the paramount consideration in resolving disputes and ensures that the child's physical, emotional, psychological, and moral needs are prioritised above all other factors. In the context of recognising and enforcing foreign judgments on child custody, support, and cases of international child abduction, Philippine courts also take into account international treaties and domestic laws.

The best interest of the child principle is the cornerstone of all child-related judgments in the Philippines. It is enshrined in both international and domestic legal frameworks. One key international instrument is the Convention on the Rights of the Child (CRC), which the Philippines ratified in 1990. The CRC obliges the state to prioritise the best interest of the child in all decisions affecting children. Specifically, Article 3(1) of the CRC states that '[i]n all actions concerning children, whether undertaken by public or private social welfare institutions, courts of law, administrative authorities, or legislative bodies, the best interests of the child shall be a primary consideration.' Domestically, the Family Code of the Philippines supports this principle, particularly in custody disputes, where Article 231 thereof emphasises that the welfare of the child is the primary concern on matters of parental authority. Also, Article 213 stipulates that in cases of parental separation, '[n]o child under seven years of age shall be separated from the mother unless there are compelling reasons to order otherwise'. Additionally, the Rule on Custody of Minors (A.M. No. 03-04-04-SC) guides Philippine courts in prioritising the child's best interests in custody cases. Section 14 of this rule outlines criteria for determining the child's best interest, such as the child's age, health, emotional ties to parents, and the parents' ability to provide care.

In both domestic and international contexts, the principle is applied to the recognition of foreign judgments. When considering foreign custody or support orders, Philippine courts closely scrutinise whether these orders align with the child's best interests before granting recognition or enforcement. This ensures that international decisions regarding a child's welfare are consistent with the fundamental legal standard of prioritising the child's well-being.

A. Recognition of Foreign Custody and Support Orders

The recognition and enforcement of foreign judgments on custody and support in the Philippines are governed by Rule 39, Section 48 of the Rules of Court. A foreign judgment may be recognised if it satisfies certain criteria, including being final and executory, consistent with Philippine laws, rendered by a competent court, and compliant with procedural requirements. Specifically, the foreign judgment must be final, meaning it is not subject to further appeal in the jurisdiction where it was issued. Additionally, it must not contravene Philippine public policy, particularly the best interest of the child principle, and must be rendered by a court with proper jurisdiction. Furthermore, the judgment must be authenticated and proven in Philippine courts.

When it comes to custody orders, foreign custody judgments are carefully evaluated to ensure they are consistent with Philippine laws and the best interest of the child. While the Philippines upholds the principle of comity of nations, foreign custody orders are not automatically enforced if they conflict with Philippine public policy or laws.

For support orders, foreign support judgments may also be recognised and enforced if they meet the requirements set out in Rule 39. In the Philippines, the child's right to financial support is protected under the Family Code of the Philippines, which obligates parents to support their legitimate and illegitimate children. Moreover, Republic Act No. 9262, or the Anti-Violence Against Women and Their Children Act of 2004, makes it a punishable offence for parents to fail to provide support, which may and could constitute economic abuse. Philippine courts ensure that the support ordered by a foreign court is sufficient to meet the child's needs, and they will not recognise foreign support orders that violate Philippine policies on child welfare.

In cases of international child abduction, the Philippines addresses such issues through a combination of international treaties and domestic laws. The Hague Convention on the Civil Aspects of International Child Abduction, to which the Philippines acceded, and, pertinently, Republic Act No. 10364 (the Expanded Anti-Trafficking in Persons Act of 2012), aims for the prompt return of abducted children to their habitual residence and ensures the enforcement of custody rights across member states. Additionally, Republic Act No. 7610 (Special Protection of Children Against Abuse, Exploitation, and Discrimination Act) provides legal protection for children against abuse and exploitation. The Rule on Custody of Minors (A.M. No. 03-04-04-SC) further directs the expeditious resolution of custody disputes, including those involving international child abduction.

In international child abduction cases, Philippine courts apply the principle of the best interest of the child, ensuring that the child's welfare is the primary consideration when determining whether to return a child to their habitual residence under the Hague Convention or other applicable laws. Under Article 13 of the Hague Convention, the child must be returned promptly unless there is evidence of a grave risk to the child's physical or psychological health. Courts also examine whether the removal or retention of the child violated a parent's custody or visitation rights.

Challenges in the recognition of foreign judgments arise from conflicts of laws, public policy considerations, and procedural hurdles. Differences between Philippine family laws and foreign laws can complicate the recognition of custody and support orders. For instance, countries that prioritise parental rights over child welfare may issue judgments that conflict with the Philippine best interest standard. Philippine courts also refuse to recognise foreign judgments that violate public policy, such as those granting custody to an unfit parent. Additionally, the requirement to prove foreign law and authenticate foreign judgments can delay the recognition process.

In conclusion, judgments on matters relating to the well-being of the child, such as custody, support, and welfare, are governed by the best interest of the child principle in the Philippines. The recognition and enforcement of foreign judgments are subject to stringent requirements under Philippine law, ensuring that they align with domestic policies and prioritise the child's welfare. Philippine courts uphold the rights and welfare of children through a careful application of domestic law, international treaties, and jurisprudence, even in cross-border disputes.

11

International Commercial Arbitration

ANGELA RAY T ABALA

I. Introduction

Arbitration is the most dominant method of resolving international disputes between states, individuals, and businesses. This is due to increased globalisation and cross-border investment. Arbitration has been an attractive form of dispute settlement for commercial parties from different countries, cultures, and legal systems who find themselves in conflict. Through arbitration, parties can opt to have their disputes definitively resolved by independent, non-government decision-makers, who are generally selected by the parties themselves.

A survey published in 2022 shows that corporate users (described as corporate executives and in-house counsel) and external lawyers (described as dispute resolution lawyers and corporate lawyers) find the direct enforceability of arbitral awards, confidentiality, procedural flexibility, speed, finality, and impartiality as important factors in choosing to arbitrate their international commercial disputes.[1] Because of the flexibility that arbitration offers, it has been described as the 'preferred means of resolving international commercial disputes.'[2] It is seen as an inexpensive, speedy and amicable process.[3]

The Philippines has long recognised the utility of arbitration as an alternative dispute resolution method.[4] It has been a state-party to the Convention on the Recognition and Enforcement of Foreign Arbitral Awards (the 'New York Convention')[5] since 1967. It also has specific legislation and rules to govern arbitration. Domestic arbitration is governed by Republic Act No. 876.[6] Executive Order No. 1008 (1985) governs construction disputes, including construction arbitration in the Philippines.[7] International commercial arbitration is governed by Republic Act No. 9285,[8] or the Alternative Dispute Resolution ('ADR') Act of 2004. With the ADR Act

[1] Singapore International Dispute Resolution Academy, SIDRA International dispute Resolution Survey: 2022 Final Report, see sidra.smu.edu.sg/sites/sidra.smu.edu.sg/files/survey-2022/index.html.

[2] G Born, *International Arbitration: Law and Practice*, 2nd edn (Wolters Kluwer, 2016).

[3] *LM Power Engineering Corporation v Capitol Industrial Construction Groups, Inc.*, G.R. No. 141833, 26 March 2003, citations omitted.

[4] *National Union Fire Insurance Company of Pittsburg, PA/American International Underwriter (Phil.) Inc. v Stolt-Nielsen Philippines Inc. and Court of Appeals*, G.R. No. 87958, 26 April 1990.

[5] The Philippines acceded to the New York Convention in 1965.

[6] An Act to Authorize the Making of Arbitration and Submission Agreements, to Provide for the Appointment of Arbitrators and the Procedure for Arbitration in Civil Controversies, and for Other Purposes, Republic Act No. 876 (1953).

[7] Executive Order No. 1008 Creating an Arbitration Machinery in the Construction Industry of the Philippines (1985).

[8] An Act to Institutionalize the Use of an Alternative Dispute Resolution System in the Philippines and to Establish the Office for Alternative Dispute Resolution, and for Other Purposes [ADR Act of 2004], Republic Act No. 9284 (2004).

of 2004 coming into law, the Philippines also adopted the 1985 United Nations Commission on International Trade Law Model Law on International Commercial Arbitration ('UNCITRAL Model Law') in its entirety.[9]

In 2009, the Department of Justice issued Department Circular No. 98, or the Implementing Rules and Regulations of the Alternative Dispute Resolution Act of 2004 ('IRR of ADR Act of 2004'). Implementing rules and regulations are administrative regulations enacted by administrative agencies to implement and interpret the law which it is entrusted to enforce.[10] Such rules have the same force and effect as binding legislation.[11] The IRR of the ADR Act of 2004 supplements and further enforces the said law.

The Philippine Supreme Court has also taken an active role in encouraging arbitration.[12] It promulgated the Special Rules of Court on Alternative Dispute Resolution ('Special ADR Rules') in 2009. The Special ADR Rules applies to both domestic and international arbitration.[13] The Supreme Court also conducts regular capacity building activities to equip the Judiciary with knowledge and expertise in handling matters relevant to international arbitration.[14]

The Philippines has consistently encouraged the use of arbitration, as well as other alternative forms of dispute resolution such as mediation, to parties who find themselves in conflict. It sees arbitration as a means to achieve speedy and impartial justice, which also helps declog court dockets.[15] The Philippine Supreme Court itself has called arbitration as 'the "wave of the future" in international civil and commercial disputes'.[16]

This chapter focuses on international commercial arbitration in the Philippines. It begins with a definition of international arbitration (Section II). Section III covers arbitration agreements. Section IV discusses the jurisdiction of arbitral tribunals. Section V discusses choice of law issues. Finally, Section VI covers the recognition and enforcement regime in the Philippines.

II. Definition of International Commercial Arbitration

International commercial arbitration is governed by the ADR Act of 2004, which defines arbitration as a voluntary dispute resolution process in which one or more arbitrators, appointed in accordance with the agreement of the parties or rules under the Act, resolve a dispute by rendering an award.[17] Commercial arbitration is defined as that which covers matters arising from all relationships of a commercial nature, whether contractual or not.[18] As such, arbitration is a private and consensual method to resolve disputes.[19]

[9] ibid s 19, Ch 4.

[10] *Abakada Guro Party List v Purisima*, G.R. No. 16671, 14 August 2008.

[11] ibid.

[12] Special Rules of Court on Alternative Dispute Resolution, A.M. No. 07-11-08-SC, 1 September 2009, Rule 2.1.

[13] ibid Rule 1.1.

[14] AP Autea, 'Philippine Arbitration Reform: Fresh Breathing Space from Congested Litigation' in A Reyes and W Gu (eds), *The Developing World of Arbitration: A Comparative Study of Arbitration Reform in the Asia Pacific* (Bloomsbury, 2018) 172–73.

[15] ADR Act of 2004, Ch 1, s 2.

[16] *LM Power Engineering Corporation* (n 3).

[17] ADR Act of 2004, Ch 1, s 3(d).

[18] ibid Ch 1, s 3(g).

[19] N Blackaby, C Partasides et al, *Redfern and Hunter on International Arbitration*, 6th edn (Oxford University Press, 2015).

In the Philippines, all matters are susceptible to arbitration, save for (a) labour disputes covered by the Labour Code of the Philippines, (b) the civil status of persons, (c) the validity of a marriage, (d) any ground for legal separation, (e) the jurisdiction of courts, (f) future legitime, (g) criminal liability, and (h) those which by law cannot be compromised.[20] In *Maynilad Water Services, Inc. v National Water Resources Board, et al.*,[21] the Supreme Court held that disputes concerning changes in water rates charged to consumers are arbitrable and that arbitral awards that would be injurious to the public at large cannot be enforced under the public policy exception.

A. Voluntary and Consensual Dispute Resolution Process

Fundamentally, arbitration is a voluntary process that requires the concurrence of the parties.[22] Arbitration is often described as a 'creature of consent,' as parties agree to submit all or certain disputes to a private dispute resolution mechanism. An agreement to arbitrate can be in a standalone arbitration agreement or in a dispute resolution clause in a contract.

B. Party Autonomy in Choosing Arbitrators, Substantive Law, Procedural Rules

Unlike litigation, parties retain more control over their disputes. Parties to an arbitration have the autonomy to choose their own non-governmental decision-maker, or the arbitrator. Parties are free to choose the best arbitrator that will suit their needs, in terms of expertise and availability. The arbitrator is usually selected by the parties themselves or, in the absence of an agreement by the parties, selected for them by an arbitral institution chosen by the parties.[23]

Parties can opt to have a sole arbitrator or several arbitrators to sit on an arbitral tribunal. The arbitrator or tribunal is tasked with rendering a final and binding award, which can be enforced by national courts.

Parties can also decide on the specific law governing their commercial relationship and their dispute.[24]

Parties themselves can choose the procedural rules to be followed during the conduct of the arbitration. This means that parties have the option to choose a documents-only proceeding or hearings to be conducted in-person, virtually, or both. This also gives the parties the freedom to set up their own procedural calendar and decide on deadlines, as well as hearing dates.

C. Confidentiality

Compared to litigation where proceedings are conducted in open court and judgments are published, parties to an arbitration have the option to keep the entire proceeding, including the

[20] ADR Act of 2004, s 6.
[21] G.R. No. 181764, 7 December 2021.
[22] Born (n 2) 3.
[23] ibid.
[24] See Section V below.

arbitral award, confidential. The confidentiality that arbitration offers may help parties maintain their business relationships and keep them from further aggravating their dispute. It may help parties focus more on an amicable resolution of their disputes.

A number of international businesses opt to arbitrate their disputes because of the confidentiality and privacy of the process.[25] But some businesses seek out public dispute resolution mechanisms, especially if it may want to have its contractual stipulations interpreted publicly.

D. Finality and Enforceability of Arbitral Awards

Awards rendered by an arbitral tribunal are considered final and binding. Philippine courts adopt the principle of minimal curial intervention – courts will rarely interfere with arbitral awards. It will not disturb the arbitral tribunal's determination of facts and/or interpretation of law.[26]

The New York Convention covers the recognition and enforcement of international arbitral awards.[27] It specifies expeditious processes to enforce awards in different jurisdictions, as well as limited grounds for denying recognition and enforcement. To date, there are 172 state-parties to the New York Convention. As such, international arbitral awards are portable in a sense that parties can seek to enforce such award in those jurisdictions that are parties to the New York Convention.

In any event, courts may refuse recognition and enforcement of awards based on a narrow set of grounds. As the Philippines is a state-party to the New York Convention and an UNCITRAL Model Law country, it follows the grounds for refusing enforcement and recognition of a foreign arbitral award found in those instruments.[28]

E. Neutral Dispute Resolution Mechanism

Arbitration is removed from domestic courts to a certain extent. Parties to cross-border commercial disputes tend to prefer international arbitration as they view it as a neutral forum to resolve disputes.

III. International Arbitration Agreements

Given that arbitration is a consensual process, the foundation of international arbitration is the agreement to arbitrate.[29] Without an agreement to arbitrate, no valid arbitration can take place. Any arbitral award obtained through a process without a valid arbitration agreement cannot be enforced.[30]

[25] SIDRA Survey: 2022 Final Report (n 1) 12.

[26] *Mabuhay Holdings Corporation v Sembcorp Logistics Limited*, G.R. No. 212734, 5 December 2018 & Special Rules of Court on Alternative Dispute Resolution, Rule 13.11.

[27] United Nations Convention on the Recognition and Enforcement of Foreign Arbitral Awards, *adopted* 1958, 330 U.N.T.S. 3 (hereinafter New York Convention), Article I(1).

[28] See Section VI below.

[29] Blackaby and Partasides (n 19) 72 and Born (n 2) 45.

[30] ibid.

The IRR of the ADR Act of 2004 defines an arbitration agreement as:

> an agreement by the parties to submit to arbitration all or certain disputes which have arisen or which may arise between them in respect of a defined legal relationship, whether contractual or not. An arbitration agreement may be in the form of an arbitration clause in a contract or in the form of a separate agreement.[31]

Additionally, the agreement should be in writing. It is considered in writing if:

> it is contained in a document signed by the parties or in an exchange of letters, telex, telegrams or other means of telecommunication which provide a record of the agreement, or in an exchange of statements of claim and defense in which the existence of an agreement is alleged by one party and not denied by another. The reference in a contract to a document containing an arbitration clause constitutes an arbitration agreement provided that the contract is in writing and the reference is such as to make that clause part of the contract.[32]

An arbitration agreement usually contains (1) a statement that expressly states that disputes are to be referred to arbitration, (2) the scope of disputes submitted to arbitration, (3) the arbitral seat or place of arbitration, (4) the number, qualifications, and method of selection of arbitrators, (5) the language of arbitration, (6) choice-of-law clauses, and (7) institutional arbitration rules, if any, or procedural rules.

In the Philippines, agreements to arbitrate are considered contracts.[33] Contracts are the law between parties and must be followed in good faith. Therefore, where parties have agreed to submit their dispute to arbitration, courts are mandated to refer the parties to arbitration.[34] The Supreme Court has ruled that 'courts should liberally construe arbitration clauses. Provided such clause is susceptible of an interpretation that covers the asserted dispute, an order to arbitrate should be granted. Any doubt should be resolved in favor of arbitration'.[35] For instance, in *Korea Technologies v Hon. Lerma and Pacific General Steel Manufacturing Corporation*, the Supreme Court ruled that a stipulation in an arbitration clause that the arbitration must be done in a different country is not contrary to public policy and must be upheld. In *BF Corporation v Court of Appeals, et al.*,[36] the Court upheld an arbitration agreement even though one of the parties failed to initial a portion of the main contract between the parties. As such, courts will uphold an arbitration clause so long as it was mutually and voluntarily agreed upon by both parties and has not been shown to be contrary to law, morals, good customs, public order, or public policy.[37] However, courts will refuse to recognise an arbitration agreement only if it is invalid, void, unenforceable, or nonexistent.[38]

Arbitration clauses are considered to be independent of the main contract in which they are found.[39] Following the principle of separability, the Special ADR Rules provides that a decision

[31] Implementing Rules and Regulations of the Alternative Dispute Resolution Act of 2004, Republic Act No. 9285, Ch 1, Rule 2, Art 1.6 (A) (4) (2004).

[32] ibid. Ch 4, Rule 2, Art 4.7.

[33] *Gonzales v Climax Mining Ltd.*, G.R. No. 161957 and G.R. No. 167994, 22 January 2007, citing *Manila Electric Co. v Pasay Transportation Co.*, 57 Phil. 600 (1932).

[34] Special Rules of Court on Alternative Dispute Resolution, Part I, Rule 2.2.

[35] *LM Power Engineering* (n 3).

[36] G.R. No. 143581, 7 January 2008.

[37] *Korea Technologies v Hon. Lerma and Pacific General Steel Manufacturing Corporation*, G.R. No. 143581, 7 January 2008.

[38] ADR Act of 2004, Ch 4, s 24, & Special Rules of Court on Alternative Dispute Resolution, Part II, Rule 3.5, Part II.

[39] *Cagayan De Oro City Water District v Pasal*, G.R. No. 202305, 11 November 2021.

that the contract is null and void shall not automatically entail the invalidity of the arbitration clause.[40]

IV. Jurisdiction of the Arbitral Tribunal

In determining the jurisdiction of an arbitral tribunal, the Philippines adopts the competence-competence principle, which provides that tribunals may presumptively rule on their own jurisdiction, including any objections with respect to the existence or validity of the arbitration agreement or any condition precedent to the filing of a request for arbitration.[41]

Accordingly, Rule 2.4 of the Special ADR Rules states that:

> The arbitral tribunal shall be accorded the first opportunity or competence to rule on the issue of whether or not it has the competence or jurisdiction to decide a dispute submitted to it for decision, including any objection with respect to the existence or validity of the arbitration agreement. When a court is asked to rule upon issue/s affecting the competence or jurisdiction of an arbitral tribunal in a dispute brought before it, either before or after the arbitral tribunal is constituted, the court must exercise judicial restraint and defer to the competence or jurisdiction of the arbitral tribunal by allowing the arbitral tribunal the first opportunity to rule upon such issues.
>
> Where the court is asked to make a determination of whether the arbitration agreement is null and void, inoperative or incapable of being performed, under this policy of judicial restraint, the court must make no more than a prima facie determination of that issue.
>
> Unless the court, pursuant to such prima facie determination, concludes that the arbitration agreement is null and void, inoperative or incapable of being performed, the court must suspend the action before it and refer the parties to arbitration pursuant to the arbitration agreement.

Chapter 4, Rule 4, Article 4.16 of the IRR of the ADR Rules provides a similar rule and also refers to the principle of separability, specifically that a decision by the arbitral tribunal that the contract is null and void shall not entail *ipso jure* the invalidity of the arbitration clause.

Thus, arbitral tribunals have the authority to rule on its own jurisdiction. Courts are mandated to exercise judicial restraint, even when a tribunal is still in the process of being constituted, when faced with an issue regarding the jurisdiction of an arbitral tribunal.

Once a tribunal renders a ruling regarding its jurisdiction, a dissatisfied party may question the same before a court but such party cannot seek an injunction as judicial recourse to the court shall not prevent the arbitral tribunal from continuing the proceedings and rendering its award.[42]

Arbitral tribunals also have the power to issue interim relief as soon as it has been constituted.[43] Such interim measures may include, but are not limited to, a preliminary injunction directed against a party, appointment of receivers or detention, preservation, and inspection of property that is the subject of the dispute in arbitration.[44] Parties can only seek interim relief from courts when: (1) the necessity for interim relief arises before the constitution of the tribunal, or (2) the

[40] Special Rules of Court on Alternative Dispute Resolution, Part I, Rule 2.2.

[41] *Mubuhay Holdings Corporation*, G.R. No. 212734.

[42] Special Rules of Court on Alternative Dispute Resolution, Part II, Rule 3.18.

[43] ADR Act of 2004, Ch 4, ss 28 and 29.

[44] ADR Act of 2004, Ch 4, s 29 & Implementing Rules and Regulations of the Alternative Dispute Resolution Act of 2004, Ch 4, Rule 4, Art 4.17.

tribunal, after it has been constituted, has no power to act or is unable to act effectively on the request for interim relief.[45]

V. Choice of Law

Clearly, international arbitration does not exist in a legal vacuum. Different laws may govern different parts of an arbitration, such as the law governing the arbitration agreement, the law of the seat or place of arbitration, and the law governing the merits of the dispute, or the substantive law.[46] Philippine law allows parties to choose what specific legal regime they think is best for their particular needs.

The law governing the arbitration agreement can be the very same law governing the underlying contract. But following the principle of separability, it is also possible that the law governing the arbitration agreement is different from the law governing the underlying agreement.

As for the arbitral seat or place of arbitration, it is 'the state where the arbitration has its formal legal or juridical seat, and where the arbitral award will formally be made.'[47] It must be noted that the arbitral seat or place of arbitration is not the same as the *actual* geographical location where hearings or meetings are to take place. As such, 'the conduct of hearings outside the arbitral seat does not affect the location of the seat or the applicability of the arbitration legislation of the seat to the arbitration.'[48]

The law of the seat governs the procedural law of the arbitral proceedings, including the rules relevant to the appointment of arbitrators and the rules for annulment of arbitral awards.[49] Clearly, the seat also determines which national court would be responsible for applying such procedural law. Chapter 4, Section 30 of the ADR Act of 2004 specifically provides that:

> The parties are free to agree on the place of arbitration. Failing such agreement, the place of arbitration shall be in Metro Manila, unless the arbitral tribunal, having regard to the circumstances of the case, including the convenience of the parties shall decide on a different place of arbitration.
>
> The arbitral tribunal may, unless otherwise agreed by the parties, meet at any place it considers appropriate for consultation among its members, for hearing witnesses, experts, or the parties, or for inspection of goods, other property or documents.

Finally, as for the law governing the merits of the dispute or the substantive law, Article 4.28 of the IRR of the ADR Act of 2004 states that:

> (a) [t]he arbitral tribunal shall decide the dispute in accordance with such rules of law as are chosen by the parties as applicable to the substance of the dispute. Any designation of the law or legal system of a given state shall be construed, unless otherwise expressed, as directly referring to the substantive law of that state and not to its conflict of laws rules.
>
> (b) [f]ailing any designation by the parties, the arbitral tribunal shall apply the law determined by the conflict of laws rules, which it considers applicable.

[45] ADR Act of 2004, Ch 4, s 28.
[46] Born (n 2) 41.
[47] ibid 37.
[48] ibid 113.
[49] Blackaby and Partasides (n 19) 99.

(c) [t]he arbitral tribunal shall decide *ex aequo et bono* or as *amiable compositeur* only if the parties have expressly authorized it to do so.
(d) [i]n all cases, the arbitral tribunal shall decide in accordance with the terms of the contract and shall take into account the usages of the trade applicable to the transaction.

VI. Recognition and Enforcement of Foreign Arbitral Awards

The New York Convention governs the recognition and enforcement of foreign arbitral awards in the Philippines.[50] But courts may still, upon grounds of comity and reciprocity, recognise and enforce a foreign arbitral award made in a country that is not a signatory to the New York Convention as if it were a Convention award.[51]

Any party who wishes to have an arbitral award recognised and enforced in the Philippines may petition the proper court to do so.[52] Courts will presume that a foreign arbitral award was made and released in due course of arbitration and is subject to enforcement.[53] Further, courts will recognise and enforce a foreign arbitral award unless a ground to refuse recognition or enforcement of the foreign arbitral award is fully established. The decision of the court recognising and enforcing a foreign arbitral award is immediately executory.[54]

Courts may refuse recognition and enforcement of an award based only on the grounds enumerated in Article V of the New York Convention.[55] As such, courts may set aside or refuse enforcement only if:

(a) The party making the application furnishes proof that:
  (i) A party to the arbitration agreement was under some incapacity, or the said agreement is not valid under the law to which the parties have subjected it or, failing any indication thereof, under Philippine law; or
  (ii) The party making the application to set aside or resist enforcement was not given proper notice of the appointment of an arbitrator or of the arbitral proceedings or was otherwise unable to present his case; or
  (iii) The award deals with a dispute not contemplated by or not falling within the terms of the submission to arbitration, or contains decisions on matters beyond the scope of the submission to arbitration; provided that, if the decisions on matters submitted to arbitration can be separated from those not so submitted, only that part of the award which contains decisions on matters not submitted to arbitration may be set aside or only that part of the award which contains decisions on matters submitted to arbitration may be enforced; or
  (iv) The composition of the arbitral tribunal or the arbitral procedure was not in accordance with the agreement of the parties, unless such agreement was in conflict with a provision of Philippine law from which the parties cannot derogate, or, failing such agreement, was not in accordance with Philippine law;

[50] ADR Act of 2004, s 42.
[51] Special Rules of Court on Alternative Dispute Resolution, Rule 13.4.
[52] Rule 13.3 of the Special Rules of Court on Alternative Dispute Resolution provides that: 'The petition to recognize and enforce a foreign arbitral award shall be filed, at the option of the petitioner, with the Regional Trial Court (a) where the assets to be attached or levied upon is located, (b) where the act to be enjoined is being performed, (c) in the principal place of business in the Philippines of any of the parties, (d) if any of the parties is an individual, where any of those individuals resides, or (e) in the National Capital Judicial Region.'
[53] Special Rules of Court on Alternative Dispute Resolution, Rule 13.11.
[54] ibid.
[55] ADR Act of 2004, s 45.

(b) The court finds that:
   (i) The subject-matter of the dispute is not capable of settlement by arbitration under the law of the Philippines; or
   (ii) The recognition or enforcement of the award would be contrary to public policy.[56]

Any other ground not found in the enumeration above shall be disregarded by the court.[57] In *Tuna Mining Processing, Inc. v Philippine Kingford, Inc.*,[58] Tuna Processing, a foreign corporation not licensed to do business in the Philippines, but which collected royalties from entities in the Philippines, sought to enforce a foreign arbitral award. The Regional Trial Court refused to recognise and enforce the award on the ground that Tuna Mining lacked legal capacity to sue in the Philippines. The Regional Trial Court relied on the Philippine Corporation Code which states that no foreign corporation transacting business in the Philippines without a licence shall be permitted to maintain or intervene in any action, suit or proceeding in any court. The Supreme Court reversed the decision of the trial court, holding that not one of these exclusive grounds under Article V of the New York Convention touched on the capacity to sue of the party seeking the recognition and enforcement of the award. The Court further explained that:

> it is in the best interest of justice that in the enforcement of a foreign arbitral award, we deny availment by the losing party of the rule that bars foreign corporations not licensed to do business in the Philippines from maintaining a suit in our courts. When a party enters into a contract containing a foreign arbitration clause and, as in this case, in fact submits itself to arbitration, it becomes bound by the contract, by the arbitration and by the result of arbitration, conceding thereby the capacity of the other party to enter into the contract, participate in the arbitration and cause the implementation of the result.

Following the principle of minimal curial intervention, Philippine courts will rarely interfere with the enforcement of arbitral awards. No challenges based on merit will be allowed to refuse recognition and enforcement of an award.

As to the power of Philippine courts to refuse recognition and enforcement of an award should it be contrary to public policy, the Supreme Court held in *Mabuhay Holdings Corporation v Sembcorp Logistics Limited* that:

> pursuant to the State's policy in favor of arbitration and enforcement of arbitral awards, the Court adopts the majority and narrow approach in determining whether enforcement of an award is contrary to Our public policy. Mere errors in the interpretation of the law or factual findings would not suffice to warrant refusal of enforcement under the public policy ground. The illegality or immorality of the award must reach a certain threshold such that, enforcement of the same would be against Our State's fundamental tenets of justice and morality, or would blatantly be injurious to the public, or the interests of the society.[59]

In a later case, the Court found that an arbitral award would be contrary to public policy if it would be injurious to the public at large and would result in an unequal protection of two groups of consumers, despite the lack of substantial distinction between them.

[56] New York Convention, Article V; & Special Rules of Court on Alternative Dispute Resolution, Rule 12.4.
[57] ADR Act of 2004, s 45.
[58] G.R. No. 185582, 29 February 2012.
[59] *Mabuhay Holdings Corporation*, G.R. No. 212734.

12

Investment Treaty Arbitration

ANGELA RAY T ABALA

I. Introduction

One of the specialised forms of arbitration involves disputes between investors and states. An investor-state arbitration or investment arbitration is conducted pursuant to an arbitration clause found in a bilateral investment treaty ('BIT') or multilateral investment treaty. States enter into these treaties to promote and protect investments of the nationals and companies of the signatory states in each other's territory. BITs are meant to provide 'protection of the investor and the stimulation of economic activity in the host.'[1] Investment protection standards that are typically included in BITs that signatory states must mutually uphold are non-arbitrariness, non-discrimination, expropriation only with compensation, fair and equitable treatment, and full protection and security. A derogation from any of these standards may give rise to a dispute, where a foreign investor may submit the dispute to arbitration against the state hosting its investment.

Arbitration, whether administered by an arbitration institution or done ad hoc, is the most commonly used mechanism to resolve investor-state disputes.[2] This comes as no surprise as arbitration clauses are prevalent in BITs and contracts, resulting in a mandatory obligation to participate in arbitration should a party institute one.[3]

The Philippines is a party to 39 BITs. In 2022, it signed treaties with Israel and the United Arab Emirates.[4] Out of those 39 BITs, 32 are in force. The Philippines is also a party to another 17 treaties with investment provisions, such as regional investment treaties and free trade agreements, that include similar investment protections and dispute settlement mechanisms found in BITs. All but one of the Philippine treaties with investment provisions are in force.[5]

The Philippines has been a party to the binding investor-state dispute settlement mechanisms found in these BITs or other international investment agreements. To date, the Philippines has been involved in six international investment arbitration cases, five of which have been concluded, one which is currently pending,[6] and one investment mediation case.[7]

[1] KN Schefer, *International Investment Law: Text, Cases and Materials*, 2nd edn (Edward Elgar, 2016).

[2] Singapore International Dispute Resolution Academy, SIDRA International dispute Resolution Survey: 2022 Final Report, see sidra.smu.edu.sg/sites/sidra.smu.edu.sg/files/survey-2022/index.html.

[3] ibid.

[4] UNCTAD, Investment Policy Hub, International Investment Agreements Navigator, Philippines, see investmentpolicy.unctad.org/international-investment-agreements/countries/166/philippines.

[5] ibid.

[6] ICSID, Cases Database, see icsid.worldbank.org/cases/case-database.

[7] LE Peterson, 'In an Apparent First, Investor and Host-State Agree to Try Mediation Under IBA Rules to Resolve an Investment Treaty Dispute' (*Inv. Arb. Rep.*, 14 April 2016) see www.iareporter.com/articles/in-an-apparent-first-investor-and-host-state-agree-to-try-mediation-under-iba-rules-to-resolve-an-investment-treaty-dispute/.

This chapter covers consent to an investment arbitration (Section II). It also discusses investment arbitration under the Convention on the Settlement of Investment Disputes between States and Nationals of Other States, or the 'ICSID Convention' (Section III), and ad hoc arbitration (Section IV). Section V covers the jurisdiction of investment arbitration tribunals. Section VI refers to the recognition and enforcement of investment arbitration awards.

II. Consent to Arbitrate

BITs and multilateral investment treaties contain dispute settlement provisions. Different provisions offer different means of resolving disputes, such as through negotiation, conciliation, mediation or litigation. Most of these treaties include a binding 'general consent-to-arbitrate provision.'[8] The arbitration clause found in these treaties

> functions as an offer to arbitrate that can be accepted by the investor through the submission of a request for arbitration. While the existence and scope of consent are questions of law to be determined by the tribunal, such consent is available equally to any investor from the other party to the treaty, not just to those investors and to that degree to which the host agrees.
>
> [ ] by giving its consent to be challenged by individual investors in a state treaty, the host becomes liable directly to the investor for a violation of any treaty provision.[9]

Most of the BITs that the Philippines is a party to include an investor-state dispute resolution clause, with a majority requiring parties to resolve disputes amicably via consultation and negotiation. If the dispute is not settled amicably, parties may refer the matter to the competent court or to international investment arbitration to resolve the same. Investment arbitration can be done either ad hoc under the United Nations Commission on International Trade Law ('UNCITRAL') Rules, or under the ICSID Convention. The majority of Philippine BITs allow for arbitration under the ICSID Convention.[10]

III. International Centre for Settlement of Investment Disputes (ICSID)

The ICSID Convention provides for a stand-alone regime, generally separate from national courts and national law, to conduct investment arbitration under the auspices of ICSID, one of the organisations of the World Bank Group. ICSID was created under the Convention with the goal of providing facilities for conciliation and arbitration of investment disputes between Contracting States and nationals of other Contracting States.[11] As such, it has specific rules as to the conduct of investor-state arbitration, as well as conciliation and mediation of investment disputes. The Convention also has a stand-alone regime regarding recognition and enforcement, as well as annulment, of arbitral awards rendered by a tribunal constituted following the

[8] Schefer (n 1) 436.
[9] ibid.
[10] The China – Philippines BIT (1992) and the Myanmar – Philippines BIT (1998) exclude ICSID arbitration.
[11] Convention on the Settlement of Investment Disputes between States and Nationals of Other States, adopted 18 March 1965, 575 U.N.T.S. 159 (hereinafter ICSID Convention), Article 1.2.

provisions of the ICSID Convention and its Rules. It is worth noting that the Convention does not provide for substantive protections for foreign investment; but provides for specialised procedural rules to resolve investment disputes.

Arbitration or conciliation when one or both parties are not ICSID member states may still have a dispute administered by ICSID under the Additional Facility Rules.

As of December 2023, the number of arbitration and conciliation cases that ICSID has registered under its Convention and Additional Facility Rules was 967, with 53 cases registered in 2023 as ICSID Convention arbitration cases.[12]

The Philippines signed the ICSID Convention in September 1978 and it entered into force shortly thereafter in December 1978. All five investment arbitration cases involving the Philippines were conducted under the Convention and administered by ICSID.

IV. Ad Hoc Arbitration

An ad hoc arbitration is one where no arbitration institution, such as ICSID, is appointed to administer the same. There are a number of Philippine BITs that allow for ad hoc arbitration and most reference the UNCITRAL Arbitration Rules, which includes provisions on the composition of the arbitral tribunal, the arbitral proceedings, and the award. Examples of Philippine BITs that permit ad hoc arbitration include those concluded with Argentina, Canada, India, Portugal, and Sweden.

V. Jurisdiction of Investment Arbitration Tribunals

Investment arbitration tribunals, similar to commercial arbitration tribunals, follow the principle of competence-competence, which provides that tribunals have the power to determine their own jurisdiction. This principle is enshrined in both the ICSID Convention and the UNCITRAL Arbitration Rules.

Article 41 of the ICSID Convention provides that:

(1) The Tribunal shall be the judge of its own competence.
(2) Any objection by a party to the dispute that that dispute is not within the jurisdiction of the Centre, or for other reasons is not within the competence of the Tribunal, shall be considered by the Tribunal which shall determine whether to deal with it as a preliminary question or to join it to the merits of the dispute.

Article 23 of the 2021 UNCITRAL Arbitration Rules states that '[t]he arbitral tribunal shall have the power to rule on its own jurisdiction, including any objections with respect to the existence or validity of the arbitration agreement.'[13]

The applicable law relevant to jurisdictional issues is international law. Tribunals may look into the underlying BIT of a particular dispute, customary international law, and the Vienna Convention on the Law of Treaties.

[12] The ICSID Caseload – Statistics Issue 2024-1, see icsid.worldbank.org/sites/default/files/publications/ENG_The_ICSID_Caseload_Statistics_Issue%202024.pdf.

[13] United Nations Commission on International Trade Law Arbitration Rules (2021), Art 23.

VI. Recognition and Enforcement of Investment Arbitration Awards

Recognition and enforcement of an investment arbitration award depends on the treaty under which the arbitration is pursued. There are differences between arbitral awards rendered under the ICSID Convention and non-ICSID awards.

An ICSID award is binding on the parties and not subject to any appeal.[14] However, parties can move to annul an award based on a limited set of grounds, specifically:

(a) that the Tribunal was not properly constituted;
(b) that the Tribunal has manifestly exceeded its powers;
(c) that there was corruption on the part of a member of the Tribunal;
(d) that there has been a serious departure from a fundamental rule of procedure; or
(e) that the award has failed to state the reasons on which it is based.[15]

A request for annulment of the arbitral award is heard by a three-member *ad hoc* annulment committee appointed from ICSID's Panel of Arbitrators.[16] An annulment committee does not hear an appeal. It only has the power to annul the award or any part thereof based on the grounds enumerated above.[17]

The Philippines has been involved in one ICSID arbitration where the arbitral award was referred to an annulment committee. In *Fraport AG Frankfurt Airport Services Worldwide v Republic of the Philippines*,[18] Fraport AG Frankfurt Airport Services Worldwide ('Fraport'), a German company, instituted an ICSID arbitration case under the Philippines-Germany BIT over a concession agreement to build and operate the Ninoy Aquino International Airport Passenger Terminal III.[19] The said concession agreement was voided by the Philippine Supreme Court on the ground that it had violated the Anti-Dummy Law.[20] Fraport then claimed that the Philippine government had expropriated its investment and violated the fair and equitable treatment clause under the Philippines-Germany BIT. The arbitral tribunal rendered an award, agreeing with the Philippines that the Anti-Dummy Law was indeed circumvented and that it lacked jurisdiction over the subject matter of the case.[21] Fraport then requested to have the award annulled. An ad hoc annulment committee was constituted to look into the matter. It found that the arbitral tribunal seriously departed from a fundamental rule of procedure and denied Fraport the right to be heard when it disregarded a Philippine Special Prosecutor's Resolution, as to whether Fraport violated the Anti-Dummy Law, which was submitted after the close of the proceedings.[22]

States must recognise an ICSID award and 'enforce the pecuniary obligations imposed by that award within its territories as if it were a final judgment of a court in that State.'[23] Article 54 of the ICSID Convention further provides that:

> [a] party seeking recognition or enforcement in the territories of a Contracting State shall furnish to a competent court or other authority which such State shall have designated for this purpose a copy of the

[14] ICSID Convention, Art 53.
[15] ibid Art 52(1).
[16] ibid Art 52(3).
[17] ibid.
[18] *Fraport AG Frankfurt Airport Services Worldwide v Republic of the Philippines* (ICSID Case No. ARB/03/25).
[19] *Fraport* Award (ICSID Case No. ARB/03/25) (16 August 2007), para 2.
[20] ibid paras 101–102.
[21] ibid para 401.
[22] *Fraport*, ICSID Case No. ARB/03/25, Decision on the Application for Annulment of Fraport AG Frankfurt Airport Services Worldwide (23 December 2010), paras 211, 218.
[23] ICSID Convention, Art 54(1).

award certified by the Secretary-General. Each Contracting State shall notify the Secretary-General of the designation of the competent court or other authority for this purpose and of any subsequent change in such designation.

[ ] Execution of the award shall be governed by the laws concerning the execution of judgments in force in the State in whose territories such execution is sought.

Enforcement is also subject to 'the law in force in any Contracting State relating to immunity of that State or of any foreign State from execution.'[24]

As for recognition and enforcement of arbitral awards rendered in a non-ICSID Convention investment arbitration, the same is subject to the recognition and enforcement provisions found under the New York Convention. As such, the recognition and enforcement of a non-ICSID Convention investment arbitration award is similar to that of an international commercial arbitration award. Such awards may be set aside in the Philippines based on the grounds and procedure found under the Philippine Alternative Dispute Resolution Act of 2004,[25] its implementing rules and regulations,[26] as well as the Special Rules of Court on Alternative Dispute Resolution Rules issued by the Supreme Court.[27]

[24] ibid Art 55.

[25] An Act to Institutionalize the Use of an Alternative Dispute Resolution System in the Philippines and to Establish the Office for Alternative Dispute Resolution, and for Other Purposes, Republic Act No. 9284 (2004).

[26] Implementing Rules and Regulations of the Alternative Dispute Resolution Act of 2004, Republic Act No. 9285 (2004).

[27] Special Rules of Court on Alternative Dispute Resolution, A.M. No. 07-11-08-SC, 1 September 2009.

13

The Harmonisation of Private International Law

THOMAS ELLIOT A MONDEZ

I. Introduction

Thomas Hobbes used an Old Testament monster, the Leviathan, to illustrate the need for a powerful sovereign to maintain peace and order within a state. This has generally been viewed as a conservative affirmation for the need of a strong centralised government. It is better for people to fear this metaphorical Leviathan than to risk life and limb in an anarchic society.

The social contract between the governed and the state is the basic structure of a society where the rule of law is supreme. The citizen is subjugated by the sovereign. However, there is an element of freedom in the execution of this social contract. Humans are, by their nature, at liberty to do whatever it is that they please. They are compulsive creatures who value self-preservation above all. But if humankind is to live and prosper in an orderly society, they must choose to submit to a Leviathan which can regulate the states of affairs among its subjects. Swearing allegiance to a Leviathan is therefore a renunciation of the basic uncivilised instincts of humankind. It creates a political obligation to vastly limit the freedoms provided by nature to an ungoverned human being.

The social contract of Hobbes is not an agreement between the sovereign and the subservient. Rather, it is a communal contract among all individuals living under the jurisdiction of the sovereign who surrender their individual rights to self-preservation to the Leviathan.[1] A citizen of a state entrusts his or her safety and well-being to the sovereign. The individuals obey the Leviathan because they know that the sovereign has absolute authority to establish and execute the laws that govern a nation.

Harmonisation of laws is therefore a practical and achievable endeavour by the sovereign. Nation-states had successfully codified various aspects of law within their respective jurisdictions. This is doable because the states are Leviathans within their areas of control.

There is no mega-Leviathan that governs the entire world.

Conflict of laws arise precisely because the concept of sovereignty is still held most holy. It is an inviolable principle that keeps regimes in power by ensuring that a Leviathan has absolute monopoly of coercive and legal forces within a territorial jurisdiction.

Nevertheless, a difficult undertaking will still see the light of day if there is sufficient compulsion for its achievement. The codification of local laws within sprawling empires was made possible because there were concrete economic advantages to standardisation.

[1] A Ristroph, 'Sovereignty and Subversion' (2015) 101(4) *Virginia Law Review* 1034–35.

Imagine that you are a merchant in seventeenth century France. Before the French Revolution, several legal entities and systems competed in the market for law.[2] It bred monopolistic competition, a turf war over jurisdictions divided by territory, creed, and allegiance. The merchant may court favour from magistrates administering regional law based on France's feudal system, which differs per territorial jurisdiction.[3] Perhaps the merchant could elevate his or her grievances before the organs implementing the King's Law. Initially, the King's Law dealt with the affairs of the French nobility. But it extended to criminal and civil procedure, beginning the seventeenth century in an attempt to expand its share over the legal market.[4] The merchant may also opt for a more pious resolution of his or her legal concerns by invoking Canon Law, which also dealt with non-spiritual affairs.[5]

To understand the difficulty, and necessity, of harmonising Philippine laws with international legal standards, it is important to study the history of the codification of laws in Europe, which ultimately led to the successful harmonisation of present-day European Union (EU) legal frameworks. It took European nations centuries to transform competing sources of law – customs, Canon law, and Roman law – into reliable codified treaties. The EU, acting as a mega-Leviathan, allowed the harmonisation of various domestic European laws. In effect, the EU mirrored the Roman Empire as a mega-Leviathan structure that empowered the establishment of a uniform legal standard throughout a vast territory. Philippine legislators and policy makers could learn from the evolution of legal codification in Europe as it moves forward towards greater integration with its fellow Association of Southeast Asian Nations (ASEAN) countries.

The experience of France is particularly relevant since its codification of private law strongly influenced the development of civil law systems in various countries, including the Philippines. The rediscovery of the comprehensive code of Roman law or *Corpus Juris Civilis* played a pivotal role in the development of European legal systems. However, since the *Corpus Juris* was in Latin, Europeans who were not literate in this language needed professional translations to interpret what it meant.[6] It was thus inaccessible to commonfolk and its translation to contemporary European languages led to unreliable legal interpretation and unpredictable litigation.[7]

Roman law was only predominantly used in the southern parts of France. The northern regions still applied local customs as the primary source of law. Charles VII of France attempted to codify regional customs in the fifteenth century.[8] In the seventeenth century, the Sun King Louis XIV commissioned the codification of law, which led to enactments covering rules of procedure, admiralty, penal law, and commercial law.[9] However, further attempts to codify other private laws were met with opposition.[10]

The Age of Enlightenment accelerated the drive to codify private law, with proponents of natural law pushing for equal legal treatment.[11] It also coincided with the American and French Revolutions of the eighteenth century. Progressive thought was no longer confined to hypothetical idealism. Practical manifestations of the universality of legal rights were no longer considered

[2] J Josselin and A Marciano, 'The Making of the French Civil Code: An Economic Interpretation' (2002) 14(3) *European Journal of Law and Economics* 194.

[3] ibid.

[4] ibid.

[5] ibid.

[6] HK Lücke, 'The European Natural Law Codes: The Age of Reason and the Powers of Government' (2012) 31(1) *University of Queensland Law Journal* 7–8.

[7] ibid.

[8] ibid 8.

[9] ibid 9.

[10] ibid.

[11] ibid 7.

products of the radical minority. The revolutionary fervour allowed Napoléon Bonaparte to push for the enactment of the Code Civil of 1804, or the Napoleonic Code.

The concept of universality in the application of law was previously used by Hugo Grotius, considered the father of international law. Grotius used two pillars to establish an international legal framework: the law of nations, which is the collective norms of states established via mutual agreements, and natural law. The law of nature applies to all since it is based on the God-given human ability to discern right from wrong. It is therefore universal in nature.

The objective of Grotius in using human reason to establish universality in law was to regulate warfare. Having experienced the Thirty Years War in seventeenth century Europe, Grotius believed that natural law is necessary to establish the basic humanitarian rules of engagement. On the other hand, the Napoleonic Code was largely associated with Napoléon's imperialistic ambitions over continental Europe and his desire to impose a universal legal system.[12] The legacy of the Napoleonic Code endured after his defeat at Waterloo, influencing the development of civil law systems in Europe, North America, and South America. Furthermore, the Napoleonic Code set a precedent that allowed Spain to freely develop its own harmonised codes.[13]

In 1889, the enforcement of the Spanish Civil Code was extended to the Philippines, Cuba, and Puerto Rico. It was retained as the primary code governing private law in the Philippines during the American period. The New Civil Code[14] only took effect on 30 August 1950, while the Family Code[15] became effective on 2 August 1988.[16]

Before discussing the challenges faced by the Philippines in harmonising private international law, it is best to review the French experience by Hobbesian metrics using the Leviathan standard.

Attempts to harmonise customary law prior to the Age of Enlightenment and the development of the Westphalian system failed due to the weak centralised governments in medieval Europe. A strong and organised central Roman government allowed the codification of Roman laws. The Dark Ages caused a power vacuum in Europe, with kingdoms struggling to rule over vast territories of the once powerful Roman Empire. For instance, the monarch of France is, on paper, the ruler of the entire kingdom. But the feudal system prevented a Leviathan from emerging since local leaders could still enforce regional laws based on domestic customs.

Harmonisation of laws became possible with the progressive ideas of the Age of Enlightenment and the growing power of the state as a Leviathan. Progressive thought may appear anathema to the perceived totalitarianism of the Hobbesian Leviathan, but the fusion of both movements in the latter part of the eighteenth century created the perfect conditions to give birth to the Napoleonic Code. First, the French Revolution (as well as the American Revolution) fostered liberty, equality, and fraternity, which allowed the proponents of natural law to push for the codification of private law. Previous efforts were thwarted, or severely limited, since the conservative establishment naturally opposed progressive legal standards that would remove their regional or sectoral legal monopoly.

Napoléon's consolidation of power in France gave rise to an authoritarian and imperialistic government under the guise of revolutionary fervour. He was in a unique position to push for a true codified French law. France was in transition. People were ready for change and Napoléon had abundant political and coercive capital to harmonise the laws of France. Napoleonic France was therefore a Leviathan in peak form.

[12] ibid 34.
[13] ibid.
[14] Republic Act No. 336. Civil Code of the Philippines (18 June 1949).
[15] Executive Order No. 209. The Family Code of the Philippines (6 July 1987).
[16] *Spouses Cueno v Spouses Bautista*, G.R. No. 246445. 2 March 2021.

The Napoleonic Code is both praised as a monumental achievement of legal codification and criticised as a product of imperialistic ambitions. However, it can be argued that Napoléon's stern approach was motivated by altruistic designs.[17] The economic benefits of the codification of laws strengthened the resolve of the French to harmonise their legal system.

The reduction of transactional costs is an attractive benefit of legal harmonisation.[18] The agreement of actors within a legislative jurisdiction to conform to a standard behaviour generates confidence and creates legal certainty.[19] Legal harmonisation aims to eliminate redundancies and suppress legal contradictions.[20] The Napoleonic Code was consistent with the principles of equality and legal uniformity advanced by the post-French Revolution regime since it replaced diverse regional customs with a consistent set of rules.[21]

Ultimately, Napoléon's dream of a continental empire faded after his defeat by an alliance of European powers. But the Napoleonic Code started a domino effect that led to the creation of civil law systems all over the world.

The Philippines in the late nineteenth century was still under the colonial rule of Spain. Hence, the Spanish colonial government functioned as a Leviathan that exercised full power to enact laws covering the entire Philippine archipelago. Apart from the Spanish Civil Code, a Royal Order was issued on 17 December 1886 to enforce in the Philippines the 1850 Penal Code of Spain, as amended by the *Codigo Penal Reformado de 1870*.[22] It was the penal code enforced in the Philippines until the enactment of Act No. 3815 or the Revised Penal Code in 1930, which took effect in 1932.[23]

The Philippines had thus reaped what was sown in the nineteenth century. The existing New Civil Code and Revised Penal Code are largely based on the codified Spanish civil and penal laws, respectively, which were in effect from the late nineteenth century until the American colonial period. In fact, Philippine jurisprudence still cites the Spanish Civil Code in discussing the effects of private law on citizens who lived and transacted before the effectivity of the New Civil Code. The Philippine Supreme Court likewise cites the *Codigo Penal* in interpreting Revised Penal Code provisions which are lifted from its Spanish predecessor. The stability of the existing Philippine legal system is therefore a product of the harmonisation efforts initiated by legal luminaries and strong-willed leaders in the nineteenth century.

II. Harmonisation of Laws in the Twentieth and Twenty-First Centuries

The Hobbesian concept of a Leviathan was initially limited to sovereign entities, traditionally defined as nation-states. It is easy to enforce uniform laws within the territorial jurisdiction of an unquestioned centralised sovereign power. The efforts of Grotius and other learned women and men were therefore concentrated on developing an international legal structure based on public international law. The general idea was that the nation-states were the undisputed rulers of their own kingdoms, but they have to surrender to a universal legal system (or at least a semblance of

[17] S Harnay, 'Was Napoleon a Benevolent Dictator? An Economic Justification for Codification' (2002) 14(3) *European Journal of Law and Economics* 237–39.

[18] ibid 238.

[19] ibid 239.

[20] ibid 245.

[21] ibid.

[22] *People v Escote, Jr.*, G.R. No. 140756. 4 April 2003.

[23] Act No. 3815. The Revised Penal Code (8 December 1930).

legal order) in the international sphere. Hence, Grotius developed his twin pillars of the law of nature (universal law) and the laws of nations based on binding agreements (*pacta sunt servanda*).

The focus was on the harmonisation of public international law since the traditional subjects of international law are nation-states. Individuals are mere objects of international law for they could only exercise or enforce their rights, if any, through the actions of their sovereign state.

The harmonisation of the law of nations through the development of public international law was premised on the perpetuation of the nation-state as the primary actor in the international sphere. The context of international relations dramatically changed in the twentieth century. The establishment of supranational and intergovernmental organisations changed the dynamics of the nation-states, as well as the creation and implementation of international law. The United Nations (UN) and other prominent intergovernmental organisations allowed greater regulation and harmonisation of international norms. But the UN still lacked the unconditional power that a traditional nation-state Leviathan exercised over its territorial jurisdiction.

While the nations of the world had committed to establishing the UN, the conservative concepts of realism in international law and the predominance of state power still governed the mindset of policy makers, legislators, and diplomats. Another key development was the loss of great power status of the European imperial nations. While France and the United Kingdom (UK) were given permanent seats in the UN Security Council, bigger and more populous nations such as the United States (US), Russia, and China began to emerge as the dominant players in the post-war world. Former European colonies such as India and Brazil are also emerging as formidable powers.

Europe was devasted after two consecutive World Wars. Most of its colonies already gained independence. The best way for European nations to stay in step with the US and Russia (and, later on, China) was to integrate and form a powerful bloc of nations.

The establishment of the EU was a key development not only in the global geopolitical landscape, but also in the harmonisation of private international law. When Grotius was developing the early concept of a law of nations, the objective was to create a pan-European legal standard in regulating the affairs of the sovereign states. Contrarily, the nation-state is no longer the primary actor in the affairs of an integrated Europe. Rather, the legal rights of the individual citizens of the member states became the focus of the integration efforts of the EU as a supranational institution. The harmonisation of private laws was made necessary to ensure the freedom of movement of goods, people, services, and capital within the EU, and to meet the transactional demands of increased cross-nation traffic within the bloc.

Europe's experience in legal integration should serve as a lesson for the Philippines. ASEAN is still decades away from the level of integration of the EU. But patience is a must since the present iteration of the EU is a product of a long evolutionary process.

Efforts to unite Europe were already broached prior to the two World Wars. Europe was at the peak of its power at the turn of the twentieth century, but it was a shell of its colonial peak by the end of World War II in 1945. Integration was seen as a solution to finally abate the endless cycle of war in Europe, particularly through a permanent Franco-German rapprochement via legal instruments integrating their economies. Post-war leaders lobbied for the creation of a new structure in Western European affairs to ensure equality and the rule of law.[24] Notably, Eastern Europe was behind the Iron Curtain during the Cold War.

The first step was the creation of economic communities. The European Coal and Steel Community (ECSC) was established by the 1951 Treaty of Paris, which became effective in 1952.[25]

[24] D Vataman, 'History of the European Union' (2010) XVII(2) *Lex Et Scientia* 112.
[25] ibid 114–15.

It created a sectoral common market for coal and steel, setting the precedent for the establishment of the EU common market. It was followed by the creation of the European Defence Community (EDC), European Economic Community (EEC), and the European Atomic Energy Community (EURATOM). One of the goals identified by the EEC is the approximation of the respective municipal laws of the member states to allow a common market to function.[26] The membership of the European Communities grew in number, which necessitated the strengthening of pan-European institutions. The 1992 Treaty of Maastricht eventually became the foundation treaty of the EU.[27]

Gomez and Ganuza's (2012) article in the European Journal of Law and Economics discussed the pathways leading to the harmonisation of European laws.[28] The authors discussed three different processes leading to the harmonisation of European private laws: legal harmonisation through convergence; legal harmonisation through coordinated action; and, legal harmonisation through political fiat. It is best for legislators and policy makers in the Philippines to take note of the various pathways to private law harmonisation.

Legal harmonisation through convergence is a spontaneous process that occurs based on the best practices of other jurisdictions. There are three ways to spontaneously harmonise laws: cascading information, competition, and knowledge transfer.[29] By cascading information, conditions requiring a legal response which are not covered by existing legal frameworks in a country may be remedied by adopting rules from other jurisdictions. It creates a herd mentality which compels a state with lacking or insufficient legal remedies to mimic successful laws from other jurisdictions.[30] The second pathway is through competition. States with diverging rules are forced to improve their existing laws by catering to the preferences of the market. For instance, if most companies prefer the legal framework of a certain country, competitive pressure will force other jurisdictions to adopt similar rules to satisfy the greatest number of 'consumers' of the legal product. In turn, the laws of various countries will eventually harmonise by adopting the most preferred or most responsive set of rules.[31] Finally, knowledge transfer occurs when legislators and the administrators of the justice system of a country acquire knowledge from their counterparts from other jurisdictions.[32] Philippine agencies involved in legislation and rule-making may send representatives to international fora to learn the best practices of other jurisdictions.

Harmonisation through coordinated action occurs when states agree to be bound by an international instrument that requires legislation to be passed in their respective jurisdictions to cover a specific matter of private law. They may agree to pattern their domestic laws with a model law or the parameters set by mutual agreement. Coordinated action may also be coursed through international organisations such as the United Nations Commission on International Trade Law (UNCITRAL).[33]

Lastly, harmonisation may be enforced via political fiat. Fragmented legal jurisdictions within a country may be compelled to adopt uniform rules by the national or federal government. Supranational institutions like the EU may also impose a legal harmonisation mandate.[34]

[26] ibid 115–16.
[27] European Union, *Treaty on European Union (Consolidated Version), Treaty of Maastricht*, 7 February 1992, Official Journal of the European Communities C 325/5; 24 December 2002.
[28] F Gomez and JJ Ganuza, 'How to build European private law: An economic analysis of the lawmaking and harmonization dimensions in European private law' (2012) 33(3) *European Journal of Law and Economics* 481–503.
[29] ibid 484.
[30] ibid 484–85.
[31] ibid 485.
[32] ibid 486.
[33] ibid 487.
[34] ibid 488.

Taking stock of the French experience, the scope of the harmonisation efforts of the ruling Leviathan depends on the reach of the governing body. In the fifteenth century, the monarchy was only able to partially codify customs in the northern part of France, particularly the ones practised in Paris, due to the limited control of the crown over the fragmented regions of the country. In the nineteenth century, France was able to produce the Napoleonic Code by relying on the political reach of a significantly more powerful Leviathan. Post-World War II France transitioned to the EU era by integrating substantial parts of its political, economic, and legal systems with a supranational body. The EU, acting as a mega-Leviathan, was able to spearhead continent-wide harmonisation efforts.

Unlike France, centralising the political and legal systems of the Philippines is much harder. There was no national identity unifying the various political units in the Philippine Islands before the Spanish conquest. While Spain had already colonised the country in the sixteenth century, the Philippines was only able to adopt a codified civil code in the nineteenth century. Filipinos were only able to develop their own harmonised legal systems in the twentieth century.

The trajectories of private law harmonisation of the French and the Filipinos are quite far apart. France benefits from a centuries-old process. The EU also had a head start of several decades over the ASEAN. Moreover, the EU already has a sophisticated supranational political system with institutions such as the European Commission, European Parliament, and the European Court of Justice having jurisdiction over the entire bloc. Contrarily, the ASEAN still relies on its consensus framework which greatly slows down the integration process. It also lacks strong centralised institutions that could hasten the harmonisation efforts.

It is therefore more difficult to harmonise private law, as it relates to conflict of laws, in the local setting.

III. Efforts of the Philippines to Harmonise Private Law with International Standards

The Hague Conference on Private International Law (HCCH) was established to attain progressive unification of the rules of private international law.[35] The Philippines joined the HCCH on 14 July 2010.[36] It is party to five HCCH instruments, *viz*:

- Convention of 5 October 1961 Abolishing the Requirement of Legalisation for Foreign Public Documents (Apostille Convention);[37]
- Convention of 15 November 1965 on the Service Abroad of Judicial and Extrajudicial Documents in Civil or Commercial Matters;[38]
- Convention of 25 October 1980 on the Civil Aspects of International Child Abduction;[39]

[35] Article 1, Statute of the Hague Conference on Private International Law. Available at www.hcch.net/en/instruments/conventions/full-text.

[36] Supreme Court Administrative Order No. 251-20 dated 11 September 2020.

[37] The Hague Convention Abolishing the Requirement of Legalization for Foreign Public Documents, 9 INT'L L. 755 (1975).

[38] The Hague Convention on the Service Abroad of Judicial and Extrajudicial Documents in Civil or Commercial Matters, 15 November 1965, 20 U.S.T. 361, 658 U.N.T.S. 163.

[39] Hague Convention on the Civil Aspects of International Child Abduction, 25 October 1980, T.I.A.S. No. 11,670, 1343 U.N.T.S. 89.

- Convention of 29 May 1993 on Protection of Children and Co-operation in Respect of Intercountry Adoption;[40] and,
- Convention of 23 November 2007 on the International Recovery of Child Support and Other Forms of Family Maintenance.[41]

The Apostille Convention came into force in the Philippines on 14 May 2019.[42] The Philippine Supreme Court immediately acted by issuing the 2019 Amendments to the 1989 Revised Rules on Evidence.[43] To harmonise the Rules on Evidence with the Apostille Convention, Section 19, Rule 132 was amended to include a provision stating that documents which are considered public documents under treaties and conventions in force between the Philippines and the country of source are also treated as public documents in the Philippines.[44]

Proof of official record under Section 24, Rule 132 was also substantially amended, to wit:

> SECTION 24. Proof of Official Record. – The record of public documents referred to in paragraph (a) of Section 19, when admissible for any purpose, may be evidenced by an official publication thereof or by a copy attested by the officer having the legal custody of the record, or by his <u>or her</u> deputy, and accompanied, if the record is not kept in the Philippines, with a certificate that such officer has the custody.
>
> <u>If the office in which the record is kept is in a foreign country, which is a contracting party to a treaty or convention to which the Philippines is also a party, or considered a public document under such treaty or convention pursuant to paragraph (c) of Section 19 hereof, the certificate or its equivalent shall be in the form prescribed by such treaty or convention subject to reciprocity granted to public documents originating from the Philippines.</u>
>
> For documents originating from a foreign country which is not a contracting party to a treaty or convention referred to in the next preceding sentence, the certificate may be made by a secretary of the embassy or legation, consul general, consul, vice-consul, or consular agent or by any officer in the foreign service of the Philippines stationed in the foreign country in which the record is kept, and authenticated by the seal of his <u>[or her]</u> office.
>
> <u>A document that is accompanied by a certificate or its equivalent may be presented in evidence without further proof, the certificate or its equivalent being prima facie evidence of the due execution and genuineness of the document involved. The certificate shall not be required when a treaty or convention between a foreign country and the Philippines has abolished the requirement, or has exempted the document itself from this formality.</u>[45] *(Amendments underscored.)*

The Supreme Court also took note of the Apostille Convention in the 2019 Rules of Procedure for Admiralty Cases.[46] For verified complaints, it is mandatory to include the specification of all evidence supporting the cause of action, including affidavits of witnesses and authenticated documentary evidence, which must be attached as object evidence. Supporting documents and evidence must be compliant with the rules on admissibility of evidence. Official documents from foreign jurisdictions are admissible if duly authenticated in accordance with the Apostille Convention.[47]

[40] Hague Conference on Private International Law, Convention on Protection of Children and Co-operation in Respect of Intercountry Adoption, 29 May 1993, 32 I.L.M. 1134.

[41] The Hague Convention on the International Recovery of Child Support and Other Forms of Family Maintenance, available at www.hcch.net/en/instruments/conventions/full-text/?cid=131.

[42] Status Table of the Apostille Convention, HCCH website available at www.hcch.net/en/instruments/conventions/status-table/?cid=41.

[43] Supreme Court Administrative Matter No. 19-08-15-SC dated 8 October 2019 (Effective 1 May 2020).

[44] ibid s 19(d), Rule 132.

[45] ibid s 24, Rule 132.

[46] Administrative Matter No. 19-08-14-SC dated 17 September 2019.

[47] ibid s 3(e), Rule 2.

The Government Procurement Policy Board (GPPB) issued GPPB Resolution No. 13-19 dated 23 May 2019 approving the amendments to various sections of the Implementing Rules and Regulations (IRR)[48] of Republic Act No. 9184 or the Government Procurement Reform Act, in view of the accession of the Philippines to the Apostille Convention. Section 8.5.2 of the said IRR provides that bidders must upload and maintain in the Philippine Government Electronic Procurement System (PhilGEPS) the required eligibility documents to participate in public bidding. For foreign bidders, the English equivalent of the eligibility documents or officially translated versions must be uploaded.[49]

Originally, the eligibility documents may only be authenticated by the appropriate Philippine foreign service establishment or equivalent office having jurisdiction over the foreign bidder's affairs in the Philippines. The GPPB introduced a new provision, stating that contracting parties to the Apostille Convention may have the documents authenticated through an apostille by the competent authority, except for countries listed by the Philippine Department of Foreign Affairs (DFA) that still require legalisation by the relevant embassy or consulate. A competent authority is defined as the authority designated by a contracting party to the Apostille Convention to issue an apostille.[50] The IRR refers prospective bidders to the HCCH official website[51] to confirm the list of competent authorities.

The same guidelines for foreign documents are reproduced under Section 23.2 of the IRR covering the eligibility requirements for the procurement of goods and infrastructure projects and Section 24.2 regarding the eligibility requirements and short listing for consulting services.[52] With the enactment of Republic Act No. 12009 or the New Government Procurement Act in 2024, and the recent approval of the Implementing Rules and Regulations of the said law (2025 IRR), foreign bidders may refer to Sections 20.2.9.2 and 52.3 of the 2025 IRR for the authentication of eligibility documents in view of the Apostille Convention.[53]

The Philippine Overseas Employment Agency (POEA), now incorporated in the new executive body called Department of Migrant Workers (DMW), issued a Memorandum Circular establishing the Guidelines in the Implementation of Apostille Convention Related to the Verification of Employment Documents for Overseas Filipino Workers (OFWs).[54] It covers the employment contracts and other documents used by licensed recruitment agencies, licensed manning agencies, employers, foreign placement agencies, foreign service contractors, ship owners, and OFWs.

The Philippine Department of Health (DOH) issued an Administrative Order setting the revised Guidelines in the Importation, Facilitation and Management of Foreign Donations Involving Health and Health-Related Products, incorporating changes necessitated by the accession of the Philippines as a party to the Apostille Convention.[55]

The Philippine Securities and Exchange Commission (SEC) issued a Memorandum Circular establishing the Guidelines on Authentication of Articles of Incorporation in Applications for

[48] The 2016 Revised Implementing Rules and Regulations (as amended) of Republic Act No. 9184, otherwise known as the Government Procurement Reform Act.

[49] ibid s 8.5.2., Rule 1. N.B. Republic Act No. 120009 or the New Government Procurement Act (2024) replaced Republic Act No. 9184. The Implementing Rules and Regulations (IRR) of the Republic Act No. 120009 was approved in February 2025. The rules on participation of foreign bidders are discussed in the 2025 IRR.

[50] ibid.

[51] Accessible at www.hcch.net/en/instruments/conventions/authorities1/?cid=41.

[52] See n 48 above, ss 23.2 and 24.2, Rule VIII N.B.

[53] The Implementing Rules and Regulations of Republic Act No. 12009 or the New Government Procurement Reform Act (2025).

[54] POEA Memorandum Circular No. 008-19 dated 29 August 2019.

[55] DOH Administrative Order No. 01-20 dated 8 January 2020.

Registration of New Domestic Corporations.[56] Section 4 of the said Memorandum Circular provides that articles of incorporation executed abroad may either be apostilled in accordance with the Apostille Convention or notarised/authenticated by a Philippine diplomatic or consular officer if executed in a non-party country. The SEC's Guidelines on the Number and Qualifications of Incorporators under the Revised Corporation Code allows application documents for registrations wherein a foreign corporation is made an incorporator to be authenticated with an apostille.[57]

The Convention on the Service Abroad of Judicial and Extrajudicial Documents in Civil or Commercial Matters (Hague Service Convention) took effect in the Philippines on 1 October 2020.[58] Shortly thereafter, the Philippine Supreme Court issued an Administrative Order setting the Guidelines on the Implementation in the Philippines of the Hague Service Convention on the Service Abroad of Judicial Documents in Civil and Commercial Matters.[59] The Supreme Court took note that the Hague Service Convention provides a streamlined transmission of judicial and extrajudicial documents from one state party to another, allows cross-border litigants to expeditiously serve documents abroad, and ensures that the recipient will be notified of the service in sufficient time.[60] The Hague Service Convention applies in the Philippines if the following are present:

- A document is to be transmitted from one state party for service to another state party;
- The address of the intended recipient in the receiving state party is known;
- The document to be served is a judicial document; and,
- The document to be served relates to a civil or commercial matter.[61]

For outbound requests for service, a party to a civil or commercial proceeding must file the necessary motion for leave of court to allow extraterritorial service. The court shall then determine if extraterritorial service through the Hague Service Convention is necessary, in accordance with Rule 13 (Filing and Service of Pleadings, Judgments and Other Papers) and Rule 14 (Summons) of the 1997 Revised Rules of Civil Procedure (as amended in 2019). The court shall issue an order granting extraterritorial service if it finds the motion to be meritorious. The order shall direct the requesting party to procure and submit a prepaid courier pouch for the transmission of court documents to the central authority of the requested state. Once all the necessary documents are submitted, and upon payment of the fees, the court shall coordinate with the central authority of the requested state for the transmission of the pertinent papers. Thereafter, the central authority of the requested state shall process the request and attempt service based on its prevailing domestic laws. A formal confirmation shall be provided, indicating whether the service was successful or unsuccessful.[62]

Inbound requests for service from other contracting states shall be referred to the Philippine Supreme Court's Office of the Court Administrator (OCA). The forwarding authority from the requesting state may send the documents via electronic transmission or physical transmission. The OCA shall forward the documents received from the requesting state to the court having

[56] SEC Memorandum Circular No. 16-20 dated 29 April 2020.

[57] Section 6, SEC Memorandum Circular No. 16-19 dated 30 July 2019.

[58] Status Table of the Convention on the Service Abroad of Judicial and Extrajudicial Documents in Civil or Commercial Matters, accessible at www.hcch.net/en/instruments/conventions/status-table/?cid=17.

[59] See n 36 above.

[60] ibid (see first whereas clause).

[61] ibid Item I (2).

[62] ibid Item 2 (Requests for Extraterritorial Service of Judicial Documents from the Philippines to Other State Parties).

jurisdiction over the area where the recipient resides. The concerned judge shall assign a sheriff, process server, or any other competent personnel to serve the documents based on the procedure provided in the Rules of Court. A return on the service shall be executed by the assigned personnel indicating whether the documents were successfully or unsuccessfully served. The judge must also execute a certificate on the return of the service. The certificate and return on the service shall then be forwarded to the requesting state.[63]

The Convention on the Civil Aspects of International Child Abduction came into force in the country on 1 June 2016.[64] The Philippine Department of Justice (DOJ) issued a Department Circular Establishing the Procedure for Processing Applications Under the 1980 Convention on the Civil Aspects of International Child Abduction.[65] The said Department Circular recognised that it is a state policy to protect the best interest of the child through measures that ensure child protection based on international standards. The Philippines is obliged to prevent a child from being forcibly separated from his or her parents, unless directed by competent authorities upon determination that such separation is necessary for the best interest of the child, pursuant to existing laws, rules, and regulations, and subject to judicial review.[66] The DOJ is the designated Philippine Central Authority for the implementation of the said Convention.[67]

The DOJ Circular covers the procedure to facilitate the prompt return of children covered by the Convention on the Civil Aspects of International Child Abduction to the country of their habitual residence if they were wrongfully removed therefore or wrongfully retained in a state that is party to the said Convention.[68] The DOJ procedure is governed by the following principles:

- The wrongful removal or retention of a child across international borders is not in his or her best interest.
- A decision to return the child to the country of origin, based on the provisions of the said Convention, is not tantamount to a determination on the merits of any legal custody issue.
- The objective of returning the child to his or her country of habitual residence is to restore the *status quo* before the wrongful removal or retention.
- The application of the said Convention is without regard to the nationalities of the child, the person who wrongfully removed or retained the child, and the person who exercised custody rights over the child prior to the breach of custody or access rights.
- The procedure only applies between the Philippines and other contracting states, as well as states who later accede to the said Convention.[69]

A Hague Child Abduction Convention (HCAC) Unit was created in the DOJ.[70] The HCAC Unit may tap other government agencies to implement the request, such as the Philippine Bureau of Immigration (BI) to check if the child entered or exited the Philippines,[71] the National Bureau of Investigation (NBI) and the Philippine National Police (PNP) to help locate the child,[72] and the

[63] ibid Item 3 (Requests for Extraterritorial Service of Judicial Documents in the Philippines from Other State Parties).
[64] Status Table of the Convention on the Civil Aspects of International Child Abduction. Available at www.hcch.net/en/instruments/conventions/status-table/?cid=24.
[65] DOJ Department Circular No. 010 dated 22 February 2022.
[66] ibid (see Whereas clauses).
[67] ibid s 5.
[68] ibid s 1.
[69] ibid s 4.
[70] ibid s 6.
[71] ibid s 12.
[72] ibid s 15.

Philippine Department of Social Welfare and Development (DSWD) to check the condition of the child and to provide counselling.[73] The HCAC may also refer concerned parties to the Public Attorney's Office (PAO) or the Integrated Bar of the Philippines (IBP) for legal assistance.[74] The PAO is an official government organ which provides free legal aid and representation to indigent litigants. The IBP is the official association of lawyers in the Philippines.

The Philippine Supreme Court also promulgated the Rule on International Child Abduction Cases on the first day of the HCCH Asia Pacific Week conference held in Manila from October 18 to 20, 2022.[75]

The Convention on Protection of Children and Co-operation in Respect of Intercountry Adoption took effect in the Philippines on 1 November 1996.[76] However, the Philippine Congress had already passed a law on intercountry adoption prior to the effectivity of the said Convention. Republic Act No. 8043 or the Inter-Country Adoption Act of 1995[77] declared a state policy to provide every neglected and abandoned child with a family that will provide love and care, as well as ample opportunities for growth and development. Inter-country adoption shall be allowed if it benefits the child's interests and if his or her fundamental rights are guaranteed.[78] Inter-country adoption pertains to the socio-legal process of adopting a Filipino child by a foreigner or a Filipino citizen who permanently resides abroad where the petition is filed, the supervised trial custody is undertaken, and the decree of adoption is issued.[79] It established an Inter-Country Adoption Board (ICAB) to act as the central authority in matters relating to inter-country adoption.[80] The ICAB was designated as the Philippine Central Authority for the implementation of the said Convention.

The Philippine Congress recently passed Republic Act No. 11642 or the Domestic Administrative Adoption and Alternative Child Care Act.[81] It replaced the ICAB with the National Authority for Child Care (NACC). All duties of the ICAB and other government agencies dealing with alternative child care and adoption were transferred to the NACC.[82] The NACC was also designated as the new Philippine Central Authority in matters concerning inter-country adoption.[83] Republic Act No. 11642 imposed a new administrative adoption process, giving the NACC quasi-judicial powers to rule on adoption matters.[84] The new administrative proceedings replaced the judicial proceedings for adoption. The NACC now has original and exclusive jurisdiction over all matters pertaining to inter-country adoption under Republic Act No. 8043.[85] Orders of Adoption issued by the NACC may be appealed before the Philippine Court of Appeals.[86]

In view of the passage of Republic Act No. 11642, the Philippine Supreme Court issued Administrative Matter No. 02-6-02-SC (Re: Rule on Adoption),[87] recognising that adoption

[73] ibid s 19.

[74] ibid s 18.

[75] Supreme Court Administrative Matter No. 22-09-15-SC dated 18 October 2022. See SC press release available at sc.judiciary.gov.ph/supreme-court-promulgates-the-rule-on-international-child-abduction-cases/.

[76] Status Table of the Convention on Protection of Children and Co-operation in Respect of Intercountry Adoption. Available at www.hcch.net/en/instruments/conventions/status-table/?cid=69.

[77] Republic Act No. 8043 (7 June 1995).

[78] ibid s 2.

[79] ibid s 3(a).

[80] ibid s 4.

[81] Republic Act No. 11642 (6 January 2022).

[82] ibid s 5.

[83] ibid s 8(j).

[84] ibid s 32.

[85] ibid ss 6 and 8(c).

[86] ibid s 35.

[87] Supreme Court Administrative Matter No. 02-6-02-SC dated 19 April 2022.

proceedings are now administrative in nature. Republic Act No. 11642 also empowered the NACC, in coordination with concerned government agencies, to determine suitable procedures for alternative care of Filipino children stranded abroad, including those in countries which are not party to the Convention on the Protection of Children and Co-Operation in Respect of Intercountry Adoption.[88]

The Convention on the International Recovery of Child Support and Other Forms of Family Maintenance came into force in the Philippines on 1 October 2022.[89] The DSWD is currently listed as the Philippine Central Authority tasked to implement the said Convention.[90] It aims to establish better coordination between the central authorities of the contracting states. Parties to the Convention are required to ensure the availability of applications for the establishment of maintenance decisions, as well as to provide recognition and prompt enforcement mechanisms.[91]

IV. Avenues to Harmonise Private International Law in the Philippines

The efforts of the Philippines to harmonise its laws with international standards are strengthened by an intergovernmental approach. The judicial, legislative, and executive branches of government are willing partners in ensuring the compliance of the Philippines with its international obligations.

Section 1, Article VI of the 1987 Philippine Constitution provides that legislative power is vested in the Congress of the Philippines, consisting of a Senate and a House of Representatives.[92] The passage of Congress of Republic Act No. 8043 and Republic Act No. 11642 allowed the Philippines to harmonise its inter-country adoption laws with the other parties to the Convention on Protection of Children and Co-operation in Respect of Intercountry Adoption. However, it is glaring that most of the recent issuances of the country relative to its legal harmonisation goals were promulgated by state organs from the other branches of government.

The Philippine Supreme Court issued the 2019 Amendments to the 1989 Revised Rules on Evidence, the 2019 Rules of Procedure for Admiralty Cases, the Guidelines on the Implementation in the Philippines of the Hague Service Convention on the Service Abroad of Judicial Documents in Civil and Commercial Matters, the Rule on International Child Abduction Cases, and Administrative Matter No. 02-6-02-SC (Re: Rule on Adoption) in the exercise of its rule-making functions. Section 5(5), Article VIII of the Constitution states that the Supreme Court has the power to promulgate rules concerning the protection and enforcement of constitutional rights, pleading, practice, and procedure in all courts, the admission to the practice of law, the Integrated Bar, and legal assistance to the underprivileged.[93]

The 1935 Constitution repealed all existing laws on pleading, practice, and procedure, which were converted as the Rules of Court which the Supreme Court may modify.[94] However, Congress

[88] See n 81, s 8(k).
[89] Status Table of the Convention on the International Recovery of Child Support and Other Forms of Family Maintenance, available at www.hcch.net/en/instruments/conventions/status-table/?cid=131.
[90] HCCH Authority, available at www.hcch.net/en/States/authorities/details3/?aid=1186.
[91] See n 41 (Article 1).
[92] Section 1, Art VI 1987 Philippine Constitution.
[93] ibid s 5(5), Art VIII.
[94] *Pimentel v Legal Education Board*, G.R. Nos. 230642 & 242954, 10 September 2019.

had the power to repeal, alter, or supplement the rules promulgated by the Supreme Court.[95] The 1973 Constitution also gave the Supreme Court the power to promulgate rules governing the integration of the Philippine Bar. Nevertheless, the *Batasang Pambansa's* authority to repeal, alter, or supplement such rules was still retained.[96] The presently governing 1987 Constitution strengthened the independence of the Judiciary by removing the authority of Congress to repeal, alter, or supplement the rules of procedure promulgated by the Supreme Court.[97]

The harmonisation of private law requires the modification of numerous remedial laws, which are under the ambit of the Philippine Supreme Court. The sole power of the Supreme Court to regulate the practice of law allowed it to issue the aforementioned rules with relative haste compared to the usual legislative process. However, the rule-making power of the Supreme Court is limited since legislative power solely belongs to Congress. Supreme Court issuances must have basis in either treaty law, such as the rules issued based on the aforementioned Conventions, or municipal law.

Government agencies under the executive branch were also able to issue rules and regulations to implement the Hague Conventions. The concerned agencies have rule-making powers under their respective organic laws. Moreover, the Republic Acts passed by Congress are often supplemented by IRRs. For instance, Section 75 of the Government Procurement Reform Act provides that the GPPB is tasked to formulate the IRR for the said law.[98] The GPPB therefore had legal basis to amend the IRR to harmonise the procurement law with the Apostille Convention even before Congress passed the New Government Procurement Act in 2024. The rule-making powers of administrative agencies allowed the concerned government organs to quickly issue new rules and regulations to comply with the Apostille Convention.

Contrarily, the legislative mill entails a long and arduous process. A bill introduced in either House of Congress must pass three readings in both chambers before it is transmitted to the President of the Philippines for approval. The President has the authority to veto a bill, which may only become law if two-thirds of both Congressional chambers agree to override the veto.[99]

A lengthy process is involved before a bill is transmitted to the plenary of either House for second reading. The respective Congressional committees must still deliberate on the merits of a proposed legislative measure. If a bill successfully hurdles committee deliberations, debates and interpellations will continue at the plenary level. The election cycle of the Philippines is every three years. Each Congress follows one election cycle. Thus, a bill must pass both chambers and be transmitted to the President within a three-year Congress. Otherwise, it has to be refiled in the succeeding Congressional cycle. The political nature of elective positions also prevents the expeditious approval of legislative measures.

Nevertheless, there are limits to the rule-making powers of the Philippine Supreme Court and other government agencies. If the IRR of a law is issued in excess of the rule-making power of an administrative office, the terms thereof may be set aside by the courts.[100] Rule-making agencies are not granted unfettered power to promulgate rules, since subordinate legislation must be germane to the objects and purposes of the law. A regulation that goes beyond the bounds of

[95] Section 13, Art VIII. 1935 Philippine Constitution.

[96] Section 5(5), Art X. 1973 Constitution. N.B. The *Batasang Pambansa* was the unicameral national legislative assembly created by the 1973 Constitution that replaced the 1935 Constitution's bicameral Congress. The bicameral Congress was reinstated in 1987.

[97] *Pimentel* (n 94).

[98] Section 77, Republic Act No. 9184 (10 January 2003).

[99] Section 27, ArtiVI. 1987 Philippine Constitution.

[100] *Department of Agrarian Reform v Carriedo*, G.R. No. 176549, 20 January 2016.

the statute is considered *ultra vires* for being issued beyond an agency's competence.[101] Hence, if the Philippines becomes party to Hague Conventions which are not covered by existing municipal laws, the Philippine Congress must act to pass legislation to ensure that local laws are in sync with the country's international commitments. Furthermore, if the harmonisation effort entails the substantial amendment of an existing law, a modification of the IRR by the implementing agency or of procedural rules in court processes by the Supreme Court would not suffice since substantial amendments to the base law would cause an intrusion on the sole province of Congress to legislate. To illustrate, the aforementioned issuances to implement the Apostille Convention are mostly procedural in nature. In the case of the Rules of Court, the recognition of the Apostille Convention is essential in presenting and authenticating foreign documentary evidence. In government procurement, it is relevant to easily establish authenticity of eligibility documents. The Supreme Court and agencies under the executive branch may act quickly to harmonise procedural aspects of private law such as the evidentiary value of documents following the Apostille Convention. However, substantial amendments that are inconsistent with municipal laws may only be introduced by Congress.

The Philippine government may also opt to harmonise its internal laws with international standards by actively participating in international organisations. The United Nations Commission on International Trade Law (UNCITRAL) was established by the United Nations (UN) General Assembly in 1966.[102] The UN General Assembly recognised that divergencies arising from different laws of member states constitute an obstacle to the development of world trade. The UN aims to promote the adoption of international conventions, uniform laws, standard contract provisions, general conditions of sale, standard trade terms, and other relevant measures in order to harmonise international trade law.[103] UNCITRAL originally had 29 members elected by the General Assembly.[104] The current membership stands at 60 States: 14 from Africa, 14 from Asia, 8 from Eastern Europe, 10 from Latin America and the Caribbean, and 14 from Western Europe and other states. The Philippines was a member of UNCITRAL from 1974 to 1986 and from 2010 to 2022.[105]

UNCITRAL is tasked to promote the progressive harmonisation and unification of international trade law by performing the following functions:

(a) Co-ordinating the work of organisations active in this field and encouraging co-operation among them;
(b) Promoting the wider participation in existing international conventions and wider acceptance of existing model and uniform laws;
(c) Preparing or promoting the adoption of new international conventions, model laws and uniform laws and promoting the codification and wider acceptance of international trade terms, provisions, customs and practices, in collaboration, where appropriate, with the organisations operating in this field;
(d) Promoting ways and means of ensuring a uniform interpretation and application of international conventions and uniform laws in the field of the law of international trade;
(e) Collecting and disseminating information on national legislation and modern legal developments, including case law, in the field of the law of international trade;

[101] *Social Weather Stations, Inc. v Commission on Elections*, G.R. No. 208062, 7 April 2015.
[102] UN General Assembly, 17 December 1966. *Establishment of the United Nations Commission on International Trade Law*. A/RES/2205(XXI).
[103] ibid.
[104] ibid II (1.).
[105] UNCITRAL Member States History, available a: uncitral.un.org/en/about/faq/mandate_composition/memberhistory.

(f) Establishing and maintaining a close collaboration with the United Nations Convention on Trade and Development;
(g) Maintaining liaison with other United Nations organs and specialised agencies concerned with international trade;
(h) Taking any other action it may deem useful to fulfil its functions.[106]

UNCITRAL employs several legislative techniques including conventions, model laws, legislative guides, and model provisions.[107] Conventions are established binding legal obligations which are designed to unify law among its parties. For instance, the Philippines is party to the New York Convention on the Recognition and Enforcement of Foreign Arbitral Awards.[108] Hence, it is bound by treaty law to accept and enforce the rulings of foreign arbitrators. Model laws are recommended legislative texts which states may adopt via local legislation.[109] The Philippines is a signatory to the Arbitration Rules of the UNCITRAL Model Law on International Commercial Arbitration, which led to the incorporation of the Model Law in Republic Act No. 9285 or the Alternative Dispute Resolution Act of 2004.[110] Majority of the provisions of Republic Act No. 8792 or the Electronic Commerce Act of 2000 are lifted from the UNCITRAL Model Law on Electronic Commerce.[111] UNCITRAL also provides legislative guides and recommendations if circumstances do not permit the adoption of a convention or model law in the national legal system of a country. Model provisions may also be used as reference for future conventions and the revision of existing instruments.[112]

Representatives from the Philippine public and private sectors are also exploring opportunities to work with the International Institute for the Unification of Private Law (UNIDROIT), an independent intergovernmental organisation which aims to harmonise and modernise private law.

V. Local Challenges in Harmonising Private International Law

A. Rights of Migrant Workers

There are local concerns that may hamper harmonisation efforts. For instance, the Philippines has strict labour laws which are generally in favour of labour protection. The 1987 Constitution provides that it is the responsibility of the Philippine government to afford full protection to labour, both local and overseas, organised and unorganised. This mandate includes assurances on security of tenure, humane conditions of work, and a living wage.[113]

There are approximately 2.16 million Filipinos working abroad.[114] Four out of ten overseas Filipino workers are employed in elementary occupations, defined by the Philippine Statistics

[106] A/RES/2205(XXI) (n 102) II(8).
[107] United Nations Commission on International Trade Law, *A Guide to UNCITRAL Basic Facts About the United Nations Commission on International Trade Law* (Vienna, 2013) 13.
[108] *Mabuhay Holdings Corp. v Sembcorp Logistics Limited*, G.R. No. 212734, 5 December 2018.
[109] ibid 14.
[110] *Korea Technologies Co., Ltd. v Lerma*, G.R. No. 143581, 7 January 2008.
[111] *Department of Health v Philippine Tobacco Institute, Inc.*, G.R. No. 200431, 31 July 2021.
[112] *A Guide to UNCITRAL* (n 107) 16–17.
[113] Section 3, Art XIV, The 1987 Philippine Constitution.
[114] Data from the Philippine Statistics Authority. Available at psa.gov.ph/statistics/survey/labor-and-employment/survey-overseas-filipinos.

Authority (PSA) as work involving simple and routine tasks such as cleaning, operation of hand-held tools, and other similar responsibilities.[115] A good number of Filipinos work as household domestic helpers, most of which are women. Saudi Arabia is the leading destination for overseas workers, accounting for 20 per cent of the total Filipino overseas workers in 2023.[116]

Around 75 per cent of reported abuses experienced by overseas Filipino workers involved female victims.[117] The Philippine Overseas Workers Welfare Administration (OWWA) reported 23,986 cases of abused workers in Middle Eastern countries in 2020.[118]

Countries in the Levant and Gulf states employ the *Kafala* system, which gives the employers of migrant workers significant power over their foreign workers, acting as their 'sponsors' in a temporary labour migration framework. It is criticised as an unbalanced system that gives the employers too much power over their migrant employees, leading to numerous cases of abuse.[119] The Philippines and Saudi Arabia experienced difficulties in resolving cases of abuse committed by Saudi employers against Filipino migrant workers. Saudi Arabia's domestic laws, reflecting the *Kafala* system, are inconsistent with the more pro-labour rules established by Philippine local laws. This resulted in the Philippines issuing a deployment ban to Saudi Arabia, which was eventually lifted in 2022 after both governments agreed to revise the standard employment contract for Filipino migrant workers to provide better protection against abuses. However, the revised contract is still criticised as insufficient to address the concerns of Filipino migrants, particularly female domestic household workers.[120]

The local law that specifically governs domestic household workers is Republic Act No. 10361 or the Domestic Workers Act.[121] Note that Filipinos working in the private sector are generally covered by the Philippine Labor Code. However, domestic household workers have a specific law addressing their particular needs since they live in the household of their employers. The Domestic Workers Act recognises that domestic household workers are more susceptible to abuses, given that they are mostly confined in the family home of their employers in the Philippines. The potential for abuse is exacerbated for those deployed abroad, since the Domestic Workers Act does not have extra-territorial application.

However, the Philippine Congress passed a specific law that governs migrant Filipino workers – Republic Act No. 8042 or the Migrant Workers Act.[122] The said law provides that the state shall only deploy workers to countries where the rights of Filipino workers are protected. The Philippines is also a signatory to the Domestic Workers Convention, which recognises the fundamental rights of migrant domestic household workers.[123] While Saudi Arabia's (and other countries following the *Kafala* system) laws are controlling within its territory, the Philippine government is still duty-bound to follow the Migrant Workers Act and its commitment to protect

[115] ibid.

[116] ibid.

[117] Per data stated in Australia Aid's ASEAN-Australia Counter Trafficking website, citing figures from the International Labour Organisation (ILO), available at www.aseanact.org/story/ople/.

[118] LJ Eugenio, 'Overseas Filipino Workers: The Modern-Day Heroes of the Philippines' (*Harvard International Review website*, 2023), hir.harvard.edu/overseas-filipino-workers-the-modern-day-heroes-of-the-philippines/.

[119] N El-Dekmak, 'Reform the Kafala System: Persistent Violations of the Rights of Migrant Domestic Workers and the Role of Private Recruitment Agencies' (*Georgetown Journal of International Affairs website*, 2025) gjia.georgetown.edu/2025/03/21/reforming-the-kafala-system-persistent-violations-of-the-rights-of-migrant-domestic-workers-and-the-role-of-private-recruitment-agencies/.

[120] LMM Ecat and ABS Libang, *Pangarap o Panganib?: A Critical Analysis of the Standard Employment Contract Between the Philippines and Saudi Arabia in Protecting Filipino Household Service Workers From All Forms of Abuse, Harassment, and Violence* (Bachelor, De La Salle University, Animo Repository, 2025).

[121] Republic Act No. 10361 (18 January 2013).

[122] Republic Act No. 8042 (7 June 1995), as amended by Republic Act No. 10022 (8 July 2010).

[123] International Labour Organization (ILO), C189 – Domestic Workers Convention, 2011, No.189, 16 June 2011, www.refworld.org/legal/agreements/ilo/2011/en/83143.

its overseas workers under the Domestic Workers Convention.[124] Nevertheless, the Philippines continues to allow its workers to be deployed in countries with numerous recorded instances of abuse, mainly out of economic necessity.

Harmonising labour standards is a difficult task. The cultural and religious nuances of countries across the globe must be considered. The Philippine government is therefore in a difficult position since it has to monitor over two million migrant workers who are deployed in countries with different legal systems and cultural norms.

Creating standardised labour rules is difficult even in the Southeast Asian region. Unlike the EU, which is a conglomerate of developed Western first world countries with shared cultural values, the ASEAN is composed of 11 countries which are not at pace with each other in terms of economic development. The EU can afford to have free movement of people and labour, although this open-border policy is already strained by mass migration and economic issues which contributed to the United Kingdom's 'Brexit' from the bloc. ASEAN only has a limited visa-free framework agreement for nationals of member states for only 14 days.[125] While ASEAN aims to enhance labour mobility, it only has a few mutual recognition agreements covering select skilled labour covering professions such as nursing and architecture. Most ASEAN nations, including the Philippines, employ protectionist policies over their local labour markets.

B. Jurisdictional Issues in Contracts Covered by Bilateral Investment Treaties

Another concern that hampers harmonisation efforts is the issue on jurisdiction over breaches in contracts involving foreign private sector entities and the Philippine government. The most prominent issue involving the Philippines is its lengthy legal battle with the German company Fraport AG Frankfurt Services Worldwide (Fraport, for brevity). Germany and the Philippines have an existing bilateral investment treaty.[126] The said treaty has a provision stating that if divergencies cannot be settled amicably between the host contracting state and the investor, the latter may either refer the matter to the competent court of the former or to the International Centre for the Settlement of Investment Disputes (ICSID). It also has a provision on expropriation and compensation, the legality of which shall be subject to review by due process of law.

In the mid-1990s, the Philippine government opened the bidding process to construct the Terminal 3 building of the Ninoy Aquino International Airport (NAIA), the country's primary aviation hub. Paircargo Consortium submitted the winning bid. It was later renamed and reorganised as Philippine International Air Terminals Co., Inc. (PIATCO).[127] Fraport acquired interest in PIATCO in 1999, and its direct and indirect ownership of the company totaled 61.44 per cent by 2001.[128] PIATCO contracted Takenaka, the local branch of a Japanese corporation, and Asahikosan, a Japanese corporation, to construct and equip the project. In 2002, PIATCO defaulted on its obligation to pay Takenaka and Asahikosan, which led to the suspension of the

[124] See LMM Ecat and ABS Libang's exhaustive discussion on the accountability of the Philippine government (n 120).

[125] ASEAN Framework Agreement on Visa Exemption (2006), available at agreement.asean.org/media/download/20160831072909.pdf.

[126] Agreement between the Federal Republic of Germany and the Republic of the Philippines for the Promotion and Reciprocal Protection of Investments (1997), available at investmentpolicy.unctad.org/international-investment-agreements/treaty-files/1392/download.

[127] *Republic v Mupas*, G.R. No. 181892, 8 September 2015.

[128] *Fraport AG Frankfurt Airport Services Worldwide v Republic of the Philippines*, ICSID Case No. ARB/03/25 (Award dated 16 August 2007).

construction of the project. In 2003, the Philippine Supreme Court voided the deal between PIATCO and the Philippine government, holding that Paircargo Consortium (PIATCO's predecessor entity) failed to meet the requisite financial capacity of the bid requirements and that the finalised concession agreement contained material and substantial amendments compared to the contract bidded upon, hence null and void for being contrary to public policy.[129] Meanwhile, Takenaka and Asahikosan filed collection suits against PIATCO in a court in London, United Kingdom. In 2005, the London court ruled in favour of Takenaka and Asahikosan.[130]

The Philippine government instituted expropriation proceedings in order to take over the NAIA Terminal 3 project. A lengthy legal joust transpired, with the government, PIATCO, Takenaka and Asahikosan, and the court-appointed Board of Commissioners submitting different appraisals for the proper amount of just compensation. Moreover, Takenaka and Asahikosan moved that part of the just compensation be set aside through an escrow account to answer for their money claims against PIATCO, which is docketed as a separate legal proceeding in the Philippines. The Philippine Supreme Court determined with finality the amount of just compensation in the 2015 case of *Republic v Mupas*,[131] but denied the prayer of Takenaka and Asahikosan to hold part of the total amount in escrow to account for their money claim against PIATCO. The Supreme Court held that only the owner of the property taken (PIATCO), not the builders of the airport terminal (Takenaka and Asahikosan), is entitled to just compensation. As for the London court's ruling, it was held that:

> While the Government refers to a judgment rendered by a London court in favor of Takenaka and Asahikosan against PIATCO in the amount of US$82 Million, it should be noted that this foreign judgment is not yet binding on Philippine courts. It is entrenched in Section 48, Rule 39 of the Rules of Civil Procedure that a foreign judgment on the mere strength of its promulgation is not yet conclusive, as it can be annulled on the grounds of want of jurisdiction, want of notice to the party, collusion, fraud, or clear mistake of law or fact. It is likewise recognized in Philippine jurisprudence and international law that a foreign judgment may be barred from recognition if it runs counter to public policy.[132]

Of equal interest are the ICSID cases filed by Fraport against the Philippine government (*Fraport AG Frankfurt Airport Services Worldwide v Republic of the Philippines*, ICSID Case No. ARB/03/25 and ICSID Case No. ARB/11/12).[133] Fraport cited the bilateral investment treaty between Germany and the Philippines and the ICSID Convention as basis for bringing the case before the ICSID. The German company claimed that the Philippine government failed to honour its obligations. It was also posited that the NAIA Terminal 3 project was fully compliant with the laws of the Philippines. On the other hand, the Philippine government claimed that ICSID had no jurisdiction over the case since Fraport allegedly violated the country's strict rules on foreign control and ownership of corporations. The Anti-Dummy Law[134] penalises violations of the limit on foreign ownership of businesses to Filipinos or corporations which are at least 60 per cent owned by Filipinos, as mandated by the 1987 Philippine Constitution. It was also alleged that Fraport participated in fraudulent and corrupt activities involving Filipino officials. The ICSID tribunal found credence in the position of the Philippine government, finding that Fraport engaged in

[129] *Agan, Jr. v Philippine International Air Terminals Co., Inc.*, G.R. Nos. 15501, 15547, & 15561, 5 May, 2003.

[130] *PIATCO v Takenaka and Asahikosan*, G.R. No. 180245, 4 July 2012.

[131] *Republic v Mupas* (n 127).

[132] ibid.

[133] *Fraport AG Frankfurt Airport Services Worldwide v Republic of the Philippines*, ICSID Case No. ARB/03/25 (Award dated 16 August 2007); *Fraport AG Frankfurt Airport Services Worldwide v Republic of the Philippines*, ICSID Case No. ARB/11/12 (Award dated 10 December 2014).

[134] Commonwealth Act No. 108 (as amended), 30 October 1936.

covert activities to circumvent Philippine foreign ownership restrictions.[135] However, this decision was annulled in a subsequent ruling issued in 2010.[136]

In ARB/11/12,[137] Fraport alleged that it has uncompensated claims against the Philippine Government due to the purported unlawful expropriation of its investment in PIATCO (this case was filed after the Philippine courts determined that expropriation can push through but before the Supreme Court determined with finality the proper just compensation). The Philippine government counters by reiterating that Fraport violated the Philippine Anti-Dummy Law and that it engaged in corrupt practices. Hence, the matter is beyond the jurisdiction of the ICSID since the agreement was null and void to begin with. The ICSID tribunal issued an award in 2014 finding that it lacked jurisdiction over the case since Fraport had violated the Anti-Dummy Law upon making its initial investment. Hence, it is not protected by the bilateral investment treaty between Germany and the Philippines because of its illegality. Curiously, the tribunal did not accept the corruption defence against ICSID jurisdiction advanced by the Philippine government due to lack of evidence.

The NAIA Terminal 3 case presents complications in private international law because it dabbled in the realm of state sovereignty and criminal law. First, it involved two courts belonging to two different legal jurisdictions (the Philippine Supreme Court and local lower courts, as well as the London court that ruled in favour of Takenaka and Asahikosan). The Philippine Supreme Court did not recognise the ruling of the London court without prejudice to the counterpart local money claim proceedings. Second, the expropriation proceedings initiated by the Philippine government were sovereign acts that, while covered by the bilateral investment treaty, were still resolved solely by Philippine courts using Philippine law. Assuming that the ICSID tribunal found that the expropriation was unlawful, how will it affect the local proceedings based on domestic laws that give Philippine courts exclusive jurisdiction over cases of expropriation? Third, the corruption defence raised by the Philippine government before the ICSID can have profound consequences over contracts covered by bilateral investment treaties had the tribunal dismissed the case based on the corruption allegation against Fraport. If corruption invalidates the protections provided by an investment treaty, could this be exploited by nation-states to reject ICSID or other arbitration proceedings in order to keep the litigated matter within the jurisdiction of local courts? On the other hand, if tribunals reject the corruption allegations and decide to take cognizance of the matter, how will it affect the local criminal prosecution of both the officers of the investing company and the country's government officials who participated in the corrupt acts?[138] Another possible issue is the quantum of evidence required in determining the presence of corruption in deciding whether a contract is void *ab initio*, hence removing it from the ambit of the terms and conditions of a bilateral investment treaty. Corruption is a specie of criminal law in the Philippines and other legal jurisdictions. To support an indictment, local prosecutors need to find probable cause that the person so charged is probably guilty of the accused crime based on the existence of facts and circumstances that would lead a reasonable person to such a conclusion. A finding of guilt by a local court requires a higher quantum of evidence, which is proof beyond reasonable doubt. In determining jurisdiction based on allegations of corruption, what metric of

[135] *Fraport AG Frankfurt Airport Services Worldwide v Republic of the Philippines*, ICSID Case No. ARB/03/25 (Award dated 16 August 2007).

[136] *Fraport AG Frankfurt Airport Services Worldwide v Republic of the Philippines*, ICSID Case No. ARB/03/25 (Decision dated 23 December 2010).

[137] *Fraport AG Frankfurt Airport Services Worldwide v Republic of the Philippines*, ICSID Case No. ARB/11/12 (Award dated 10 December 2014).

[138] TEA Mondez and JP Cruz in N Teramura, L Nottage, and B Jetin (eds), *Corruption and Illegality in Asian Investment Arbitration: The Philippines. Corruption and Illegality in Asian Investment Arbitration* (Springer, 2024) 360–62.

certainty should a tribunal organised to resolve a commercial (not criminal) dispute use to determine its competence and to decide whether a contract is indeed void *ab initio?*

C. Liberal Views on Divorce Prohibition

The Philippines and the Holy See (Vatican City) are the only sovereign entities with no law allowing absolute divorce, although Filipino Muslims may do so under the Code of Muslim Personal Laws of the Philippines.[139] According to the 2020 census conducted by the PSA, 78.8 per cent of Filipinos surveyed identify as Catholics while only 6.4 per cent are Muslim. Other religious Filipinos belong to local Christian sects, Western evangelical Christian churches, and other religious affiliations.[140] The marital tie may only be completely dissolved if one of the grounds to declare the marriage void *ab initio* are present: lack of essential and formal requisites under the Family Code (such as being underaged), bigamous and polygamous unions, incest, and psychological incapacity. These grounds void a marriage from the beginning since either or both of the spouses were disqualified to contract marriage as defined by law, or there was a defect in the actual marriage ceremony itself (such as lack of a marriage licence and lack of authority of the solemnising officer). A marriage may also be annulled, but not declared void *ab initio*, if any of the grounds under Article 46 of the Family Code are present.[141] These grounds vitiate or diminish consent when the marriage was contracted, such as lack of parental consent for those aged 18–21, fraud, and concealment by one of the spouses of a sexually transmissible disease. However, marriages that may be annulled under Article 46 are merely voidable. The marriage may be ratified by continued cohabitation. For actions that compromise the marriage or the family during the course of the marriage, the only recourse is to file for legal separation based on the grounds under Article 55 of the Family Code.[142] However, it must be noted that legal separation is not absolute divorce. The marital tie remains but the spouses may live separately, the property regime is dissolved, custody of the children may be awarded to the innocent spouse, and the offending spouse is disqualified from inheriting from the innocent spouse via intestate succession.[143]

Divorce remains a divisive issue in the Philippines. There are initiatives in the Philippine Congress to enact a law allowing absolute divorce. However, there remains significant opposition against divorce. It is also noteworthy that the 1987 Constitution explicitly provides that marriage is an inviolable social institution which must be protected by the state.[144] While this matter remains a political issue, it is observed that the Philippine Supreme Court's decisions have trended towards a more liberal interpretation of one of the grounds to declare a marriage void *ab initio* – psychological incapacity. Article 36 of the Family Code provides that if a party that contracts marriage was psychologically incapacitated to comply with the essential marital obligations expected of spouses, the marriage is void even if the incapacity only manifests after solemnisation.[145]

[139] Presidential Decree No. 1083 (4 February 1977). N.B. This was issued by former President Ferdinand Marcos, Sr. while he wielded both executive and legislative powers when the Philippines was under martial law.

[140] Data from the Philippine Statistics Authority website, available at psa.gov.ph/content/religious-affiliation-philippines-2020-census-population-and-housing.

[141] Executive Order No. 209 (6 July 1987). N.B. This Executive Order has the force and effect of law since it was issued by former President Corazon Aquino while she exercised provisional legislative powers after the ouster of former President Marcos, Sr.

[142] ibid Art 55.

[143] ibid Art 63.

[144] Section 2, Art XV. 1987 Constitution.

[145] Executive Order No. 209, Art 46 (n 141).

Early decisions of the Supreme Court rigidly interpreted psychological incapacity, emphasising that marriage is permanent, inviolable, and founded on solidarity. In the 1997 case of *Republic v Molina*, it was held that a court may only void a marriage based on psychological incapacity if it is medically or clinically identified, alleged in the complaint, sufficiently proven by experts, and clearly explained in the court's decision.[146] The Supreme Court noted in the 2009 case of *Ting v Ting*[147] that the totality of circumstances should be considered in assessing psychological incapacity, bearing in mind that the legal presumption is always in favour of the validity of marriage. Drinking and gambling vices are not necessarily incurable defects. The case also involved two conflicting assessments of experts who analysed the alleged incapacitated spouse. The Supreme Court ruled against the petition to declare the marriage void since there was insufficient proof to establish psychological incapacity.

More recent rulings have shifted towards a liberal interpretation of both the 1987 Constitution's mandate to protect marriage and psychological incapacity as a ground to void a marital union. In *Kalaw v Fernandez*,[148] the Supreme Court initially ruled in 2011 against the petition to declare a marriage void due to the alleged psychological incapacity of a spouse addicted to gambling. In a rare reversal, the Supreme Court reconsidered its 2011 decision in 2015, declaring the marriage void *ab initio* due to psychological incapacity. It was held that the constitutional mandate to protect marriage does not remove the power of Congress to define all legal aspects of marriage and prescribe the proper strategy to protect it. While the Supreme Court mentioned this under the context of guiding judges to liberally construe Article 36 of the Family Code, notwithstanding the constitutional edict to protect marriage, it can also be used as a precedent to justify a divorce law should such a legislative measure be questioned before a court of law for being unconstitutional. In the landmark 2021 case of *Tan-Andal v Andal*,[149] the Supreme Court abandoned the stringent guidelines stated in *Republic v Molina* by declaring that psychological incapacity is not a medical illness that has to be medically or clinically identified. Hence, expert opinion is no longer necessary to establish psychological incapacity. The quantum of proof necessary to establish its existence is clear and convincing evidence, which is greater than preponderant evidence but less than proof beyond reasonable doubt. Proof of the aspects of a spouse's personality which manifests through clear acts of dysfunctionality that undermine the family need not be established by expert witnesses. This is a game-changer since judges may now decide whether a spouse is incapacitated to perform his or her marital obligations based on testimonies of ordinary witnesses. However, it must still be proven that the incapacity existed at the time of the marriage ceremony, as required by Article 36 of the Family Code.

The lack of an absolute divorce law in the Philippines has consequences in private international law, given that numerous Filipinos are married to foreigners. The PSA recorded that in 2023, 15,962 marriages in the Philippines were between a Filipino and a foreign national. It accounts for 3.8 per cent of the registered marriages in the said year. This is only based on data collected from local civil registrars in the Philippines.[150] Filipinos marrying foreigners abroad are not accounted for in the aforementioned total.

The inclusion of the vaguely defined psychological incapacity ground in the Family Code is seen as a way out of a legally iron-clad marital union forged in the Philippines. The recent

[146] *Republic v Molina*, G.R. No. 108763, 13 February 1997.

[147] *Ting v Ting*, G.R. No. 166562, 31 March 2009.

[148] *Kalaw v Fernandez (Motion for Reconsideration)*, G.R. No. 166357, 14 January 2015.

[149] *Tan-Andal v Andal*, G.R. No. 196359, 11 May 2021.

[150] Data from the Philippine Statistics Authority website, available at psa.gov.ph/statistics/vital-statistics/node/1684065408.

trend to liberally interpret the definition of psychological incapacity, and the loosening of the evidentiary requirement to prove it, may come as a welcome reprieve for married couples who want to dissolve their marital tie. Nevertheless, the Supreme Court still affirms the provision in Article 36 that the incapacity must exist at the time of the marriage ceremony. Foreigners married to Filipinos, and vice versa, who want to have their marriage declared void in the Philippines must still prove this via clear and convincing evidence.

It must also be stressed that the Family Code recognises divorce obtained abroad, but with limitations, *viz:* 'Where a marriage between a Filipino citizen and a foreigner is validly celebrated and a divorce is thereafter validly obtained by the alien spouse capacitating him or her to remarry, the Filipino spouse shall have capacity to remarry under Philippine law.'[151] Based on the wording of this provision, as quoted *verbatim*, only the alien spouse can initiate the divorce proceedings. It is also unclear whether a judicial edict of a foreign court is necessary before Philippine courts could recognise the validity of the dissolution of marriage. The jurisprudential trend to interpret this Family Code provision has likewise shifted towards a more liberal view.

In *Republic v Obrecido*,[152] the Supreme Court held that citizenship is not determined at the time of the solemnisation of marriage, but at the time of the divorce. Hence, when two Filipinos marry, but one of them later on becomes a naturalised American citizen and, thereafter, obtains a divorce decree, the Filipino spouse who remained in the Philippines may also be allowed to remarry. While this goes against the letter of the law, the Supreme Court stressed that if a statute is interpreted based on its literal import, and such interpretation would lead to mischievous results or contravene its very purpose, it must be interpreted based on the spirit of the law. Legislators never intended for a Filipino to be at a disadvantage should his or her former Filipino spouse become a naturalised foreign citizen and obtain a divorce decree abroad. The *Republic v Obrecido* decision must be compared with the Supreme Court's ruling in *Corpuz v Sto. Tomas*,[153] wherein a former Filipino citizen who became a naturalised Canadian obtained a divorce in Canada to separate from his Filipina spouse, but returned to the Philippines and fell in love with another Filipina citizen whom he wanted to marry. The Supreme Court ruled that Article 26 of the Family Code only benefits the Filipino spouse who intends to remarry. Hence, the naturalised Canadian, despite being a former Filipino who obtained a divorce abroad, cannot take another Filipino for his wife. The ruling in *Corpuz* interpreted Article 26 based on the strict letter of the law.

Another interesting case which illustrates the difficulties encountered in divorce proceedings involving private international law is *Fujiki v Marinay*.[154] A Filipina married a Japanese man (first spouse) in the Philippines. Unfortunately, the parents of the first spouse did not approve of the marriage, which prevented him from bringing his Filipina spouse to Japan. They lost touch with each other. Eventually, the Filipina met and subsequently married another Japanese citizen (second spouse) without dissolving her earlier marriage. The relationship soured due to alleged physical abuse. The Filipina went to Japan and rekindled her relationship with her first spouse, who helped her obtain a declaration of nullity of her marriage with the second spouse from a Japanese court on the ground of bigamy. Thus, the Filipina is still technically married to her first Japanese spouse. The first spouse filed a petition before a local Philippine court to recognise the Japanese court's ruling which voided the marriage of the Filipina with her second spouse. A local Philippine court refused since the first spouse lacked the legal personality to initiate the

[151] Executive Order No. 209, Art 46 (n 141).
[152] *Republic v Obrecido*, G.R. No. 154380, 5 October 2005.
[153] *Corpuz v Sto. Tomas*, G.R. No. 186571, 11 August 2010.
[154] *Fujiki v Marinay*, G.R. No. 196049, 26 June 2013.

proceedings, since only the spouses of the bigamous marriage that was declared void have the right to do so. On appeal, the first spouse countered by asserting that he is merely trying to establish his status as legally married to his Filipina spouse, given that the second marriage obtained by the Filipina was declared void *ab initio* for being bigamous. The Supreme Court held that the first spouse has the right to file the petition to recognise the foreign decision since it is necessary to establish his civil status. In effect, he is still legally married to his Filipina spouse.

The case of *Republic v Manalo*[155] further liberalised the Supreme Court's interpretation of Article 26 of the Family Code. In this case, it was the Filipina spouse who obtained a divorce decree in a Japanese court in order to separate from her Japanese spouse. A literal reading of Article 26 will lead to a conclusion that it is only when the foreign spouse initiates divorce proceedings abroad that the Filipino spouse may be allowed to remarry. The Supreme Court's majority ruling, citing their previous liberal interpretation of the said provision in cases such as *Republic v Obrecido*, held that a literal interpretation is too restrictive. Hence, based on the spirit of the law, the privilege to remarry must extend to the Filipino spouse regardless of whomever initiated the divorce. The dissenting justices claimed that the court's duty to interpret the law does not include the power to determine what the law ought to be. It was also emphasised that there is still no law allowing absolute divorce in the Philippines.

The challenge in recognising a divorce obtained abroad is that Philippine courts require both the divorce decree and the applicable national law of the alien spouse to be proven based on Philippine rules on evidence. The Supreme Court held in the case of *In Re: Petition for Judicial Recognition of Divorce Decree Between Minuro Takahasi and Juliet Rendora Moraña*[156] that an official judicial decree is not necessary to establish that a competent authority abroad approved the divorce. A divorce report issued by the Office of the Mayor of Fukuyama City, the official body that granted the dissolution of marriage, was considered as sufficient proof of the divorce. However, the Japanese law on divorce was not duly established since the petitioner in this case only submitted printouts from a website of pertinent portions of the Japanese law on divorce, as translated in English. The Supreme Court ordered that the case be remanded to the trial court to give the petitioner the opportunity to prove the foreign divorce law. In *Racho v Tanaka*,[157] the Supreme Court affirmed the admission of the trial court of the pertinent Japanese divorce law based on a copy of the English version of the Civil Code of Japan, the translation of which was authorised by the Ministry of Justice and the Code of Translation Committee. However, in *Arreza v Toyo*,[158] it was ruled that the English translation of Japanese laws by a private company may not be considered as an official translation of the pertinent Japanese law on divorce. Likewise, a photocopy of the English translation of the Civil Code of Japan, with a stamp stating that it is from the library of the Japan Information and Culture Center in the Embassy of Japan in Pasay City, Philippines, was deemed inadequate to prove the pertinent Japanese divorce law.[159]

The above discussions and case law stem from just two provisions of the Family Code: Article 26 on foreign divorce and Article 36 on psychological incapacity being a ground to void a marriage. The Family Code was promulgated in 1987. The Philippine Congress failed to provide clarity on the ambiguous nature of Article 36 and the restrictive legal implications on the Filipino spouse if Article 26 was to be interpreted based strictly on the letter of the law. It can be argued

[155] *Republic v Manalo*, G.R. No. 221029, 24 April 2018 (see dissenting opinion of Justice Alfredo Benjamin S Caguioa).

[156] *In Re: Petition for Judicial Recognition of Divorce Decree Between Minuro Takahasi and Juliet Rendora Moraña*, G.R. No. 227605, 5 December 2019.

[157] *Racho v Tanaka*, G.R. No. 199515, 25 June 2018.

[158] *Arreza v Toyo*, G.R. No. 213198, 1 July 2019.

[159] *Republic v Kikuchi*, G.R. No. 243646, 22 June 2022; *Nullada v Civil Registrar of Manila*, G.R. No. 224548, 23 January 2019.

that the Supreme Court tested the limits of its power to interpret the law by engaging in what others may view as judicial legislation, as expressed by the minority in the dissenting opinion in the case of *Republic v Manalo*. On the other hand, the Supreme Court was left with no choice but to settle these matters as legitimate justiciable controversies, given the ambiguity of Article 36 and possible absurdity (in certain situations) of the literal text of Article 26.

Psychological incapacity was only defined through judicial fiat in the 1995 case of *Santos v Court of Appeals*.[160] It must be grave or serious such as to cause a spouse to be incapable of performing the ordinary duties required in marriage. It was also held that until statutory and jurisprudential parameters are established, every circumstance must be examined, including the opinions of psychiatrists and psychologists. The constitutional edict declaring marriage as an inviolable social institution was emphasised. Canon Law of the Catholic Church was also quoted in the said decision. The same conservative tenor was maintained in the *Republic v Molina* ruling. Notice the gradual change of tone as the Supreme Court tilted towards a more liberal view, which culminated in the 2021 *Tan-Andal v Andal* ruling. Ultimately, absolute divorce for non-Muslim Filipinos is still a political issue. *Republic v Manalo* and *Tan-Andal v Andal* may have liberally pushed this matter to its limits, but the Supreme Court still followed the text of the Family Code, or at least the intention of its framers.

D. Ideological Conflicts

The composition of the Philippine Supreme Court is not divided between clearly identified conservative and liberal justices, as ideological beliefs are not generally considered in the selection and appointment process. Thus, the gradual shift in matters concerning psychological incapacity and foreign divorce may be viewed as an organic process that reflects the current ideological stand of the magistrates. Nonetheless, the slow movement in Congress on matters concerning Family Law and progressive civil rights may reflect the mood and preference of the electorate. Contrarily, shifts in judicial doctrines in the United States may be directly attributed to the composition of the US Supreme Court, wherein vacant justice seats are appointed by the sitting president generally based on shared political ideology. Hence, the 2022 landmark ruling of the US Supreme Court in *Dobbs v Jackson*,[161] which overturned the constitutional right to abortion, as held in *Roe v Wade*,[162] is a reflection of the ideological stand of the current conservative majority composition of America's top court. The ruling in *Dobbs v Jackson* may be considered as a reverse-harmonisation move since it gave the individual states the authority to regulate abortion, allowing 'red states' (conservative) and 'blue states' (liberal) to have their own abortion policies. Conservatives hail it as a triumph for state autonomy in the US, while liberals condemn the decision as a set-back for women's rights.

Foreigners staying in the Philippines, especially those marrying or having romantic relationships with Filipinos, must be aware that abortion is illegal in the country. The 1987 Constitution provides that the state shall equally protect the life of the mother and of the unborn from conception.[163] The Revised Penal Code imposes prison time for those who carried out the abortion, including the mother herself if done alone or with the aid of her parents, the husband or any person through a physical act of violence (resulting in abortion, whether intended or not),

[160] *Santos v Court of Appeals*, G.R. No. 11201, 4. January 1995.
[161] *Dobbs v Jackson Women's Health Organization*, 597 U.S. 215 (2022).
[162] *Roe v Wade*, 410 U.S. 113 (1973).
[163] Section 12, Art II. 1987 Constitution.

the physician or midwife who caused or assisted to cause the abortion, and even pharmacists who dispense an abortive without proper prescription.[164] The promotion of the use of contraceptives by mandate of Republic Act No. 10354 or the Reproductive Health Law was questioned when the said law was constitutionally challenged. In *Imbong v Ochoa*,[165] the Supreme Court held that only contraceptives that kill or destroy the fertilised ovum are considered as abortifacients. Contraceptives that prevent the male sperm from reaching the female ovum are constitutionally permissible since these devices are deemed non-abortive.

Legislation on divisive matters such as divorce, same-sex marriage, and other progressive advocacies remain stagnant due to the opposing, but equally compelling, combative stands taken by both political liberals and conservatives. Religion, culture, and local values must also be considered. Harmonisation efforts concerning private law must be sensitive towards these social nuances that not only divide nations, but also fellow citizens within a country. The proliferation of opposing views is a necessary consequence of a democratic society. The key to successful harmonisation of private laws is to ensure that no sector is marginalised, and that all views are respected in formulating legal frameworks that meet both local and international expectations. Unfortunately, it is easier said than done.

VI. The Future of Private International Law

To recall the discussion on the concept of a Leviathan, the nation-state has emerged as an entity with a monopoly of political, legal, and coercive powers within a given jurisdiction, thus allowing laws within its territory to be codified and uniformly enforced. The trend towards integration gave rise to new Leviathans such as the supranational EU, which has the power to compel legal integration across multiple sovereign jurisdictions. On the other hand, the UN functions as a loose body of nation-states operating on consensus rather than compulsion.

The current Philippine Republic stands as the Leviathan over the Philippine Islands. The country's democratic and republican form of government ensures a system of checks and balances, preventing one organ of government from exercising tyrannical rule. However, the same bureaucracy that protects democracy also breeds red tape and inefficient government mechanisms. The Philippine government is not the same Leviathan as the French Empire under Napoléon. Harmonisation of laws requires greater effort in societies with diffused legislative and rule-making powers.

The various Philippine government organs exerted commendable efforts to harmonise laws, rules, and regulations with international standards. But an over-expanded government structure with multiple authorities greatly hinders the ability of the Philippines to modernise and harmonise its laws. Take for instance the ongoing codification programmes being implemented by both Congress and the Supreme Court. To date, the primary penal law of the country is still the Revised Penal Code, which came into effect in 1932, and which was primarily based on the nineteenth century Spanish *Codigo Penal*. Numerous Special Penal Laws (SPL) were introduced by the legislative branch thereafter. Instead of being incorporated in one penal code, the SPLs became piecemeal legislations that snowballed into the current bloated collection of local penal laws.

[164] Articles 255–259 (n 23).
[165] *Imbong v Ochoa*, G.R. No. 204819, 3 April 2014.

The same is true with the country's civil laws. Instead of periodically amending the New Civil Code to maintain a comprehensive legal code, multiple laws were passed to address new developments in private law. The same problem is encountered in the fields of commercial, labour, taxation, and political laws.

The accession of the Philippines to various conventions not only became the impetus to harmonise the country's legal systems with international standards, an unintended consequence is that it thickened the untamed jungle of Philippine laws. It is therefore necessary to coordinate the codification of local laws with the country's compliance with its treaty obligations. This coordinated effort is a herculean task that will require the cooperation of the three co-equal branches of government.

From a national policy perspective, the Philippines may also explore adopting other UNCITRAL conventions and model laws. The Philippines had ratified/adopted the following UNCITRAL instruments: the 1958 New York Convention, the UN Convention on the Use of Electronic Communications in International Contracts, the UNCITRAL Model Law on International Commercial Arbitration, the UNCITRAL Model Law on Electronic Commerce, and the UNCITRAL Model Law on Cross-Border Insolvency.[166] The Philippines signed, but has yet to ratify, the UN Convention on the Carriage of Goods by Sea (the 'Hamburg Rules') in 1978, the UN Convention on the Liability of Operators of Transport Terminals in International Trade in 1991, and the UN Convention on International Settlement Agreements Resulting from Mediation in 2019.[167]

The Philippines may consider the following UNCITRAL conventions:

- The UN Convention on the Limitation Period in the International Sale of Goods, which establishes when claims of a buyer and a seller against each other arising from a contract involving the international sale of goods can no longer be exercised after the expiration of a set period of time.[168]
- The UN Convention on Contracts for the International Sale of Goods, which adopts uniform rules governing contracts for the international sale of goods and promotes consistency in commercial exchanges.[169]
- The UN Convention on International Bills of Exchange and International Promissory Notes, providing a modern set of rules which only cover international bills of exchange and international promissory notes that satisfy the requisites of form identified in the Convention.[170] It is not yet in force since it only becomes effective after a year following the deposit of the tenth instrument of ratification, acceptance, approval, or accession. Only five states have acceded to the Convention.[171]
- The UN Convention on Independent Guarantees and Stand-by Letters of Credit, which facilitates the use of independent guarantees and stand-by letters of credit where only one or the

[166] Overview of the Status of UNCITRAL Conventions and Model Laws (v. 23 January 2023), available at uncitral.un.org/sites/uncitral.un.org/files/media-documents/uncitral/en/overview-status-table.pdf.

[167] ibid.

[168] United Nations, Treaty Series, vol. 1511, No. 26119, p 3.

[169] United Nations, Treaty Series, vol. 1489, No. 25567, p 3.

[170] UN General Assembly, 9 December 1988. *United Nations Convention on International Bills of Exchange and International Promissory Notes*. A/RES/43/165.

[171] Status: United Nations Convention on International Bills of Exchange and International Promissory Notes. Available at uncitral.un.org/en/texts/payments/conventions/bills_of_exchange/status.

other of those instruments is traditionally in use. It provides a common umbrella of rules for both instruments.[172]

- The UN Convention on the Assignment of Receivables in International Trade, promoting the availability of affordable credit and capital across national borders to facilitate easier cross-border movement of goods and services. It also aims to lessen legal uncertainty involving receivables financing transactions.[173] It requires the approval of five nations before it enters into force. Four States have signed the instrument, but only two had ratified/acceded to the Convention.[174]
- The UN Convention on Contracts for the International Carriage of Goods Wholly or Partly by Sea (the 'Rotterdam Rules'), providing uniformity in modern transport practices in international carriage of goods involving a sea leg to promote legal certainty, efficiency, and access to remote parties and markets.[175] It requires 20 actions for entry into force. There are currently only five parties to the Convention.[176]
- The UN Convention on Transparency in Treaty-based Investor-State Arbitration (the 'Mauritius Convention on Transparency'), allowing public access to information on investor-state arbitrations under investment treaties to promote the fair and efficient settlement of international investment disputes, transparency and accountability, and good governance.[177]

UNCITRAL also has a Model Law on Public Procurement, although the Philippines already has its existing New Government Procurement Act, which recently replaced the Government Procurement Reform Act. The UN General Assembly recommended to all states to use the said Model Law in enacting or revising their local procurement laws.[178] It may serve as a guide for both the Philippine Congress and the GPPB in introducing revisions to the law and its IRR, respectively, if needed based on the prevailing circumstances.

The Philippines may also consider the UNCITRAL Model Law on Electronic Signatures,[179] in view of the increasing use of electronic transactions and exchange of electronic documents in the country prompted by the restrictions caused by the COVID-19 pandemic. The UN General Assembly endorsed the said Model Law since it is a must to have uniformity of applicable law to alternatives to traditional paper-based communications, storage, and information authentication.[180] The Philippines has an existing Electronic Commerce Act that recognises electronic signatures, although it was drafted and passed into law before the proliferation of remote transactions via the internet.[181]

[172] United Nations, Treaty Series, vol. 2169, No. 38030, p 163.

[173] UN General Assembly, 12 December 2001. *United Nations Convention on the Assignment of Receivables in International Trade*. A/RES/56/81.

[174] Status: United Nations Convention on the Assignment of Receivables in International Trade. Available at uncitral.un.org/en/texts/securityinterests/conventions/receivables/status.

[175] UN General Assembly, 11 December 2008. *United Nations Convention on Contracts for the International Carriage of Goods Wholly or Partly by Sea*. A/RES/63/122.

[176] Status: United Nations Convention on Contracts for the International Carriage of Goods Wholly or Partly by Sea. Available at uncitral.un.org/en/texts/transportgoods/conventions/rotterdam_rules/status.

[177] UN General Assembly, 10 December 2014. *United Nations Convention on Transparency in Treaty-based Investor-State Arbitration*. A/RES/69/116.

[178] UN General Assembly, 11 December 2011. *United Nations Commission on International Trade Law Model Law on Public Procurement*. A/RES/66/95.

[179] UN General Assembly, 12 December 2001. *Model Law on Electronic Signatures of the United Nations Commission on International Trade Law*. A/RES/56/80.

[180] ibid.

[181] Republic Act No. 8792 (14 June 2000). *N.B.* Republic Act No. 11967 (5 December 2023) or the Internet Transactions Act of 2023 was recently passed, although it does not directly cover electronic signatures.

The Philippines may also review the other conventions and instruments of the HCCH. The first HCCH conference was held in 1893. The Philippines only joined the HCCH in 2010 and is only party to five HCCH conventions. The country may also increase its engagement with UNIDROIT and eventually consider joining the organisation. The Philippine Department of Agrarian Reform (DAR) issued its Rules on Agri-Business Venture Agreements in 2016, which cites UNIDROIT principles relating to contract farming.[182]

The Philippines must also grow its legal system as a member of ASEAN. Unlike the EU, which has supranational institutions and pooled sovereignty among its members, ASEAN employs the 'ASEAN Way' of working through informal institutional dialogue and decision-making based on consensus. The EU functions on a region-wide institutional level with a rigid legal system, as opposed to ASEAN's non-binding and consensus-driven framework.[183] ASEAN instruments are made in the form of declarations, plans of action, memoranda of agreement, and other documents of questionable or weak binding nature.[184] The consensus system of ASEAN generally avoids antagonism among member states, but often leads to a conclusion based on the lowest common denominator. This leads to weaker institutional action based on what is acceptable to all member states. On the other hand, the majoritarian system of the EU allows legally binding agreements to have greater reach,[185] notwithstanding opposition from the minority. ASEAN also prefers mutual recognition of legal systems or harmonisation of technical rules and regulations rather than establishing a region-wide community law as basis for harmonised national laws.[186]

The 2007 ASEAN Charter, which came into force in 2008, gave legal personality to ASEAN as an intergovernmental organisation.[187] The language of describing ASEAN as an intergovernmental body was deliberate since the member states had no intention of creating a supranational organisation like the EU.[188] The ASEAN Charter established new organisations with specific functions which should help the member states move closer to achieving their goal of creating a single market and production base.

It is also important for the Philippines to harmonise its private laws with the greater East Asian region. The Philippines joined the Asian Principles of Private International Law (APPIL) initiative of private international law scholars from ten Southeast Asian and East Asian jurisdictions.[189] Seven of the ten participating jurisdictions (Thailand, the Philippines, Vietnam, Taiwan, Mainland China, South Korea, and Japan) have private law codifications or principal statutes based on civil law tradition, including the New Civil Code of the Philippines. Singapore and the Hong Kong Special Administrative Region (SAR) follow common law tradition. Indonesia has a mixed legal system.[190] The diversity of private laws makes cross-border litigation unpredictable due to conflicting legal bases.[191] Harmonisation of laws in Southeast Asia and East Asia is a more realistic option since it is highly difficult to create a convention establishing a uniform private international law in the region, given the heterogenous legal systems of the covered jurisdictions.[192]

[182] See Prefatory Statement and Section 16, DAR Administrative Order No. 04-16 dated 27 May 2016.

[183] L Henry, 'The ASEAN Way and Community Integration: Two Different Models of Regionalism' (2007) 13(6) *European Law Journal* 859–60.

[184] ibid 866.

[185] ibid 867.

[186] ibid 868.

[187] Association of Southeast Asian Nations, Treaty Series, vol 2624, no 46745, p 223.

[188] W Woon, 'The ASEAN Charter Ten Years On' (2017) 39(2) *Contemporary Southeast Asia* 246.

[189] W Chen and G Goldstein, 'The Asian Principles of Private International Law: objectives, contents, structure and selected topics on choice of law' (2017) 13(2) *Journal of Private International Law* 411.

[190] ibid 413–14.

[191] ibid 415.

[192] ibid 417–18.

The Philippines continues to labour in codifying its existing rules and updating body of laws to conform to its international obligations. The country's leaders and policy makers should account for the new realities of the twenty-first century, especially the increased traffic in international trade, the greater mobility of people, marital ties between spouses of different nationalities, and the growing number of cross-border transactions. The harmonisation of private international law must be prioritised to keep the country in step with the global movement towards legal standardisation.

TABLE OF SECONDARY RESOURCES

Journal Articles

Adjami, M and Harrington, J, 'The Scope and Content of Article 15 of the Universal Declaration of Human Rights' (2008) 27(3) *Refugee Survey Quarterly*, ssrn.com/abstract=1443012.

Akkermans, B, 'Lex Rei Sitae and the EU Internal Market – Towards Mutual Recognition of Property Relations' (2018) 7(3) *European Property Law Journal* 246–66, doi.org/10.1515/eplj-2018-0012.

Akkermans, B, 'The Influence of the Four (or five) Freedoms on Property Law' *Research Handbook on European Union Property Law* (2022), dx.doi.org/10.2139/ssrn.4232332.

Balane, RF, 'The Spanish Roots of Philippine Law' (2018) 66(1) *Estudios de Deusto* 23–31.

Bennett, TW, 'Choice of Law Rules in Claims of Unjust Enrichment' (1990) 39(1) *The International and Comparative Law Quarterly* 136–68, www.jstor.org/stable/760323.

Chong, A, 'Choice of Law for Unjust Enrichment/Restitution and the Rome II Regulation' (2008) 57(4) *The International and Comparative Law Quarterly* 863–98, www.jstor.org/stable/20488256.

Columbia Law Review Association, 'Conflict of Laws: "Party Autonomy" in Contracts' (1957) 57(4) *Columbia Law Review* 553–76, doi.org/10.2307/1119750.

'Conflict of Laws in Negotiable Instruments' (1902) 2(4) *Columbia Law Review* 253–55, doi.org/10.2307/1109884.

De Nova, R, 'New Trends in Italian Private International Law' (1963) 28(4) *Law and Contemporary Problems*, doi.org/10.2307/1190566.

Gandhi, S, 'Theories of Private International Law and Their Application' (2021) II(1) *Indian Journal of Integrated Research in Law*.

Gewolb, R, 'The Law Applicable to International Letters of Credit' (1966) 11(4) *Villanova Law Review* 742–70, digitalcommons.law.villanova.edu/vlr/vol11/iss4/9.

Gomez, F and Ganuza, JJ, 'How to Build European Private Law: An Economic Analysis of the Lawmaking and Harmonization Dimensions in European Private Law' (2012) 33(3) *European Journal of Law and Economics* 481–503.

Gotlieb, AE, 'The Incidental Question in Anglo-American Conflict of Law' (1955) *The Canadian Bar Review* 33.

Harnay, S, 'Was Napoleon a Benevolent Dictator? An Economic Justification for Codification' (2002) 14(3) *European Journal of Law and Economics* 237–39.

Johnston, R, 'Party Autonomy in Contracts Specifying Foreign Law' (1966) 7(1) *William & Mary Law Review* 37–60, scholarship.law.wm.edu/wmlr/vol7/iss1/3/.

Josselin, J and Marciano, A, 'The Making of the French Civil Code: An Economic Interpretation' (2002) 14(3) *European Journal of Law and Economics* 194.

Klepper, S, 'Choice of Law for CGL Insurance Policies: Toward a Uniform Rule' (2009) 45(1) *Tort Trial & Insurance Practice Law Journal* 31–56, www.jstor.org/stable/25763950.

Lorenzen, EG and Huber, 'Huber's De Conflictu Legum' (1918) *Illinois Law Review* 13, openyls.law.yale.edu/bitstream/handle/20.500.13051/4068/Huber_s_De_Conflictu_Legum.pdf.

Lücke, HK, 'The European Natural Law Codes: The Age of Reason and the Powers of Government' (2012) 31(1) *University of Queensland Law Journal* 7–8.

Markstein, A, 'The Law Governing Letters of Credit' (2010) 16 *Auckland University Law Review* 138–63, www.nzlii.org/nz/journals/AukULawRw/2010/7.html.

Marshall, B, 'Reconsidering the Proper Law of the Contract' (2012) 13 *Melbourne Journal of International Law* 505–39, ssrn.com/abstract=2718853.

Michaels, R, (n.d.), 'Forthcoming in Elgar Encyclopedia of Private International Law', scholarship.law.duke.edu/cgi/viewcontent.cgi?article=6387&context=faculty_scholarship.

Miralao, VA, 'The Family, Traditional Values and the Sociocultural Transformation of Philippine Society' (1994) 45(1) *Philippine Sociological Review* 189–215.

Mondez, TEA and Cruz, JP, 'Corruption and Illegality in Asian Investment Arbitration: The Philippines' in N Teramura, L Nottage and B Jetin (eds), *Corruption and Illegality in Asian Investment Arbitration* (Springer, 2024).
Morris, W, 'Some Conflict of Laws Problems Relating to Negotiable Instruments' (1964) 66(2) *West Virginia Law Review* 91–108, researchrepository.wvu.edu/wvlr/vol66/iss2/3.
Özel, S, 'The Determination of Applicable Law to Torts Based on "the Law Which Is More Closely Connected"' (2021) 41(2) *Public and Private International Law Bulletin* 483–515, doi.org/10.26650/ppil.2021.41.2.939398.
Pangalanan, EA, 'International Judicial Cooperation through The Hague Conference on Private International Law (HCCH) Conventions' (2017) *Philippine Yearbook of International Law* 158–60, law.upd.edu.ph/wp-content/uploads/2021/09/IJC-The-Hague.pdf.
Phukon, B, 'The Concept of Lex Situs and Tangible Movable Properties under Private International Law' (2021) 4(3) *International Journal of Law Management and Humanities* 385–393, doij.org/10.10000/IJLMH.11486.
Ristroph, A, 'Sovereignty and Subversion' (2015) 101(4) *Virginia Law Review* 1034–35.
Rodger, B, 'Ascertaining the Statutory Lex Loci Delicti: Certain Difficulties under the Private International Law (Miscellaneous Provisions) Act 1995' (1998) 47(1) *The International and Comparative Law Quarterly* 205–11, doi.org/10.1017/S0020589300061625.
Roosevelt, K, (2006). 'Choice of Law Issues in the Nonprofit Arena' (2006) *New York University School of Law*, ncpl.law.nyu.edu/wp-content/uploads/pdfs/2006/Conf2006_Roosevelt_FINAL.pdf.
Ruhl, G, 'Consumer Protection in Choice of Law' (2011) 44(3) *Cornell International Law Journal* 570–601, scholarship.law.cornell.edu/cilj/vol44/iss3/4/.
Thomas, CD, 'Secret Prior Art – Get Your Priorities Straight' (1996) 9 *Harvard Journal of Law & Technology* 147.
Vataman, D, 'History of the European Union' (2010) XVII(2) *Lex Et Scientia* 112.
Wallace, A, 'Choice of Law for Trusts in Australia and the United Kingdom' (1987) 36(3) *The International and Comparative Law Quarterly* 454–82, www.jstor.org/stable/760478.
Woodhouse, A, 'The Importance of Jurisdiction and Choice of Law Clauses: A European Perspective' (2007) 42(4) *Tort Trial & Insurance Practice Law Journal* 1027–41, www.jstor.org/stable/25763867.
Yntema, HE, 'The Historic Bases of Private International Law' (1953) 2(3) *The American Journal of Comparative Law* doi.org/10.2307/837480.

Textbooks and Treatises

American Law Institute, *Restatement of the Law of Conflicts of Law*, Introductory Note to Ch XII, § 585 (1934).
Aquino TB and Aquino MAA, *Commentaries and Jurisprudence on the Revised Corporation Code of the Philippines* (Quezon City, Rex Printing Company Inc, 2020)
Autea, AP, 'Philippine Arbitration Reform: Fresh Breathing Space from Congested Litigation' in A Reyes and W Gu (eds), *The Developing World of Arbitration: A Comparative Study of Arbitration Reform in the Asia Pacific* (2018).
Balane, RF, *Civil Law Florilegium: Essays on the Philippine Variant of the Civil Law Tradition* (Quezon City, University of the Philippines College of Law, 2012).
Balane, RF, *Jottings and Jurisprudence in Civil Law (Succession)* (2016).
Blackaby, N, Partasides, C et al, *Redfern and Hunter on International Arbitration*, 6th edn (Oxford, Oxford University Press, 2015).
Born, G, *International Arbitration: Law and Practice*, 2nd edn (Alphen aan den Rijn, Wolters Kluwer, 2016).
Caguioa, EP, *Comments and Cases on Civil Law* (Quezon City, Central Law Book Publishing 1970).
Coquia, JR and Aguiling-Pangalangan, E, *Conflict of Laws: Cases, Materials and Comments* (Quezon City, Central Book Supply, 2000).
Coquia, JR and Pangalanan, EA, *Conflict of Laws, Materials and Cases* (Central Books, 2000).
De Leon, HS and De Leon, HM Jr, *Comments and Cases on Credit Transactions* (Quezon City, Rex Printing Company Inc., 2016).
De Leon, HS and De Leon, HM Jr, *Comments and Cases on Obligations and Contracts* (Manila, Rex Bookstore, 2014).
Herbosa, TJ and Recalde, ER, *The Revised Corporation Code of the Philippines (Its Theories and Applications)* (Quezon City, Rex Printing Company Inc., 2020).
Jurado, DP, *Comments and Jurisprudence on Succession* (2009).
Nachura, AEB and Gatdula, J, *Outline Introduction to Public International Law* (Manila, Rex Bookstore, 2017).
Palfrey, J, *Intellectual Property Strategy* (Massachusetts, The MIT Press Knowledge Series, 2012).
Pe Benito, G, *Conflicts of Law* (Manila, Rex Bookstore, 2020).
Salonga, J, *Private International Law* (Pasig, Regina Publishing, 1995).

Salonga, J, 'Private International Law' (Manila, Rex Bookstore, 1995).
Schefer, KN, *International Investment Law: Text, Cases and Materials*, 2nd edn (Cheltenham, Edward Elgar, 2016).
Sempio-Diy, AV, *Handbook on Conflict of Laws* (Quezon, Joer Printing, 2004).
World Intellectual Property Organization, *Collective Management of Copyright and Related Rights*, WIPO Pub. No. L450CM(E) (Geneva, Switzerland, 2013).
World Intellectual Property Organization, *Making Intellectual Property Work for Business*, WIPO Pub. No. 956–E (Geneva, Switzerland, 2011).

Web Resources

Amjad, R, 'How To Get Married Online in Utah (Step-by-Step Guide)' (2024) available at: www.courtly.com/resources/how-to-get-married-online-in-utah-step-by-step-guide.
Asia Business Law Journal, 'Philippine Commission Blocks Merger' available at: law.asia/philippine-commission-blocks-merger/.
Commission of Overseas Filipinos, 'Statistics' available at: cfo.gov.ph/statistics-2/?appgw_azwaf_jsc=x9sXAV2D4Zr0Gy7_-m0K_QOLfR91NujnnRvN7MMYzBM.
Ford, D. & American Society of International Law, 'Private International Law' (*Electronic Source Guide* 2013) available at: www.asil.org/sites/default/files/ERG_PRIVATE_INT.pdf.
HCCH Authority, 'Designated Central Authorities' available at: www.hcch.net/en/States/authorities/details3/?aid=1186.
Immediate Cause, *Legal Dictionary* available at: legal-dictionary.thefreedictionary.com/Immediate+Cause.
International Legal Research, 'Private International Law' (n.d.) available at: law.duke.edu/ilrt/def_terms_3.htm.
IPOPHL, *Manual for Patent Examination Procedure*.
Legal Information Institute, 'Negotiable Instruments' available at: www.law.cornell.edu/wex/negotiable_instruments.
Legal Information Institute, 'Tort' available at: www.law.cornell.edu/wex/tort.
LibGuides, UCLA School of Law Hugh and Hazel Darling Law Library, 'Private International Law' (n.d.) available at: libguides.law.ucla.edu/privateinternational.
Peterson, LE, 'In an Apparent First, Investor and Host-State Agree to Try Mediation Under IBA Rules to Resolve an Investment Treaty Dispute' (*Inv. Arb. Rep.*, 14 April 2016) available at: www.iareporter.com/articles/in-an-apparent-first-investor-and-host-state-agree-to-try-mediation-under-iba-rules-to-resolve-an-investment-treaty-dispute/.
Pew Research Center, 'Filipino Americans: A Survey Data Snapshot' (accessed 14 Mar. 2025) available at: www.pewresearch.org/race-and-ethnicity/2024/08/06/filipino-americans-a-survey-data-snapshot/.
Regular Processing of SEC-ESPARC (with uploading of documents) *User Guide*, Securities and Exchange Commission, available at: esparc.sec.gov.ph/docs/UserGuide-esparc.pdf.
SIDRA International Dispute Resolution Survey: *2022 Final Report*, available at: sidra.smu.edu.sg/sites/sidra.smu.edu.sg/files/survey-2022/index.html.
Status Table of the Apostille Convention, HCCH website, available at: www.hcch.net/en/instruments/conventions/status-table/?cid=41.
Status Table of the Convention on Protection of Children and Co-operation in Respect of Intercountry Adoption, HCCH website, available at: www.hcch.net/en/instruments/conventions/status-table/?cid=69.
Status Table of the Convention on the International Recovery of Child Support and Other Forms of Family Maintenance, HCCH website, available at: www.hcch.net/en/instruments/conventions/status-table/?cid=131.
Status Table of the Convention on the Service Abroad of Judicial and Extrajudicial Documents in Civil or Commercial Matters, HCCH website, available at: www.hcch.net/en/instruments/conventions/status-table/?cid=17.
The Economist, 'Why the Philippines Is the Only Country Where Divorce Is Illegal' (15 Feb. 2020) available at: www.economist.com/asia/2020/02/13/why-the-philippines-is-the-only-country-where-divorce-is-illegal.
Trademark FAQ, Intellectual Property Office of the Philippines, available at: www.ipophil.gov.ph/help-and-support/trademark/.
Types of Nuisances, *US Legal Information* available at: nuisances.uslegal.com/types-of-nuisances/.
U.S. Federal Trade Commission, 'Price Fixing' available at: www.ftc.gov/advice-guidance/competition-guidance/guide-antitrust-laws/dealings-competitors/price-fixing.
World Intellectual Property Organization, 'What Is Intellectual Property?' (2020).

INDEX

References are to page number.